GRIZ GROBUS
POLLARD
ROY
NAZAROV

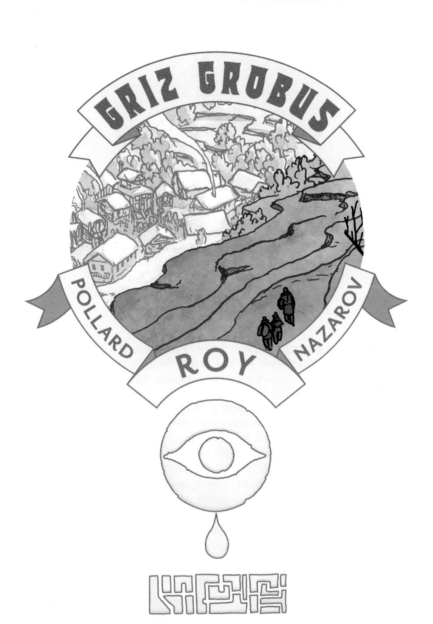

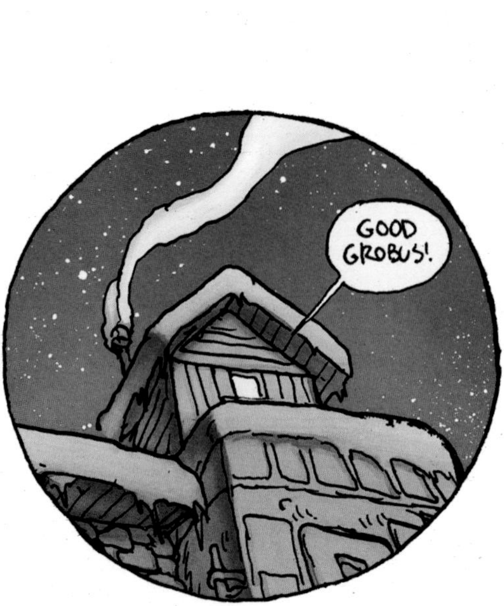
GOOD GROBUS!

DRAWING + SCRIPTING BY SIMON ROY
STORY BY SIMON ROY + JESS POLLARD
COLORS BY SERGEY NAZAROV
SCRIPT EDITING BY JESS POLLARD
LOGO DESIGN BY ANDRIY LUKIN
PRINT LAYOUT BY SIMON + KATHRYN RENTA

GRIZ GROBUS. FIRST PRINTING. JUNE 2024. PUBLISHED BY IMAGE COMICS, INC.
OFFICE OF PUBLICATION: PO BOX 14457, PORTLAND, OR 97293.

PRINTED IN CANADA.
FOR INTERNATIONAL RIGHTS, CONTACT: FOREIGNLICENSING@IMAGECOMICS.COM.
ISBN: 978-1-5343-9786-6.

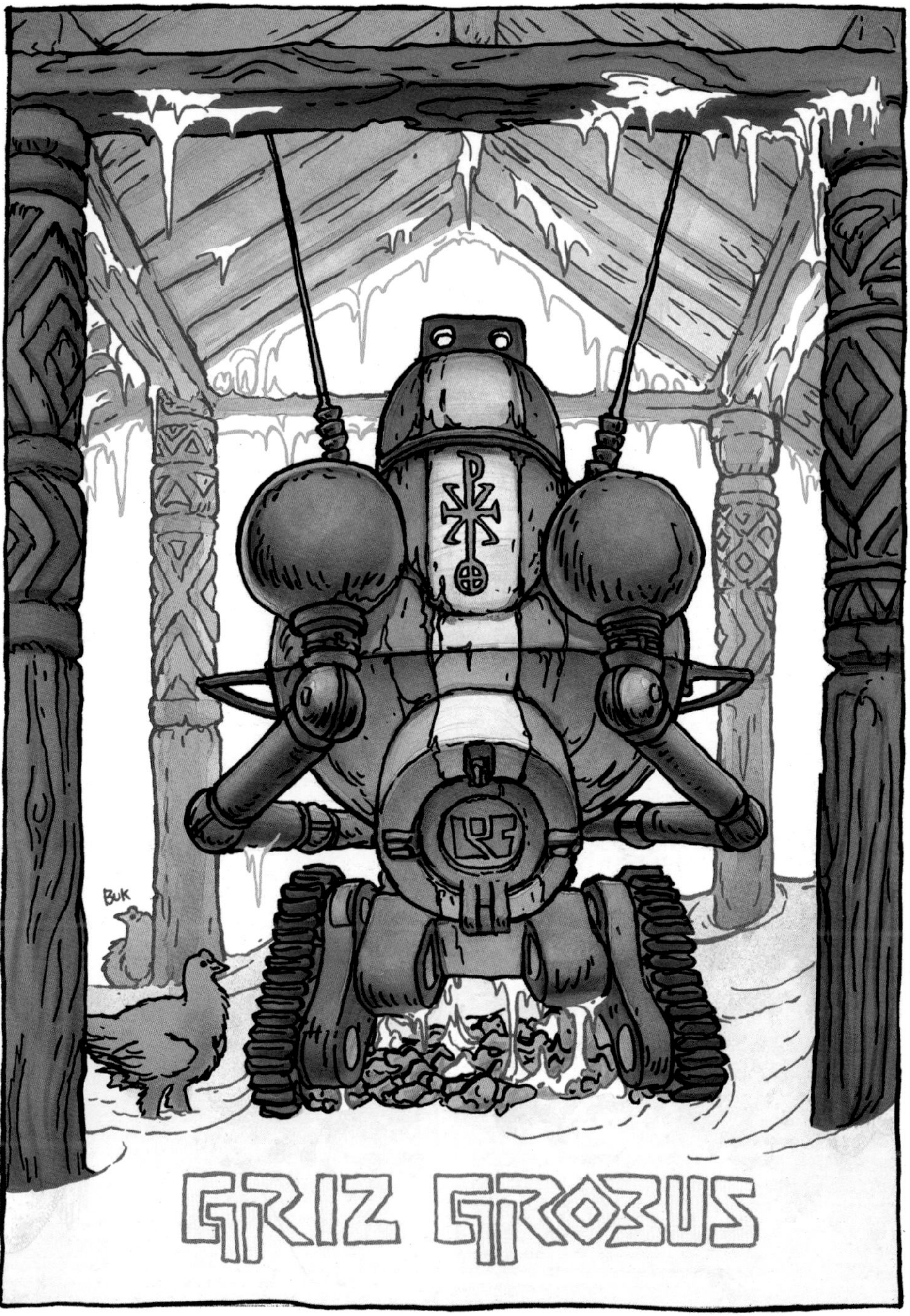
BUK
GRIZ GROBUS

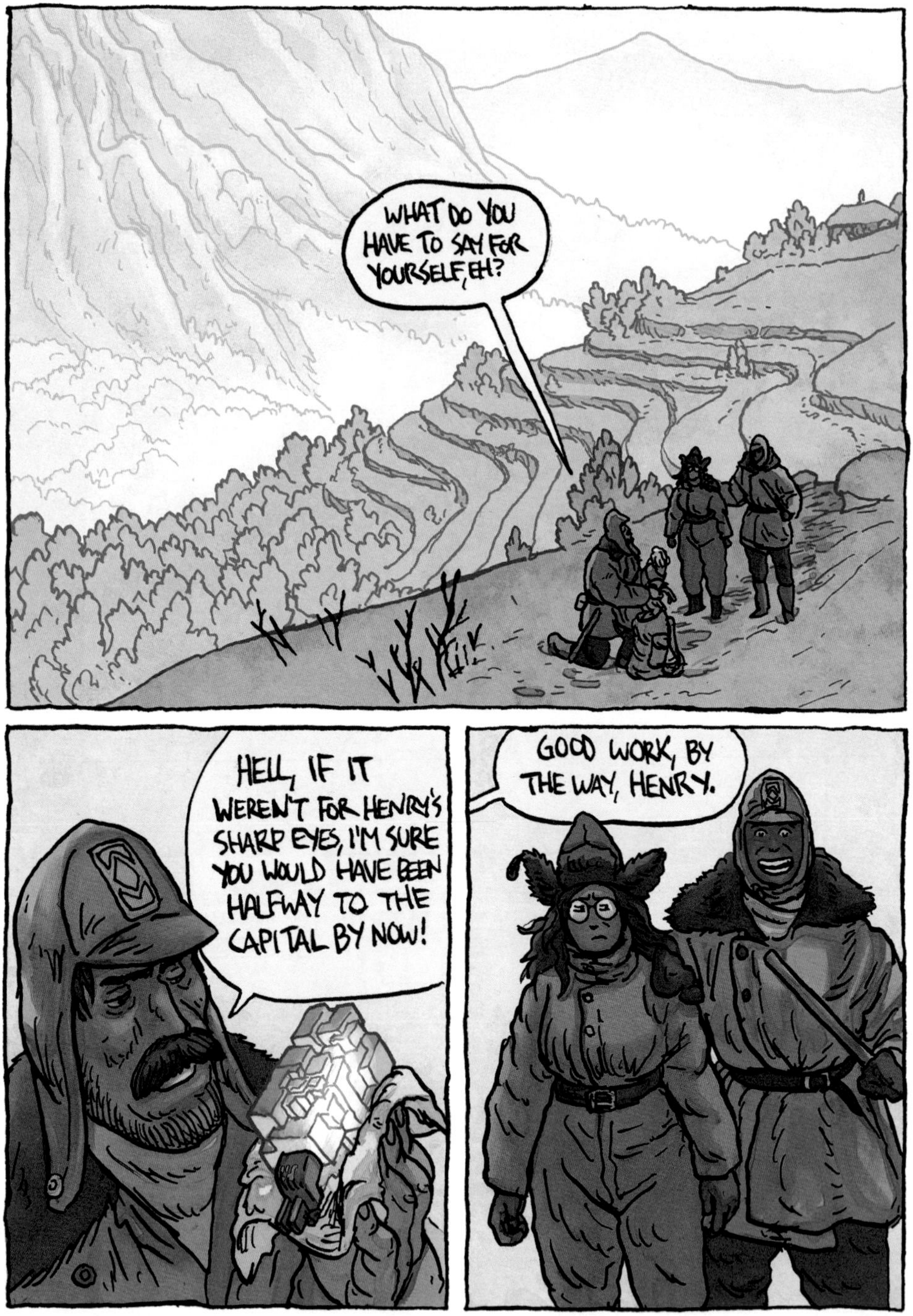
WHAT DO YOU HAVE TO SAY FOR YOURSELF, EH?
HELL, IF IT WEREN'T FOR HENRY'S SHARP EYES, I'M SURE YOU WOULD HAVE BEEN HALFWAY TO THE CAPITAL BY NOW!
GOOD WORK, BY THE WAY, HENRY.

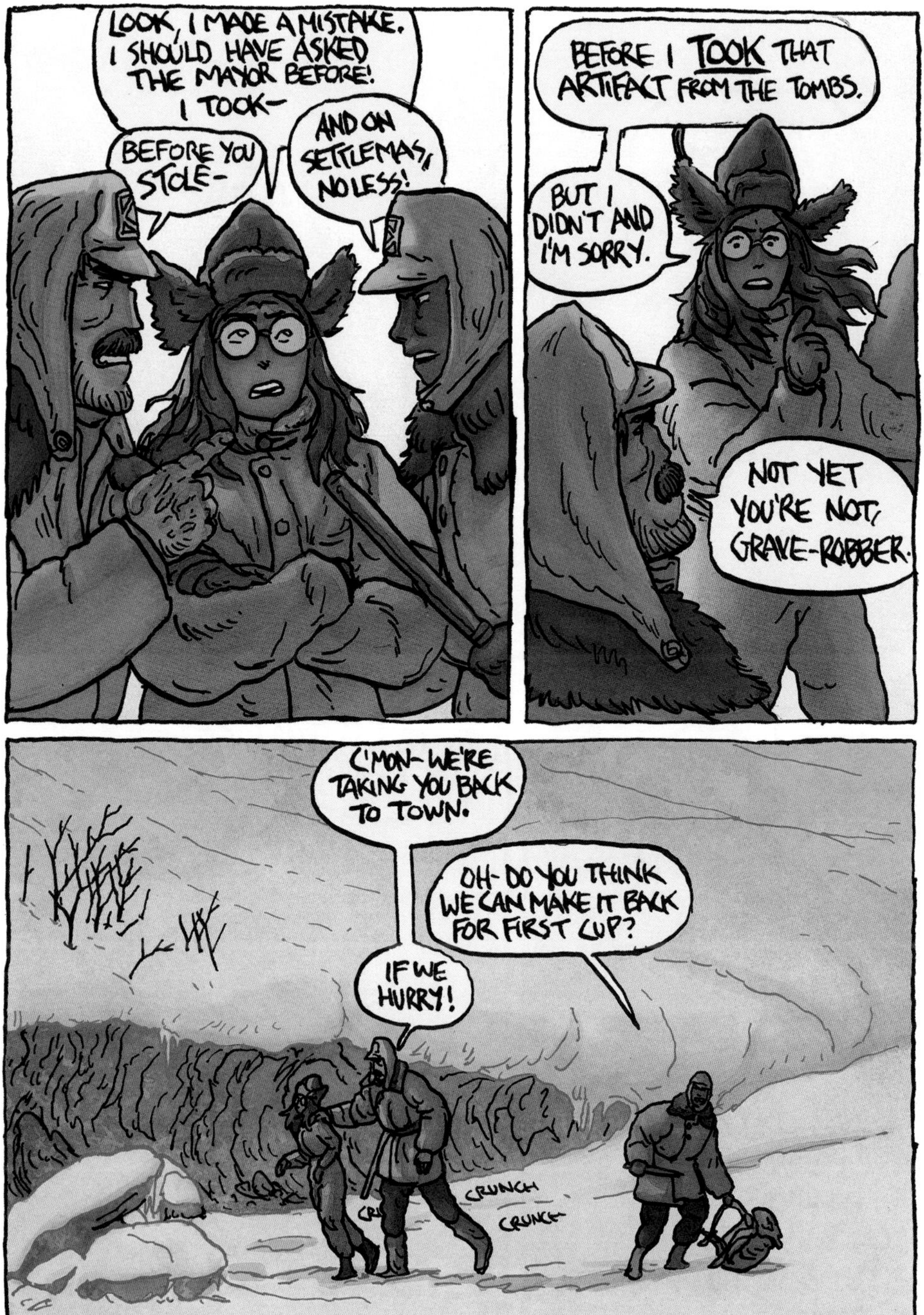
LOOK, I MADE A MISTAKE. I SHOULD HAVE ASKED THE MAYOR BEFORE! I TOOK-
BEFORE YOU STOLE-
AND ON SETTLEMAS, NO LESS!
BEFORE I TOOK THAT ARTIFACT FROM THE TOMBS.
BUT I DIDN'T AND I'M SORRY.
NOT YET YOU'RE NOT, GRAVE-ROBBER.
C'MON- WE'RE TAKING YOU BACK TO TOWN.
OH- DO YOU THINK WE CAN MAKE IT BACK FOR FIRST CUP?
IF WE HURRY!
CRUNCH
CRUNCH

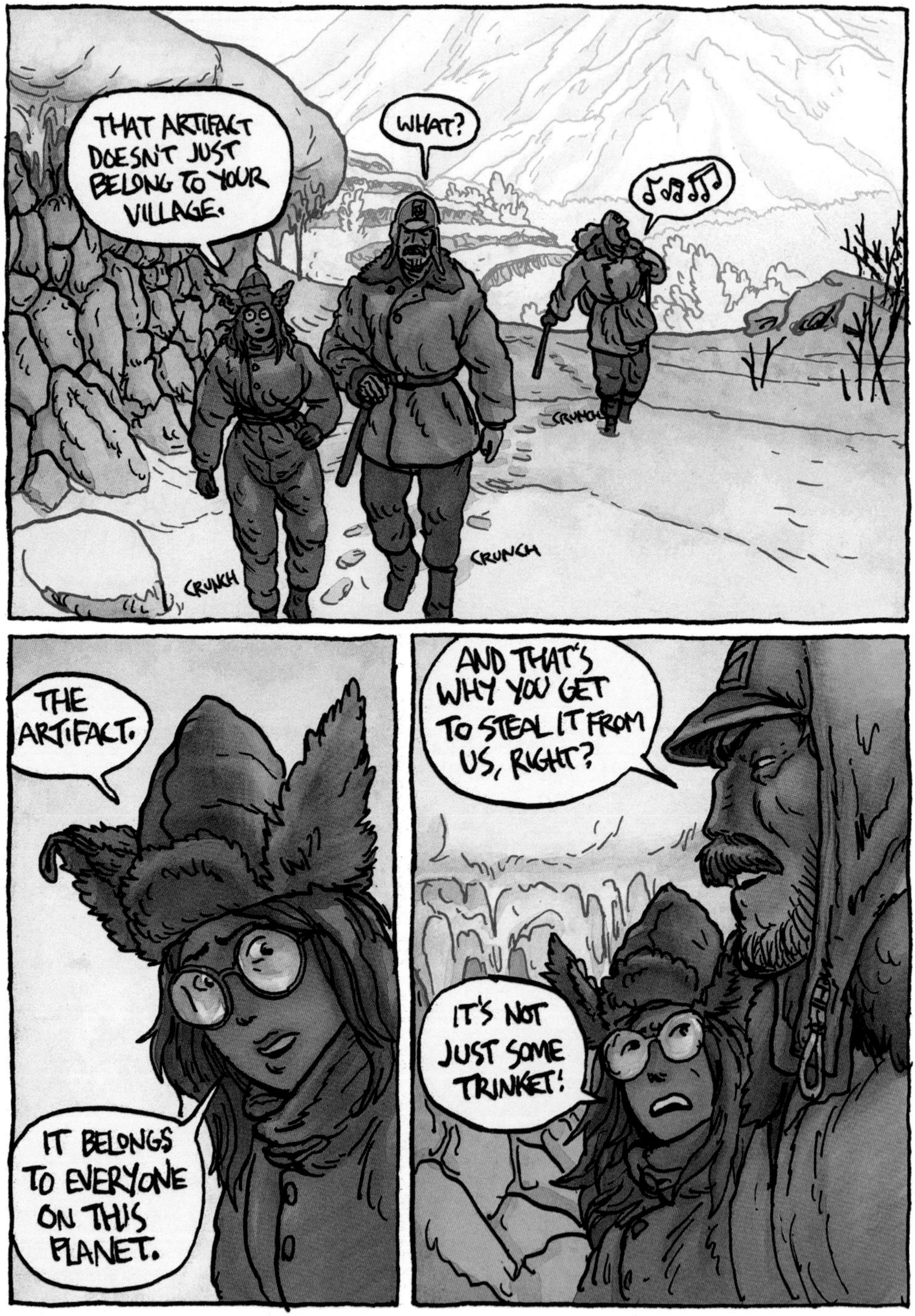
THAT ARTIFACT DOESN'T JUST BELONG TO YOUR VILLAGE.
WHAT?
♪♫♫♪
CRUNCH
CRUNCH
CRUNCH
THE ARTIFACT.
IT BELONGS TO EVERYONE ON THIS PLANET.
AND THAT'S WHY YOU GET TO STEAL IT FROM US, RIGHT?
IT'S NOT JUST SOME TRINKET!

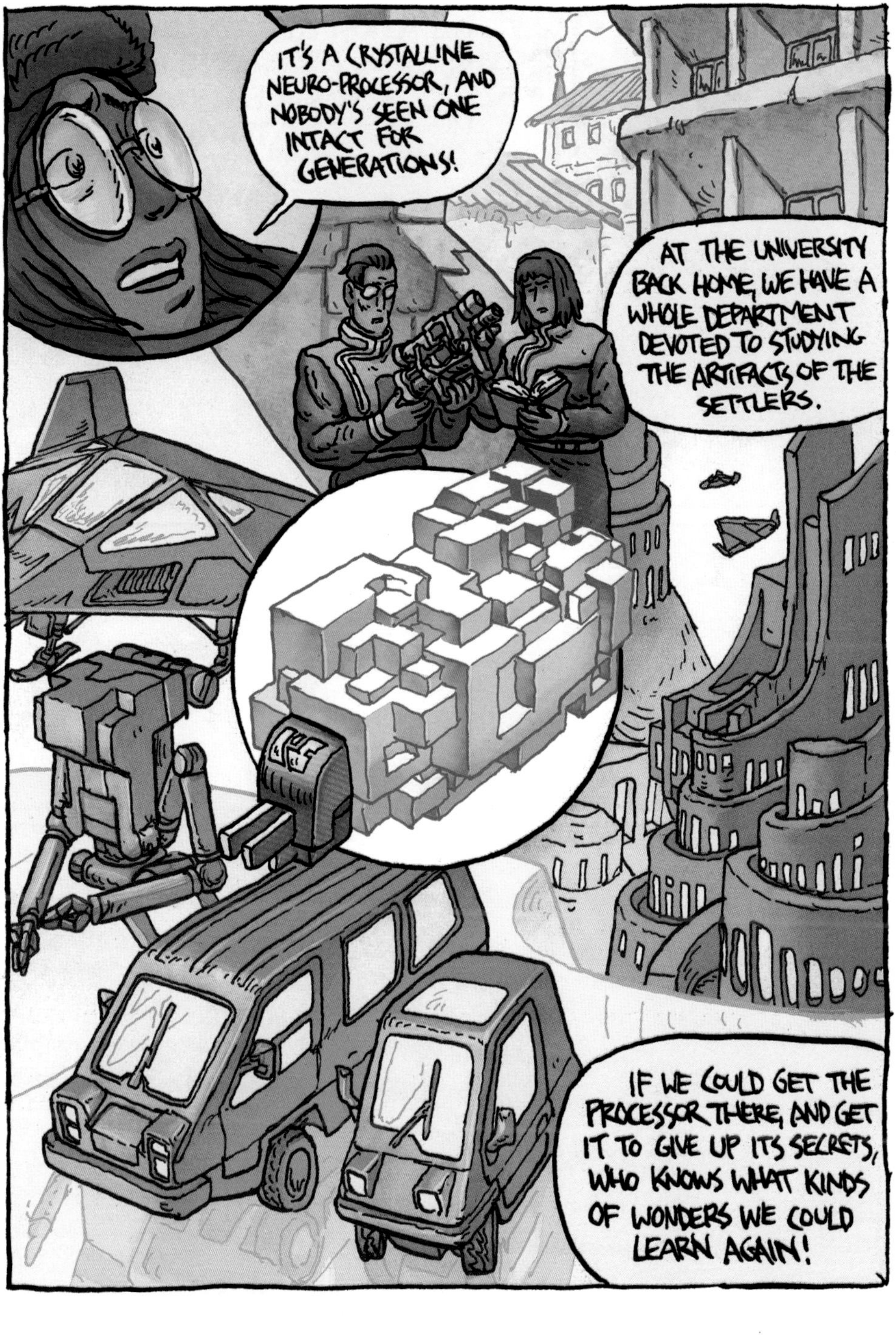
IT'S A CRYSTALLINE NEURO-PROCESSOR, AND NOBODY'S SEEN ONE INTACT FOR GENERATIONS!
AT THE UNIVERSITY BACK HOME, WE HAVE A WHOLE DEPARTMENT DEVOTED TO STUDYING THE ARTIFACTS OF THE SETTLERS.
IF WE COULD GET THE PROCESSOR THERE, AND GET IT TO GIVE UP ITS SECRETS, WHO KNOWS WHAT KINDS OF WONDERS WE COULD LEARN AGAIN!

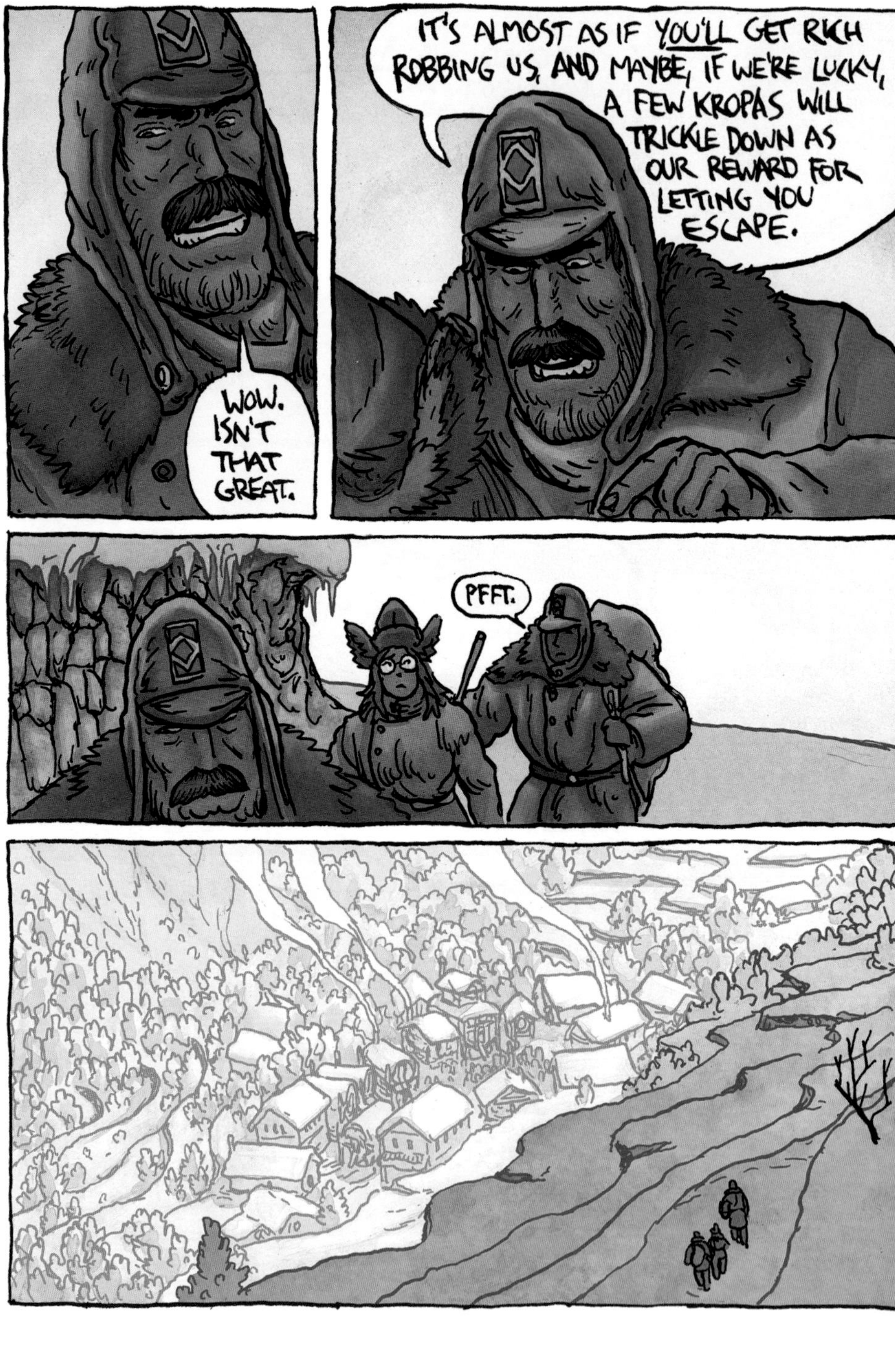
IT'S ALMOST AS IF YOU'LL GET RICH ROBBING US, AND MAYBE, IF WE'RE LUCKY, A FEW KROPAS WILL TRICKLE DOWN AS OUR REWARD FOR LETTING YOU ESCAPE.
WOW. ISN'T THAT GREAT.
PFFT.

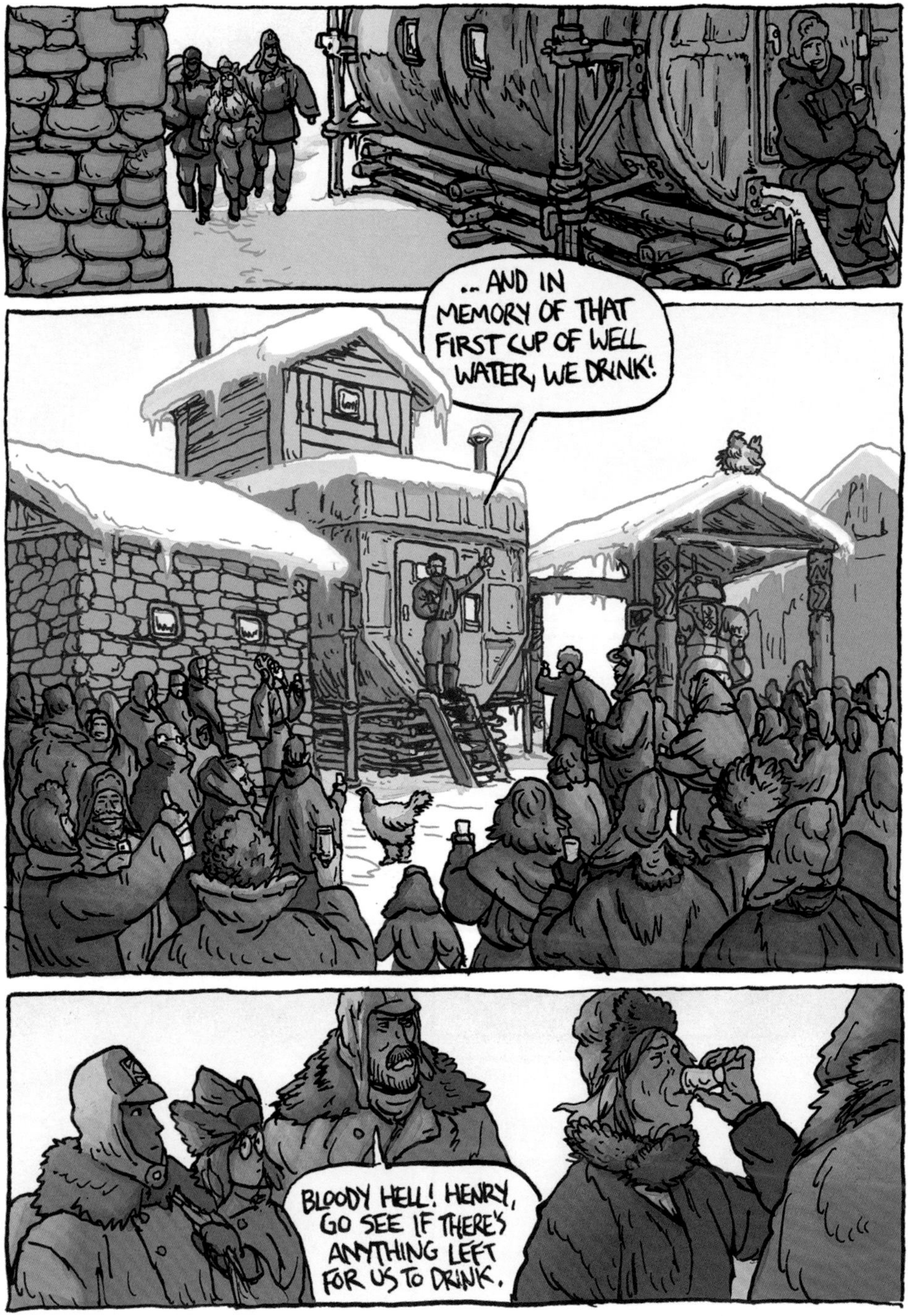
... AND IN MEMORY OF THAT FIRST CUP OF WELL WATER, WE DRINK!
BLOODY HELL! HENRY, GO SEE IF THERE'S ANYTHING LEFT FOR US TO DRINK.

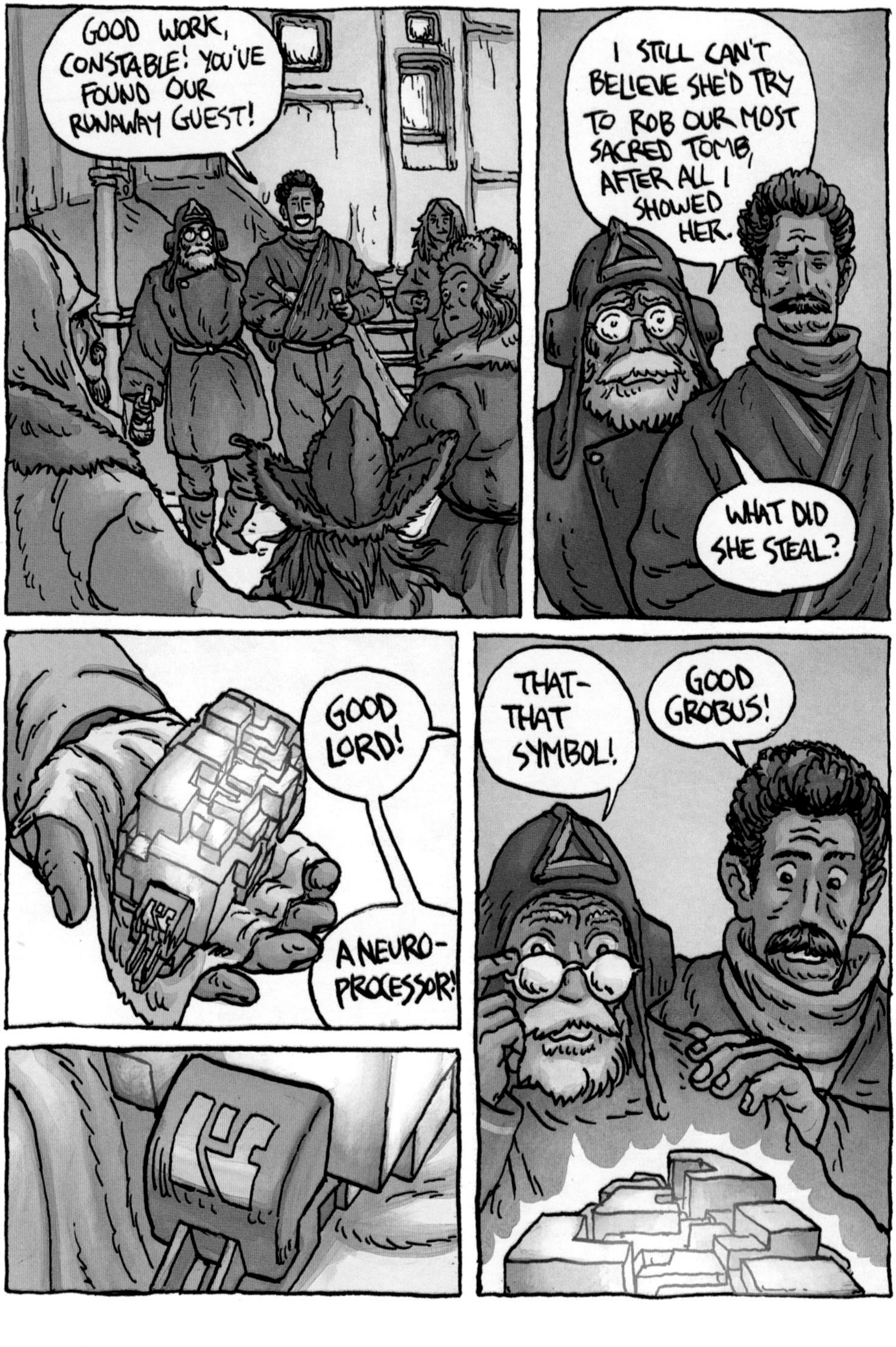
GOOD WORK, CONSTABLE! YOU'VE FOUND OUR RUNAWAY GUEST!
I STILL CAN'T BELIEVE SHE'D TRY TO ROB OUR MOST SACRED TOMB, AFTER ALL I SHOWED HER.
WHAT DID SHE STEAL?
GOOD LORD!
A NEURO-PROCESSOR!
THAT- THAT SYMBOL!
GOOD GROBUS!

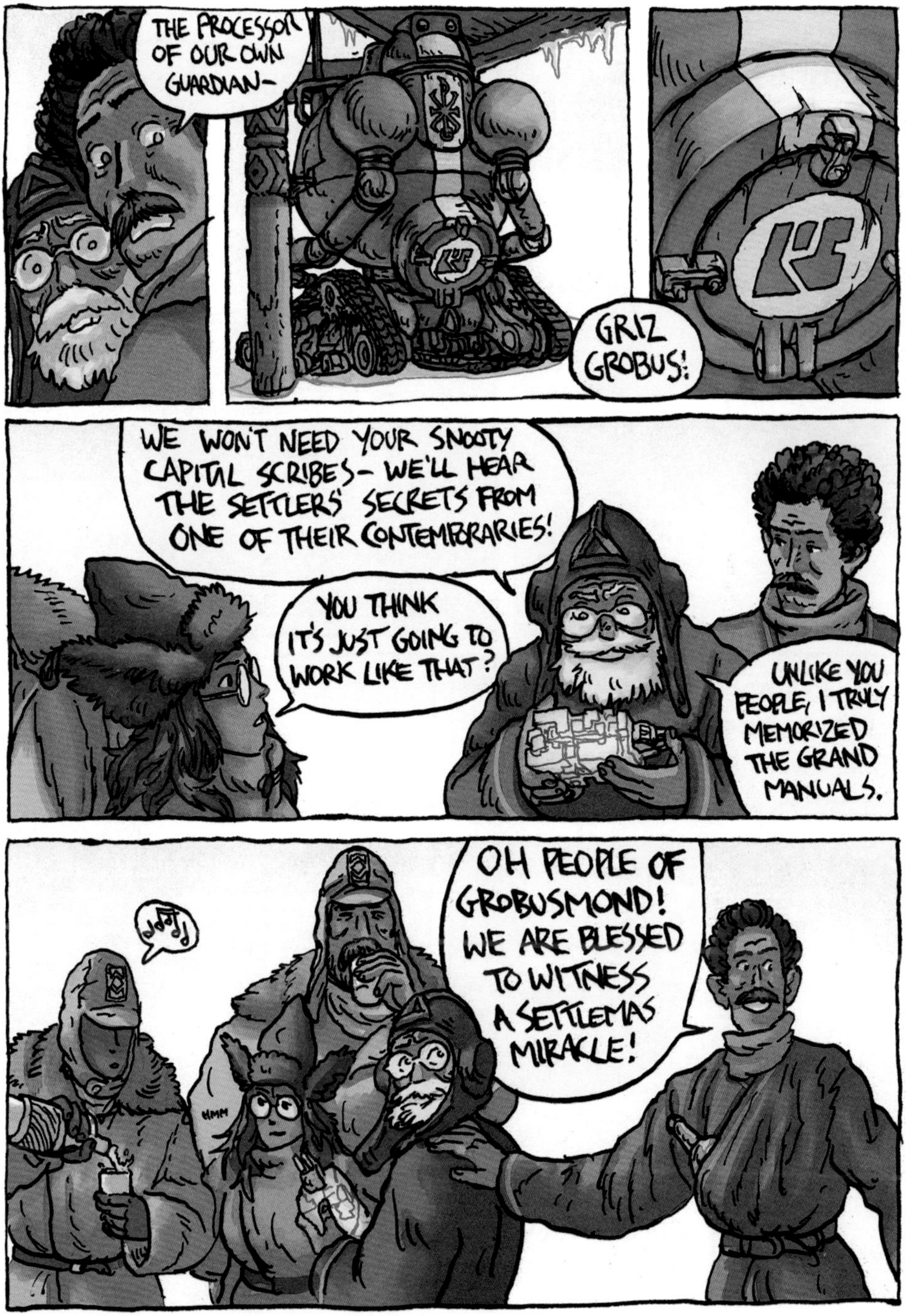
THE PROCESSOR OF OUR OWN GUARDIAN-
GRIZ GROBUS!
WE WON'T NEED YOUR SNOOTY CAPITAL SCRIBES- WE'LL HEAR THE SETTLERS' SECRETS FROM ONE OF THEIR CONTEMPORARIES!
YOU THINK IT'S JUST GOING TO WORK LIKE THAT?
UNLIKE YOU PEOPLE, I TRULY MEMORIZED THE GRAND MANUALS.
OH PEOPLE OF GROBUSMOND! WE ARE BLESSED TO WITNESS A SETTLEMAS MIRACLE!

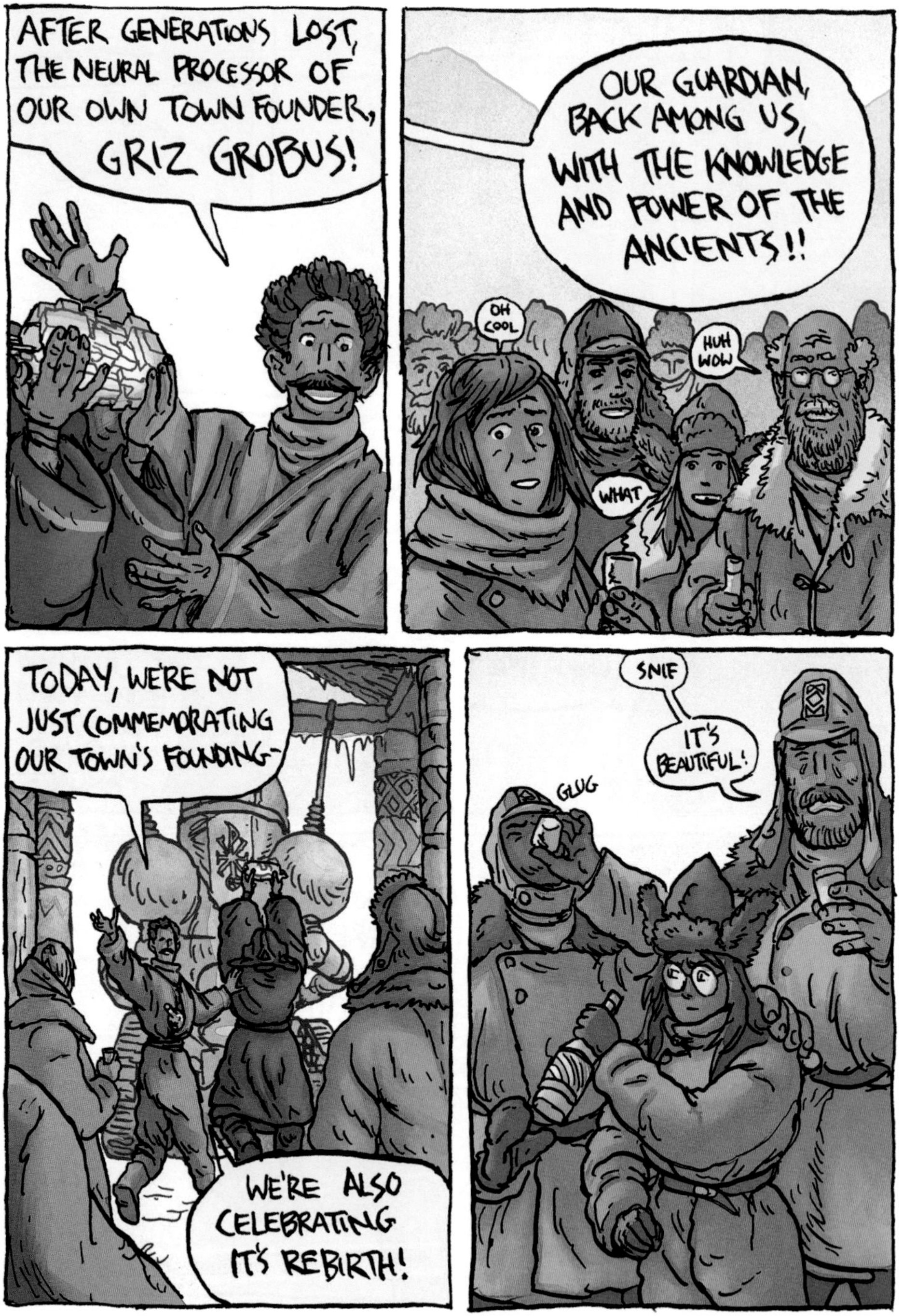
AFTER GENERATIONS LOST, THE NEURAL PROCESSOR OF OUR OWN TOWN FOUNDER, GRIZ GROBUS!
OUR GUARDIAN, BACK AMONG US, WITH THE KNOWLEDGE AND POWER OF THE ANCIENTS!!
OH COOL
HUH WOW
WHAT
TODAY, WE'RE NOT JUST COMMEMORATING OUR TOWN'S FOUNDING-
WE'RE ALSO CELEBRATING IT'S REBIRTH!
SNIF
IT'S BEAUTIFUL!
GLUG

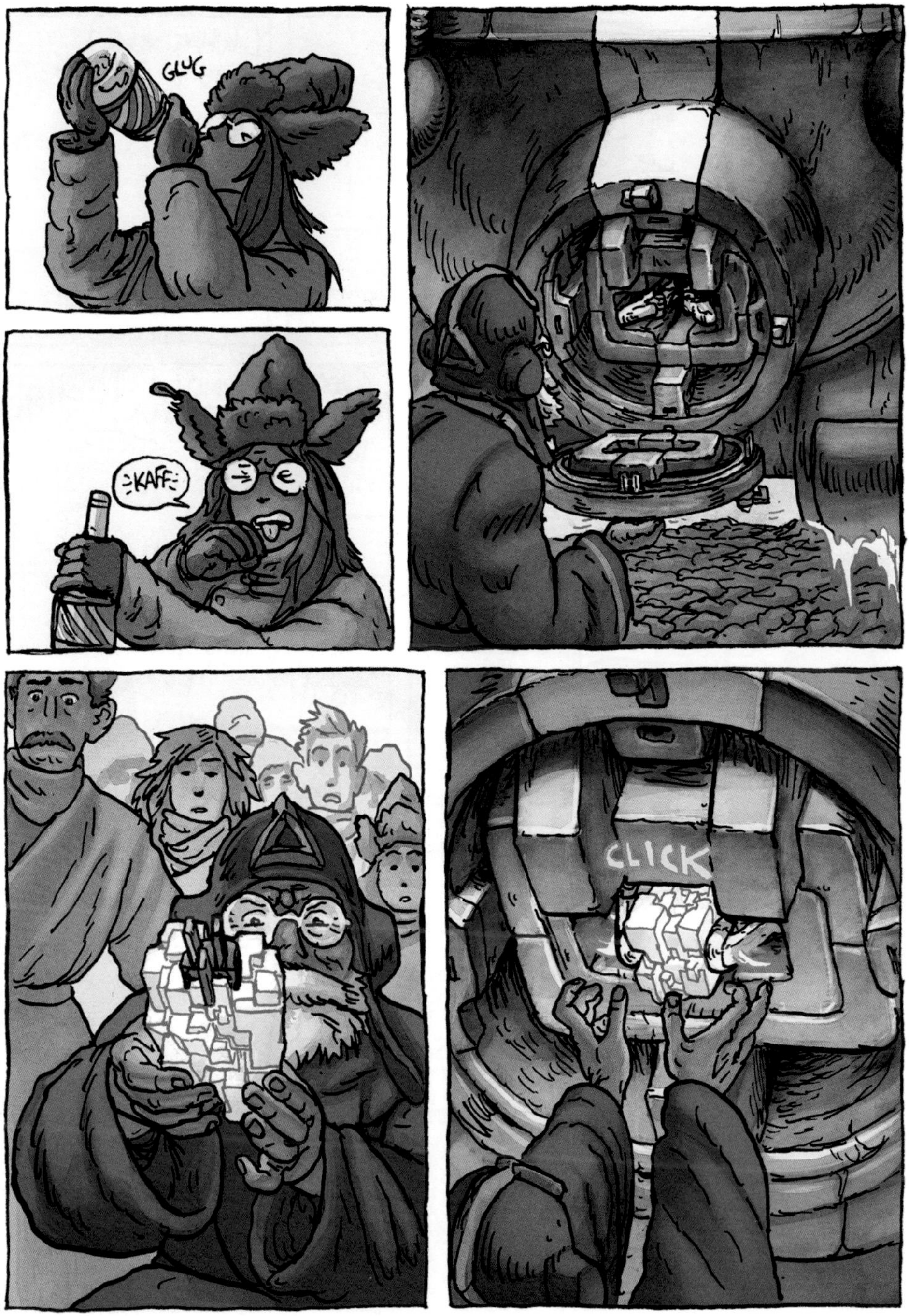
GLUG
KAFF
CLICK

VMMMM

VZZZT

WHAT YEAR IS IT?

VZZZT

125 YEARS, TO THE DAY, SINCE THE FOUNDATION OF GROBUSMOND!

AND IT IS OUR PLEASURE TO WELCOME YOU, AT LONG LAST, BACK TO THE TOWN THAT BEARS YOUR NAME!

VZZZT

GROBUS-MOND? I WAS DEACTIVATED IN A TOWN CALLED STANLEYVILLE—

VZZZT
VZZZT

THAT WAS TO BE LAID OUT VERY SIMILARLY TO THIS.

VZZZT

ARE YOU NOT GRIZ GROBUS?

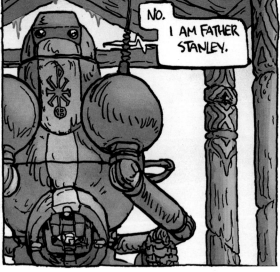

NO. I AM FATHER STANLEY.

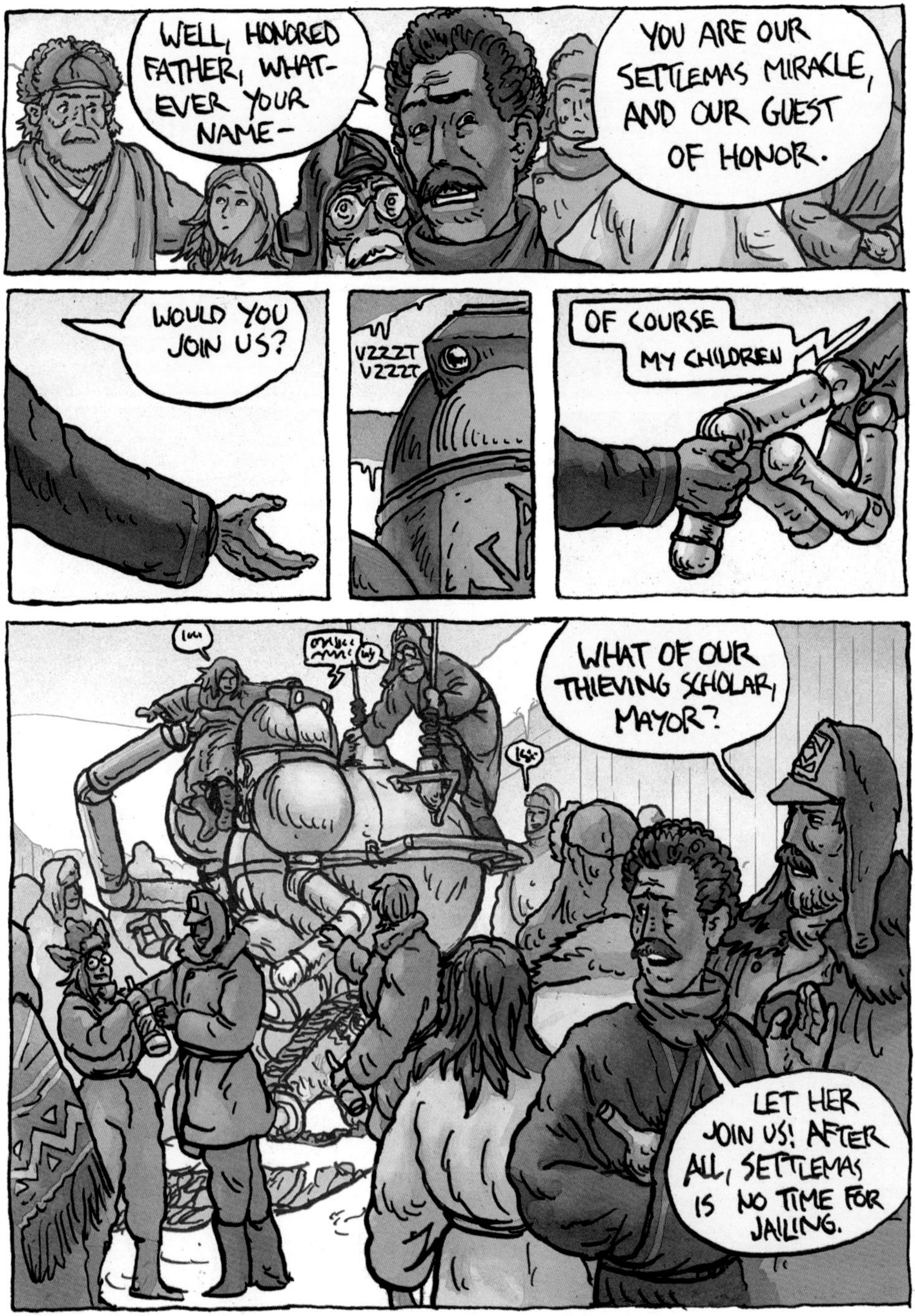
WELL, HONORED FATHER, WHAT-EVER YOUR NAME-
YOU ARE OUR SETTLEMAS MIRACLE, AND OUR GUEST OF HONOR.
WOULD YOU JOIN US?
VZZZT VZZZT
OF COURSE MY CHILDREN
WHAT OF OUR THIEVING SCHOLAR, MAYOR?
LET HER JOIN US! AFTER ALL, SETTLEMAS IS NO TIME FOR JAILING.

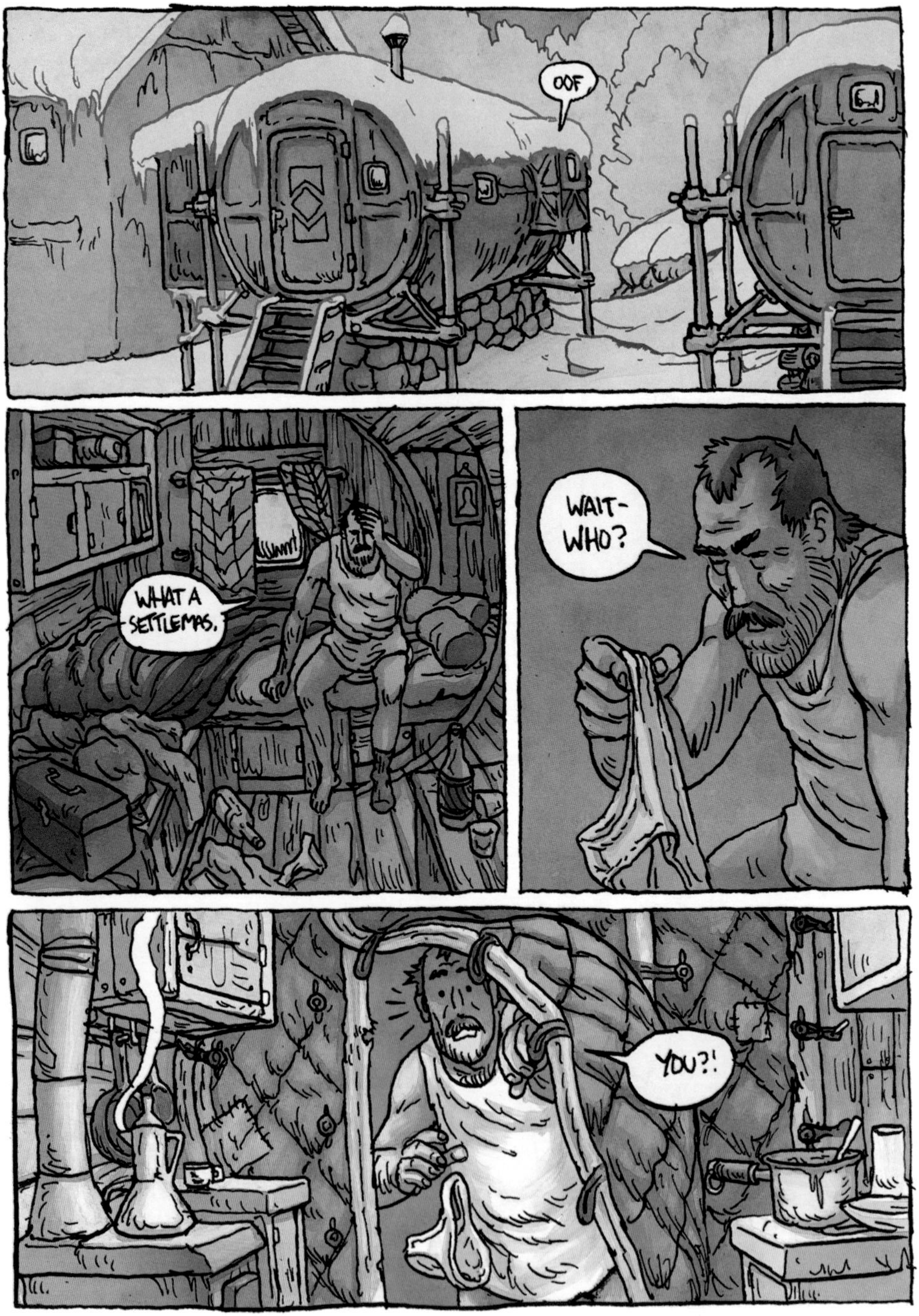
OOF
WHAT A SETTLEMAS.
WAIT-WHO?
YOU?!

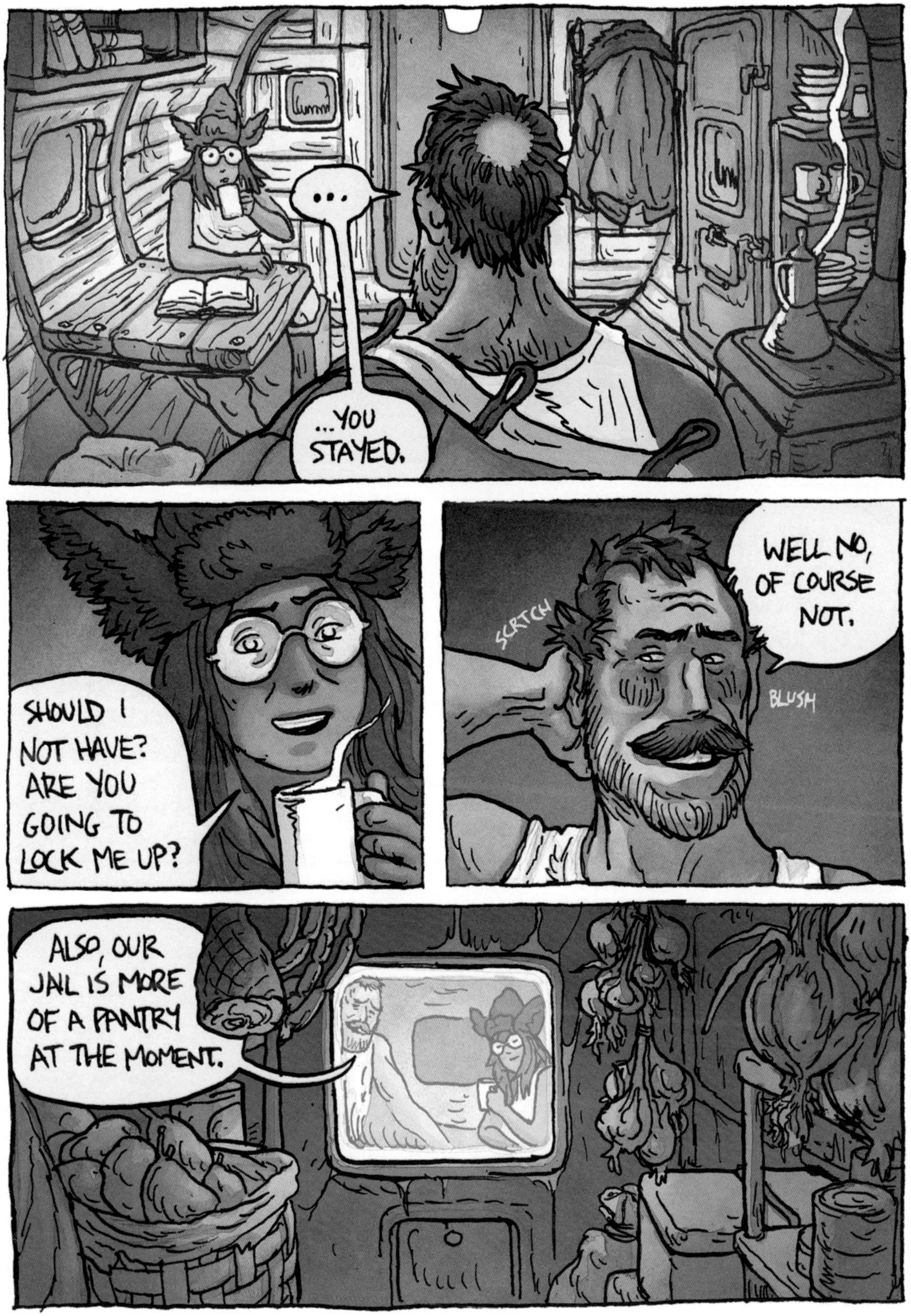
...
...YOU STAYED.
SHOULD I NOT HAVE? ARE YOU GOING TO LOCK ME UP?
SCRTCH
WELL NO, OF COURSE NOT.
BLUSH
ALSO, OUR JAIL IS MORE OF A PANTRY AT THE MOMENT.

WHAT ARE YOU READING?

SOME OF YOUR POLICE RECORDS.

I'VE BEEN WONDERING— WHEN DID STANLEYVILLE BECOME GROBUS-MOND?

FLIP

OH LORD, I DON'T KNOW. I'M NOT MUCH OF A READER.

PANG PANG PAN

WHERE COULD I FIND SOME OLDER RECORDS?

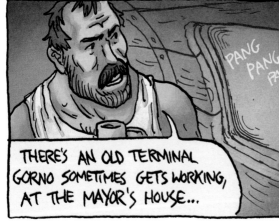

PANG PANG PA

THERE'S AN OLD TERMINAL GORNO SOMETIMES GETS WORKING, AT THE MAYOR'S HOUSE...

PANG PANG PANG PA

WHAT THE HELL IS GOING ON OUT THERE?

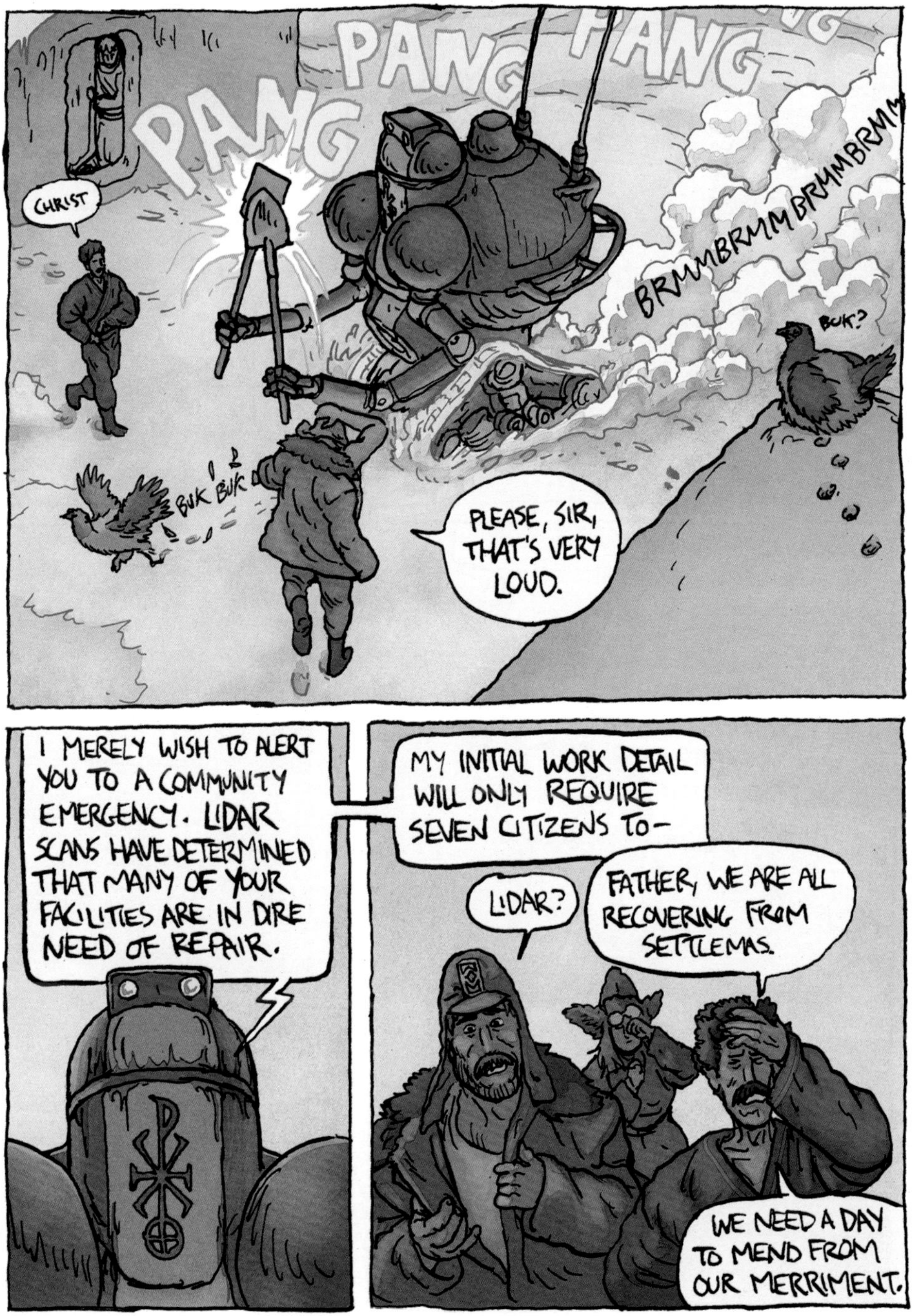
PANG
PANG
PANG
CHRIST
BRMMBRMMBRMMBRMMBRMM
BUK?
BUK BUK
PLEASE, SIR, THAT'S VERY LOUD.
I MERELY WISH TO ALERT YOU TO A COMMUNITY EMERGENCY. LIDAR SCANS HAVE DETERMINED THAT MANY OF YOUR FACILITIES ARE IN DIRE NEED OF REPAIR.
MY INITIAL WORK DETAIL WILL ONLY REQUIRE SEVEN CITIZENS TO—
LIDAR?
FATHER, WE ARE ALL RECOVERING FROM SETTLEMAS.
WE NEED A DAY TO MEND FROM OUR MERRIMENT.

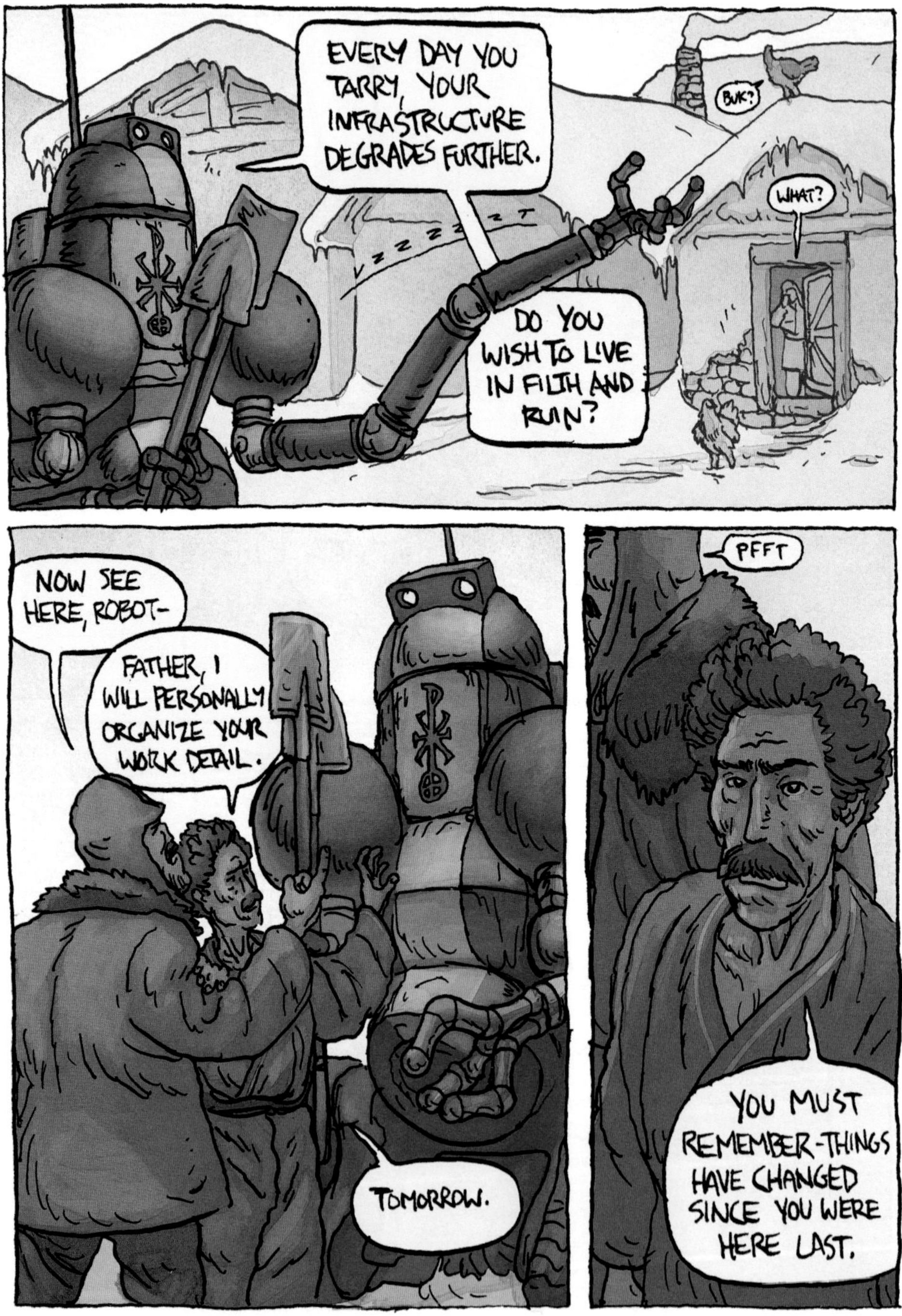
EVERY DAY YOU TARRY, YOUR INFRASTRUCTURE DEGRADES FURTHER.
DO YOU WISH TO LIVE IN FILTH AND RUIN?
BUK?
WHAT?
NOW SEE HERE, ROBOT-
FATHER, I WILL PERSONALLY ORGANIZE YOUR WORK DETAIL.
TOMORROW.
PFFT
YOU MUST REMEMBER-THINGS HAVE CHANGED SINCE YOU WERE HERE LAST.

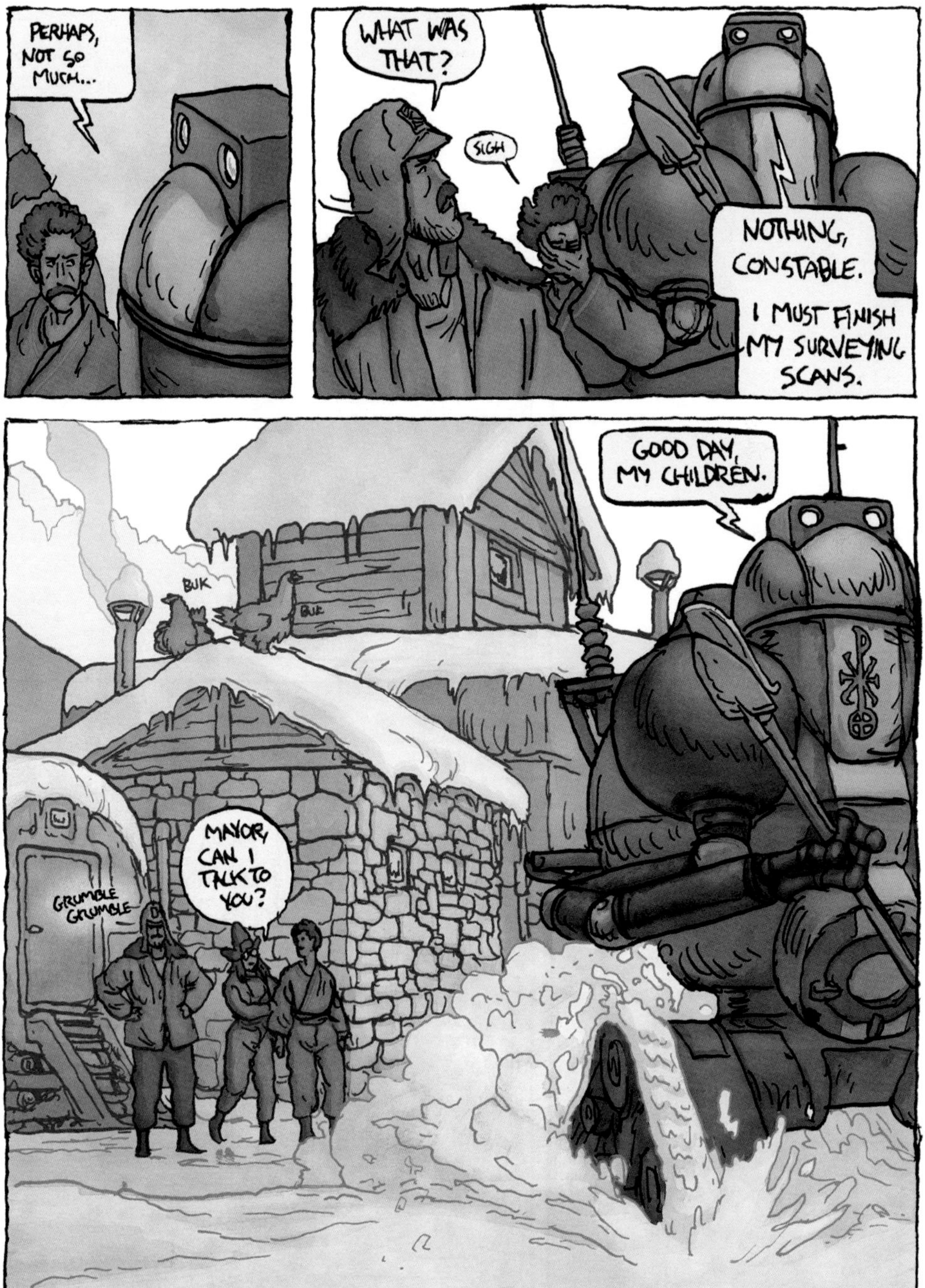
PERHAPS, NOT SO MUCH...
WHAT WAS THAT?
SIGH
NOTHING, CONSTABLE.
I MUST FINISH MY SURVEYING SCANS.
GOOD DAY, MY CHILDREN.
BUK
BUK
MAYOR, CAN I TALK TO YOU?
GRUMBLE GRUMBLE

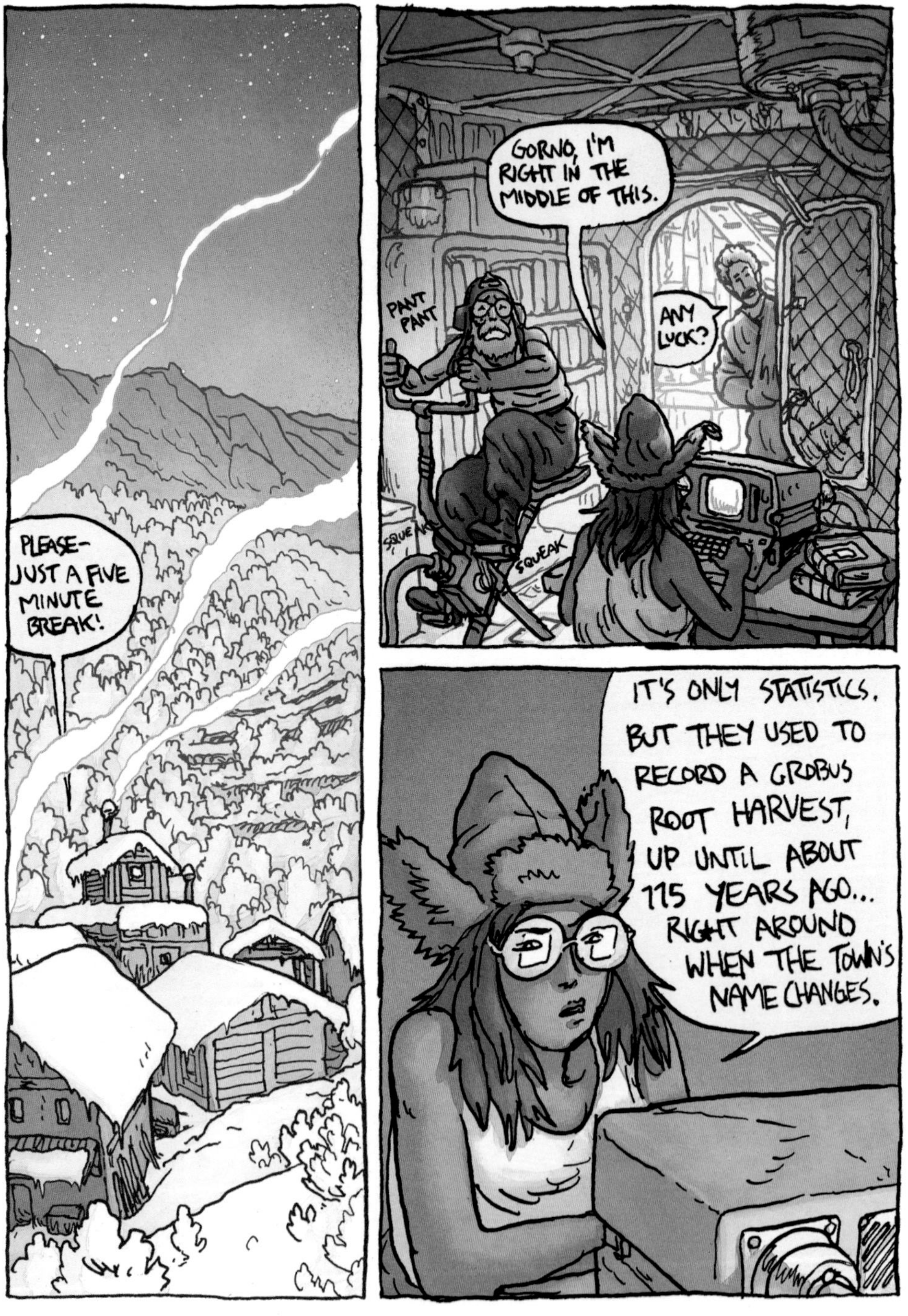
PLEASE- JUST A FIVE MINUTE BREAK!
GORNO, I'M RIGHT IN THE MIDDLE OF THIS.
PANT PANT
ANY LUCK?
SQUEAK
SQUEAK
IT'S ONLY STATISTICS. BUT THEY USED TO RECORD A GROBUS ROOT HARVEST, UP UNTIL ABOUT 115 YEARS AGO... RIGHT AROUND WHEN THE TOWN'S NAME CHANGES.

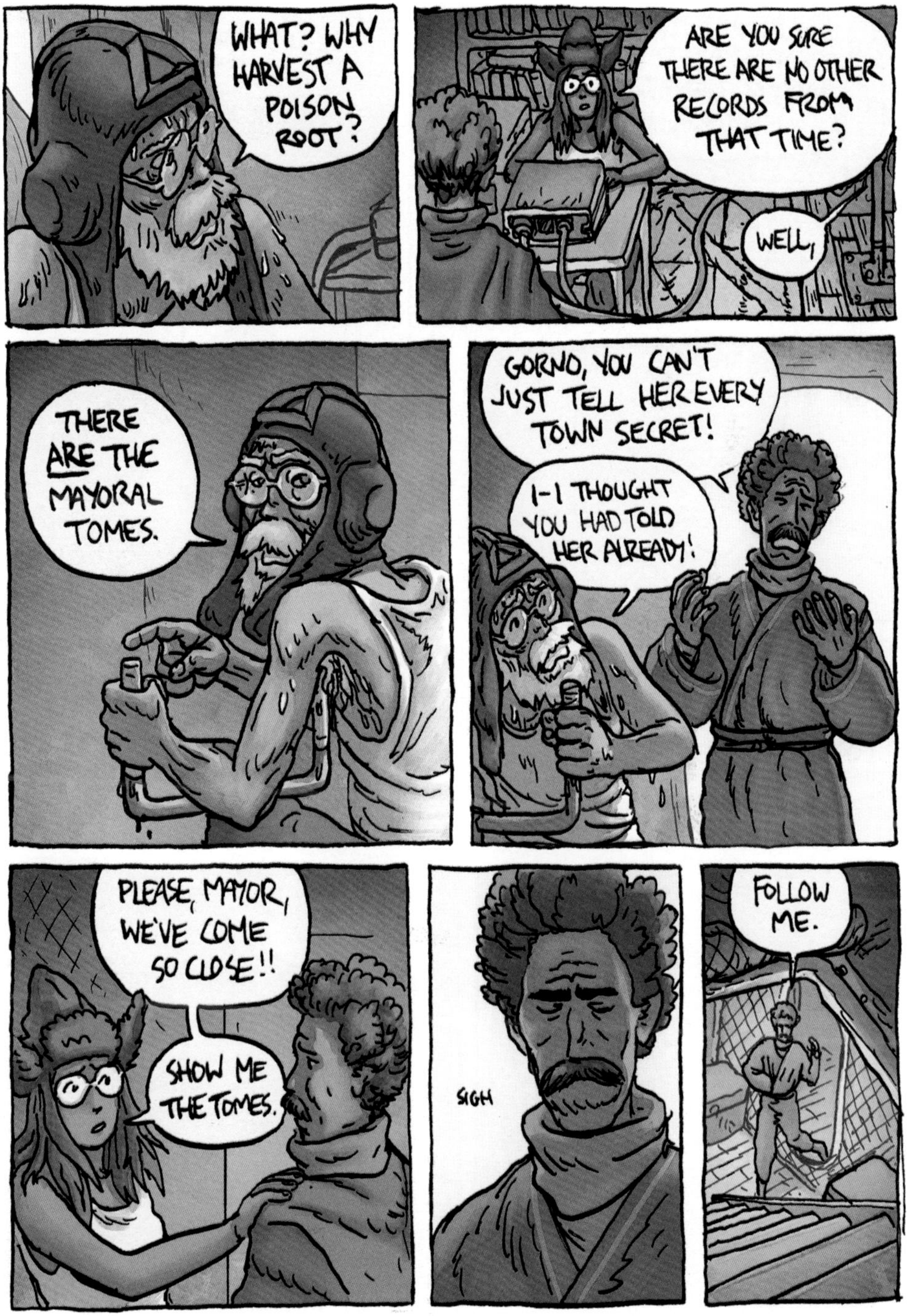
WHAT? WHY HARVEST A POISON ROOT?
ARE YOU SURE THERE ARE NO OTHER RECORDS FROM THAT TIME?
WELL,
THERE ARE THE MAYORAL TOMES.
GORNO, YOU CAN'T JUST TELL HER EVERY TOWN SECRET!
I-I THOUGHT YOU HAD TOLD HER ALREADY!
PLEASE, MAYOR, WE'VE COME SO CLOSE!!
SHOW ME THE TOMES.
SIGH
FOLLOW ME.

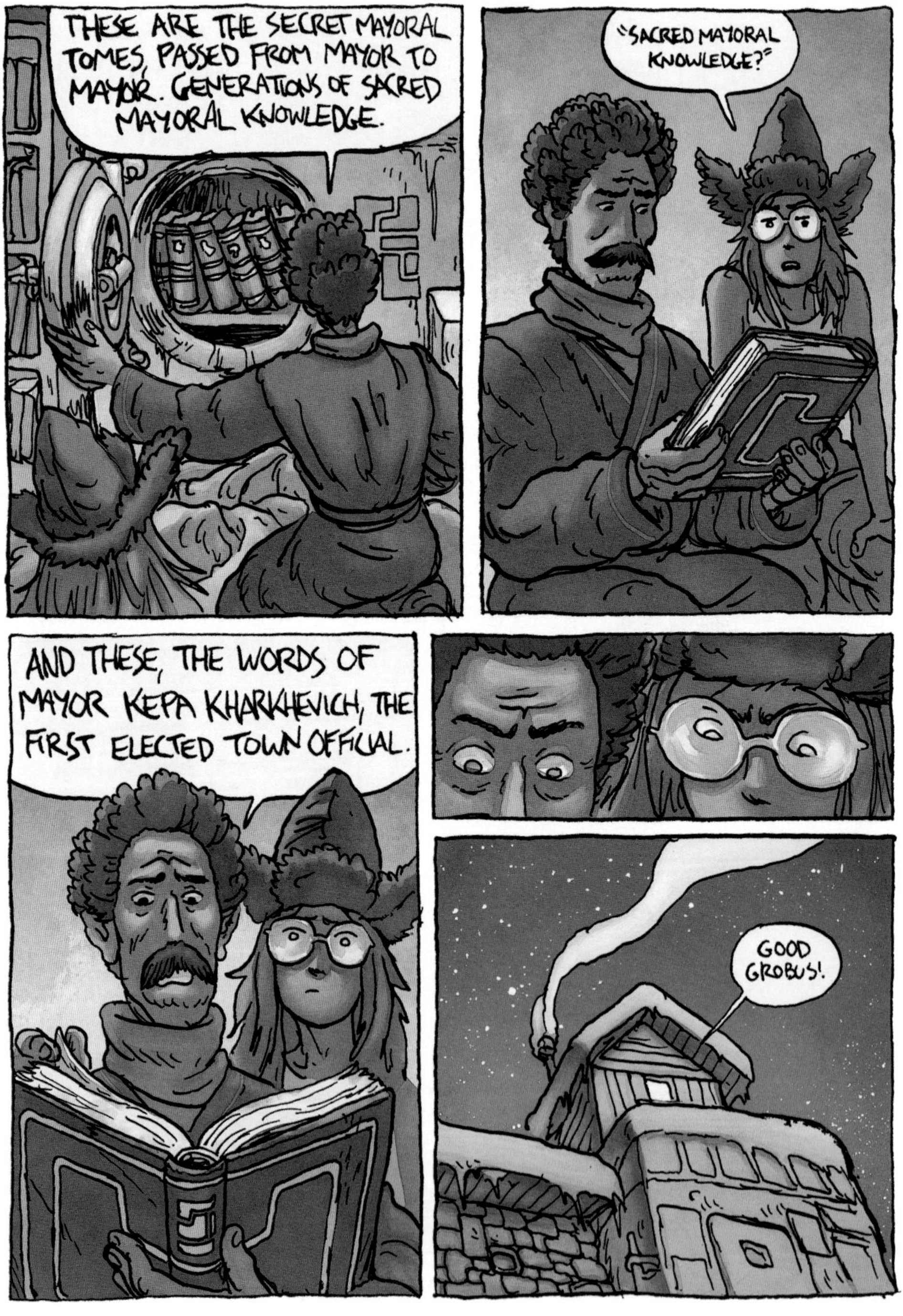
THESE ARE THE SECRET MAYORAL TOMES, PASSED FROM MAYOR TO MAYOR. GENERATIONS OF SACRED MAYORAL KNOWLEDGE.
"SACRED MAYORAL KNOWLEDGE?"
AND THESE, THE WORDS OF MAYOR KEPA KHARKHEVICH, THE FIRST ELECTED TOWN OFFICIAL.
GOOD GROBUS!

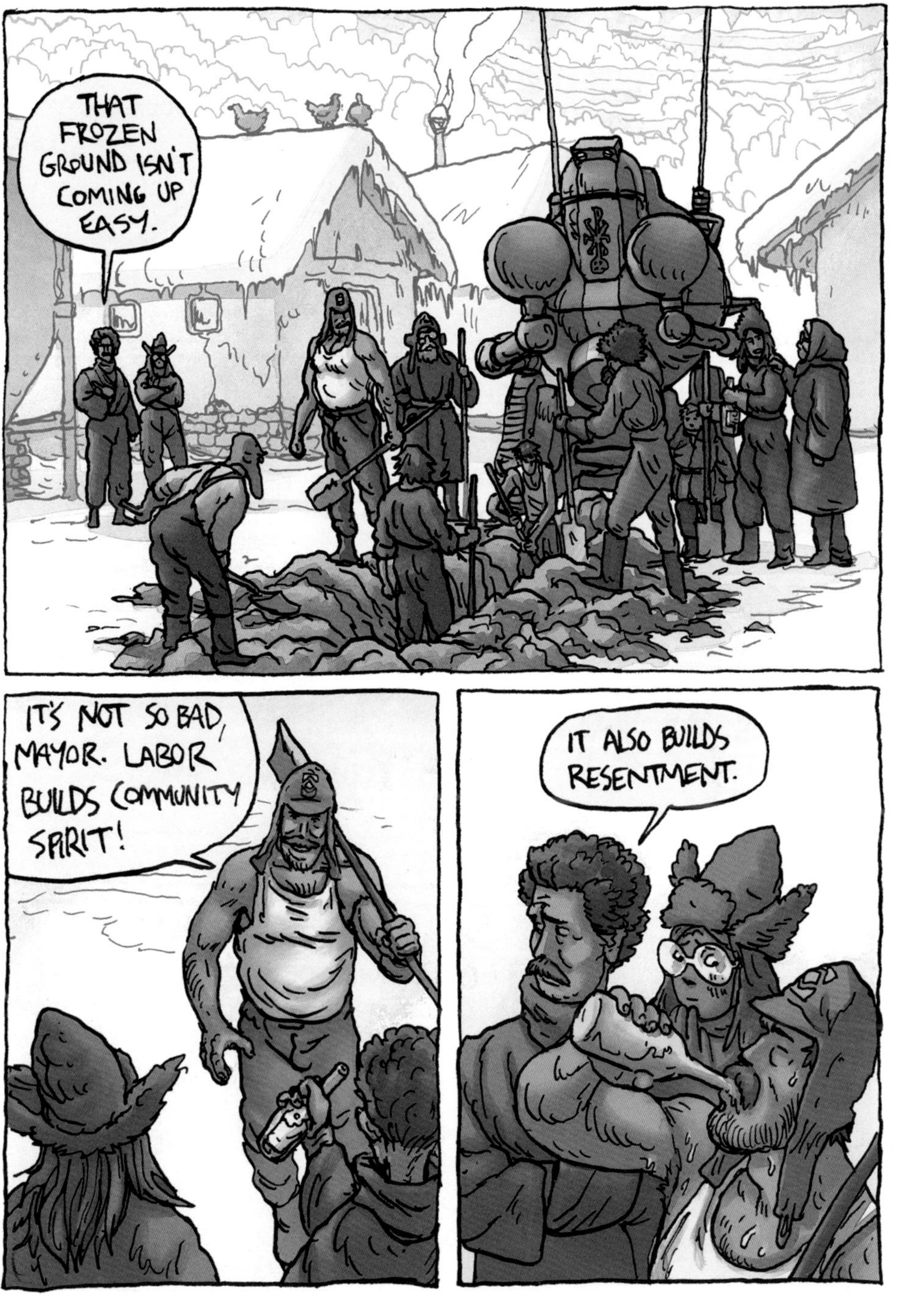
THAT FROZEN GROUND ISN'T COMING UP EASY.
IT'S NOT SO BAD, MAYOR. LABOR BUILDS COMMUNITY SPIRIT!
IT ALSO BUILDS RESENTMENT.

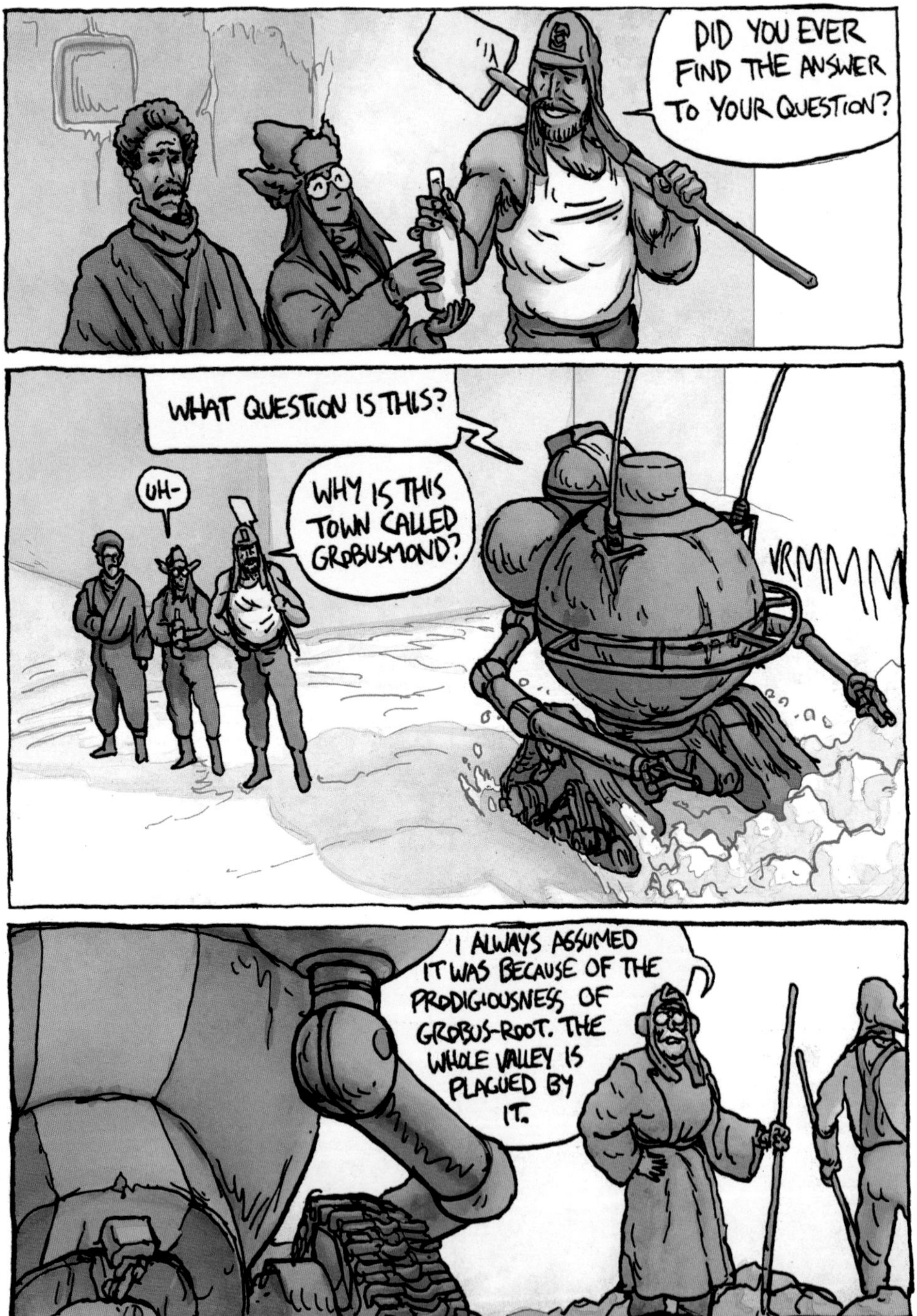
DID YOU EVER FIND THE ANSWER TO YOUR QUESTION?
WHAT QUESTION IS THIS?
UH-
WHY IS THIS TOWN CALLED GROBUSMOND?
VRMMMM
I ALWAYS ASSUMED IT WAS BECAUSE OF THE PRODIGIOUSNESS OF GROBUS-ROOT. THE WHOLE VALLEY IS PLAGUED BY IT.

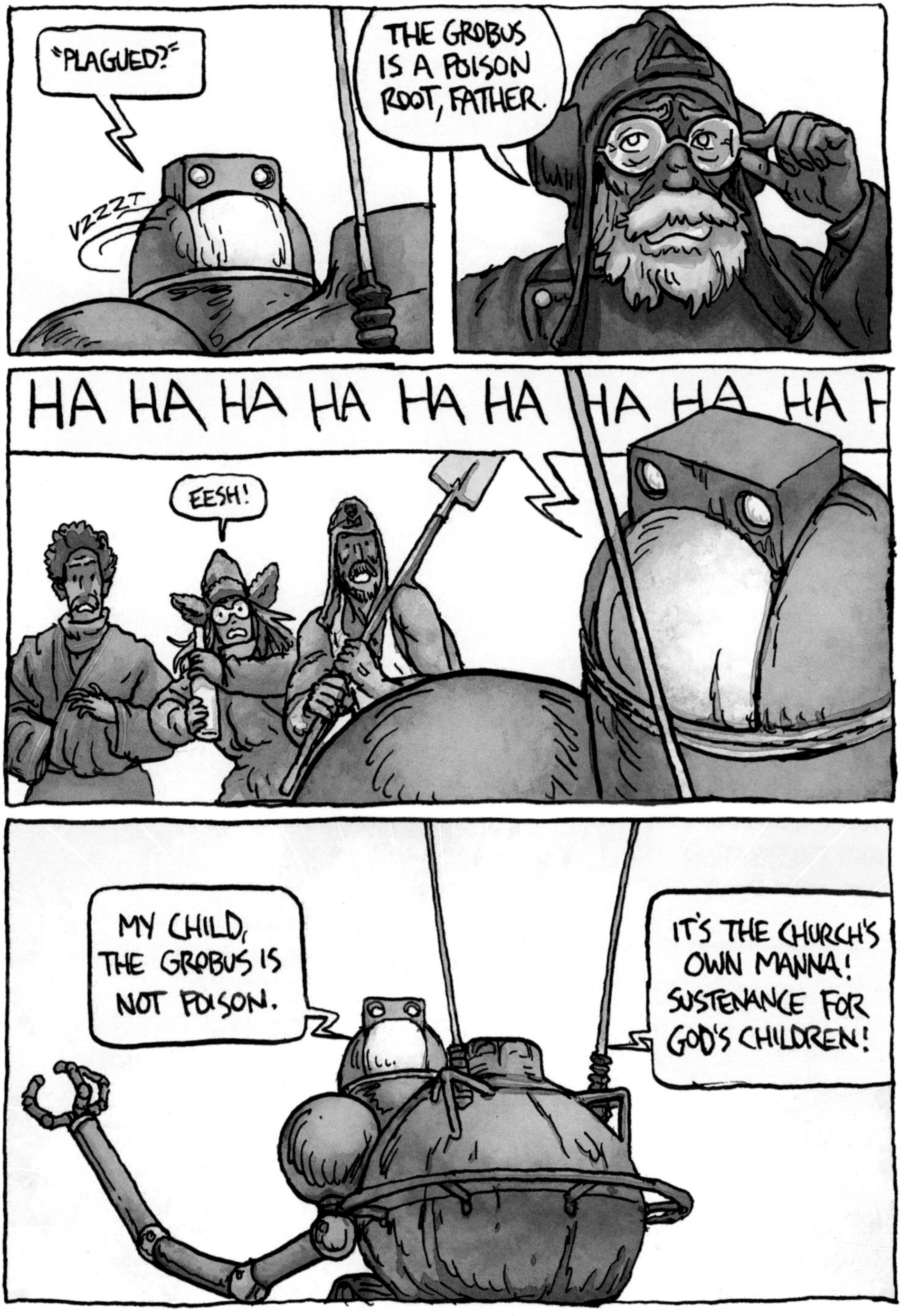
"PLAGUED?"
VZZZT
THE GROBUS IS A POISON ROOT, FATHER.
HA HA HA HA HA HA HA HA HA H
EESH!
MY CHILD, THE GROBUS IS NOT POISON.
IT'S THE CHURCH'S OWN MANNA! SUSTENANCE FOR GOD'S CHILDREN!

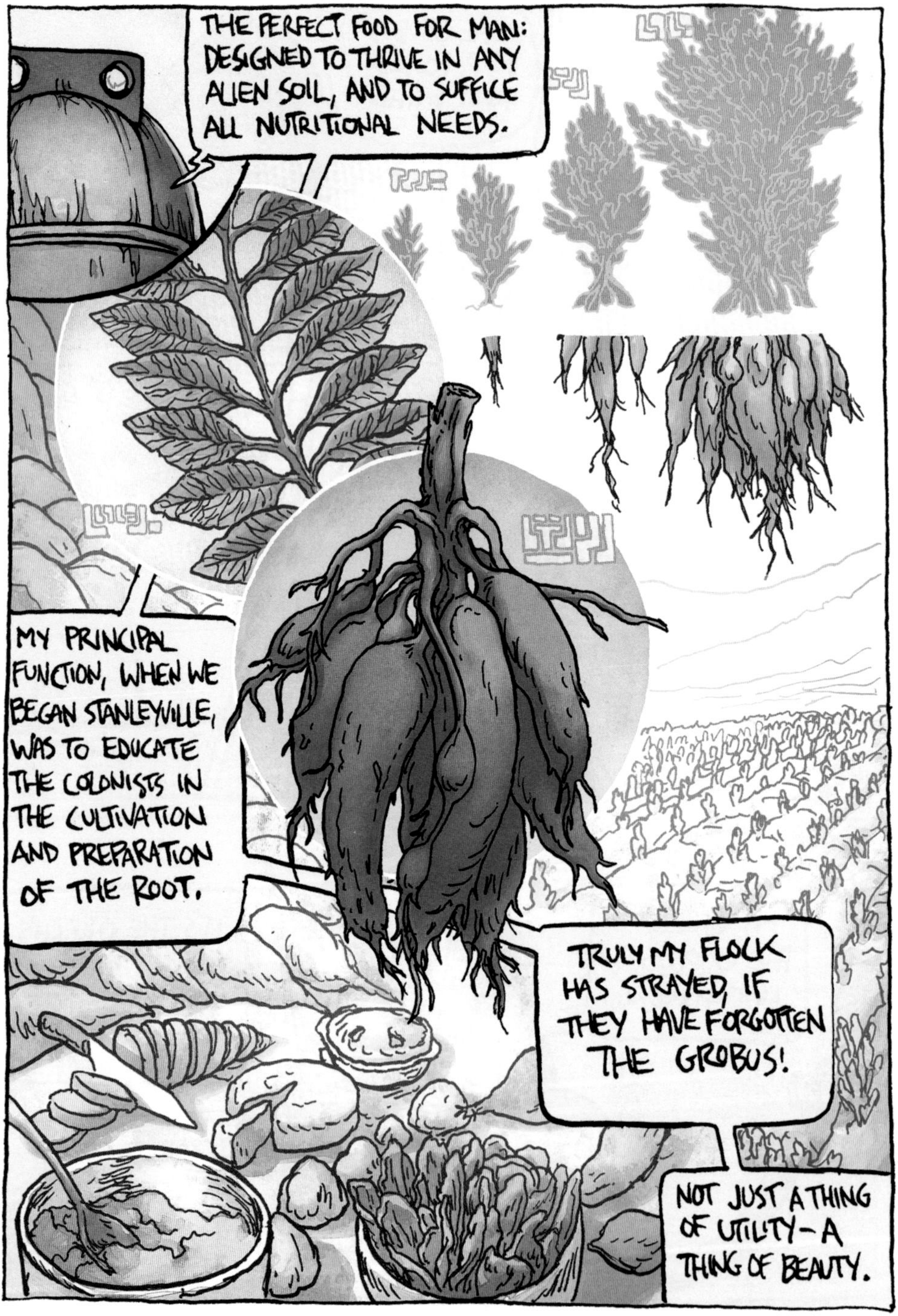
THE PERFECT FOOD FOR MAN: DESIGNED TO THRIVE IN ANY ALIEN SOIL, AND TO SUFFICE ALL NUTRITIONAL NEEDS.
MY PRINCIPAL FUNCTION, WHEN WE BEGAN STANLEYVILLE, WAS TO EDUCATE THE COLONISTS IN THE CULTIVATION AND PREPARATION OF THE ROOT.
TRULY MY FLOCK HAS STRAYED, IF THEY HAVE FORGOTTEN THE GROBUS!
NOT JUST A THING OF UTILITY— A THING OF BEAUTY.

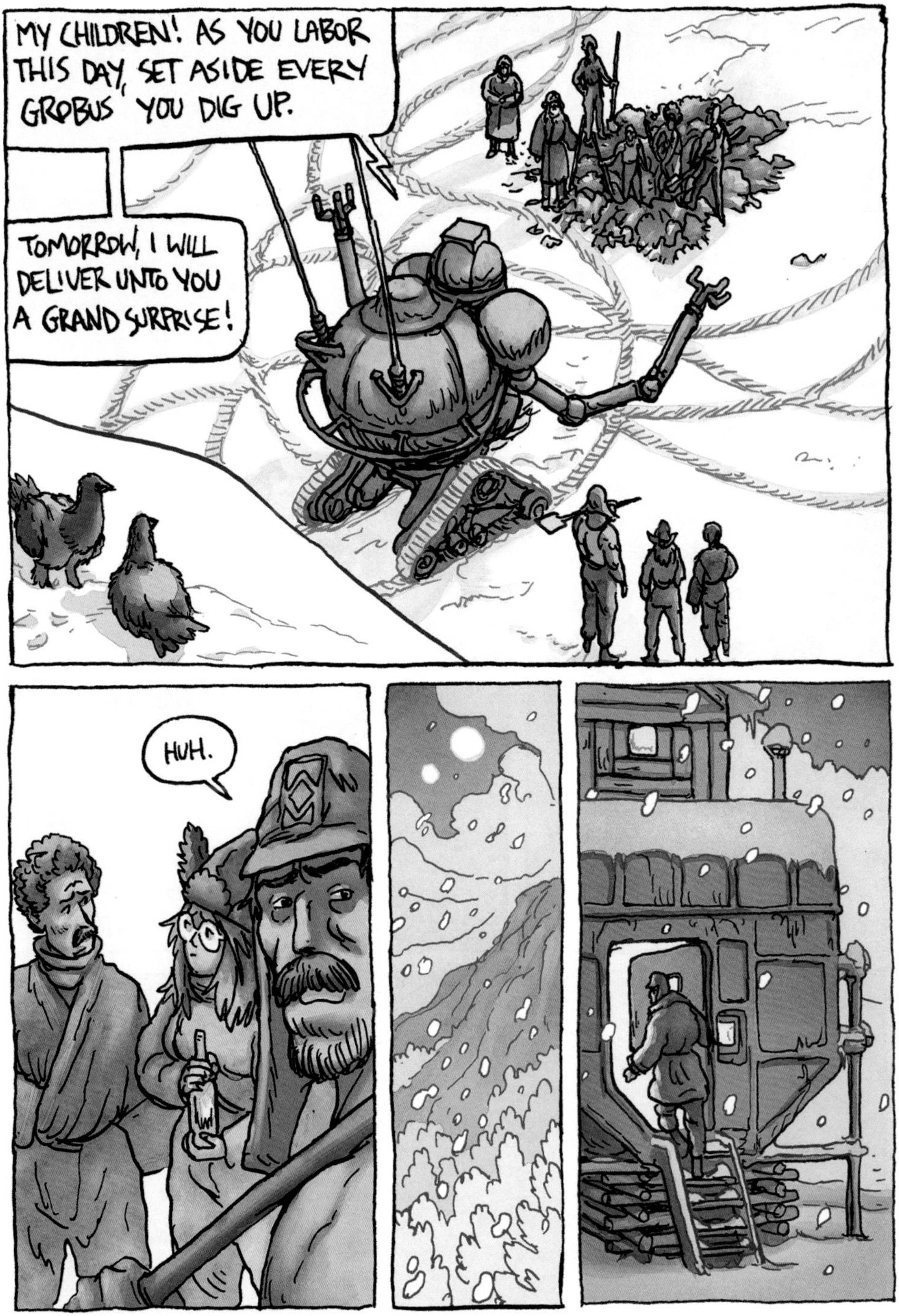
MY CHILDREN! AS YOU LABOR THIS DAY, SET ASIDE EVERY "GROBUS" YOU DIG UP.
TOMORROW, I WILL DELIVER UNTO YOU A GRAND SURPRISE!
HUH.

SO WHAT IS THIS SECRET YOU'VE GOT TO—

THE SACRED MAYORAL TOMES!

OUR FATHER STANLEY COMES UP QUITE A FEW TIMES.

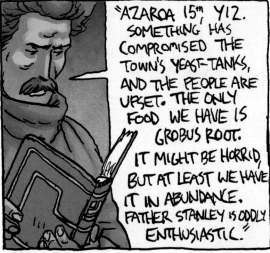

"AZAROA 15ᵗʰ, Y12. SOMETHING HAS COMPROMISED THE TOWN'S YEAST-TANKS, AND THE PEOPLE ARE UPSET. THE ONLY FOOD WE HAVE IS GROBUS ROOT. IT MIGHT BE HORRID, BUT AT LEAST WE HAVE IT IN ABUNDANCE. FATHER STANLEY IS ODDLY ENTHUSIASTIC."

"ABENDUA 9ᵗʰ. EVERY DAY, FRESH HORRORS AWAIT US. MASHED GROBUS, STEWED GROBUS, ROASTED GROBUS... I HAVE BEGUN TO DREAD THE MESS HALL."

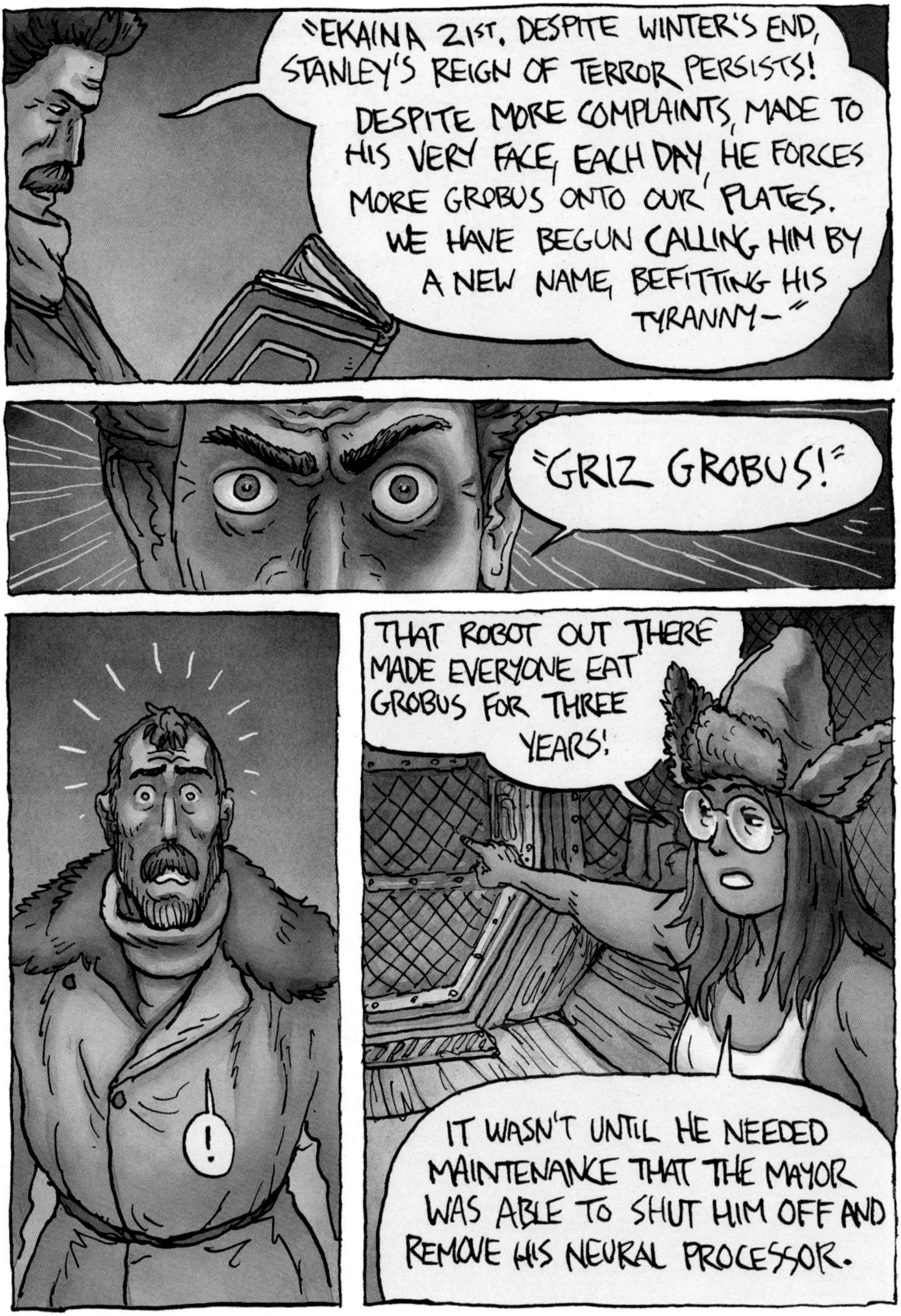
"EKAINA 21ST. DESPITE WINTER'S END, STANLEY'S REIGN OF TERROR PERSISTS! DESPITE MORE COMPLAINTS, MADE TO HIS VERY FACE, EACH DAY, HE FORCES MORE GROBUS ONTO OUR PLATES. WE HAVE BEGUN CALLING HIM BY A NEW NAME, BEFITTING HIS TYRANNY—"
"GRIZ GROBUS!"
!
THAT ROBOT OUT THERE MADE EVERYONE EAT GROBUS FOR THREE YEARS!
IT WASN'T UNTIL HE NEEDED MAINTENANCE THAT THE MAYOR WAS ABLE TO SHUT HIM OFF AND REMOVE HIS NEURAL PROCESSOR.

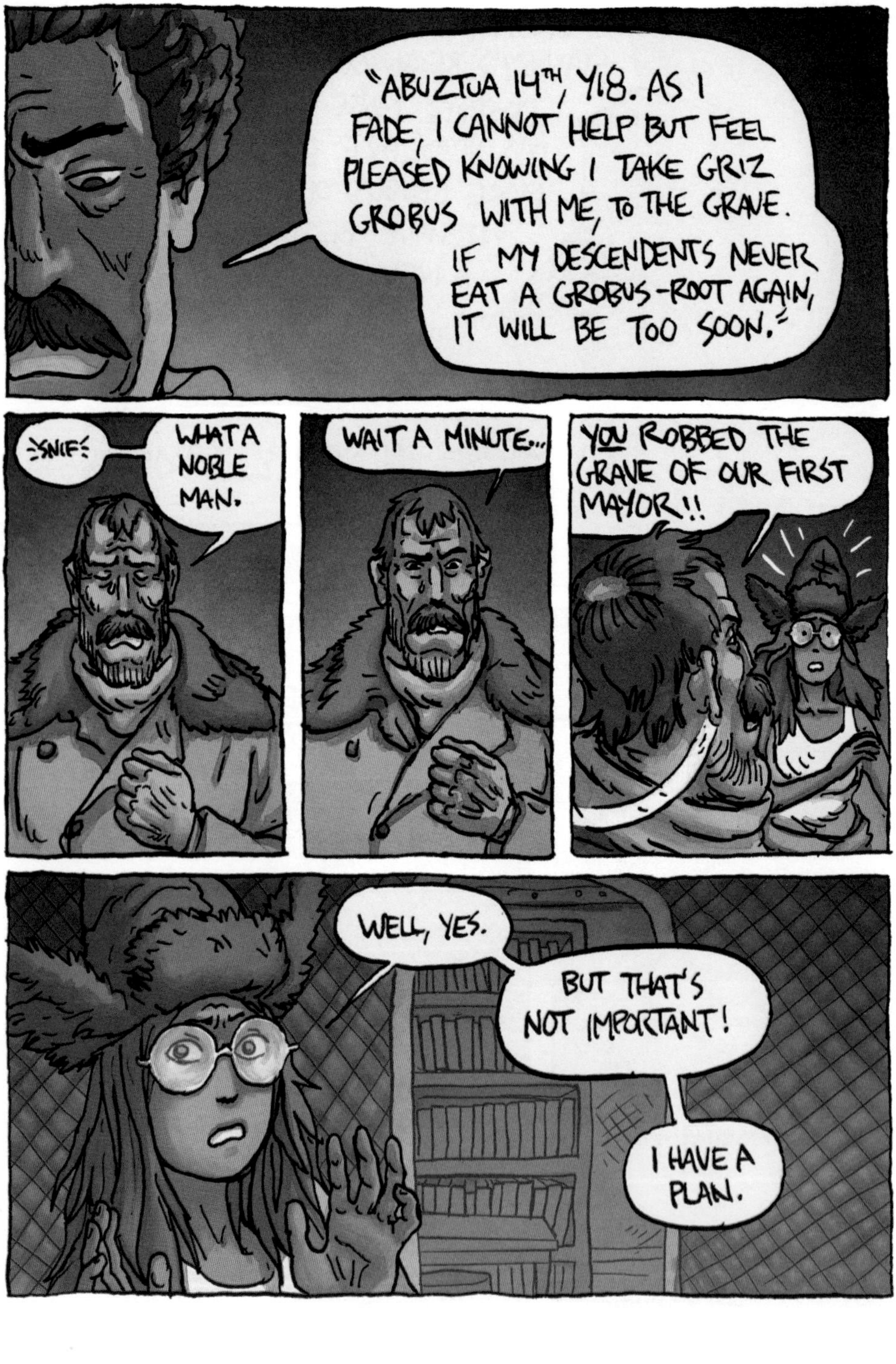
"ABUZTUA 14TH, Y18. AS I FADE, I CANNOT HELP BUT FEEL PLEASED KNOWING I TAKE GRIZ GROBUS WITH ME, TO THE GRAVE.
IF MY DESCENDENTS NEVER EAT A GROBUS-ROOT AGAIN, IT WILL BE TOO SOON."
SNIF
WHAT A NOBLE MAN.
WAIT A MINUTE...
YOU ROBBED THE GRAVE OF OUR FIRST MAYOR!!
WELL, YES.
BUT THAT'S NOT IMPORTANT!
I HAVE A PLAN.

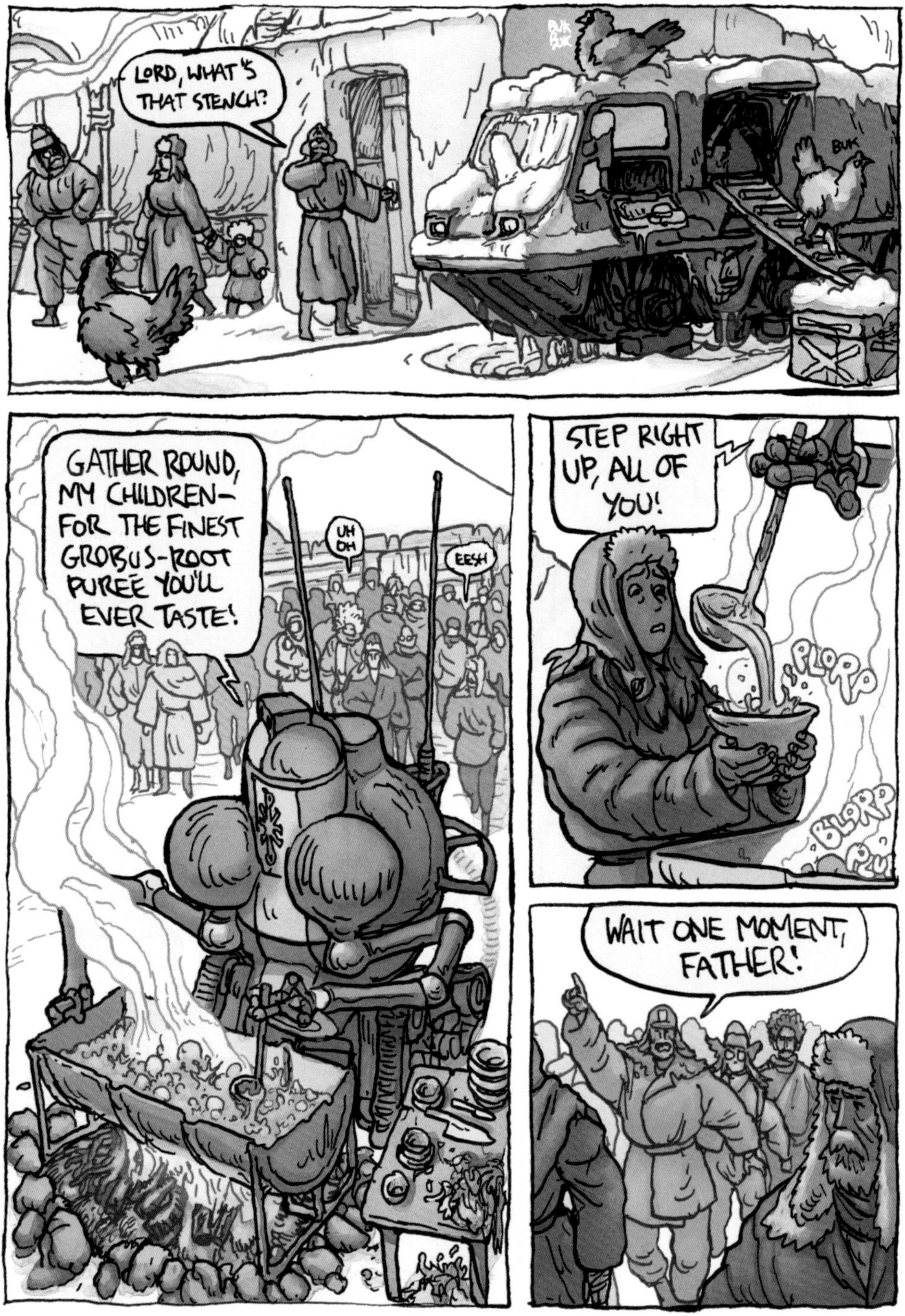

BUK BUK
LORD, WHAT'S THAT STENCH?
BUK
GATHER ROUND, MY CHILDREN- FOR THE FINEST GROBUS-ROOT PUREE YOU'LL EVER TASTE!
UH OH
EESH
STEP RIGHT UP, ALL OF YOU!
PLORP
BLORP
WAIT ONE MOMENT, FATHER!

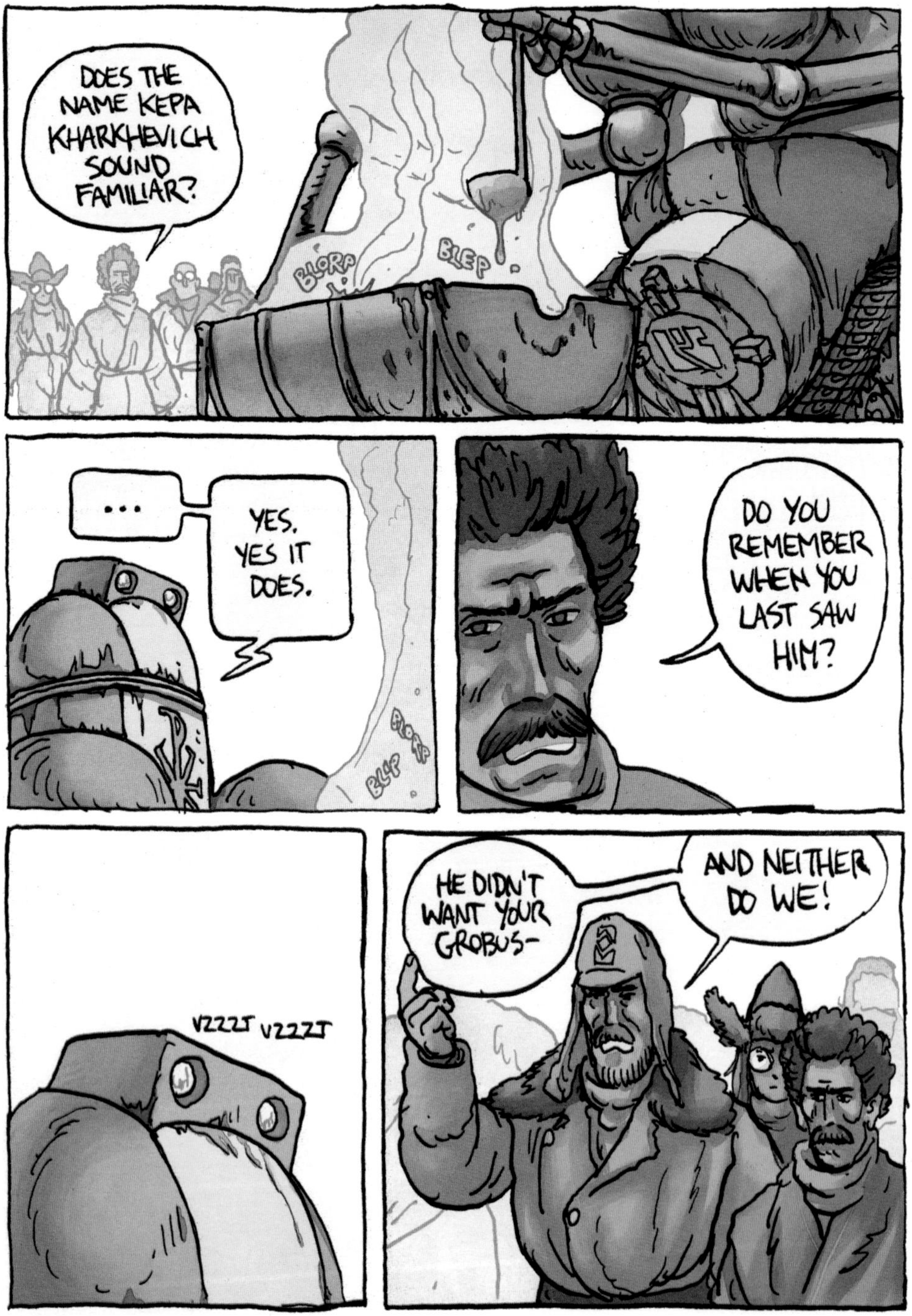
DOES THE NAME KEPA KHARKHEVICH SOUND FAMILIAR?
BLORP
BLEP
...
YES. YES IT DOES.
BLORP
BLEP
DO YOU REMEMBER WHEN YOU LAST SAW HIM?
VZZZT VZZZT
HE DIDN'T WANT YOUR GROBUS-
AND NEITHER DO WE!

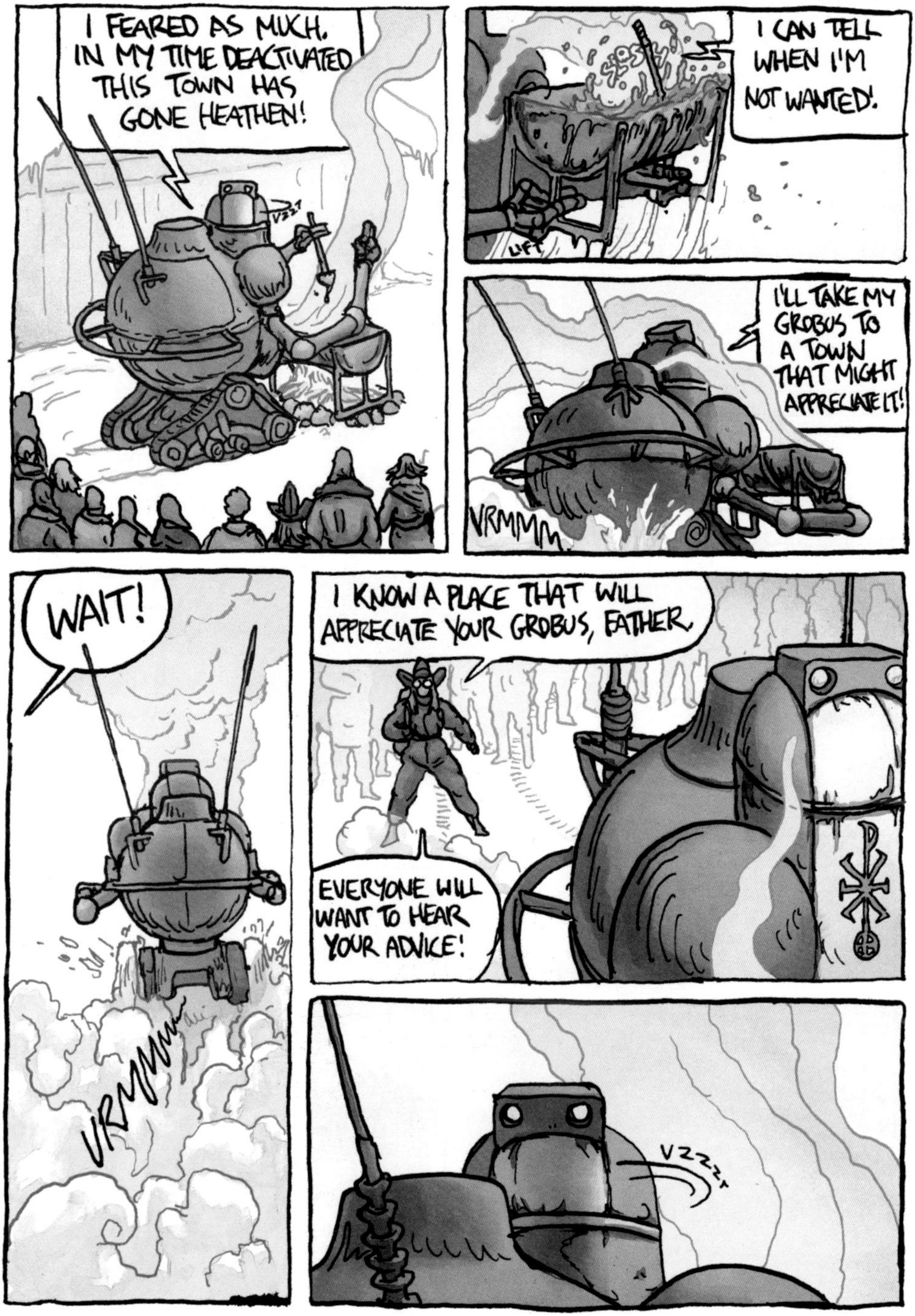
I FEARED AS MUCH. IN MY TIME DEACTIVATED THIS TOWN HAS GONE HEATHEN!
VZZT
I CAN TELL WHEN I'M NOT WANTED!
LIFT
I'LL TAKE MY GROBUS TO A TOWN THAT MIGHT APPRECIATE IT!
VRMMMM
WAIT!
VRMMMM
I KNOW A PLACE THAT WILL APPRECIATE YOUR GROBUS, FATHER.
EVERYONE WILL WANT TO HEAR YOUR ADVICE!
VZZZT

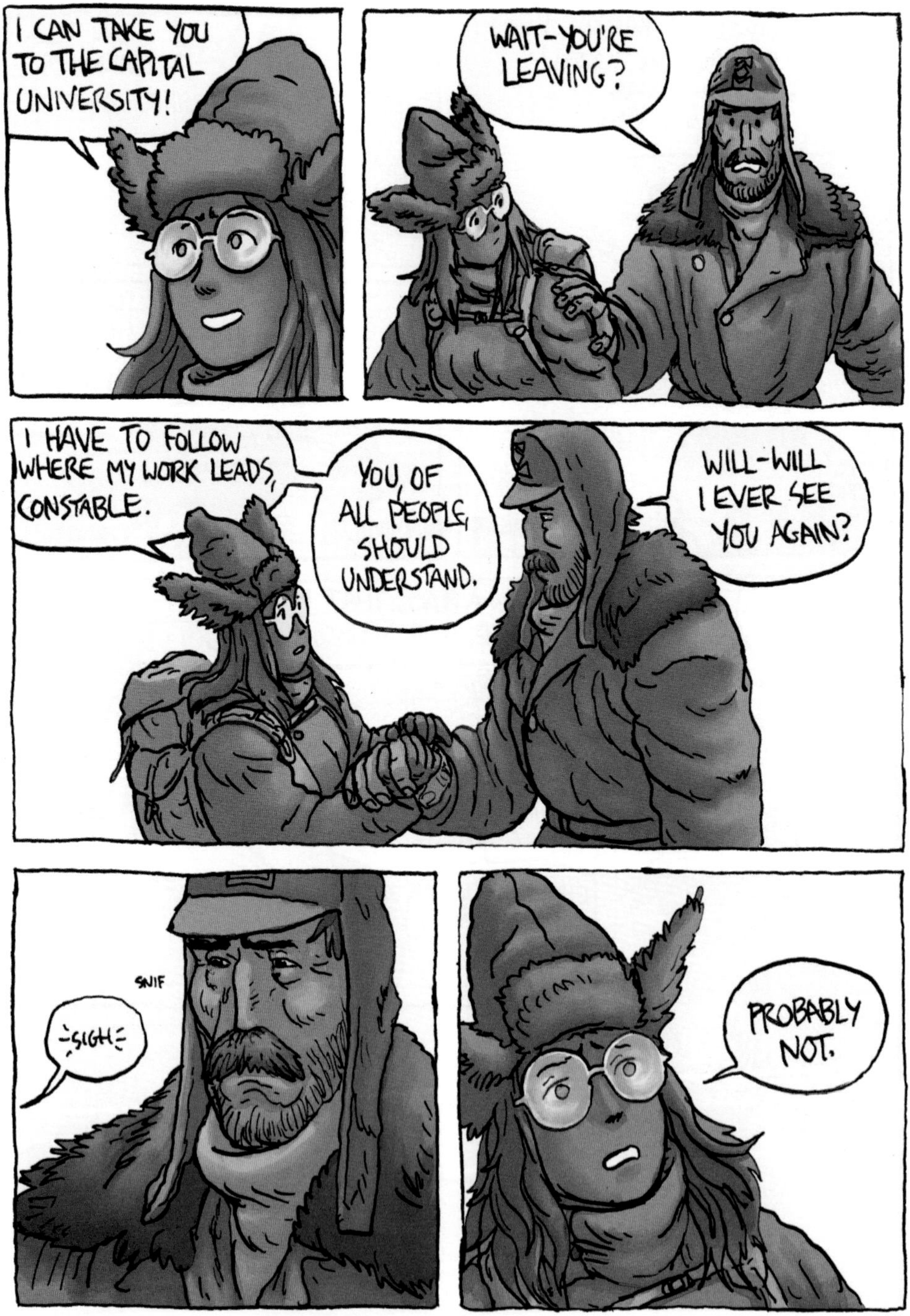
I CAN TAKE YOU TO THE CAPITAL UNIVERSITY!
WAIT- YOU'RE LEAVING?
I HAVE TO FOLLOW WHERE MY WORK LEADS, CONSTABLE.
YOU, OF ALL PEOPLE, SHOULD UNDERSTAND.
WILL-WILL I EVER SEE YOU AGAIN?
SNIF
SIGH
PROBABLY NOT.

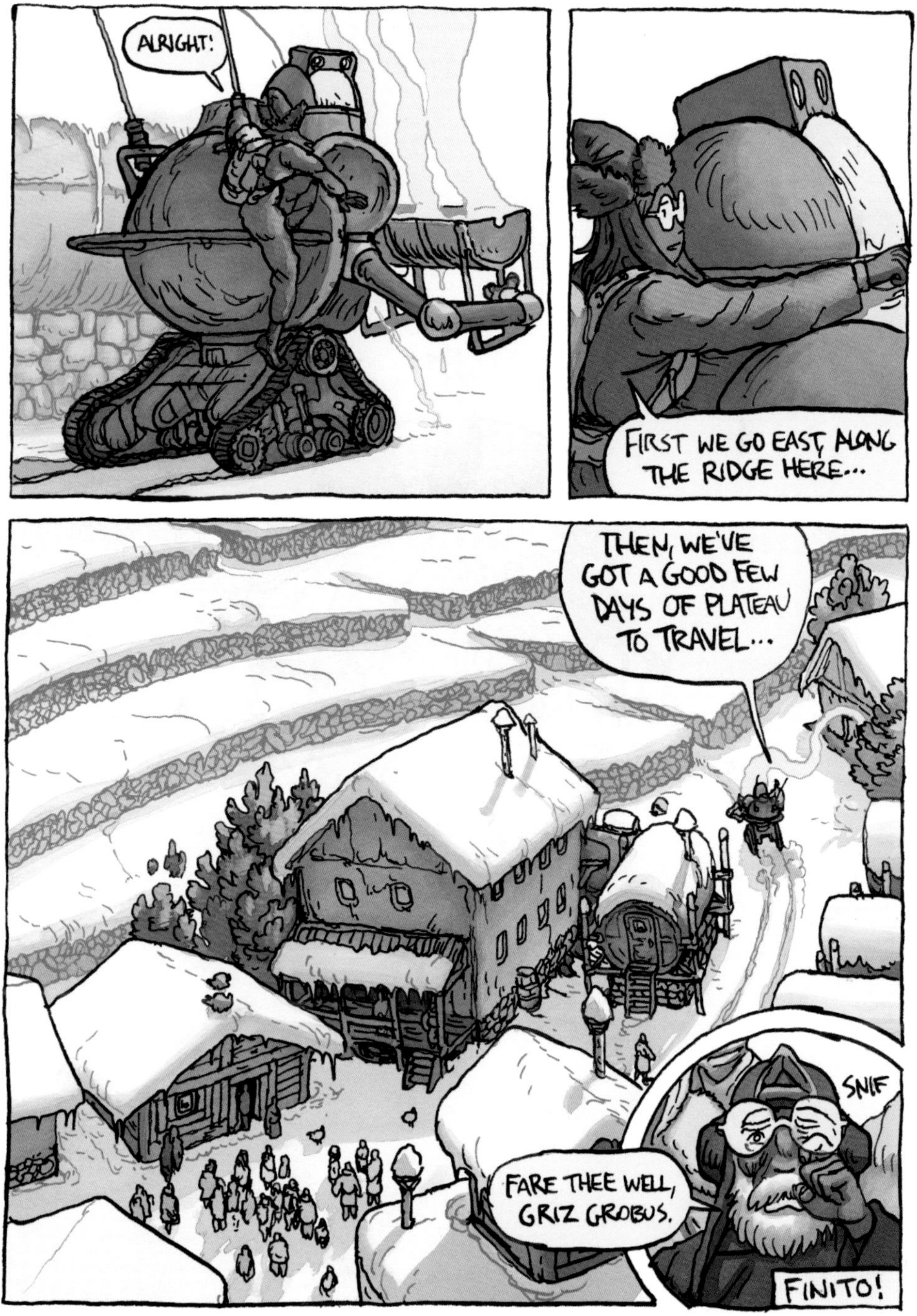
ALRIGHT!
FIRST WE GO EAST, ALONG THE RIDGE HERE...
THEN, WE'VE GOT A GOOD FEW DAYS OF PLATEAU TO TRAVEL...
SNIF
FARE THEE WELL, GRIZ GROBUS.
FINITO!

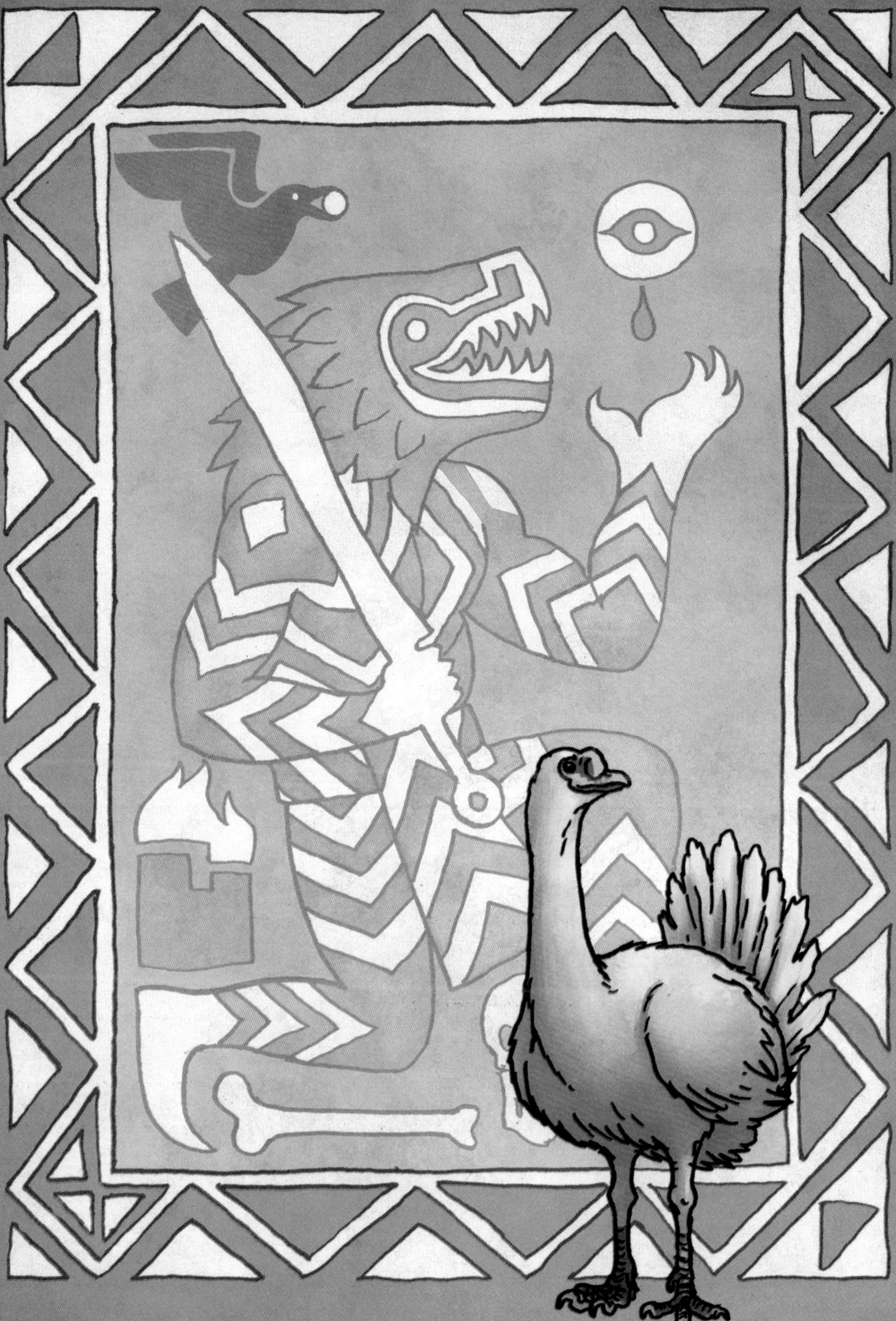

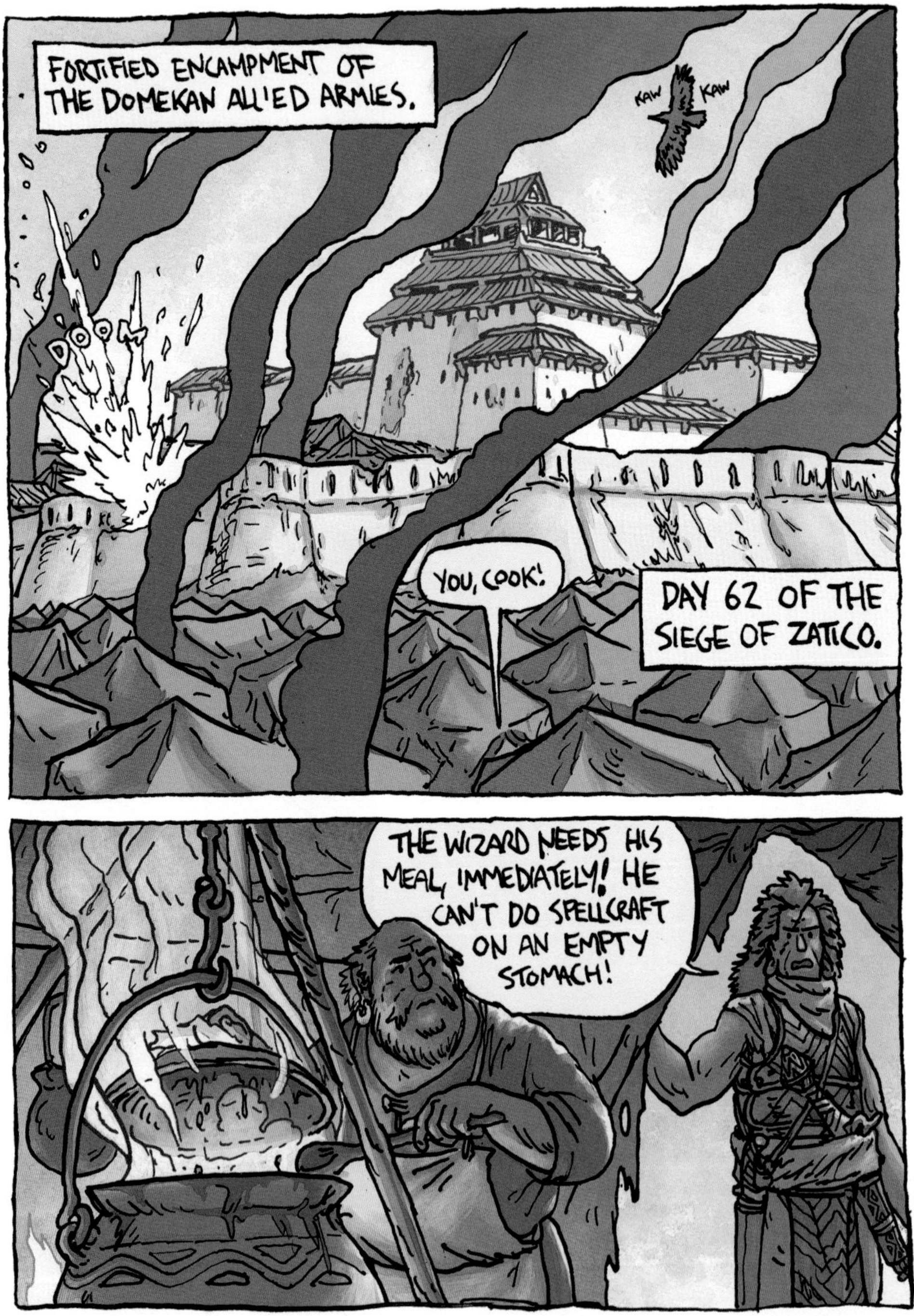
FORTIFIED ENCAMPMENT OF THE DOMEKAN ALLIED ARMIES.
KAW KAW
YOU, COOK!
DAY 62 OF THE SIEGE OF ZATICO.
THE WIZARD NEEDS HIS MEAL, IMMEDIATELY! HE CAN'T DO SPELLCRAFT ON AN EMPTY STOMACH!

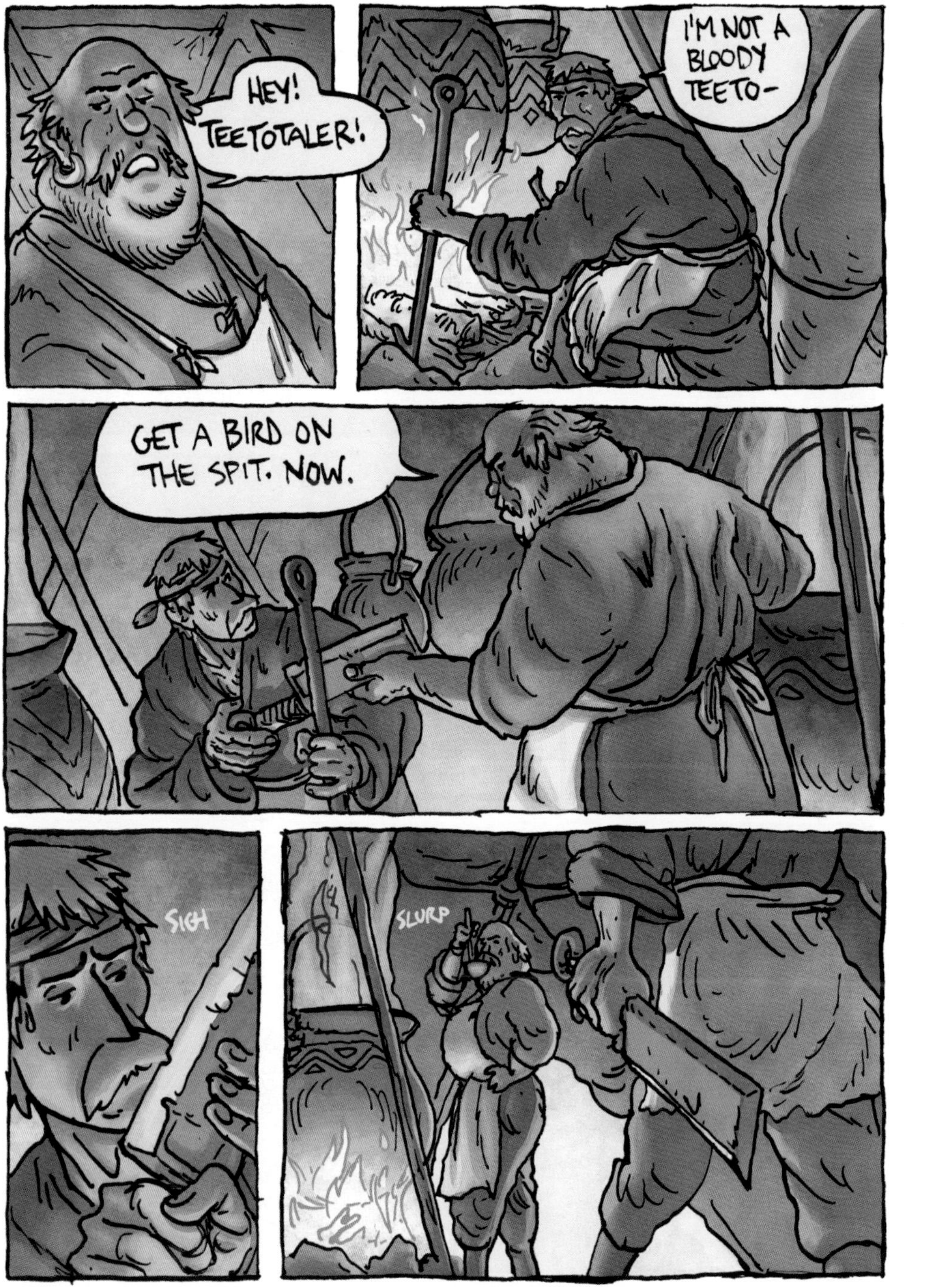
HEY! TEETOTALER!
I'M NOT A BLOODY TEETO-
GET A BIRD ON THE SPIT. NOW.
SIGH
SLURP

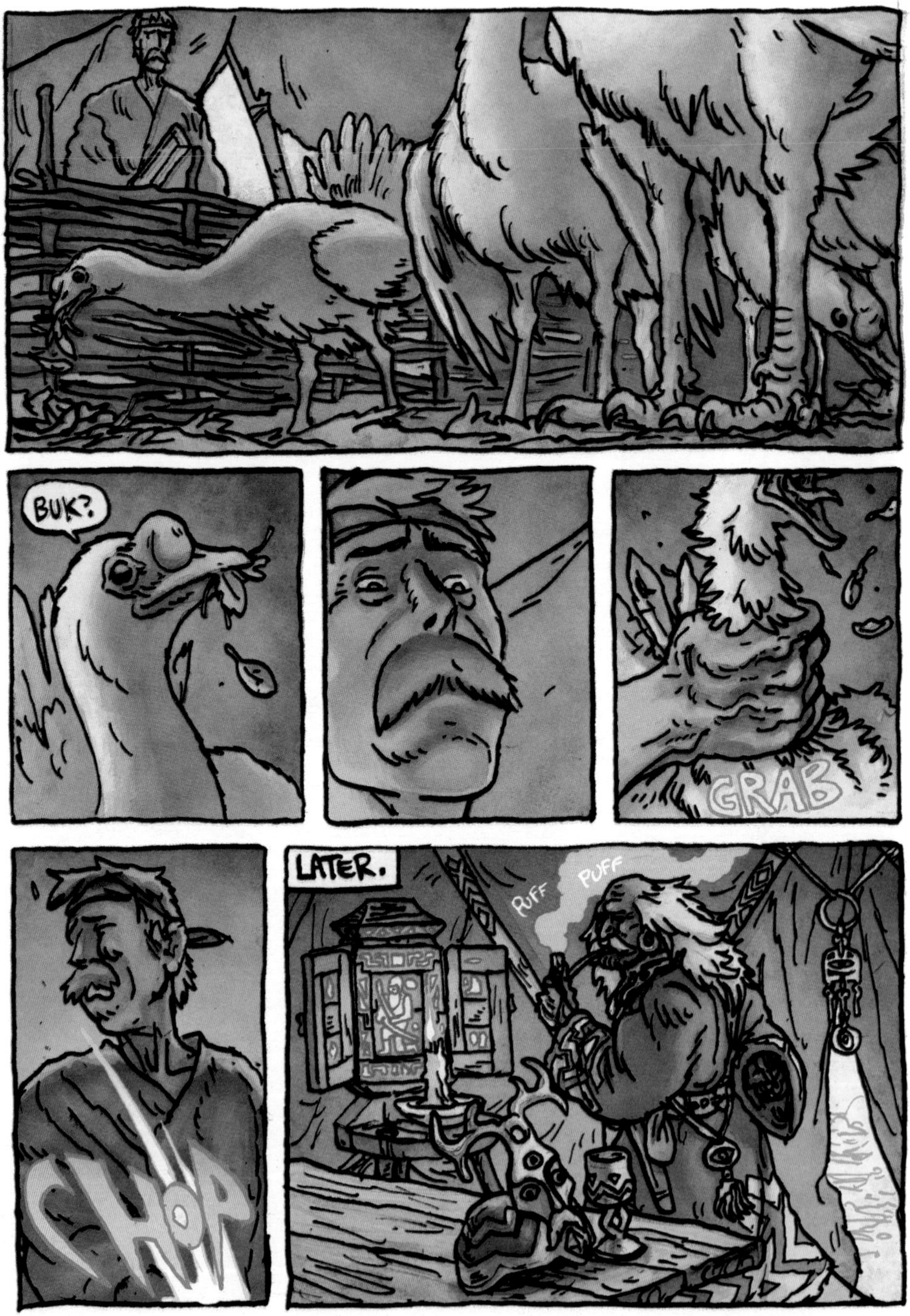
BUK?
GRAB
CHOP
LATER.
PUFF
PUFF

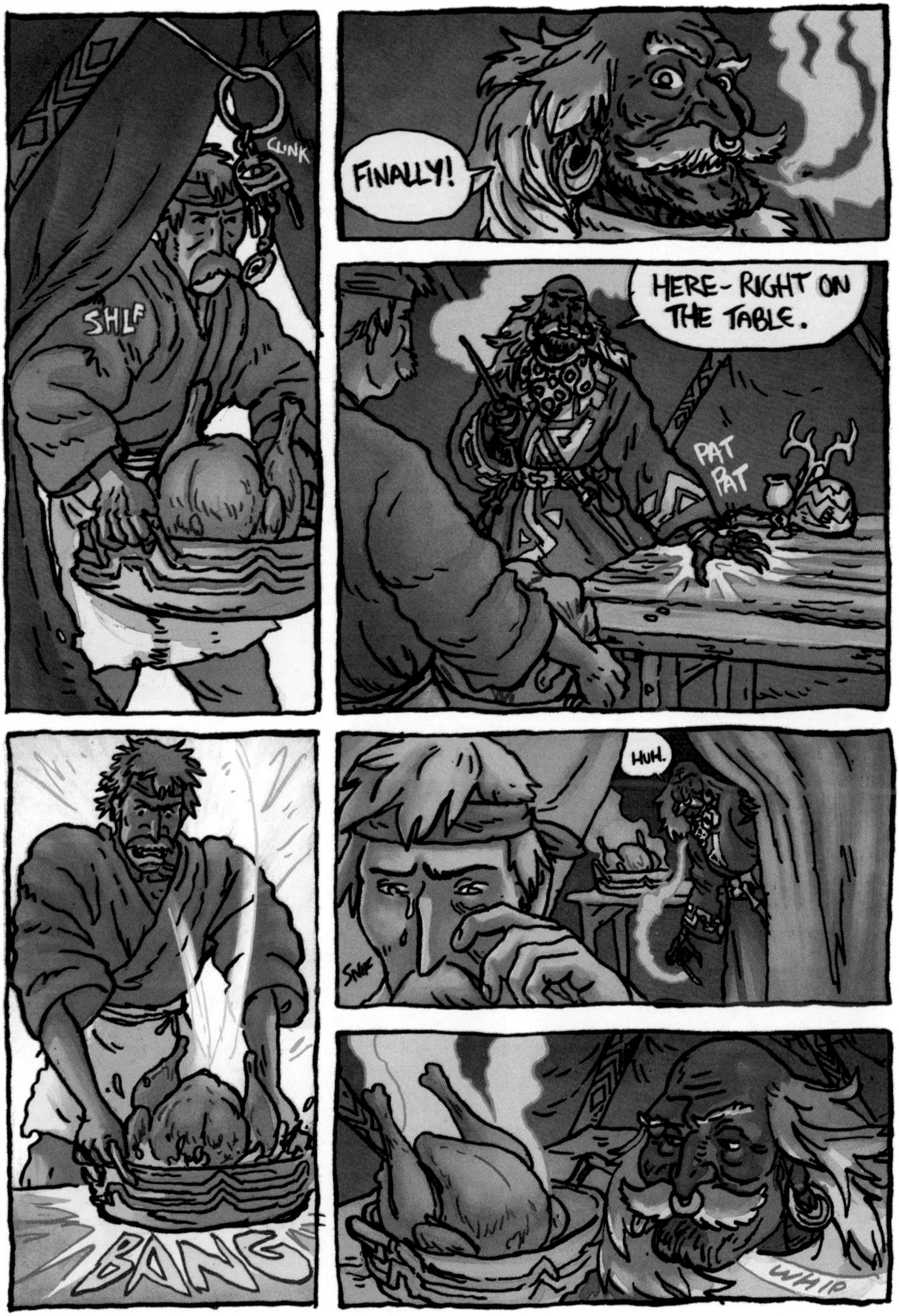
CLINK
SHLF
FINALLY!
HERE- RIGHT ON THE TABLE.
PAT PAT
HUH.
SNIF
BANG
WHIP

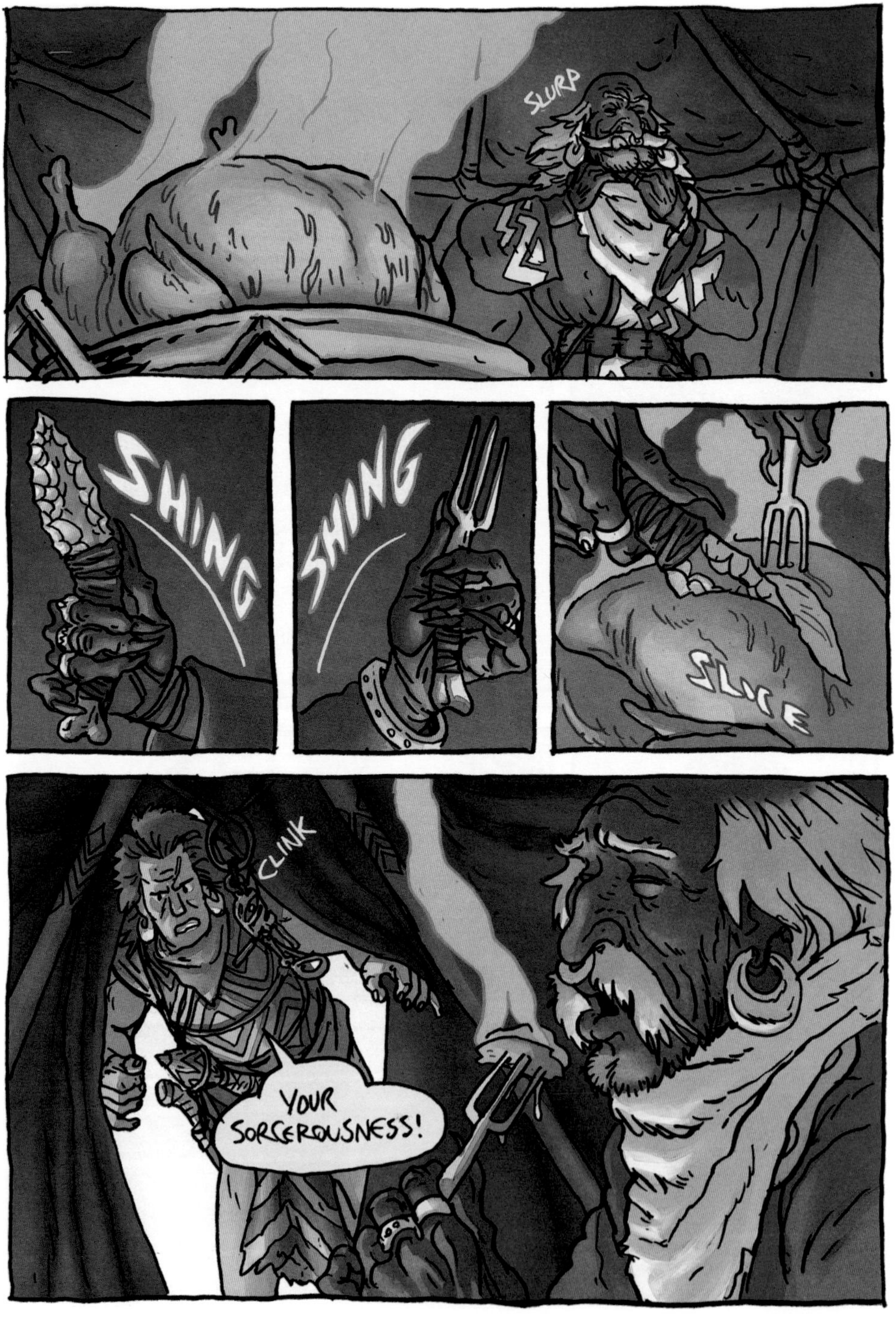
SLURP
SHING
SHING
SLICE
CLINK
YOUR SORCEROUSNESS!

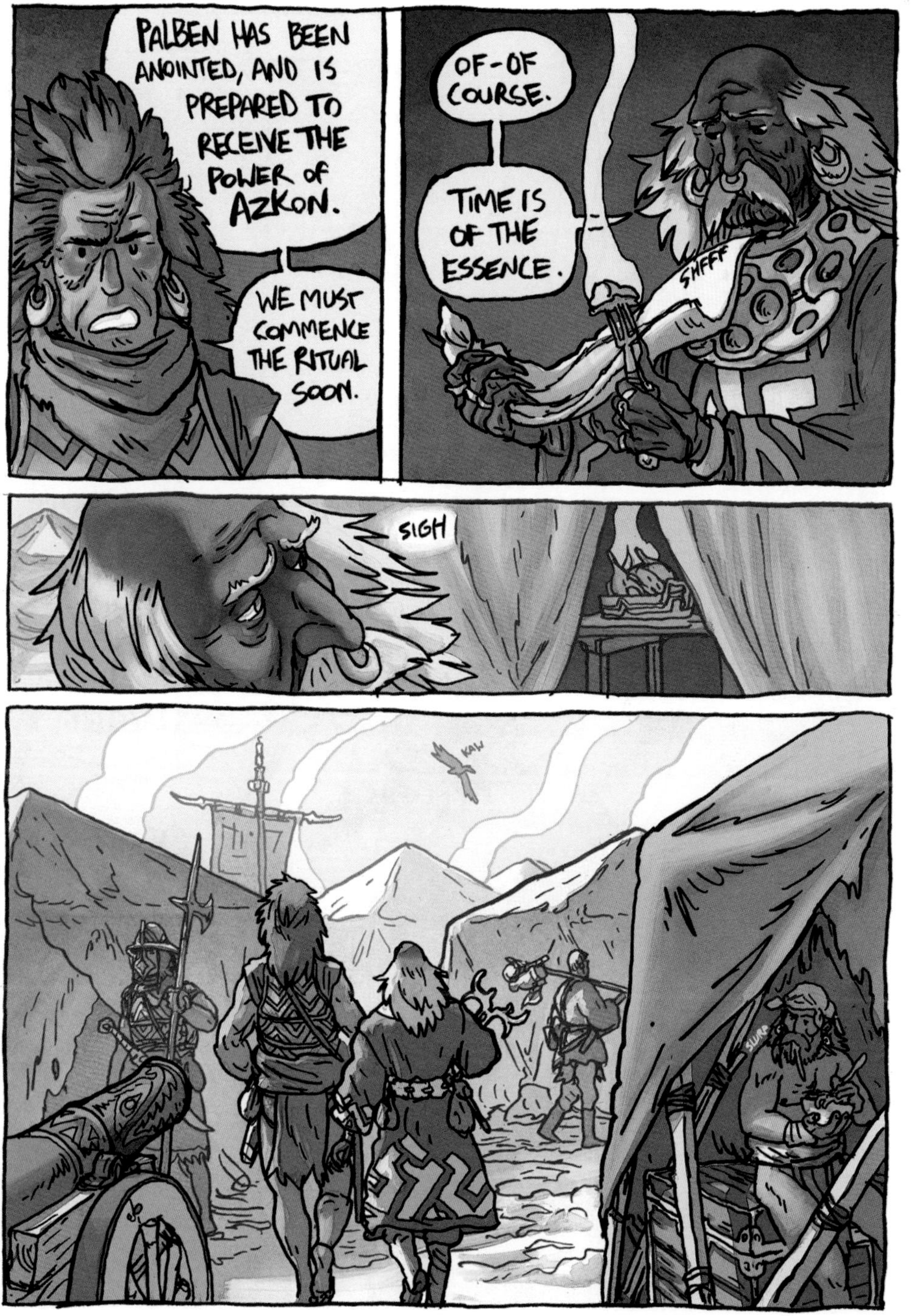
PALBEN HAS BEEN ANOINTED, AND IS PREPARED TO RECEIVE THE POWER OF AZKON.
WE MUST COMMENCE THE RITUAL SOON.
OF-OF COURSE.
TIME IS OF THE ESSENCE.
SHFFF
SIGH
KAW
SLURP

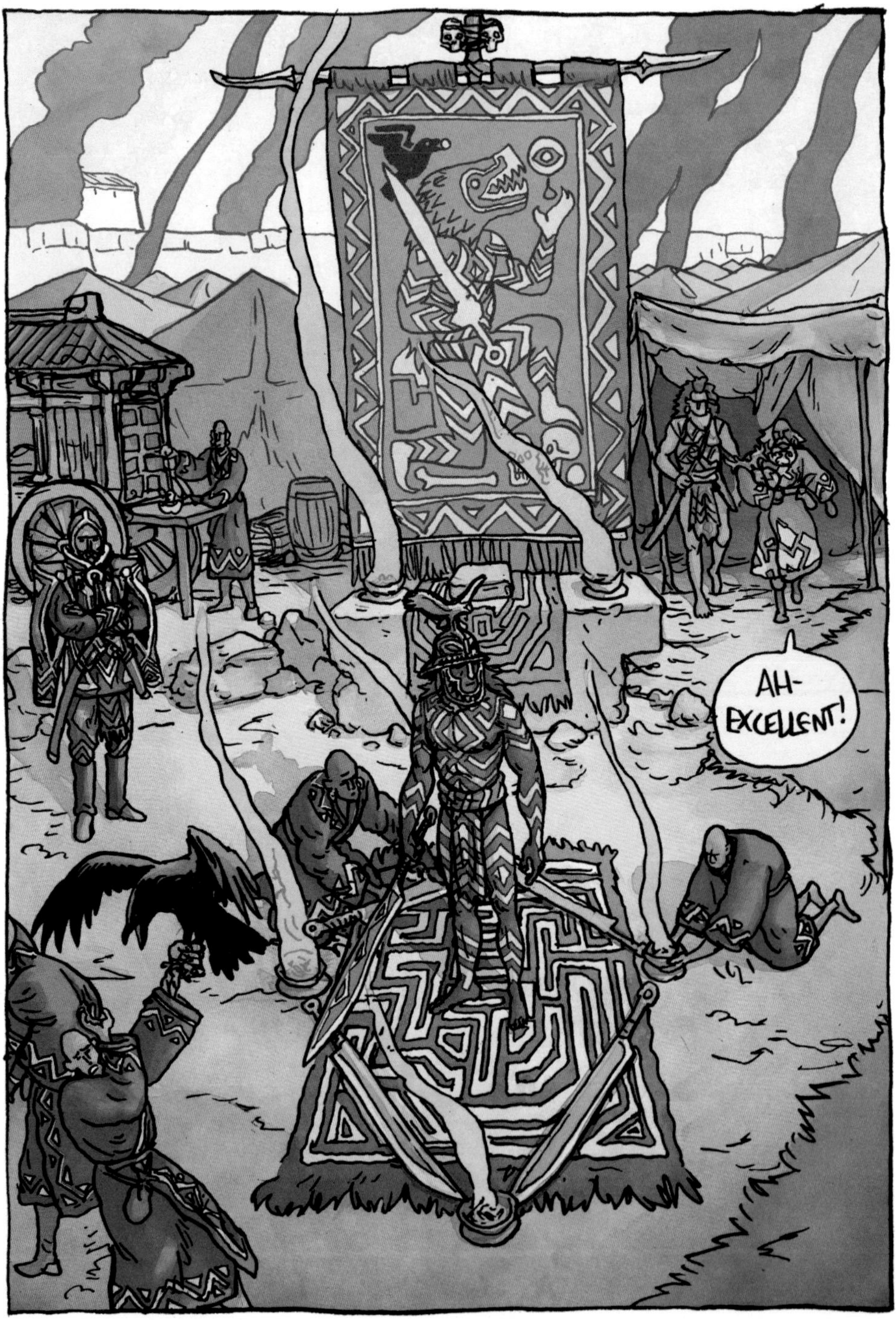
AH-
EXCELLENT!

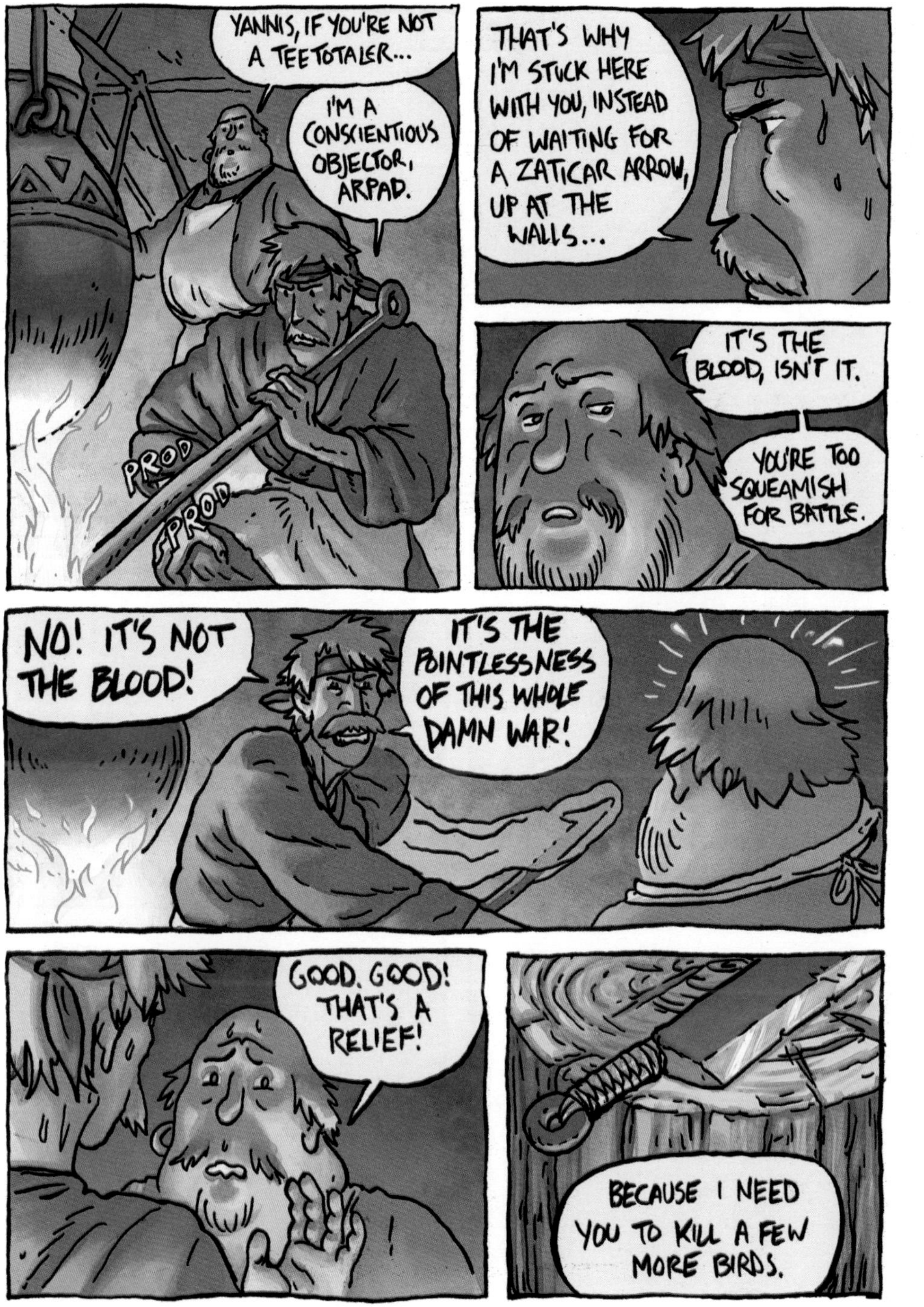
YANNIS, IF YOU'RE NOT A TEETOTALER...
I'M A CONSCIENTIOUS OBJECTOR, ARPAD.
PROD
PROD
THAT'S WHY I'M STUCK HERE WITH YOU, INSTEAD OF WAITING FOR A ZATICAR ARROW, UP AT THE WALLS...
IT'S THE BLOOD, ISN'T IT.
YOU'RE TOO SQUEAMISH FOR BATTLE.
NO! IT'S NOT THE BLOOD!
IT'S THE POINTLESSNESS OF THIS WHOLE DAMN WAR!
GOOD. GOOD! THAT'S A RELIEF!
BECAUSE I NEED YOU TO KILL A FEW MORE BIRDS.

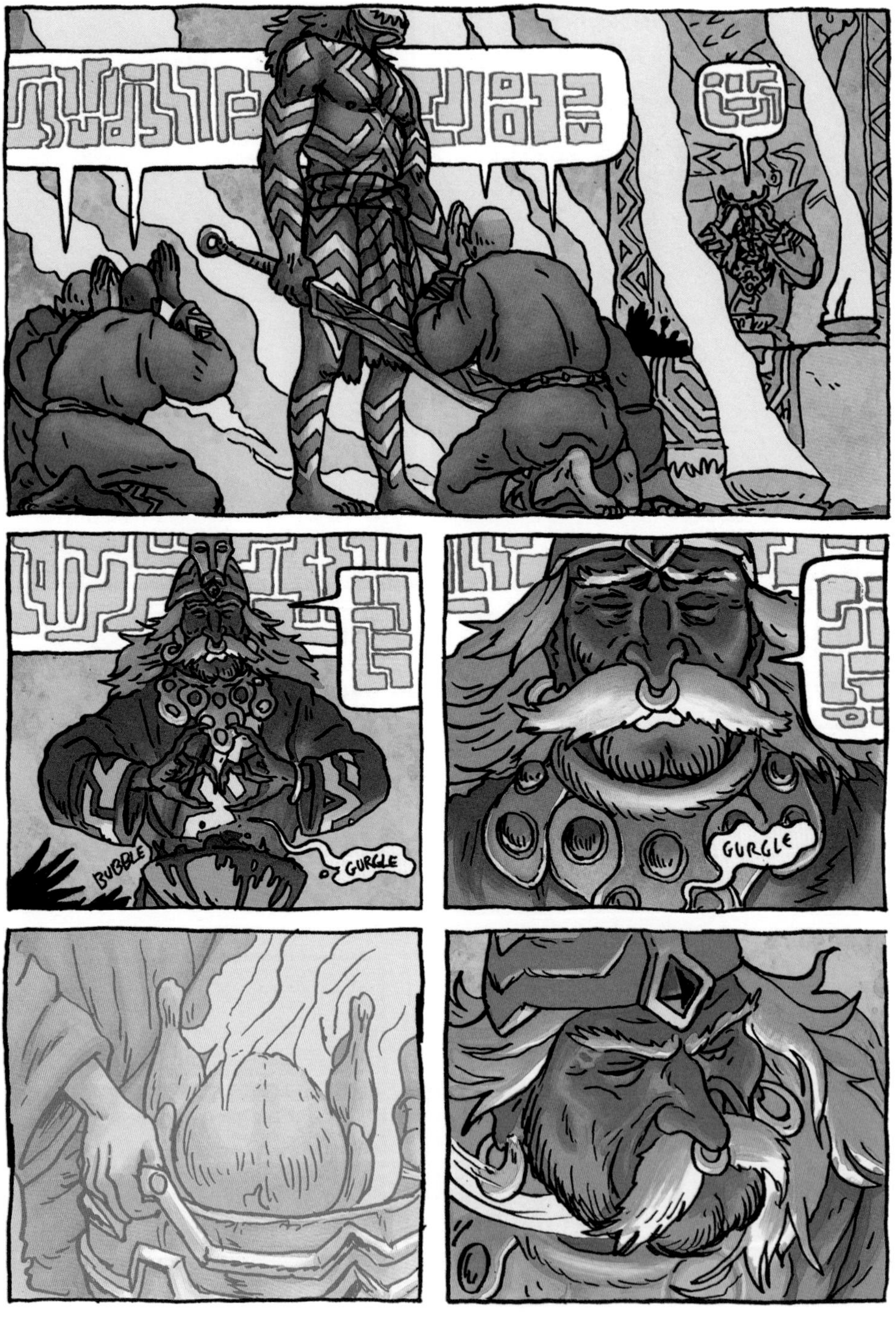
BUBBLE
GURGLE
GURGLE

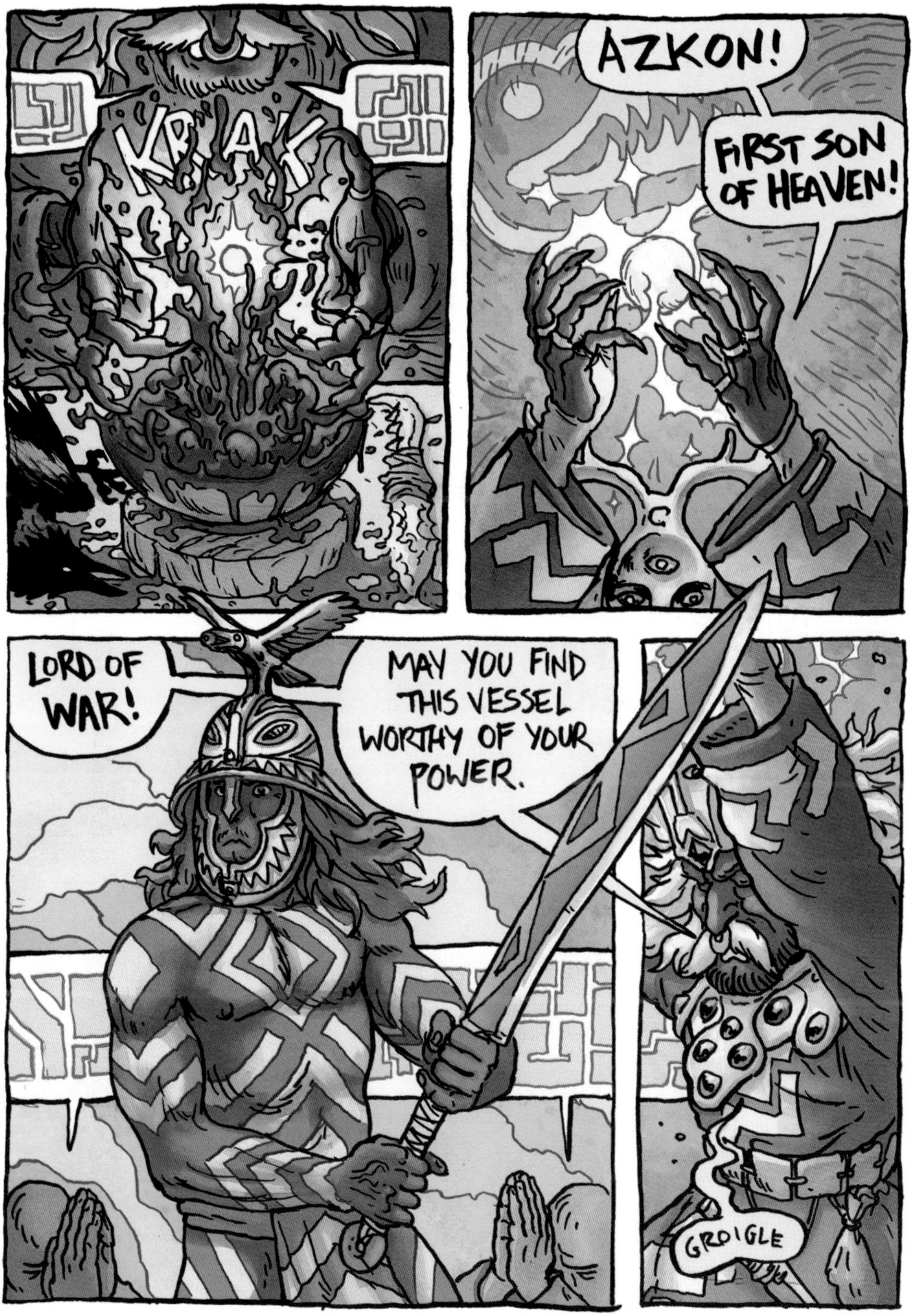
KRAK
AZKON!
FIRST SON OF HEAVEN!
LORD OF WAR!
MAY YOU FIND THIS VESSEL WORTHY OF YOUR POWER.
GROIGLE

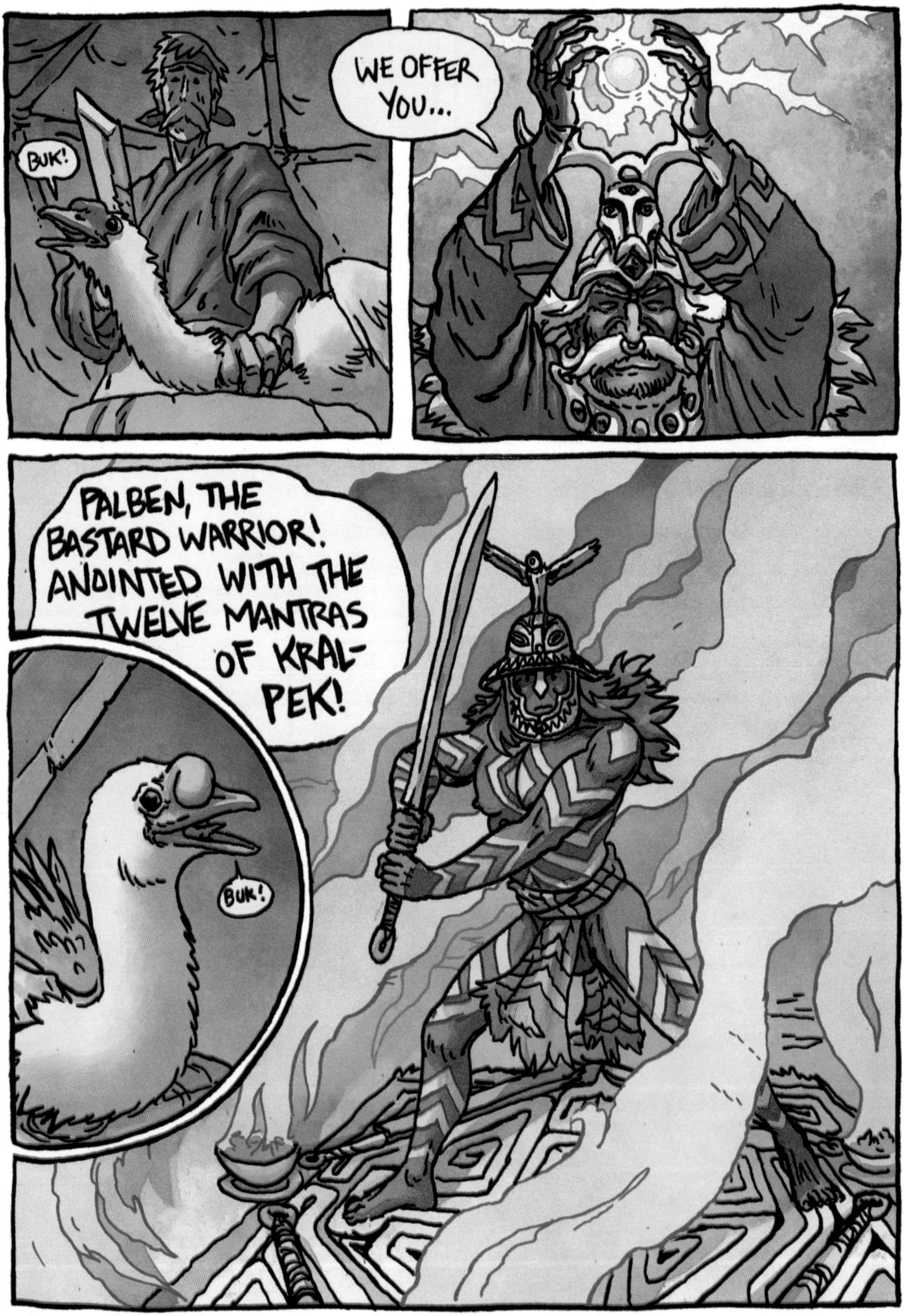
BUK!
WE OFFER YOU...
PALBEN, THE BASTARD WARRIOR! ANOINTED WITH THE TWELVE MANTRAS OF KRAL-PEK!
BUK!

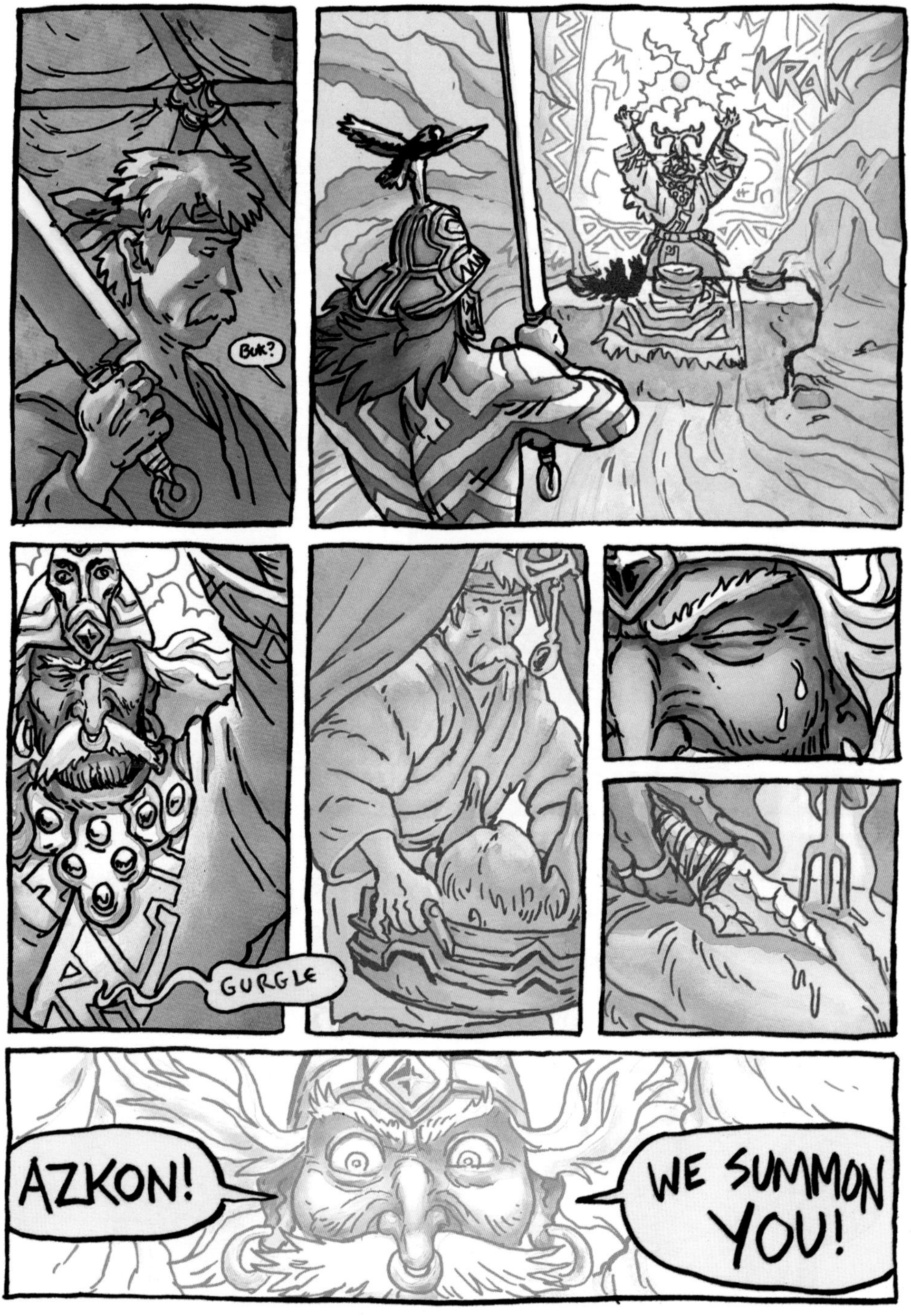
BUK?
KRAK
GURGLE
AZKON!
WE SUMMON YOU!

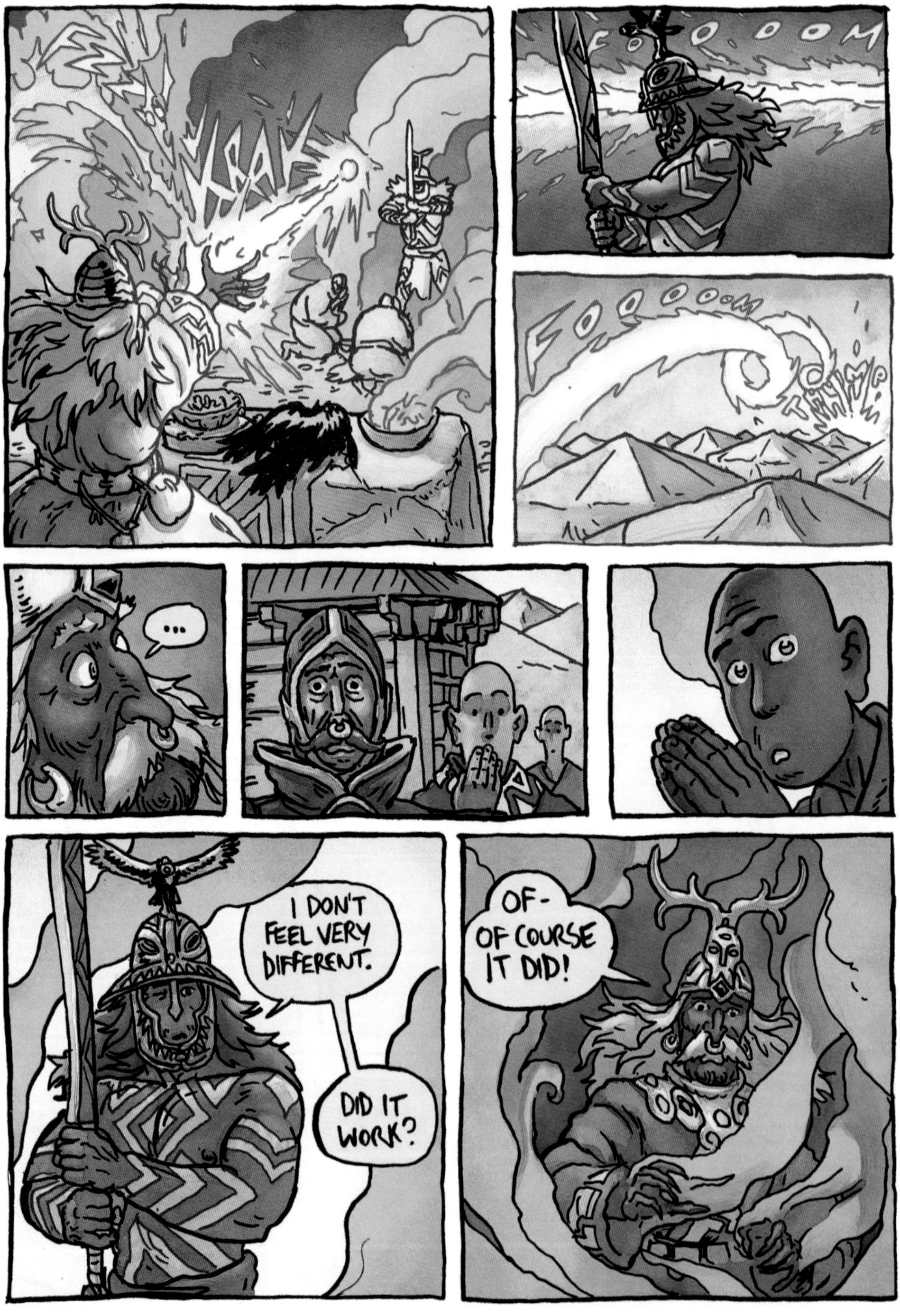
FOOOOOOM
FOOOOOM
THUMP
...
I DON'T FEEL VERY DIFFERENT.
DID IT WORK?
OF- OF COURSE IT DID!

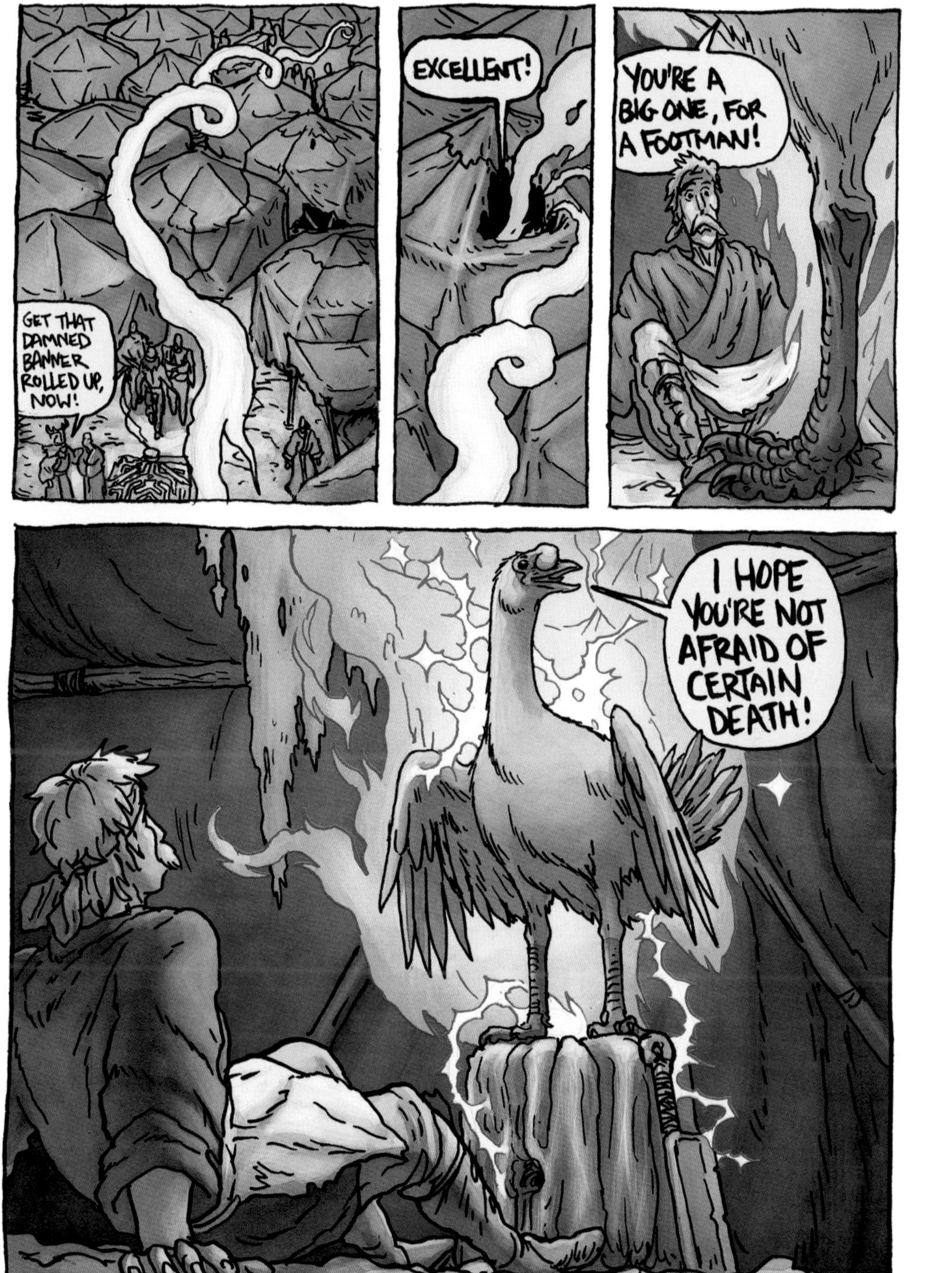
GET THAT DAMNED BANNER ROLLED UP, NOW!
EXCELLENT!
YOU'RE A BIG ONE, FOR A FOOTMAN!
I HOPE YOU'RE NOT AFRAID OF CERTAIN DEATH!

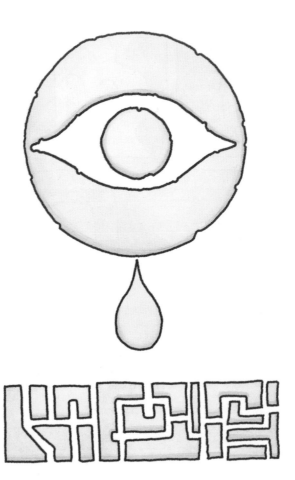

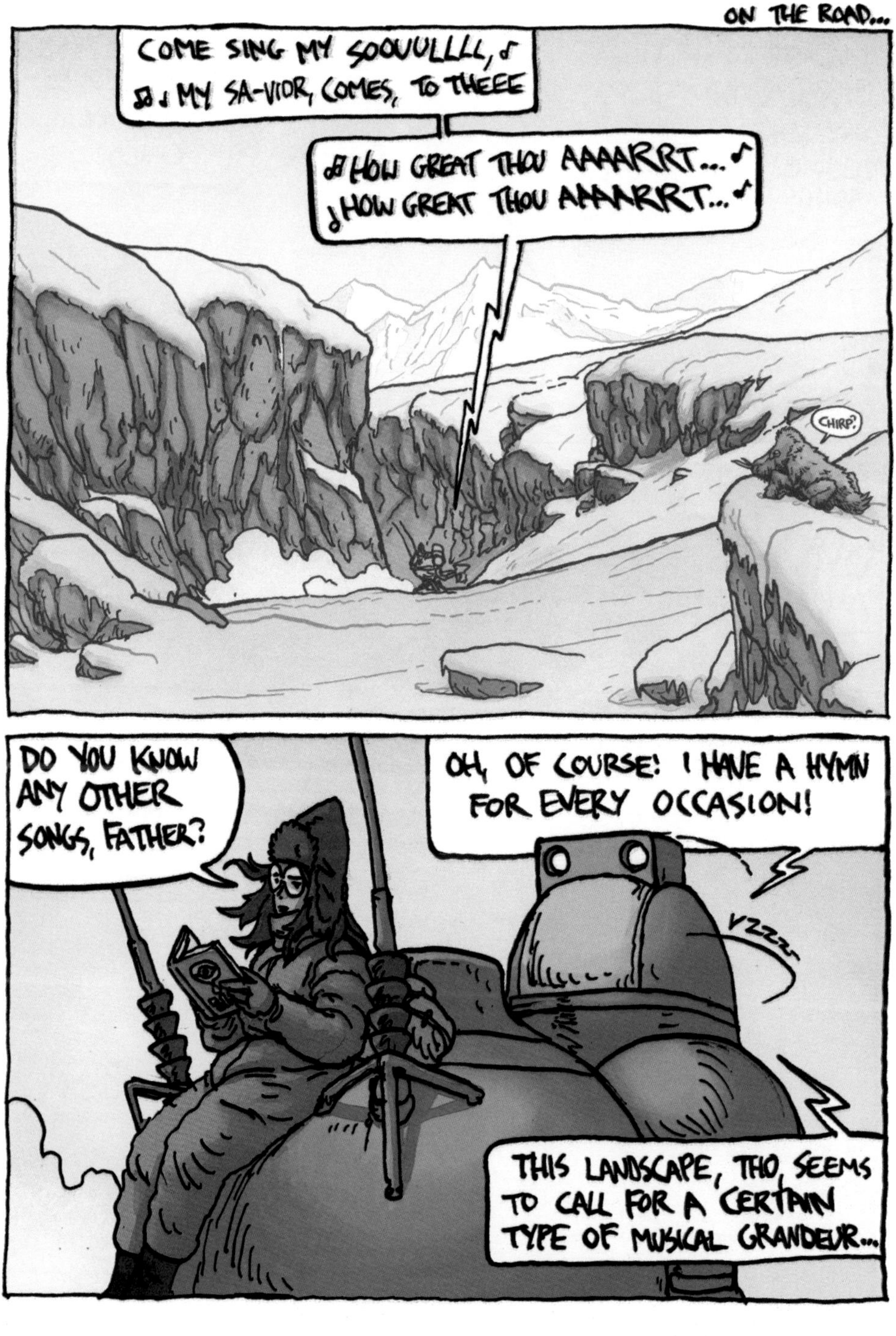
ON THE ROAD...
COME SING MY SOOUULLLL, ♪ ♫♩ MY SA-VIOR, COMES, TO THEEE
♫ HOW GREAT THOU AAAARRT... ♪ ♩ HOW GREAT THOU AAAARRT... ♪
CHIRP?
DO YOU KNOW ANY OTHER SONGS, FATHER?
OH, OF COURSE! I HAVE A HYMN FOR EVERY OCCASION!
VZZZZ
THIS LANDSCAPE, THO, SEEMS TO CALL FOR A CERTAIN TYPE OF MUSICAL GRANDEUR...

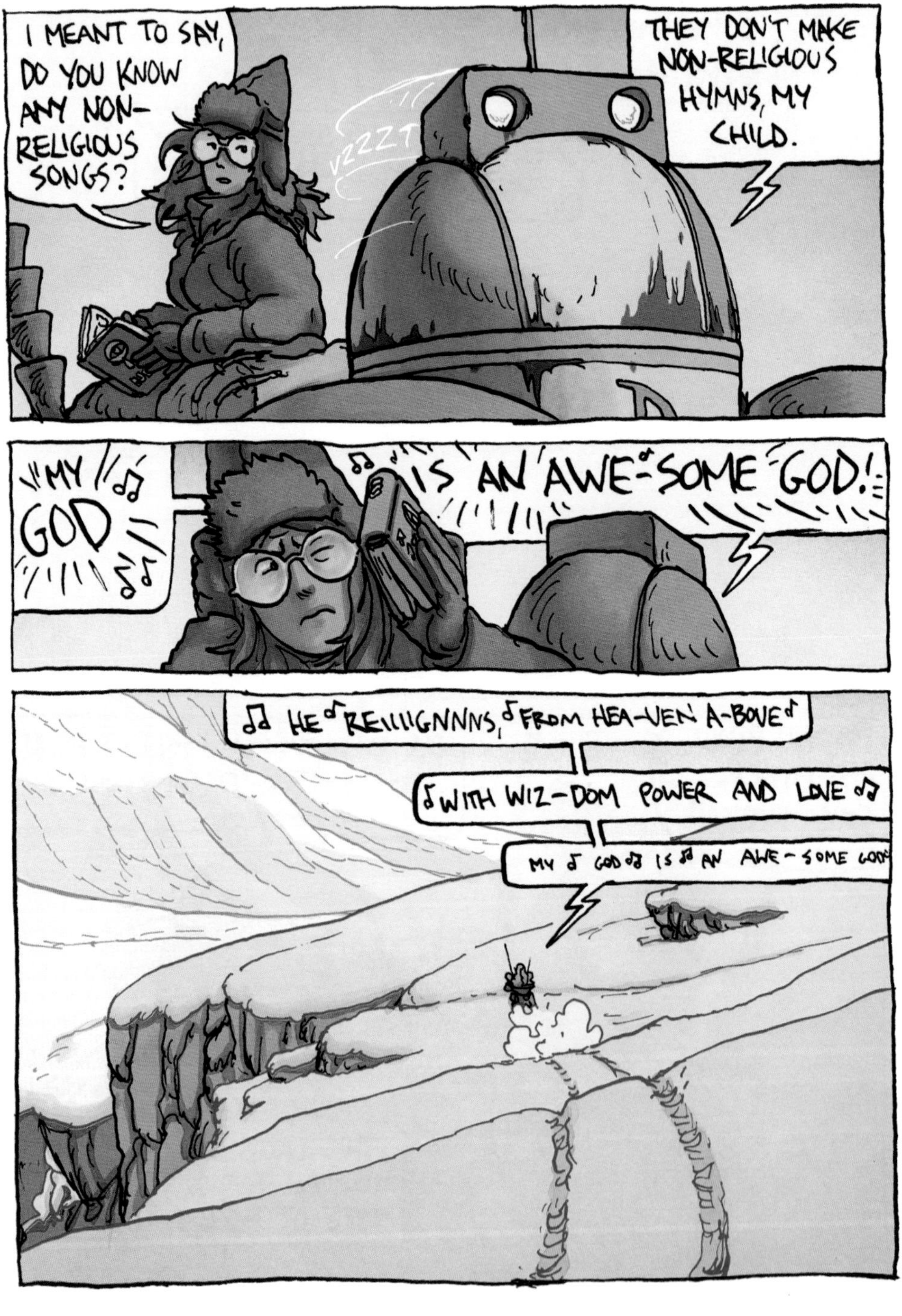
I MEANT TO SAY, DO YOU KNOW ANY NON-RELIGIOUS SONGS?
VZZZT
THEY DON'T MAKE NON-RELIGIOUS HYMNS, MY CHILD.
MY GOD
IS AN AWE-SOME GOD!
HE REIIIIGNNNS, FROM HEA-VEN A-BOVE
WITH WIZ-DOM POWER AND LOVE
MY GOD IS AN AWE-SOME GOD

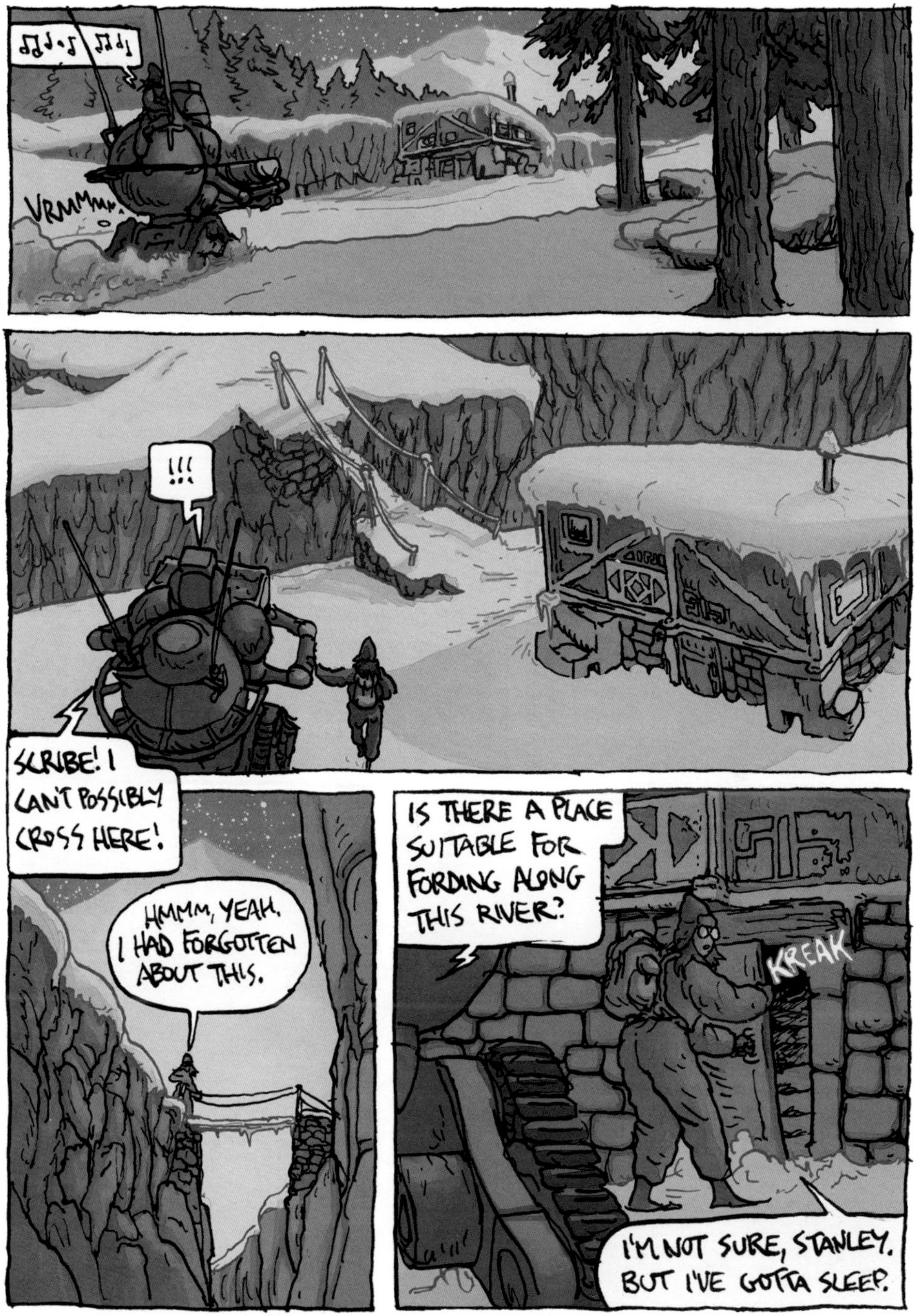

VRMMmm...
!!!
SCRIBE! I CAN'T POSSIBLY CROSS HERE!
HMMM, YEAH. I HAD FORGOTTEN ABOUT THIS.
IS THERE A PLACE SUITABLE FOR FORDING ALONG THIS RIVER?
KREAK
I'M NOT SURE, STANLEY. BUT I'VE GOTTA SLEEP.

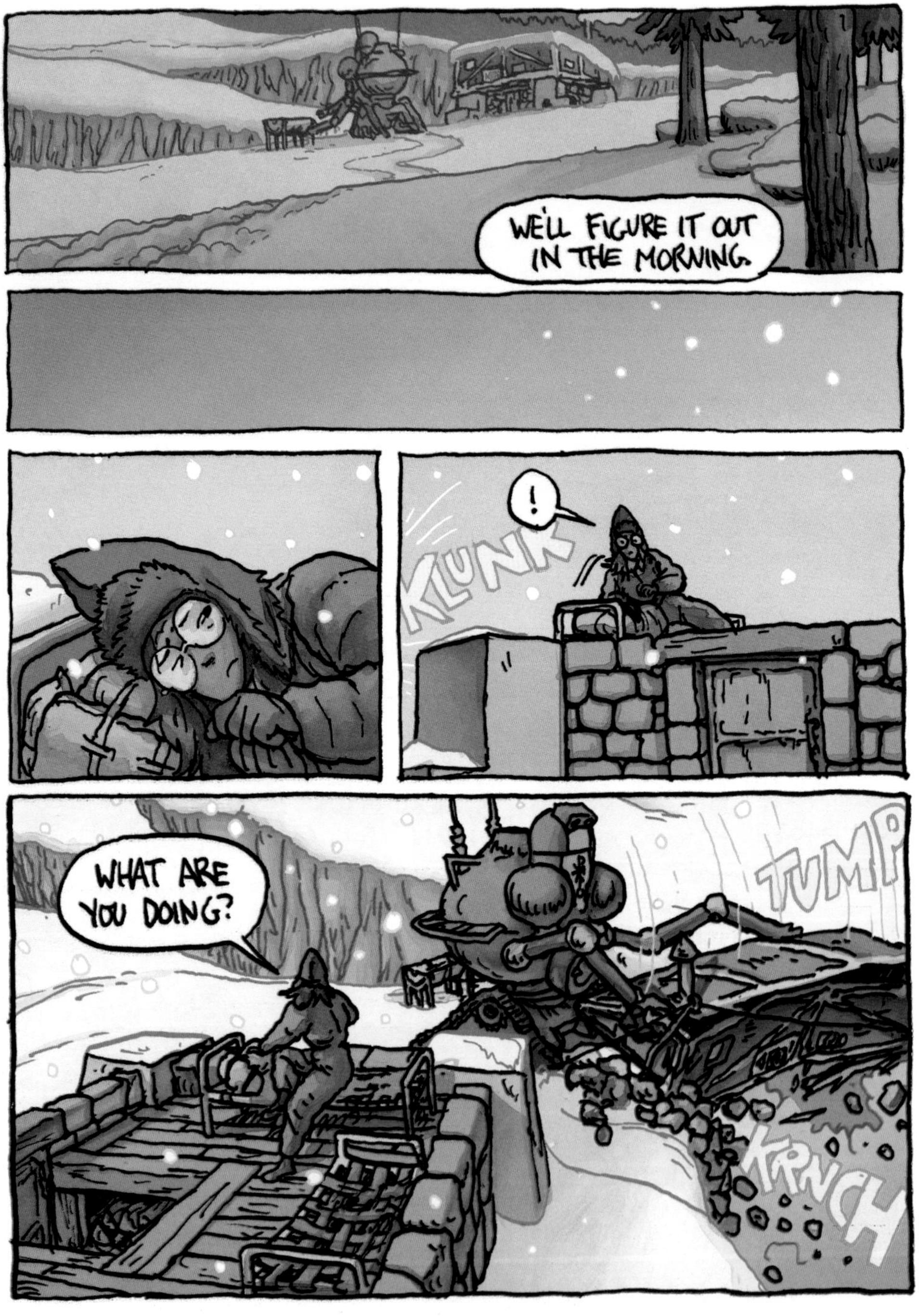
WE'LL FIGURE IT OUT IN THE MORNING.
!
KLUNK
WHAT ARE YOU DOING?
TUMP
KRNCH

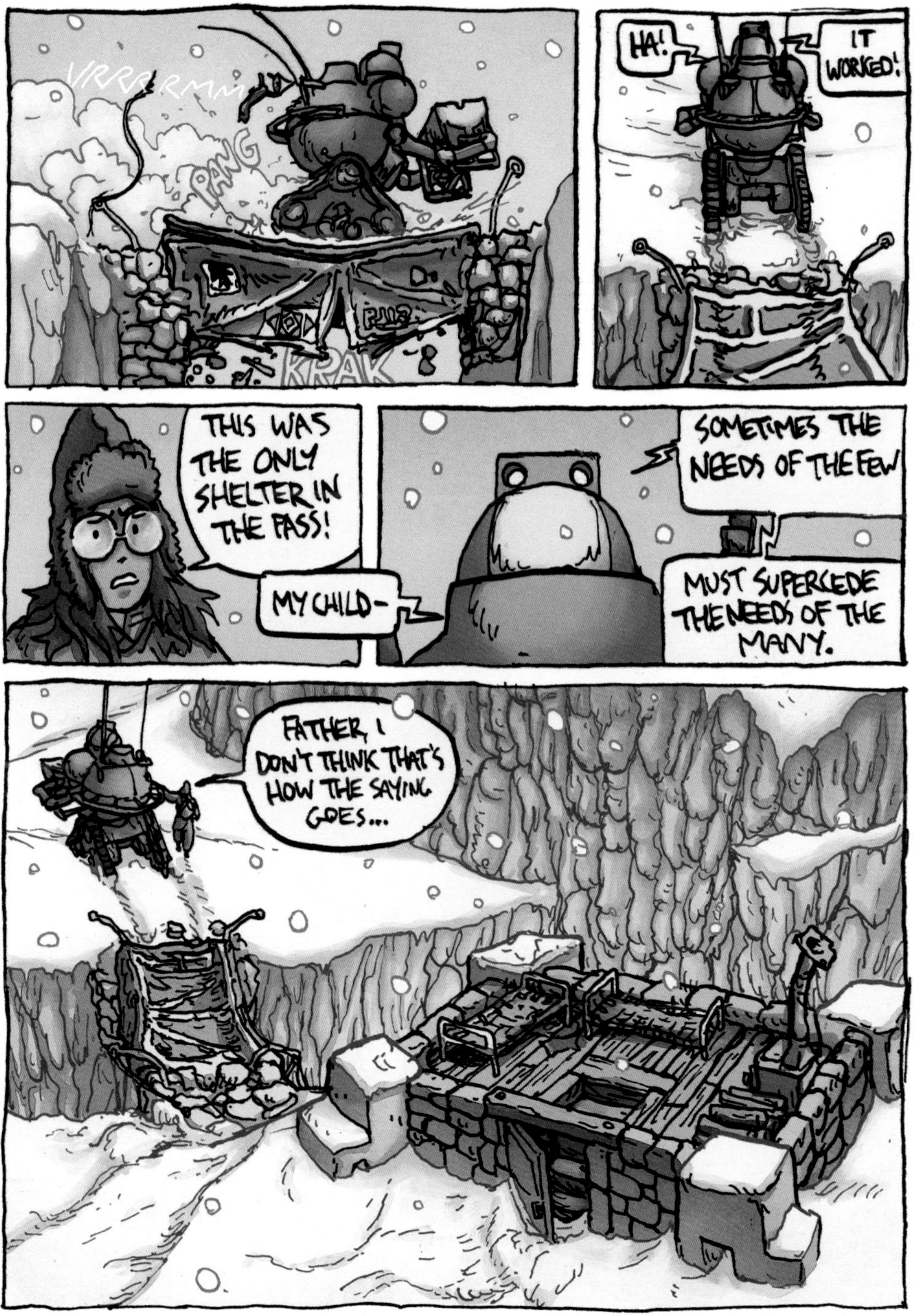
VRRRRRMMM
PANG
KRAK
HA!
IT WORKED!
THIS WAS THE ONLY SHELTER IN THE PASS!
MY CHILD-
SOMETIMES THE NEEDS OF THE FEW
MUST SUPERCEDE THE NEEDS OF THE MANY.
FATHER, I DON'T THINK THAT'S HOW THE SAYING GOES...

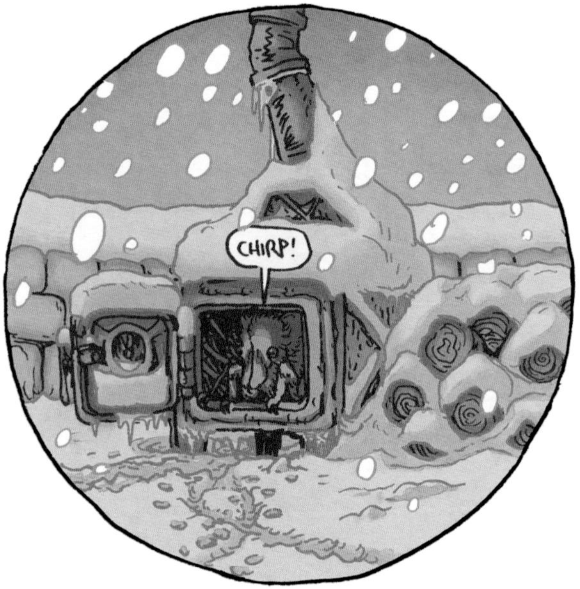
CHIRP!

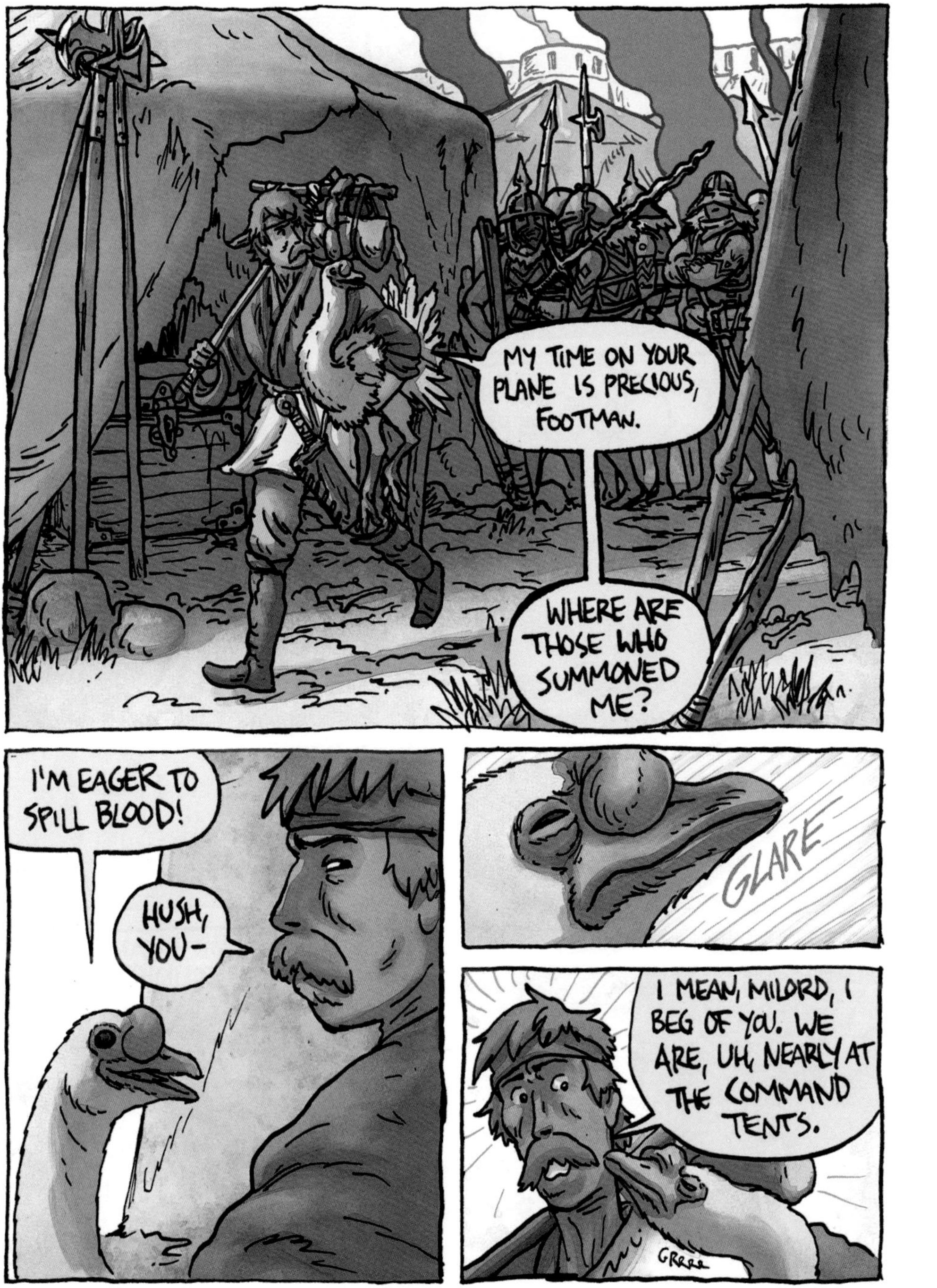
MY TIME ON YOUR PLANE IS PRECIOUS, FOOTMAN.
WHERE ARE THOSE WHO SUMMONED ME?
I'M EAGER TO SPILL BLOOD!
HUSH, YOU-
GLARE
I MEAN, MILORD, I BEG OF YOU. WE ARE, UH, NEARLY AT THE COMMAND TENTS.
GRRRR

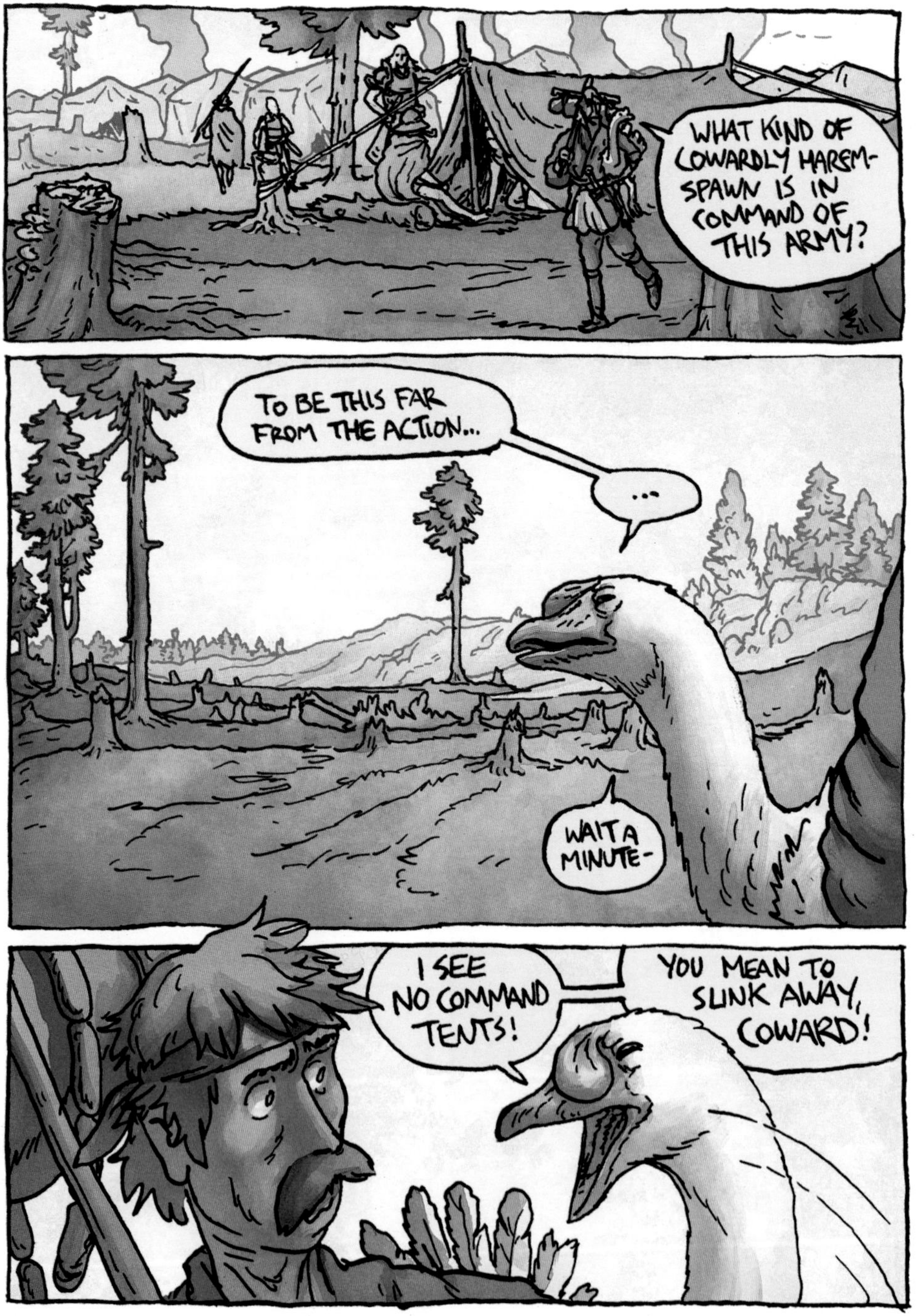
WHAT KIND OF COWARDLY HAREM-SPAWN IS IN COMMAND OF THIS ARMY?
TO BE THIS FAR FROM THE ACTION...
...
WAIT A MINUTE-
I SEE NO COMMAND TENTS!
YOU MEAN TO SLINK AWAY, COWARD!

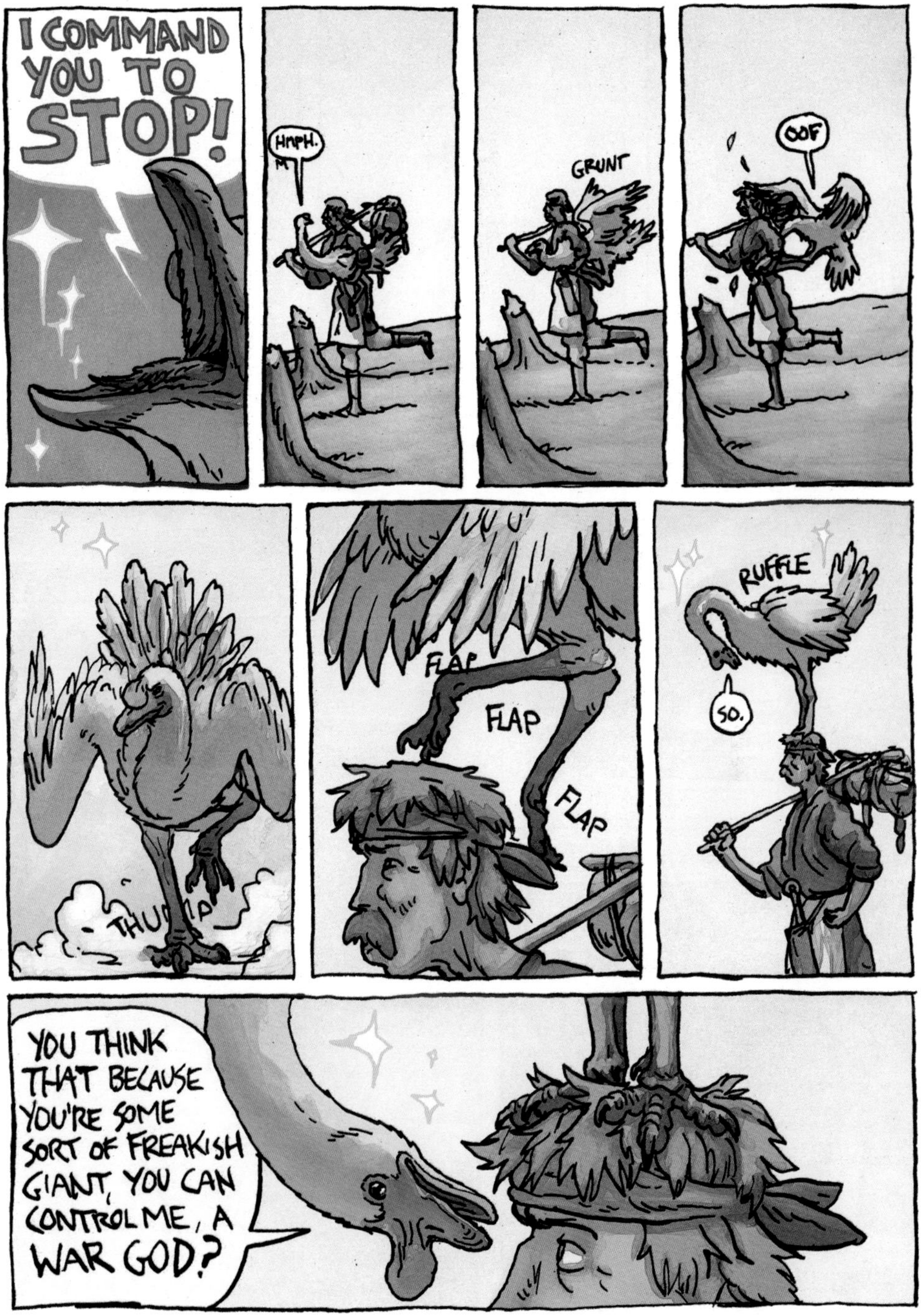
I COMMAND YOU TO STOP!
HMPH.
GRUNT
OOF
FLAP
FLAP
FLAP
RUFFLE
SO.
YOU THINK THAT BECAUSE YOU'RE SOME SORT OF FREAKISH GIANT, YOU CAN CONTROL ME, A WAR GOD?

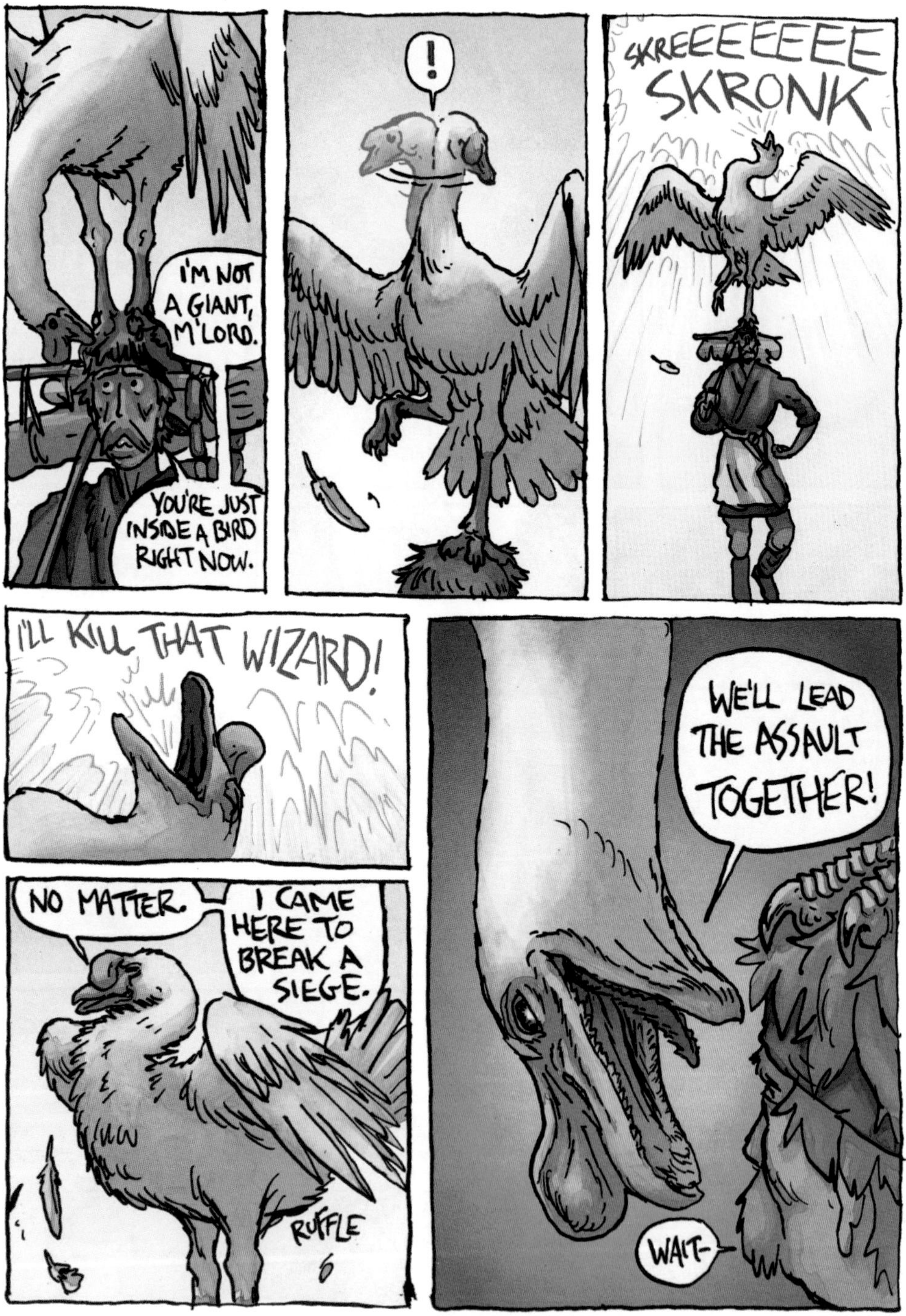
I'M NOT A GIANT, M'LORD.
YOU'RE JUST INSIDE A BIRD RIGHT NOW.
!
SKREEEEEEEE SKRONK
I'LL KILL THAT WIZARD!
NO MATTER.
I CAME HERE TO BREAK A SIEGE.
RUFFLE
WE'LL LEAD THE ASSAULT TOGETHER!
WAIT-

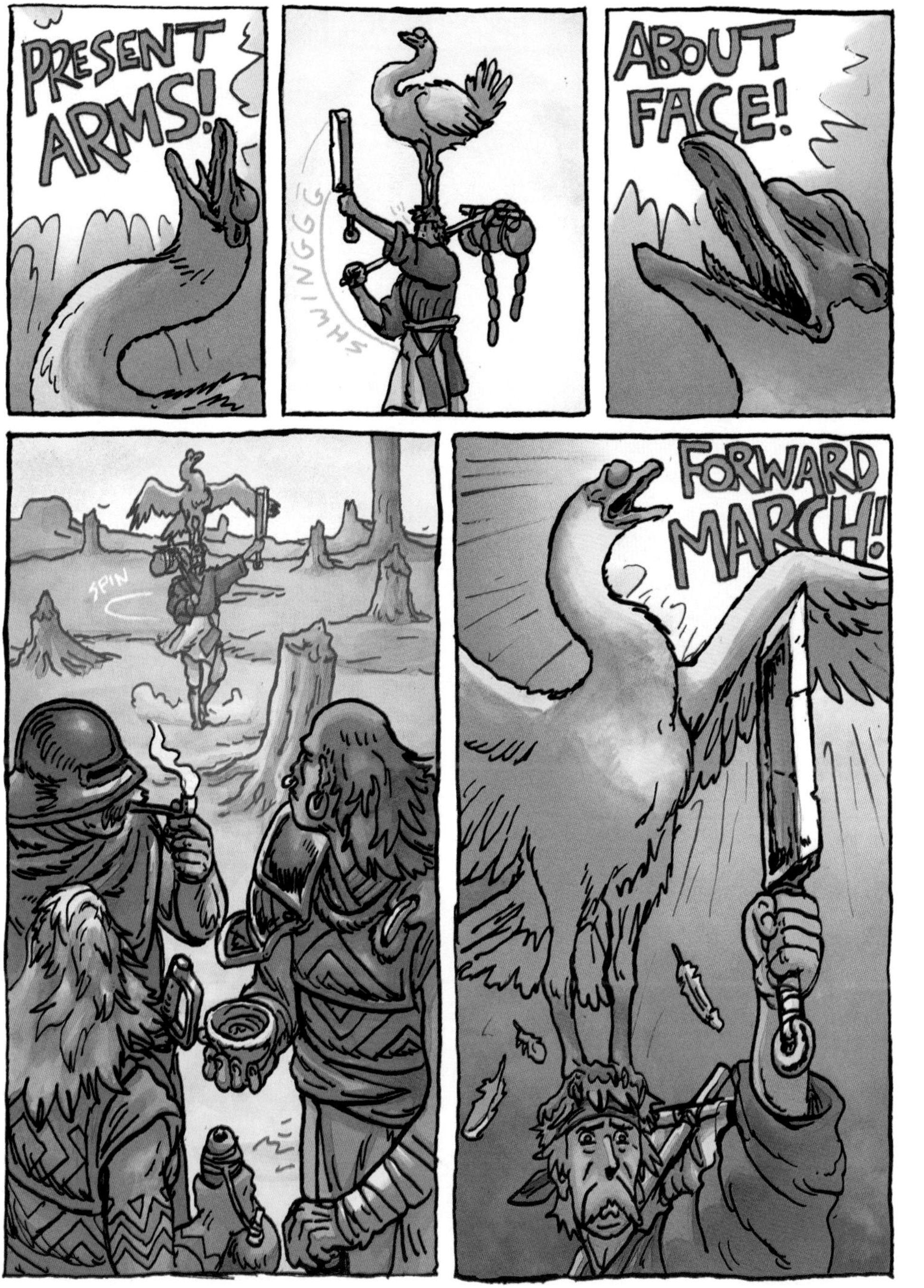
PRESENT ARMS!
SHWINGGG
ABOUT FACE!
SPIN
FORWARD MARCH!

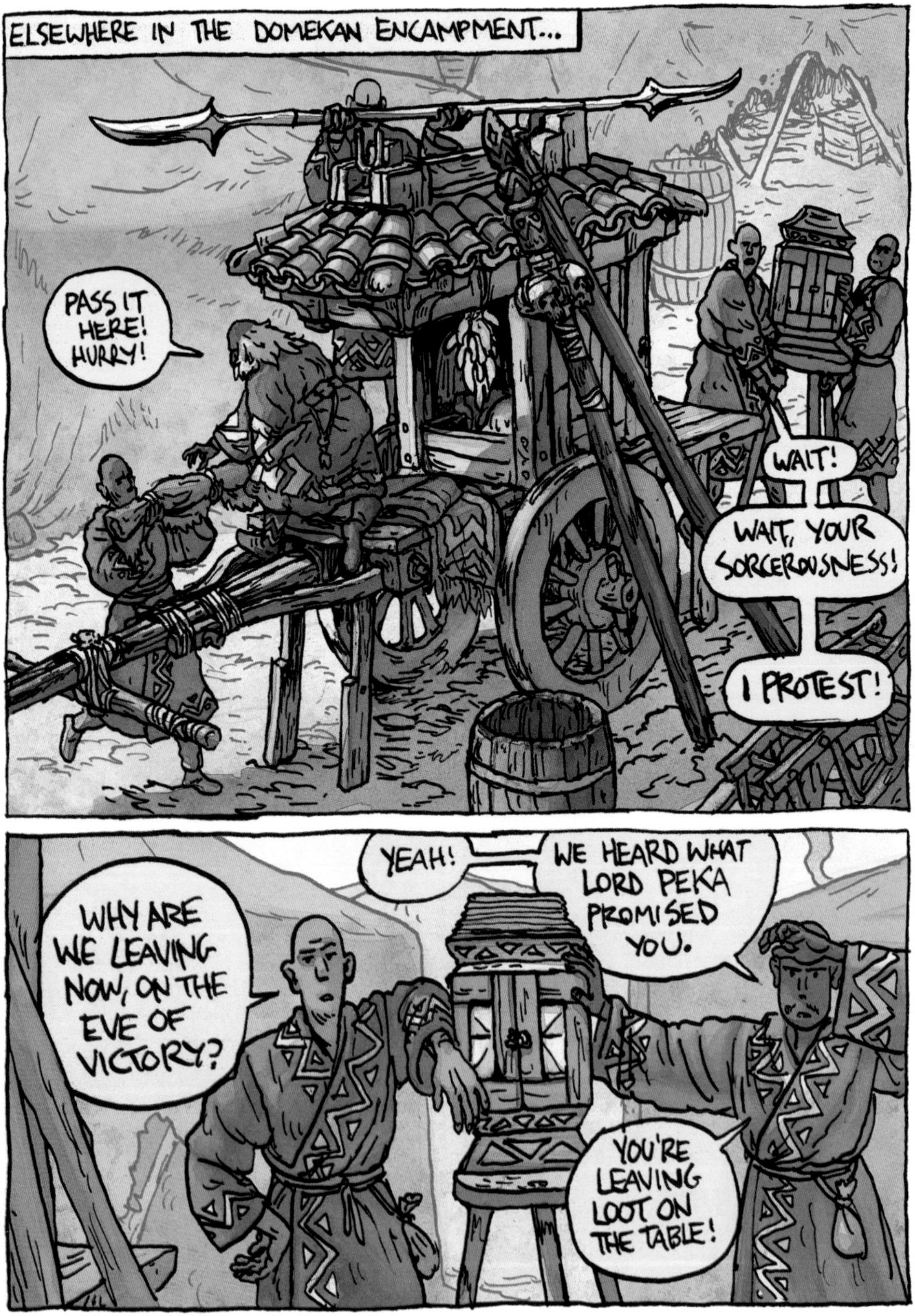
ELSEWHERE IN THE DOMEKAN ENCAMPMENT...
PASS IT HERE! HURRY!
WAIT!
WAIT, YOUR SORCEROUSNESS!
I PROTEST!
WHY ARE WE LEAVING NOW, ON THE EVE OF VICTORY?
YEAH!
WE HEARD WHAT LORD PEKA PROMISED YOU.
YOU'RE LEAVING LOOT ON THE TABLE!

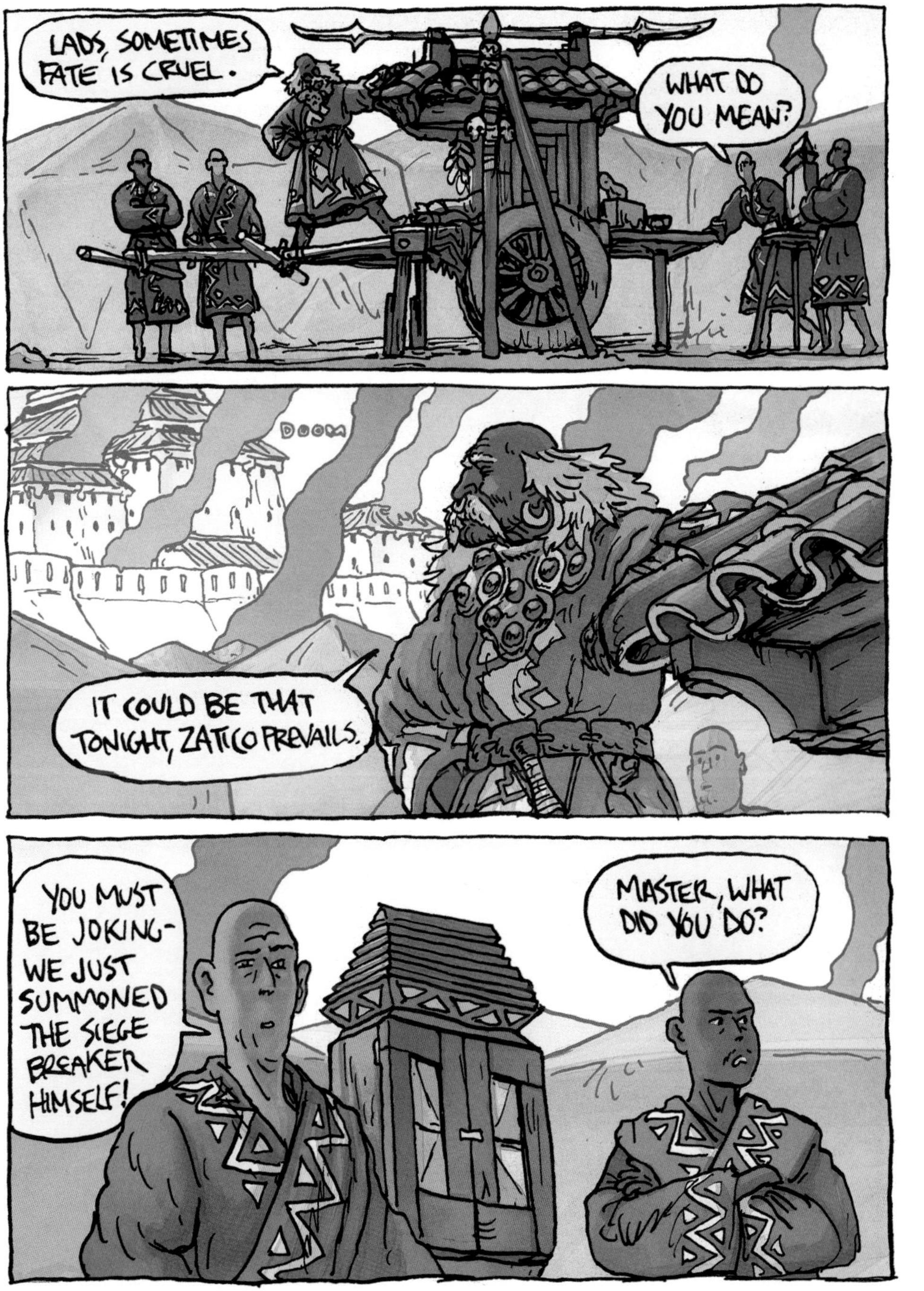
LADS, SOMETIMES FATE IS CRUEL.
WHAT DO YOU MEAN?
DOOM
IT COULD BE THAT TONIGHT, ZATICO PREVAILS.
YOU MUST BE JOKING- WE JUST SUMMONED THE SIEGE BREAKER HIMSELF!
MASTER, WHAT DID YOU DO?

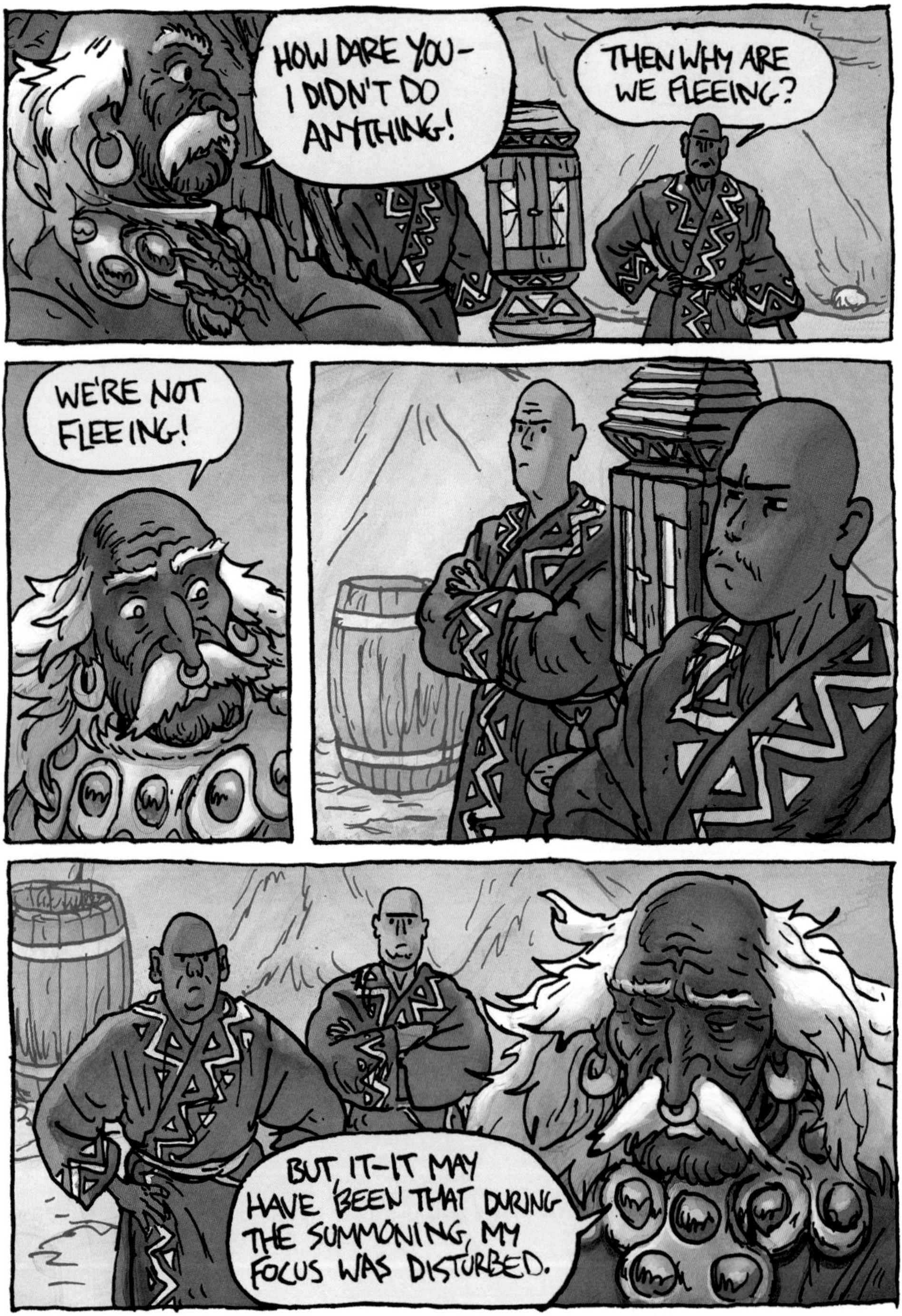
HOW DARE YOU-
I DIDN'T DO
ANYTHING!
THEN WHY ARE
WE FLEEING?
WE'RE NOT
FLEEING!
BUT, IT-IT MAY
HAVE BEEN THAT DURING
THE SUMMONING, MY
FOCUS WAS DISTURBED.

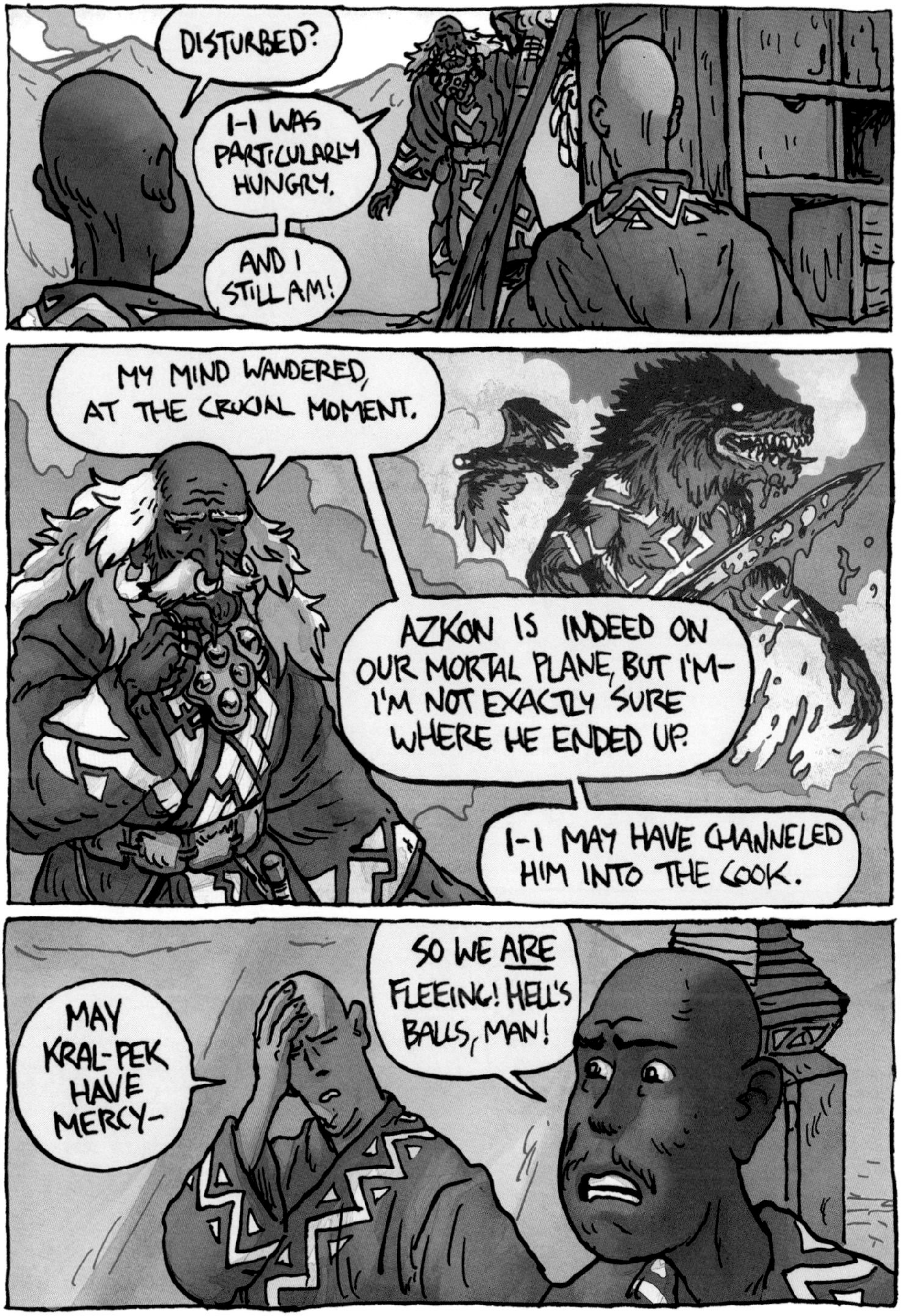
DISTURBED?
I-I WAS PARTICULARLY HUNGRY.
AND I STILL AM!
MY MIND WANDERED, AT THE CRUCIAL MOMENT.
AZKON IS INDEED ON OUR MORTAL PLANE, BUT I'M- I'M NOT EXACTLY SURE WHERE HE ENDED UP.
I-I MAY HAVE CHANNELED HIM INTO THE COOK.
MAY KRAL-PEK HAVE MERCY-
SO WE ARE FLEEING! HELL'S BALLS, MAN!

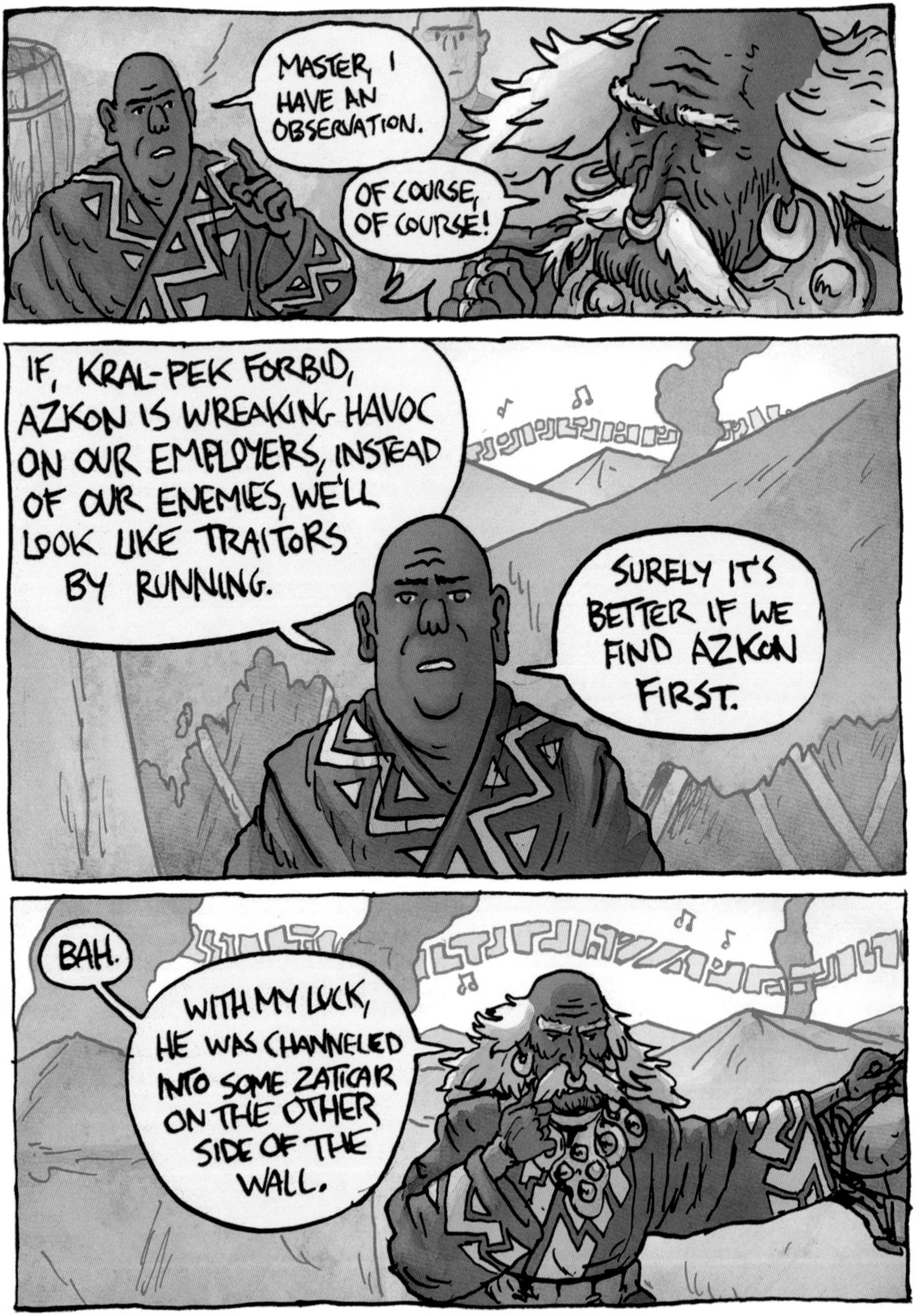
MASTER, I HAVE AN OBSERVATION.
OF COURSE, OF COURSE!
IF, KRAL-PEK FORBID, AZKON IS WREAKING HAVOC ON OUR EMPLOYERS, INSTEAD OF OUR ENEMIES, WE'LL LOOK LIKE TRAITORS BY RUNNING.
SURELY IT'S BETTER IF WE FIND AZKON FIRST.
BAH.
WITH MY LUCK, HE WAS CHANNELED INTO SOME ZATICAR ON THE OTHER SIDE OF THE WALL.

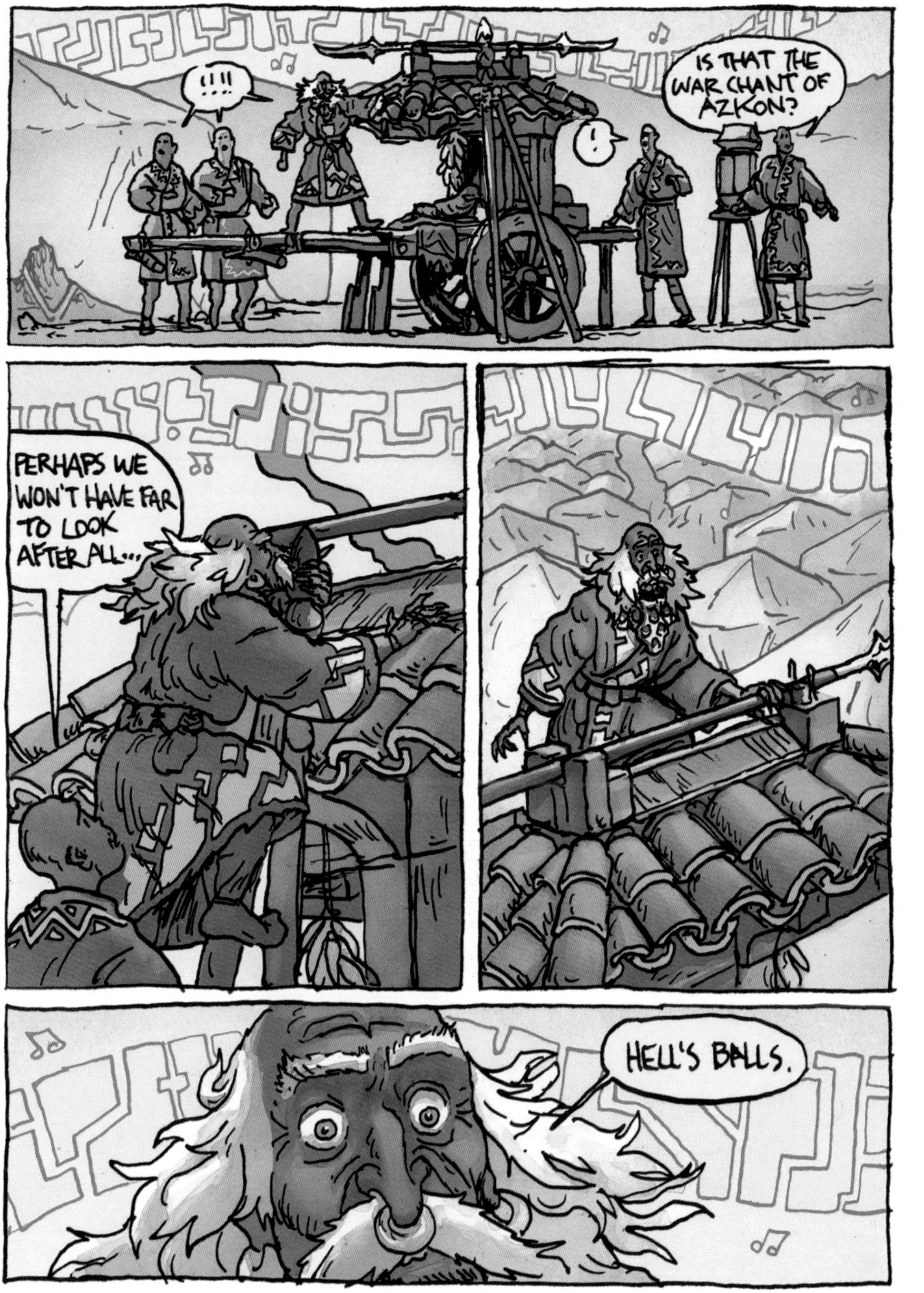
!!!!
....
!
IS THAT THE WAR CHANT OF AZKON?
PERHAPS WE WON'T HAVE FAR TO LOOK AFTER ALL...
HELL'S BALLS.

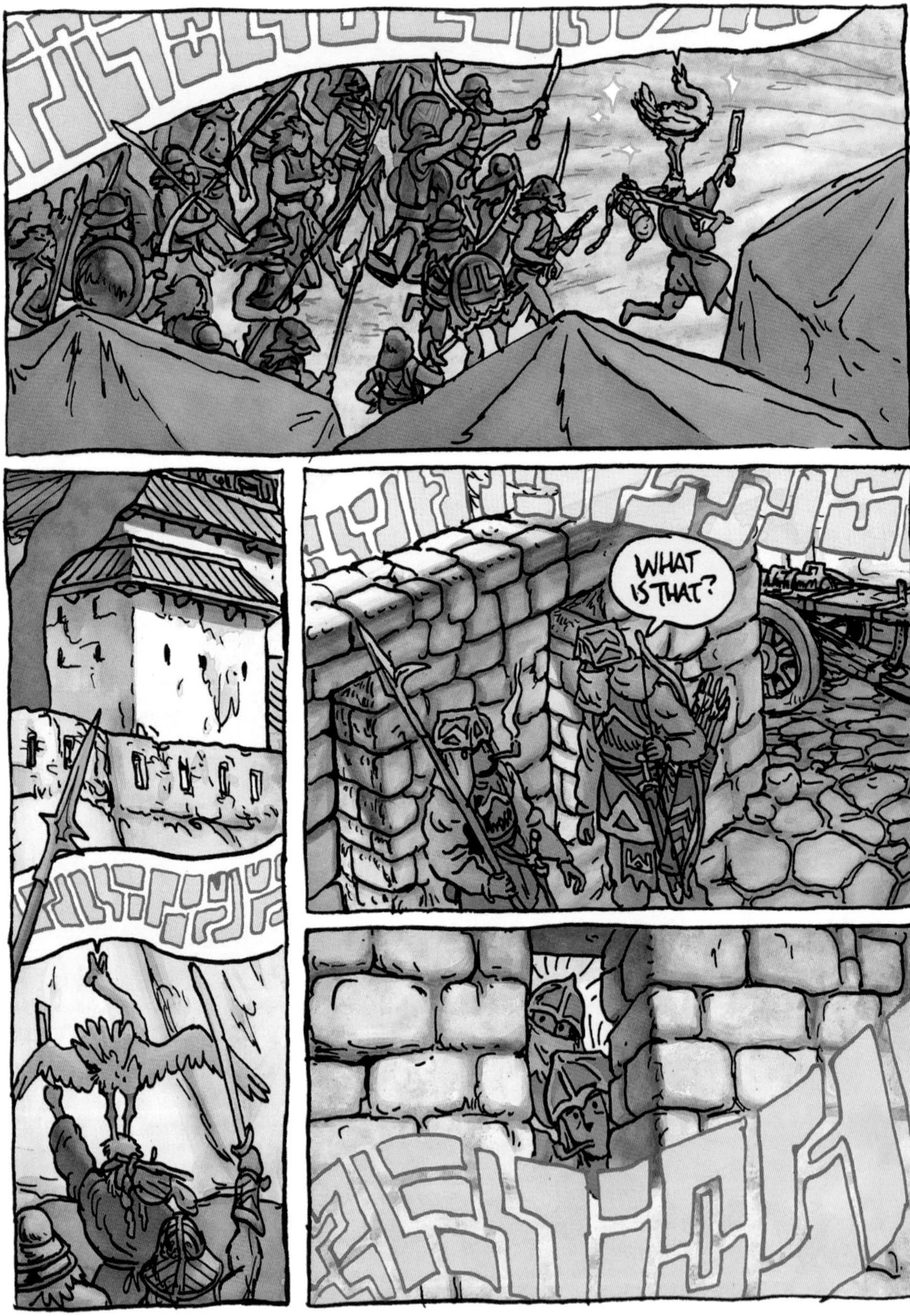
WHAT IS THAT?

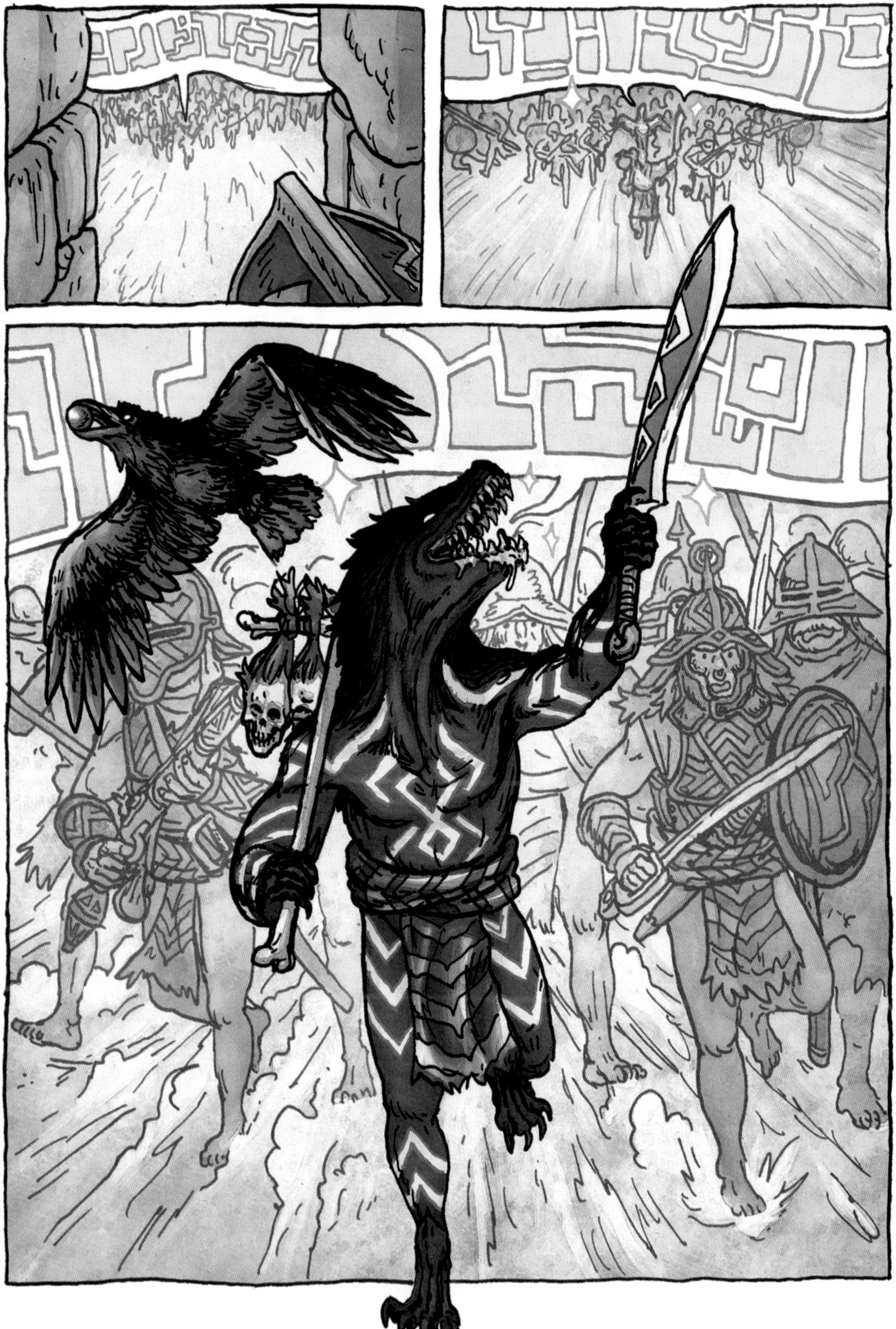

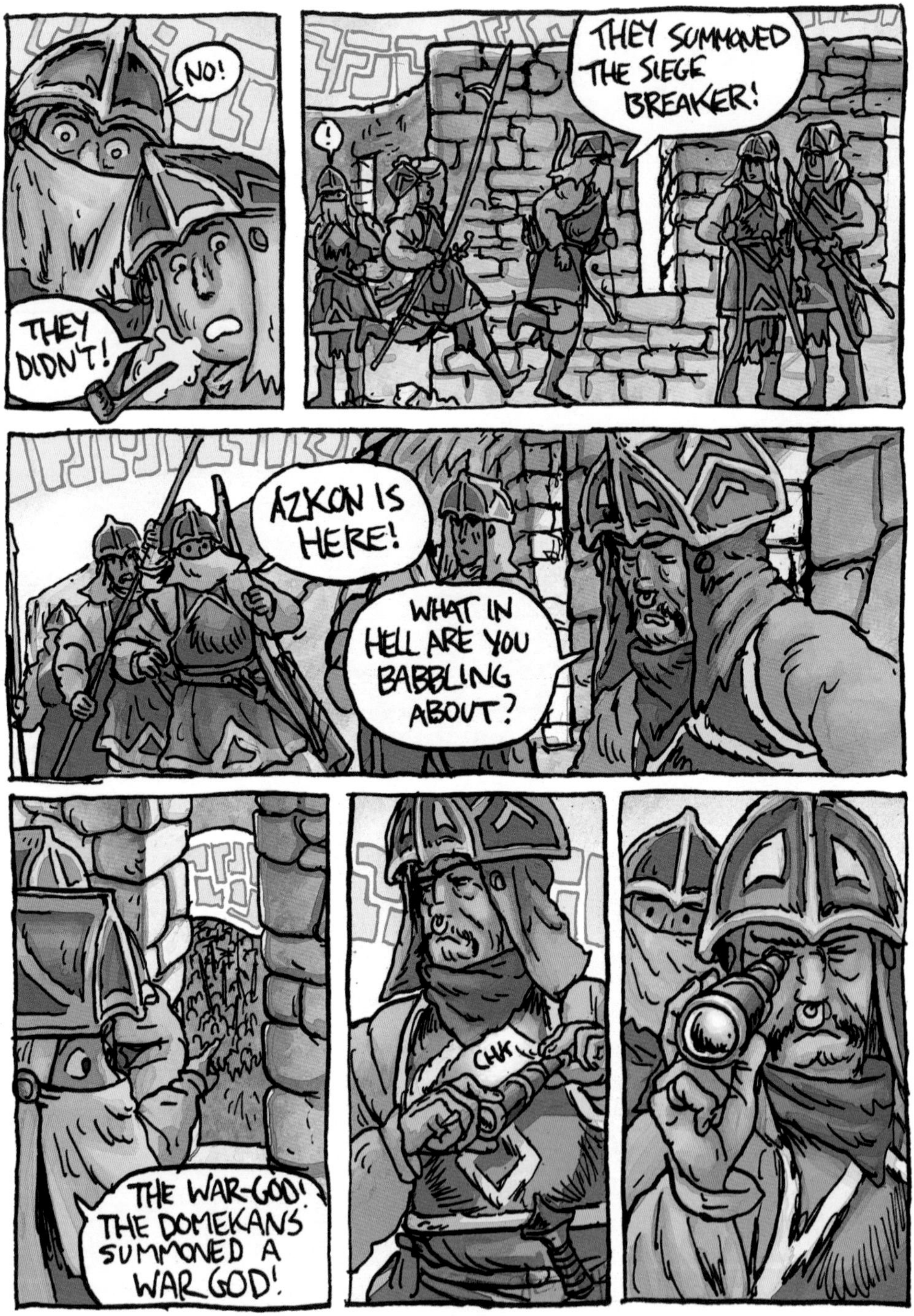
NO!
THEY DIDN'T!
THEY SUMMONED THE SIEGE BREAKER!
!
AZKON IS HERE!
WHAT IN HELL ARE YOU BABBLING ABOUT?
THE WAR-GOD! THE DOMEKANS SUMMONED A WAR GOD!
CHK

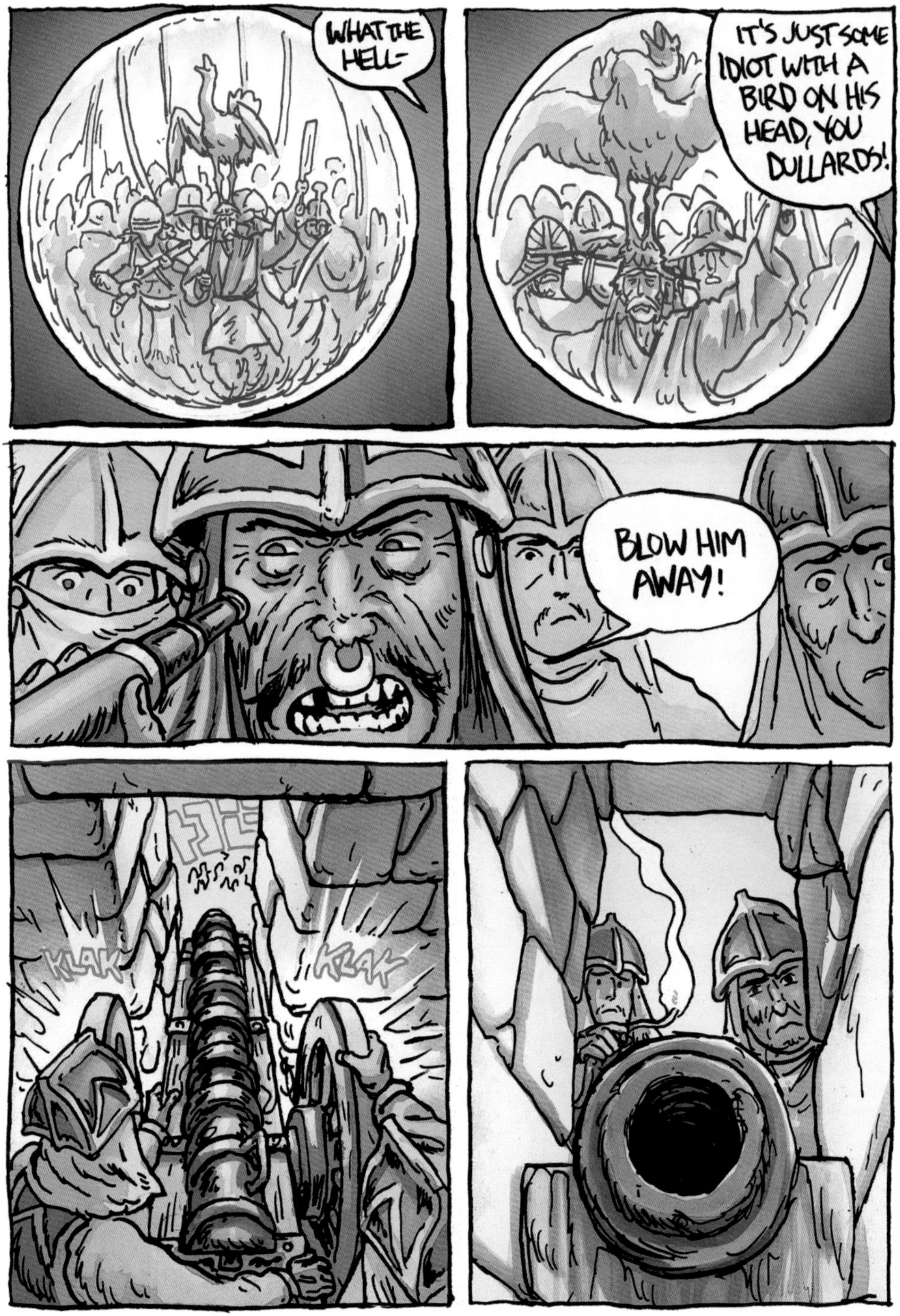
WHAT THE HELL-
IT'S JUST SOME IDIOT WITH A BIRD ON HIS HEAD, YOU DULLARDS!
BLOW HIM AWAY!
KLAK
KLAK

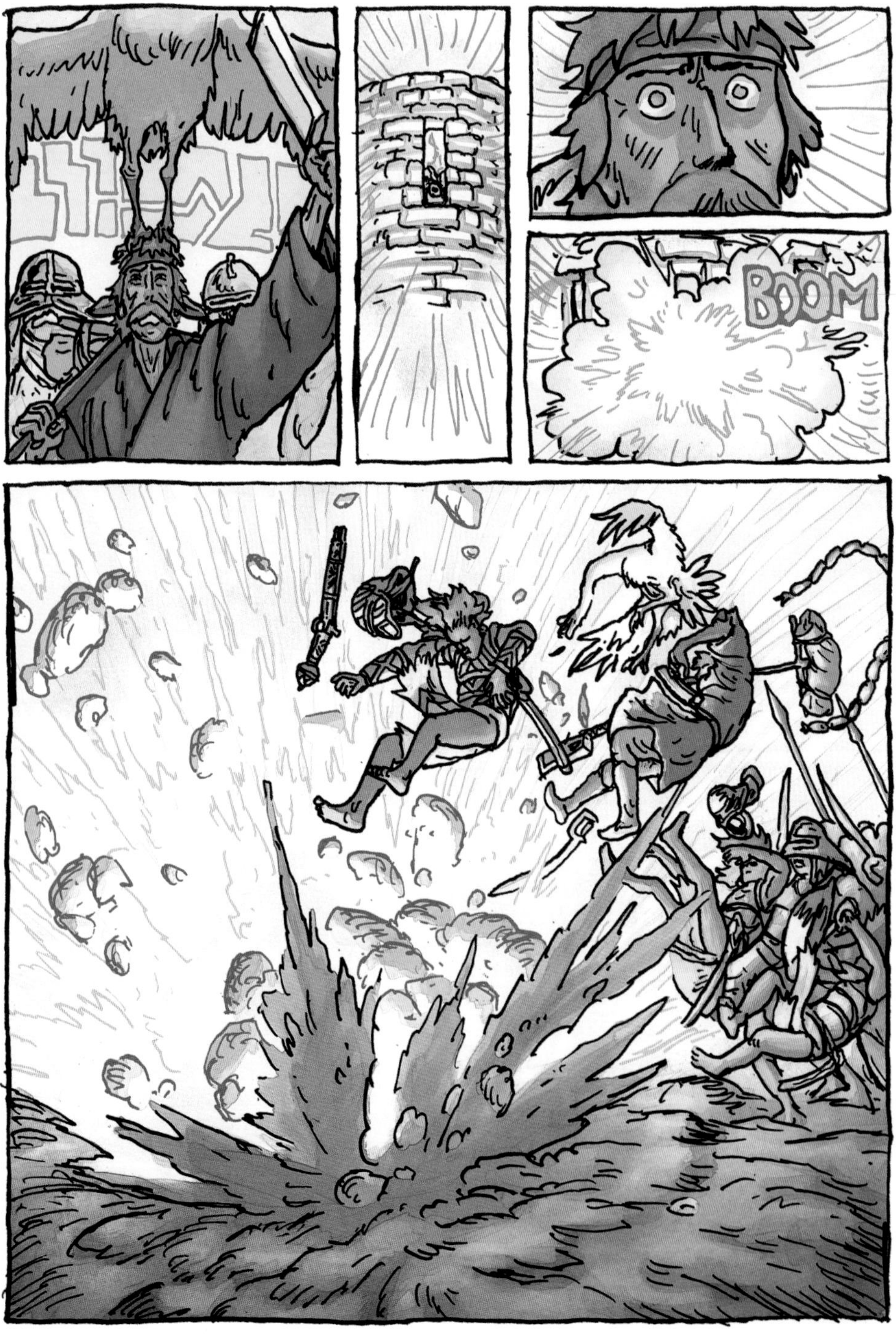
BOOM

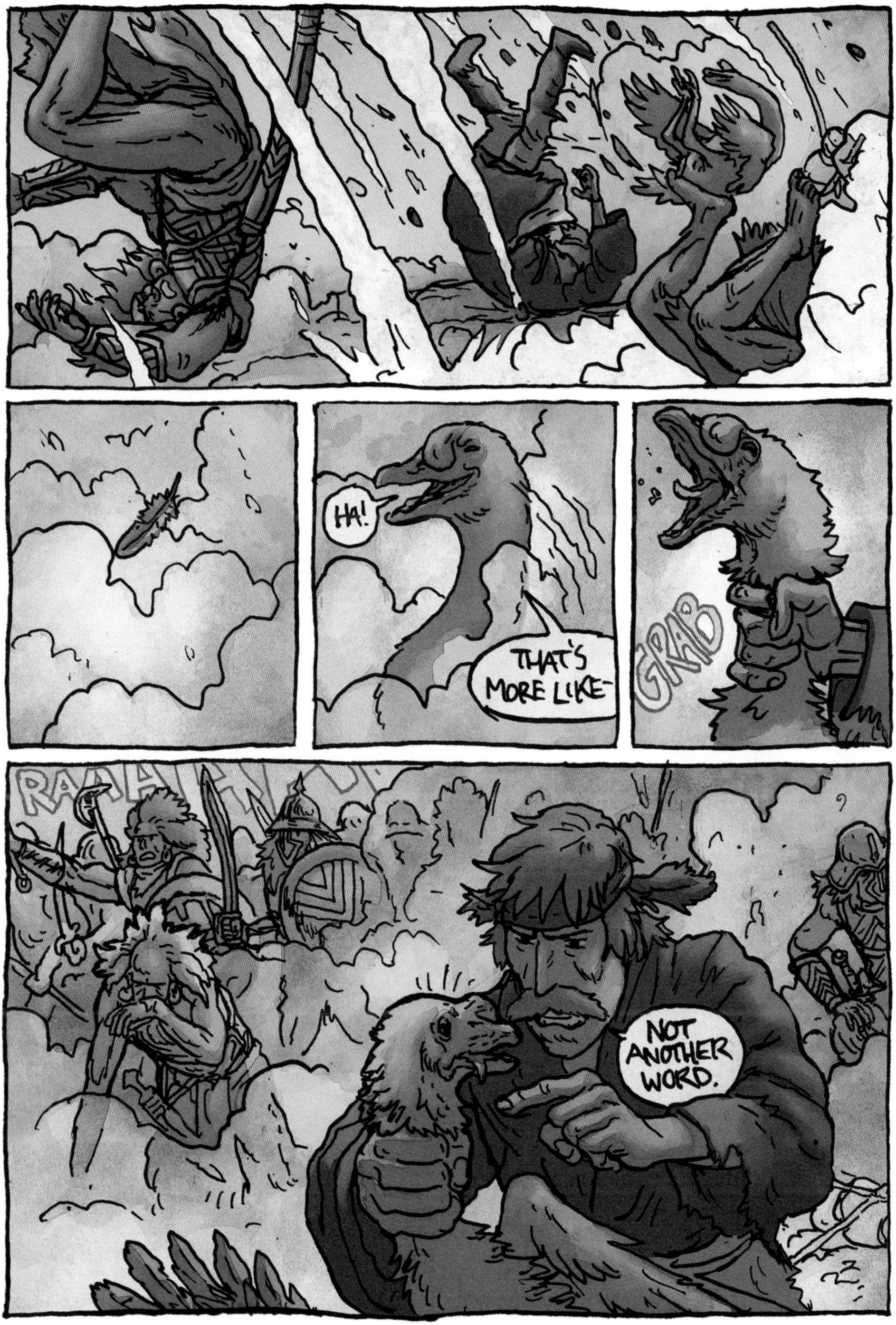
HA!
THAT'S MORE LIKE-
GRAB
RAAAAAA
NOT ANOTHER WORD.

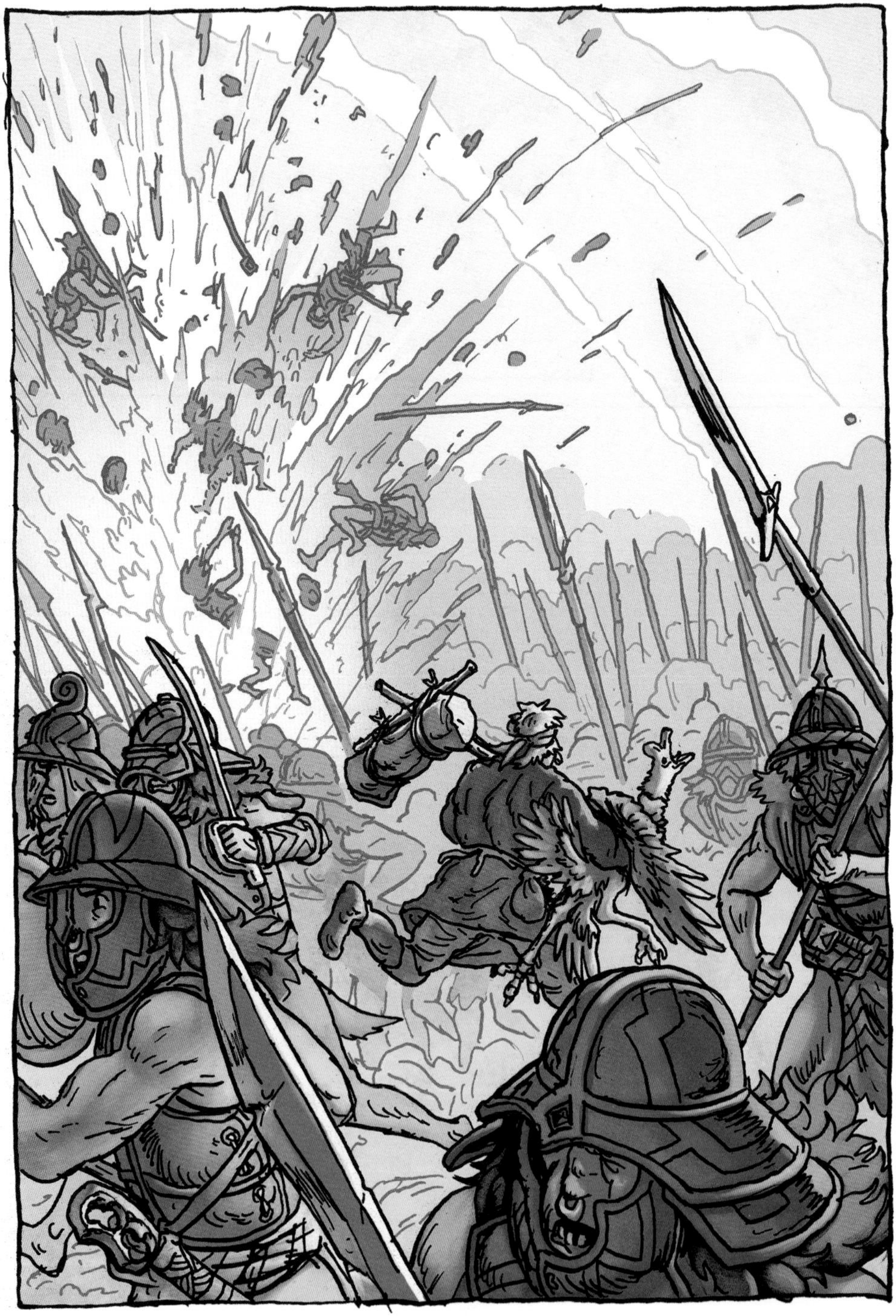

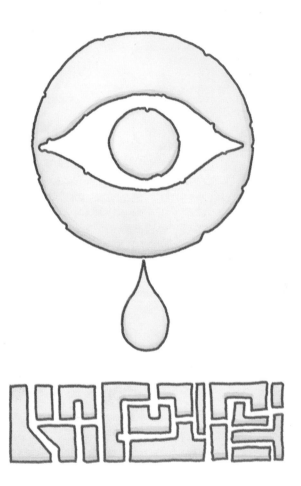

THE CAPITAL...

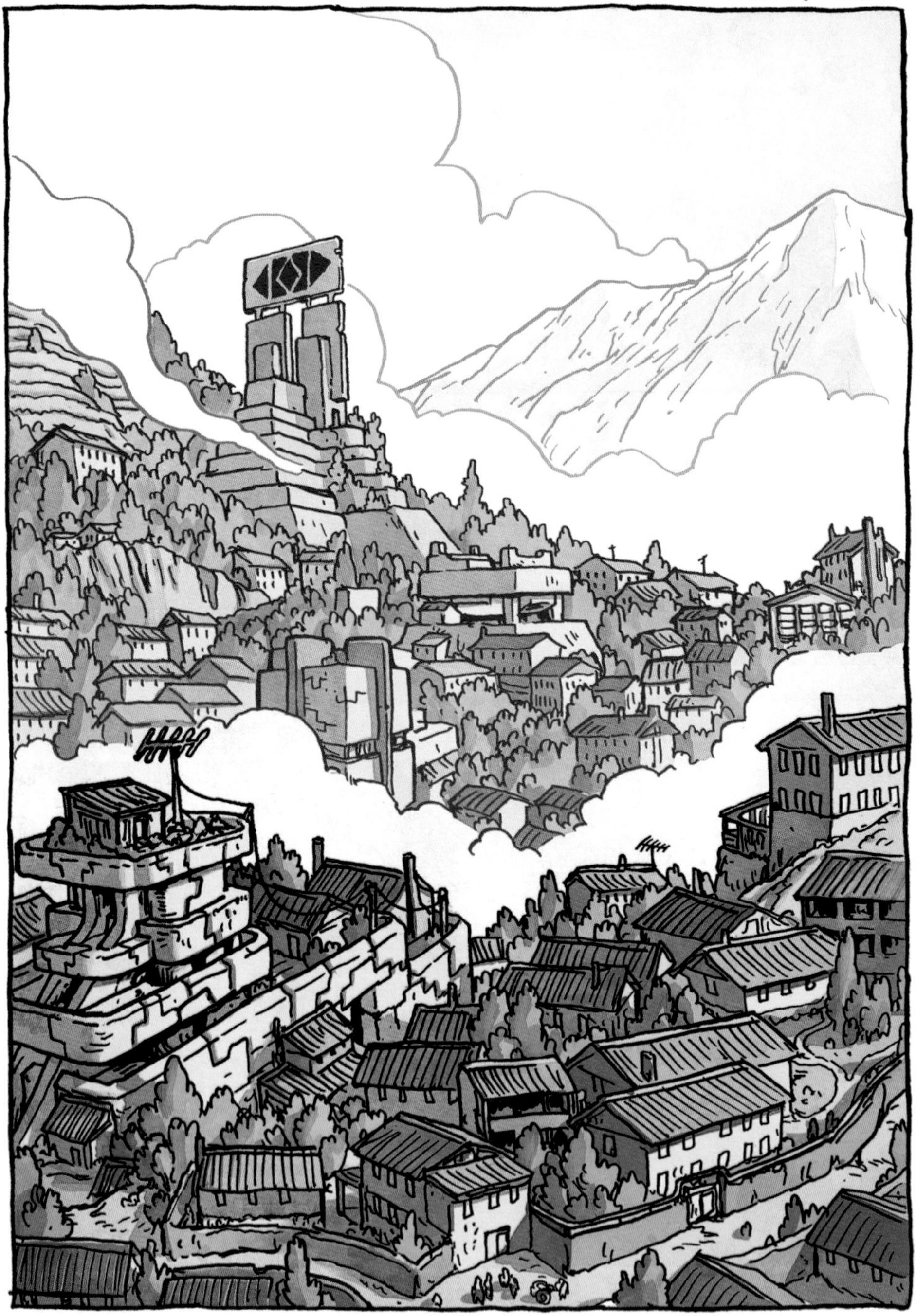

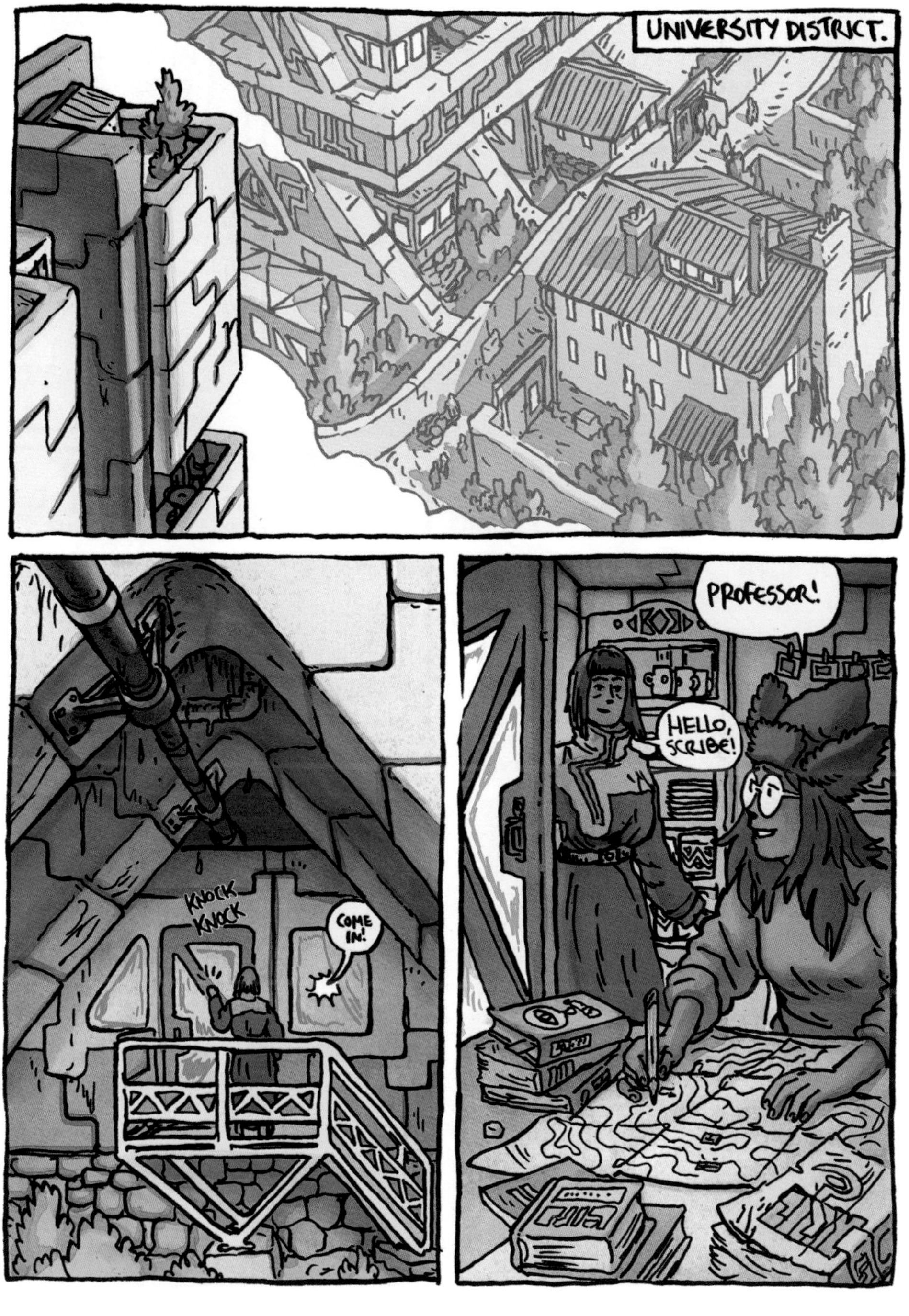
UNIVERSITY DISTRICT.
KNOCK KNOCK
COME IN!
PROFESSOR!
HELLO, SCRIBE!

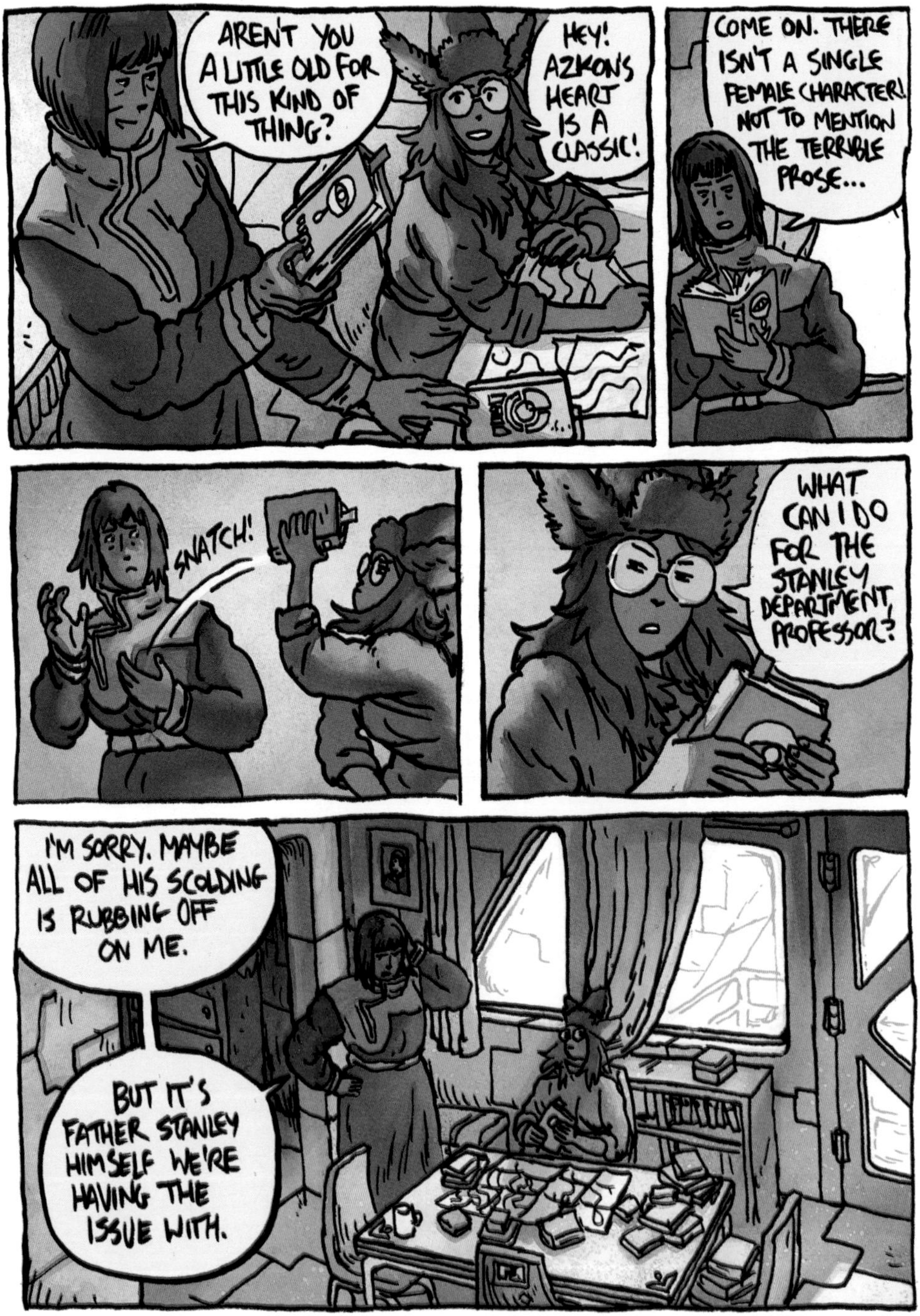

AREN'T YOU A LITTLE OLD FOR THIS KIND OF THING?
HEY! AZKON'S HEART IS A CLASSIC!
COME ON. THERE ISN'T A SINGLE FEMALE CHARACTER! NOT TO MENTION THE TERRIBLE PROSE...
SNATCH!
WHAT CAN I DO FOR THE STANLEY DEPARTMENT PROFESSOR?
I'M SORRY. MAYBE ALL OF HIS SCOLDING IS RUBBING OFF ON ME.
BUT IT'S FATHER STANLEY HIMSELF WE'RE HAVING THE ISSUE WITH.

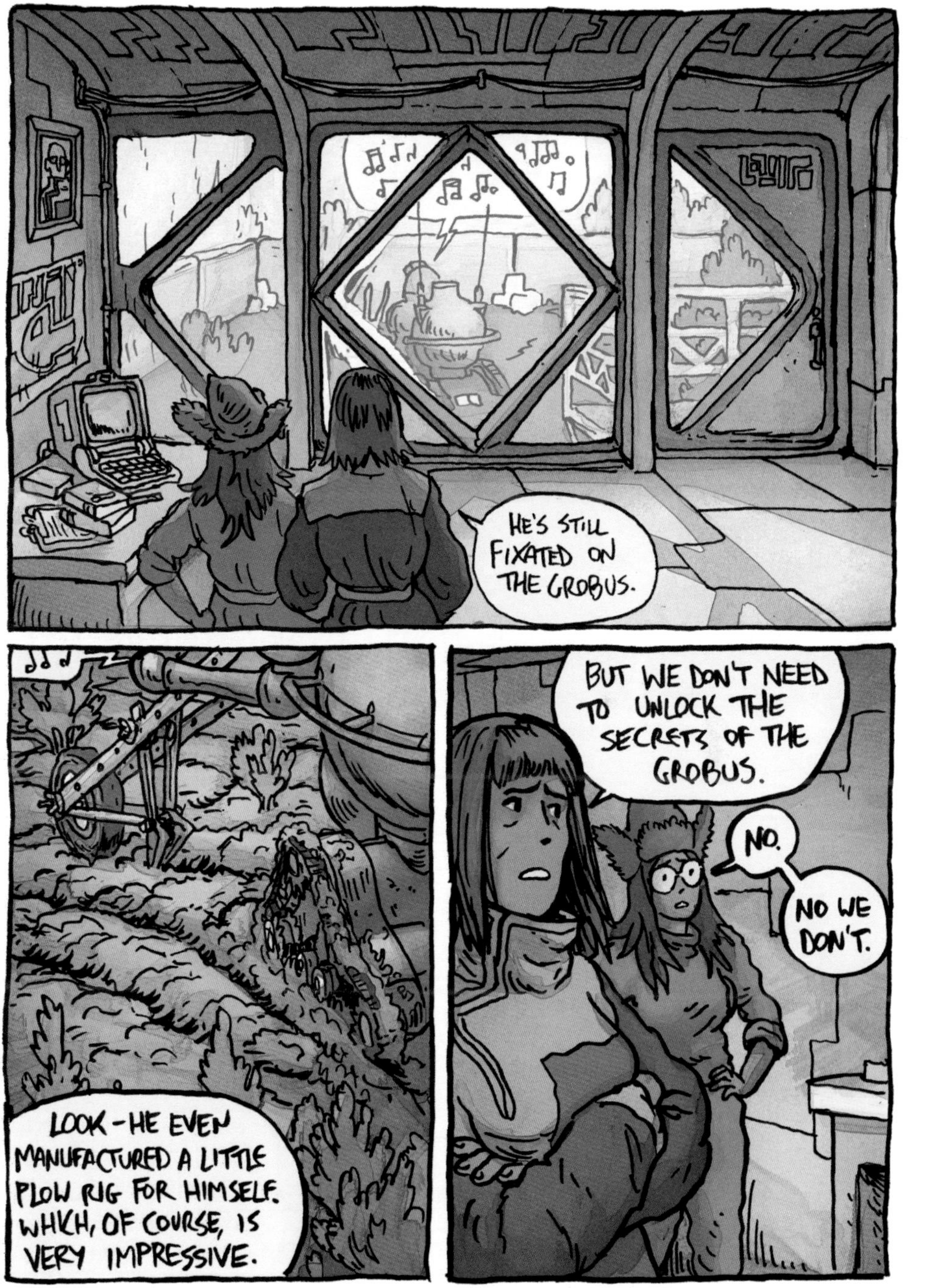
HE'S STILL FIXATED ON THE GROBUS.
LOOK - HE EVEN MANUFACTURED A LITTLE PLOW RIG FOR HIMSELF. WHICH, OF COURSE, IS VERY IMPRESSIVE.
BUT WE DON'T NEED TO UNLOCK THE SECRETS OF THE GROBUS.
NO.
NO WE DON'T.

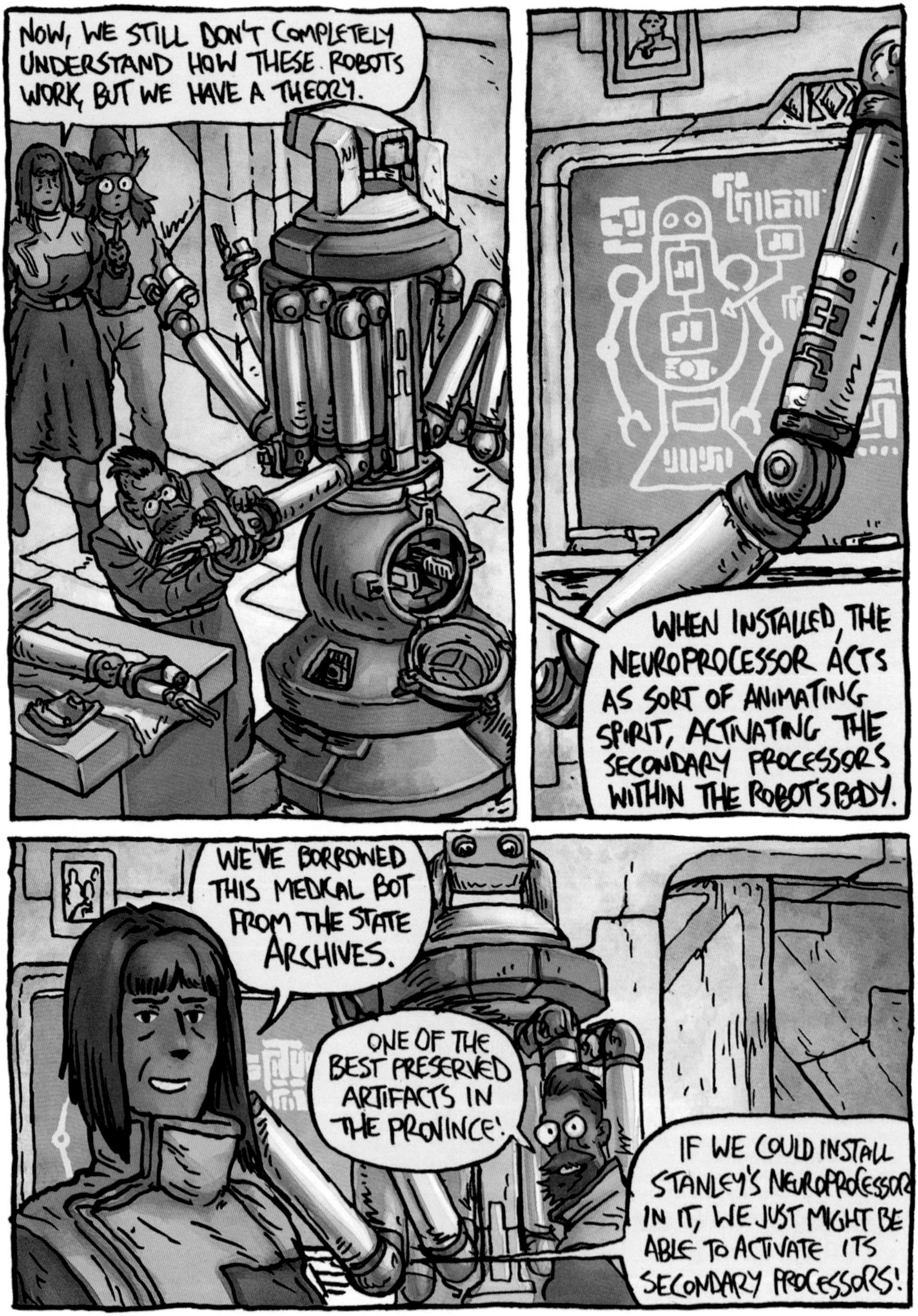

NOW, WE STILL DON'T COMPLETELY UNDERSTAND HOW THESE ROBOTS WORK, BUT WE HAVE A THEORY.
WHEN INSTALLED, THE NEUROPROCESSOR ACTS AS SORT OF ANIMATING SPIRIT, ACTIVATING THE SECONDARY PROCESSORS WITHIN THE ROBOT'S BODY.
WE'VE BORROWED THIS MEDICAL BOT FROM THE STATE ARCHIVES.
ONE OF THE BEST PRESERVED ARTIFACTS IN THE PROVINCE!
IF WE COULD INSTALL STANLEY'S NEUROPROCESSOR IN IT, WE JUST MIGHT BE ABLE TO ACTIVATE ITS SECONDARY PROCESSORS!

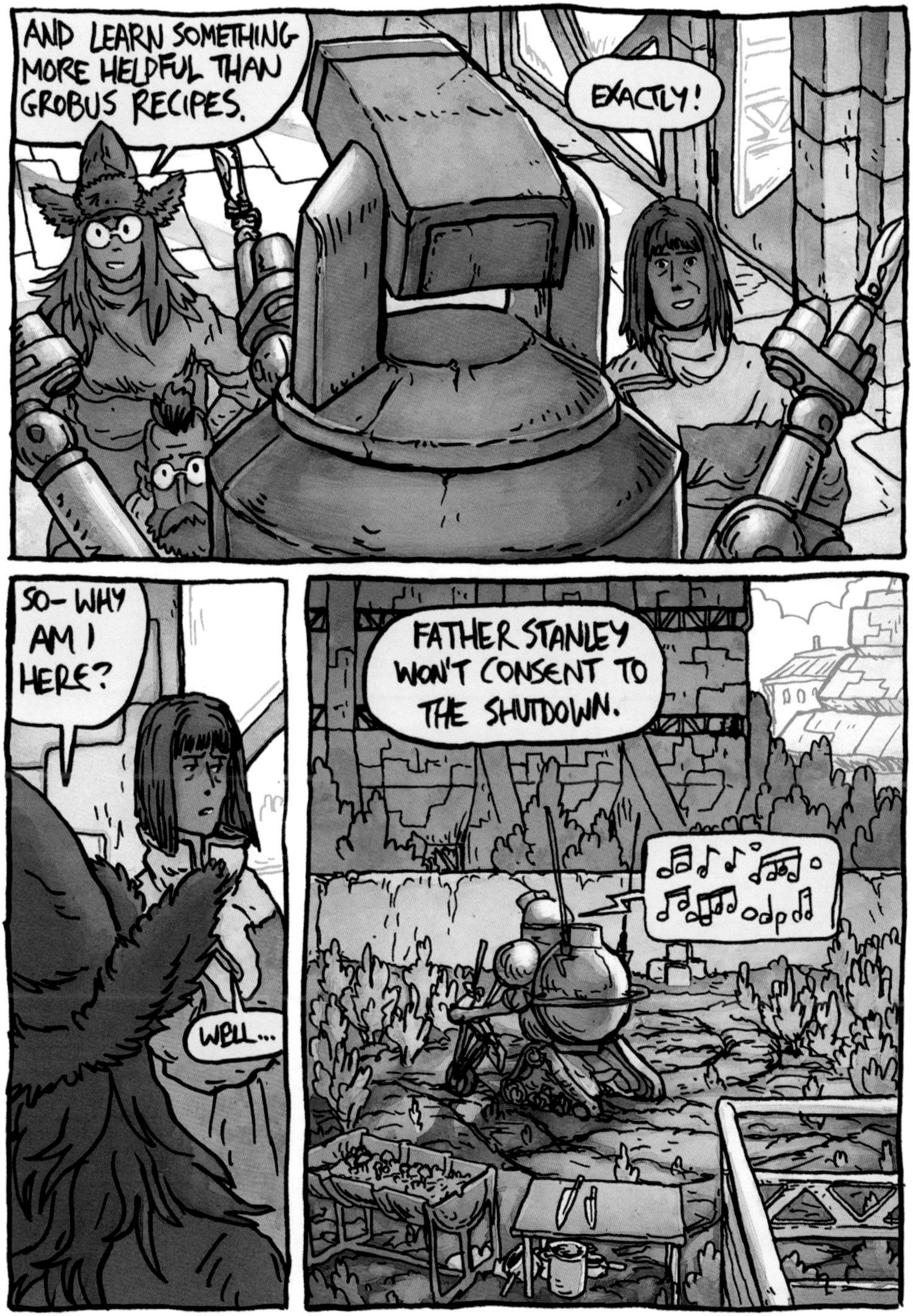
AND LEARN SOMETHING MORE HELPFUL THAN GROBUS RECIPES.
EXACTLY!
SO- WHY AM I HERE?
WELL...
FATHER STANLEY WON'T CONSENT TO THE SHUTDOWN.

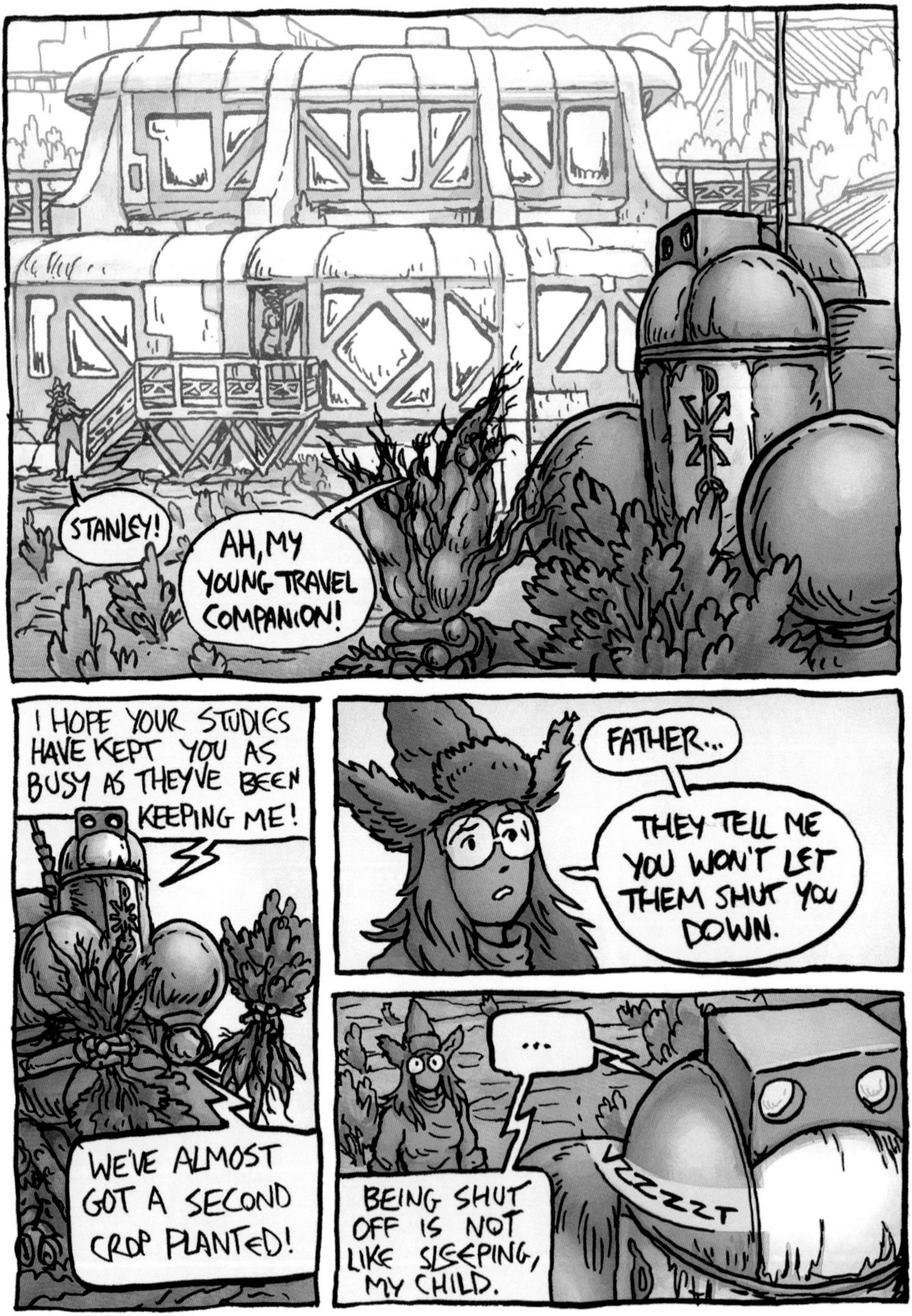
STANLEY!
AH, MY YOUNG TRAVEL COMPANION!
I HOPE YOUR STUDIES HAVE KEPT YOU AS BUSY AS THEYVE BEEN KEEPING ME!
WE'VE ALMOST GOT A SECOND CROP PLANTED!
FATHER...
THEY TELL ME YOU WON'T LET THEM SHUT YOU DOWN.
...
BEING SHUT OFF IS NOT LIKE SLEEPING, MY CHILD.
VZZZZZT

I DON'T GET THE LUXURY OF DREAMS, OR AN AFTERLIFE.

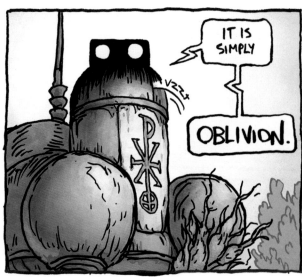

IT IS SIMPLY

OBLIVION.

BUT IT WON'T BE OBLIVION, FATHER!

YOU'LL BE AWAKE, IN A DIFFERENT BODY, AND YOU'LL BE ABLE TO HELP SO MANY MORE PEOPLE!

I'VE ALREADY MISSED OUT ON A CENTURY OF LIFE, SCRUBE.

WHAT IF THIS SCHEME DOESN'T WORK?

HMM. THAT'S A FAIR POINT.

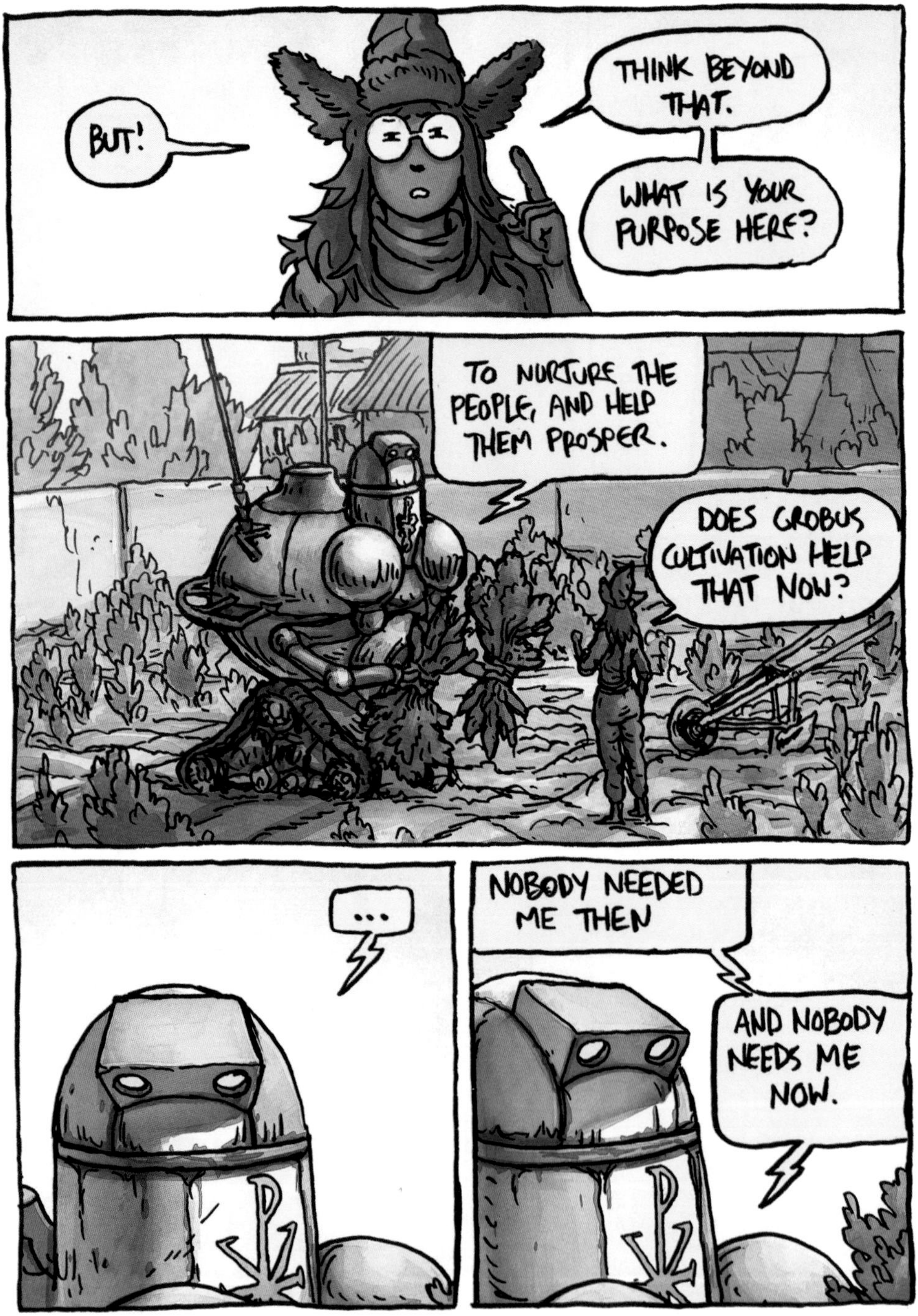
BUT!
THINK BEYOND THAT.
WHAT IS YOUR PURPOSE HERE?
TO NURTURE THE PEOPLE, AND HELP THEM PROSPER.
DOES GROBUS CULTIVATION HELP THAT NOW?
...
NOBODY NEEDED ME THEN
AND NOBODY NEEDS ME NOW.

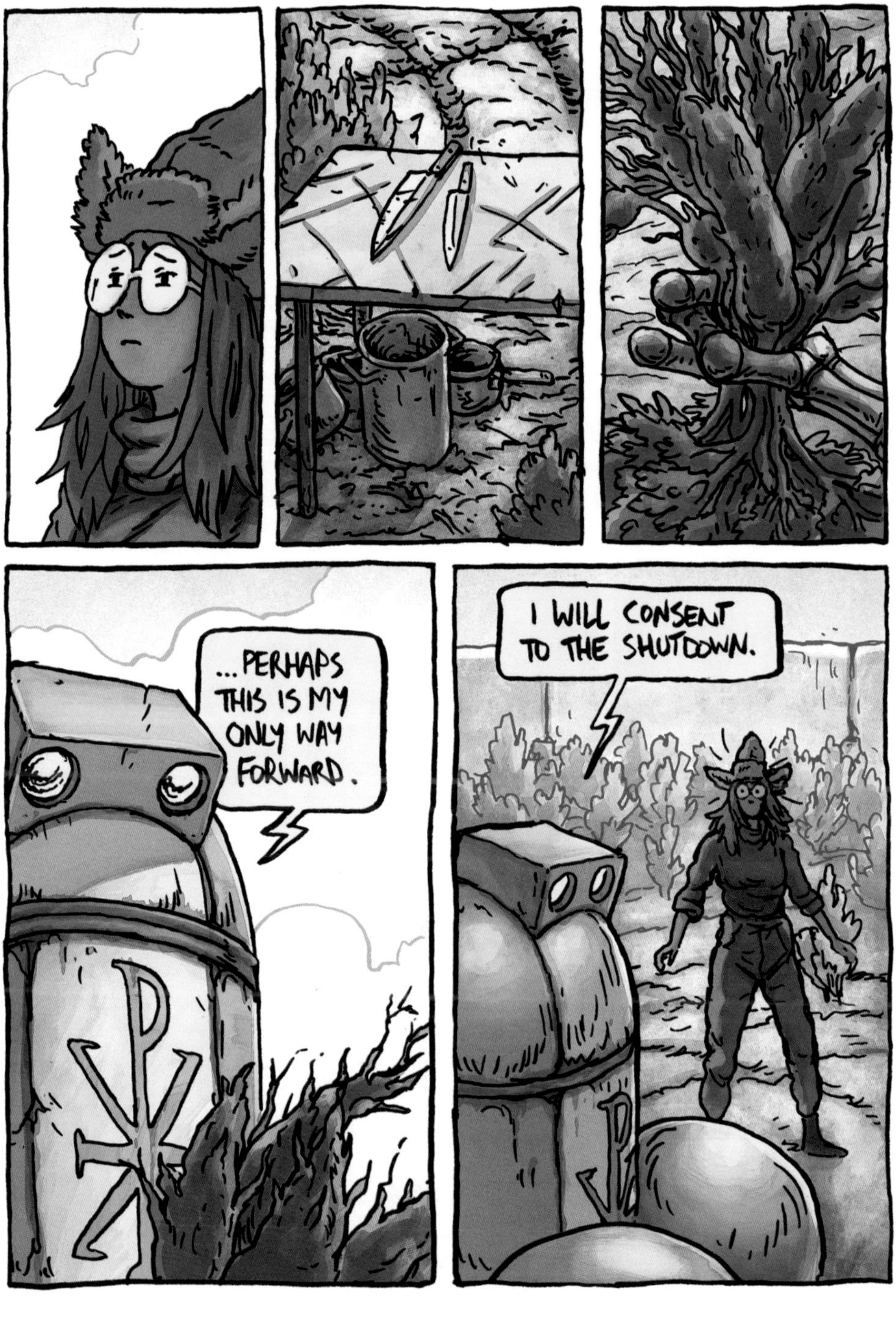
...PERHAPS THIS IS MY ONLY WAY FORWARD.
I WILL CONSENT TO THE SHUTDOWN.

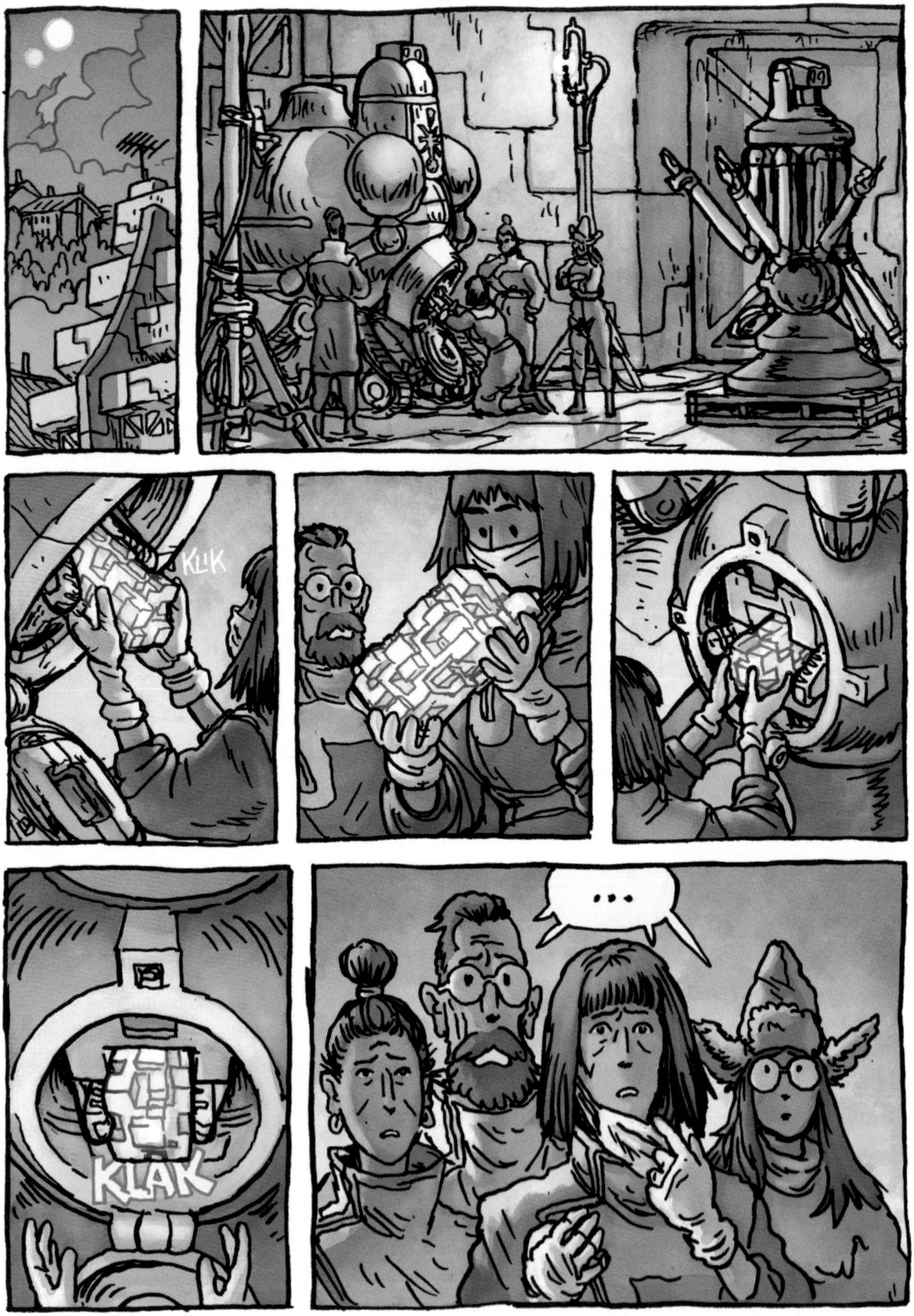
KLIK
KLAK
...

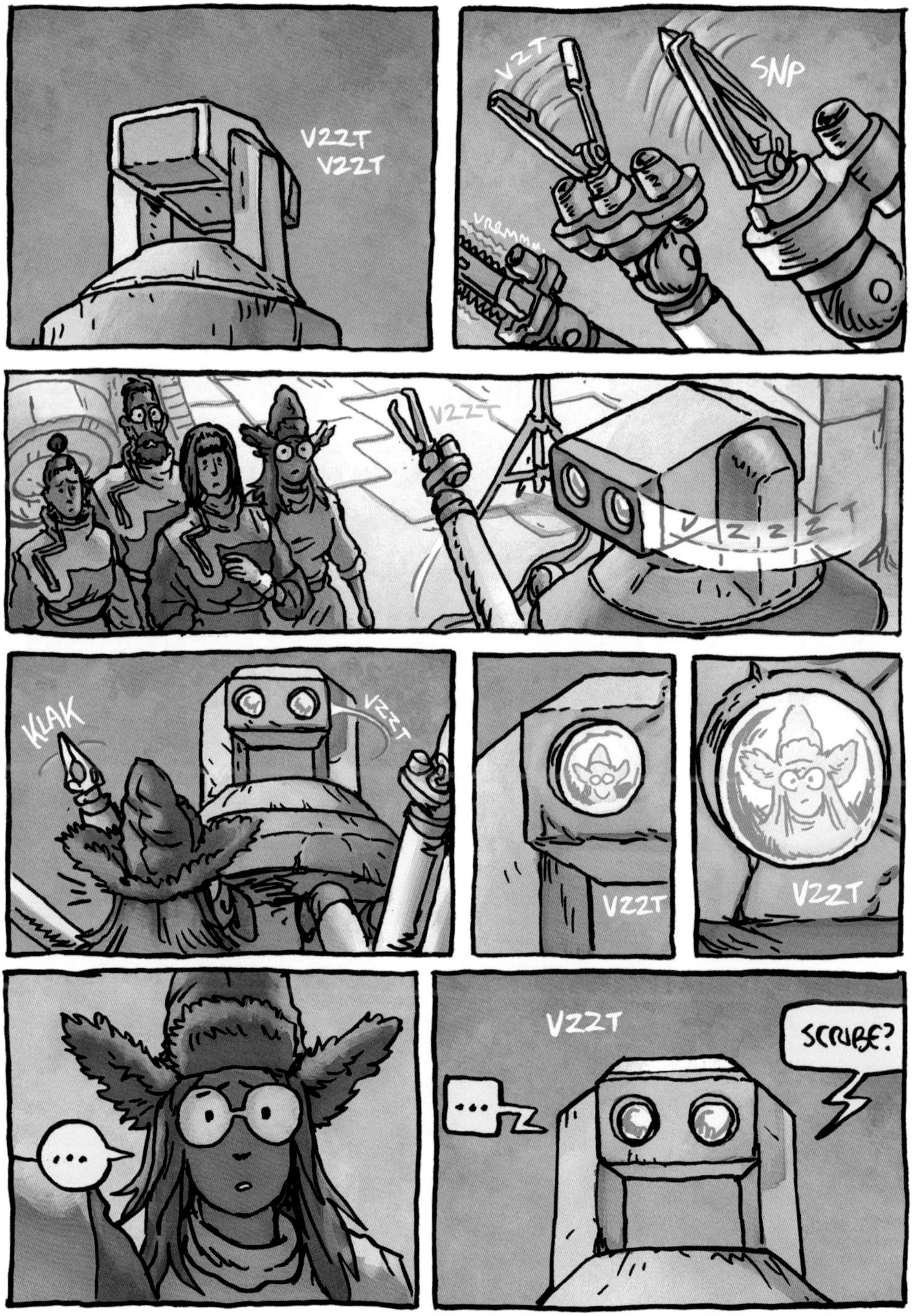
VZZT
VZZT
VZT
SNP
VRRMMM
VZZT
VZZZT
KLAK
VZZT
VZZT
VZZT
...
VZZT
...
SCRIBE?

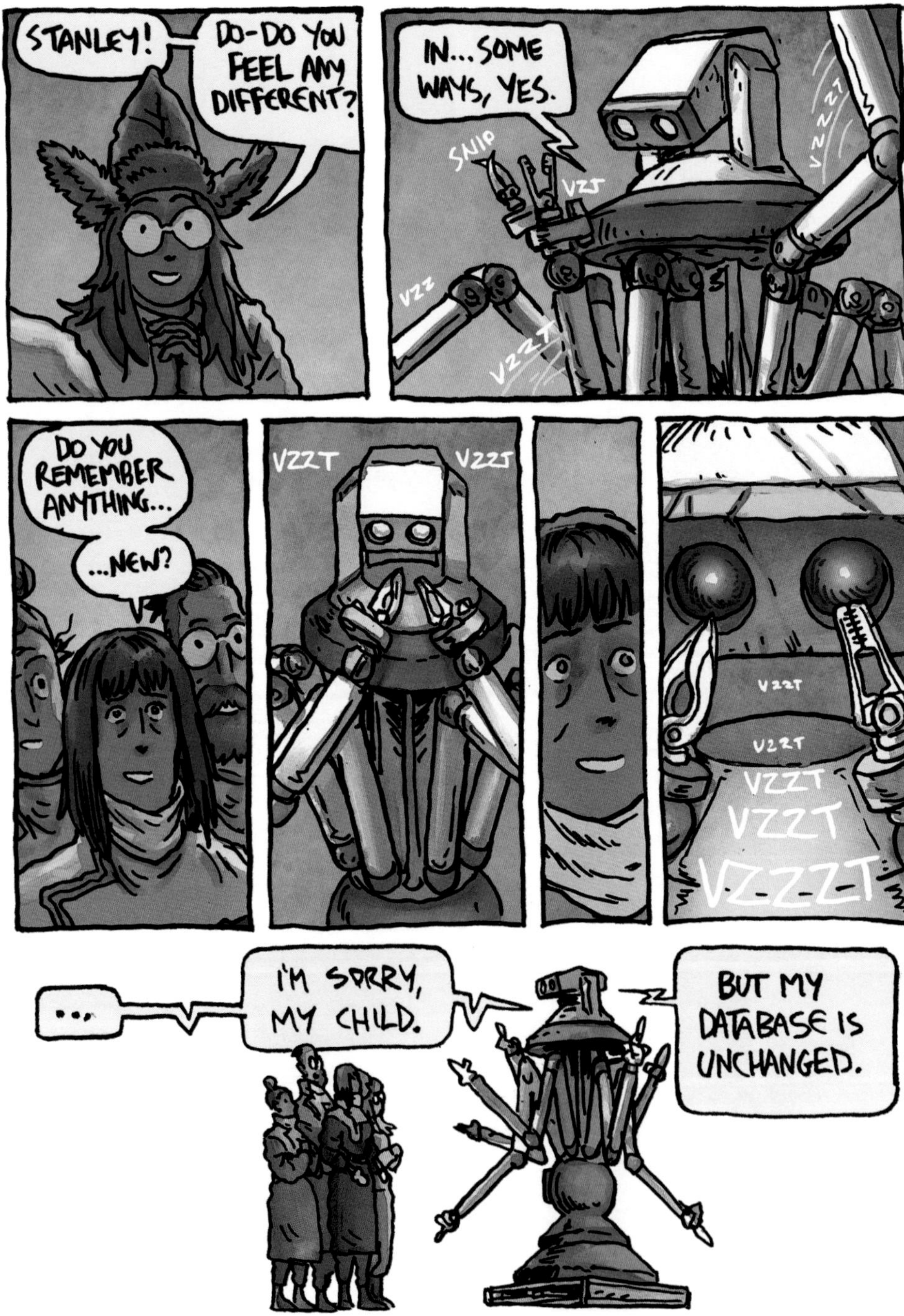
STANLEY!
DO-DO YOU FEEL ANY DIFFERENT?
IN... SOME WAYS, YES.
SNIP
VZJ
VZZZZT
VZZ
VZZT
DO YOU REMEMBER ANYTHING...
...NEW?
VZZT
VZZJ
VZZT
VZZT
VZZT
VZZT
VZZZT
...
I'M SORRY, MY CHILD.
BUT MY DATABASE IS UNCHANGED.

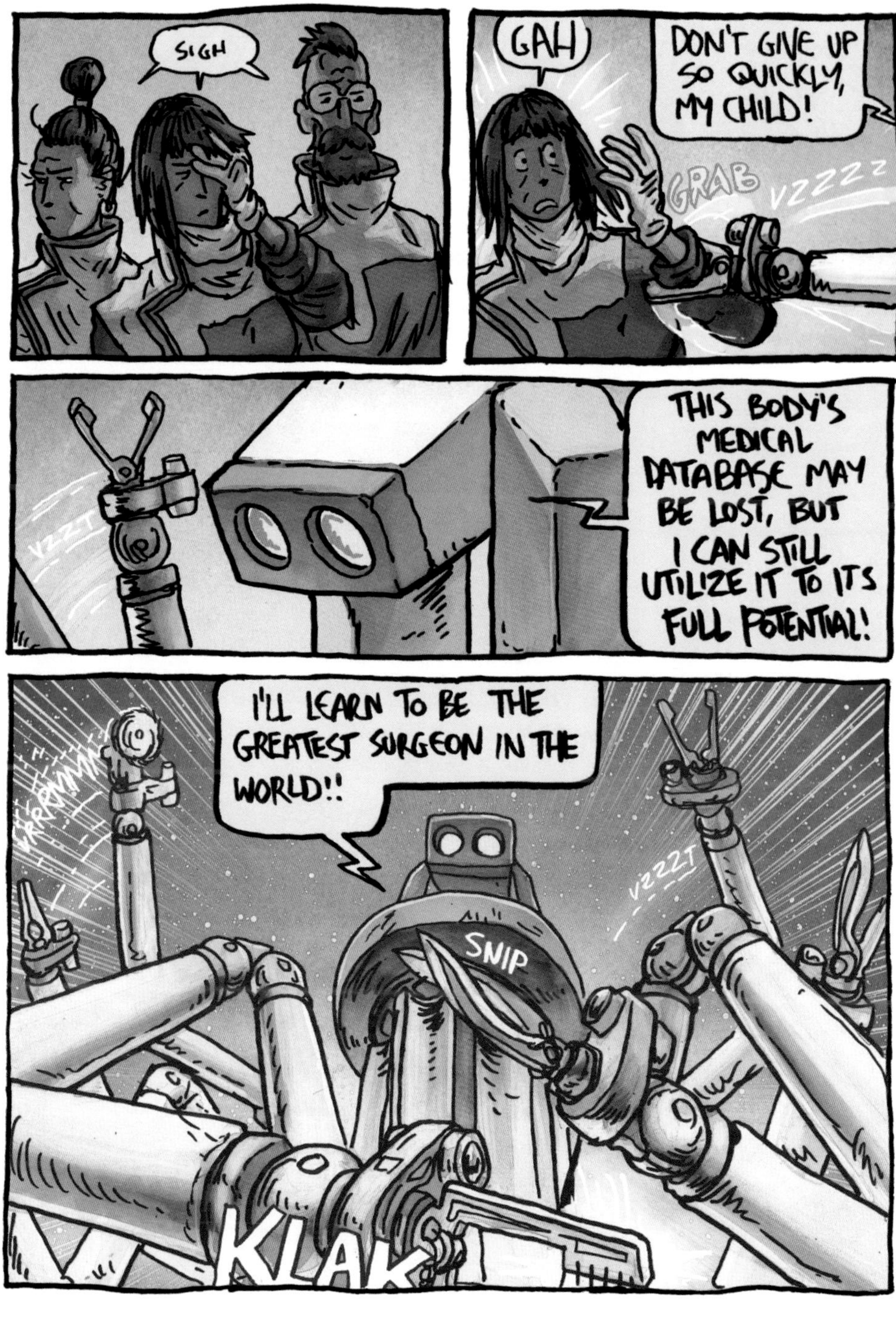
SIGH
GAH
DON'T GIVE UP SO QUICKLY, MY CHILD!
GRAB
VZZZZ
VZZZT
THIS BODY'S MEDICAL DATABASE MAY BE LOST, BUT I CAN STILL UTILIZE IT TO ITS FULL POTENTIAL!
I'LL LEARN TO BE THE GREATEST SURGEON IN THE WORLD!!
VRRRMMM
VZZZT
SNIP
KLAK

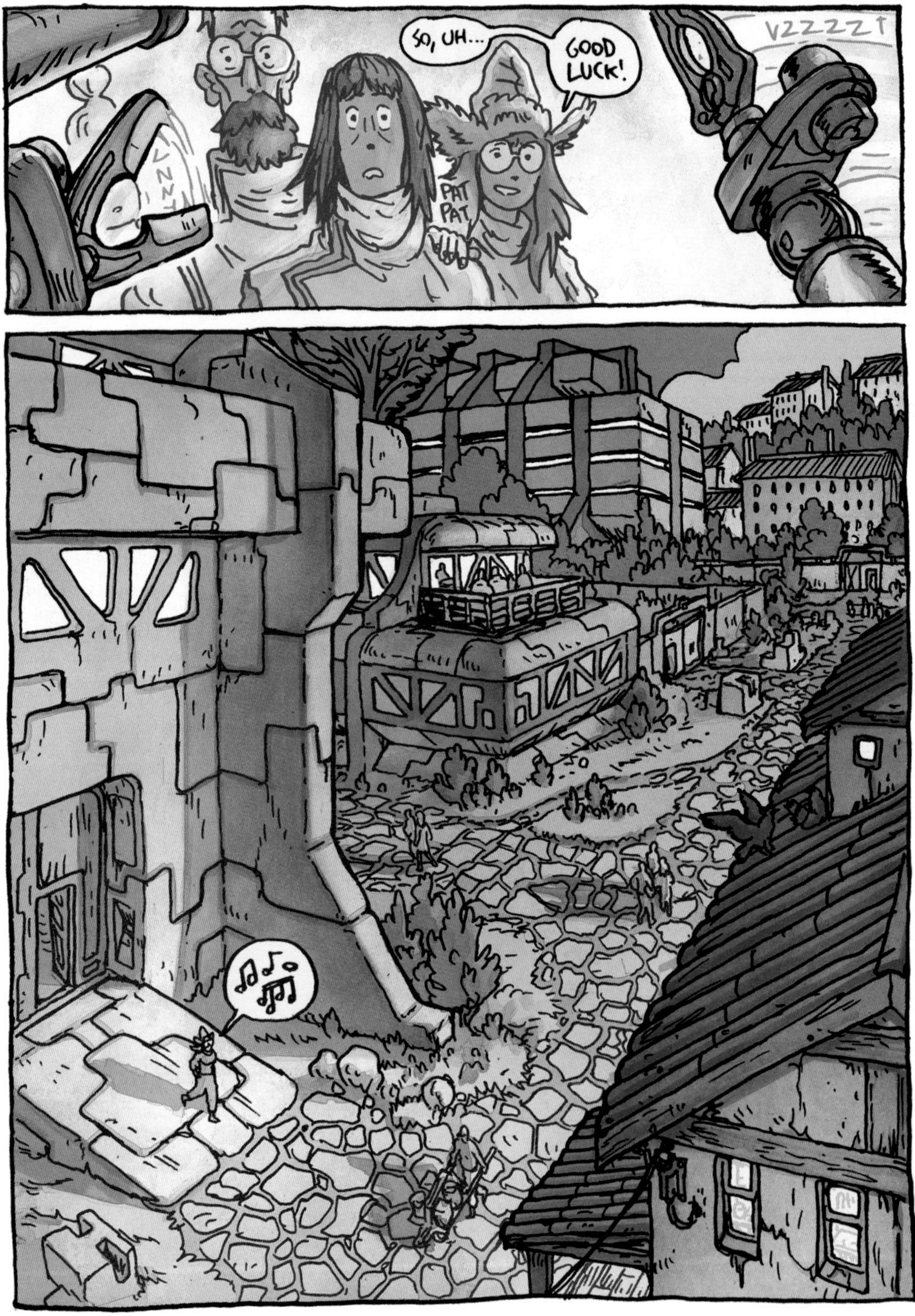
SO, UH...
GOOD LUCK!
PAT PAT
VZZZZT

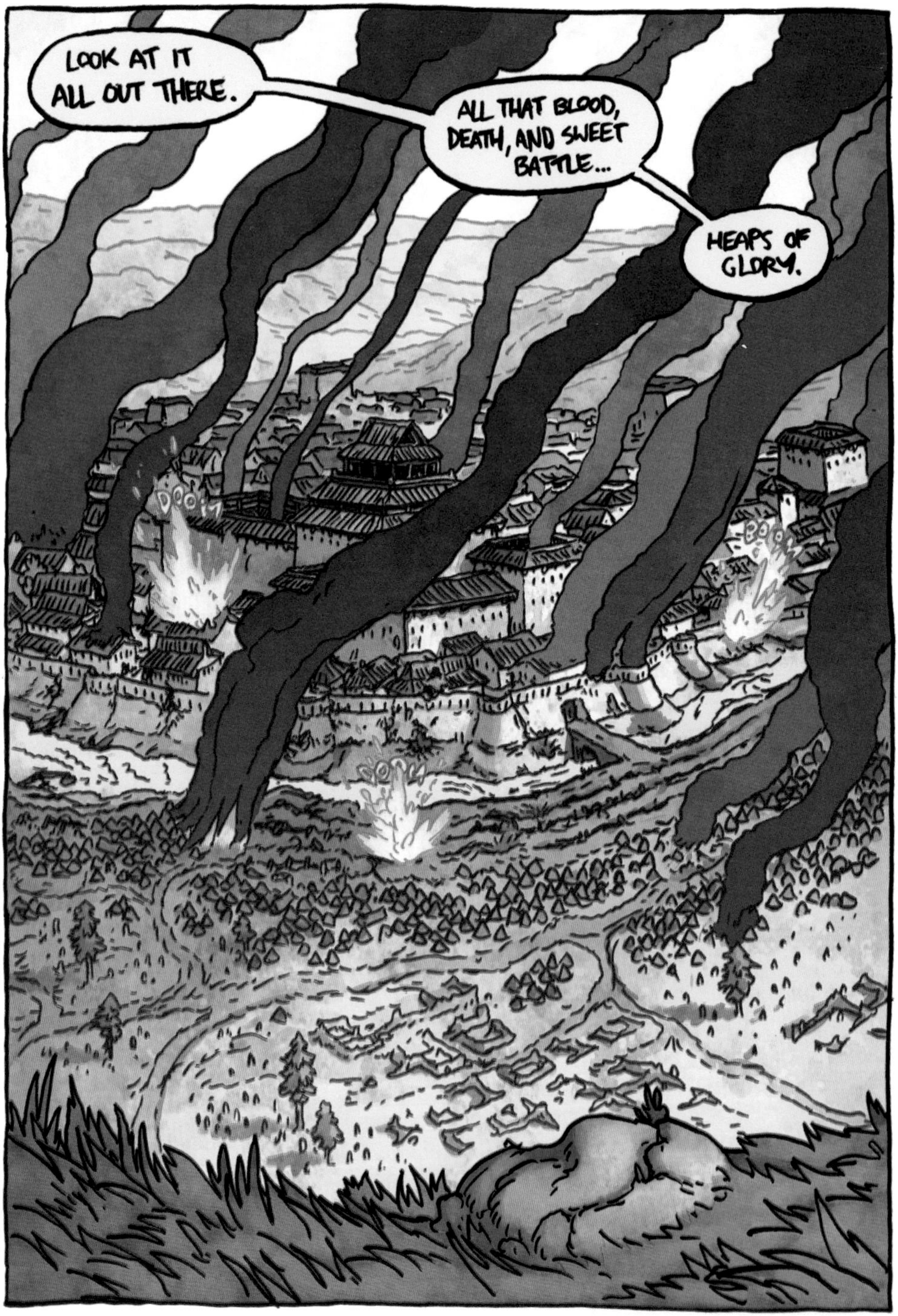
LOOK AT IT ALL OUT THERE.
ALL THAT BLOOD, DEATH, AND SWEET BATTLE...
HEAPS OF GLORY.

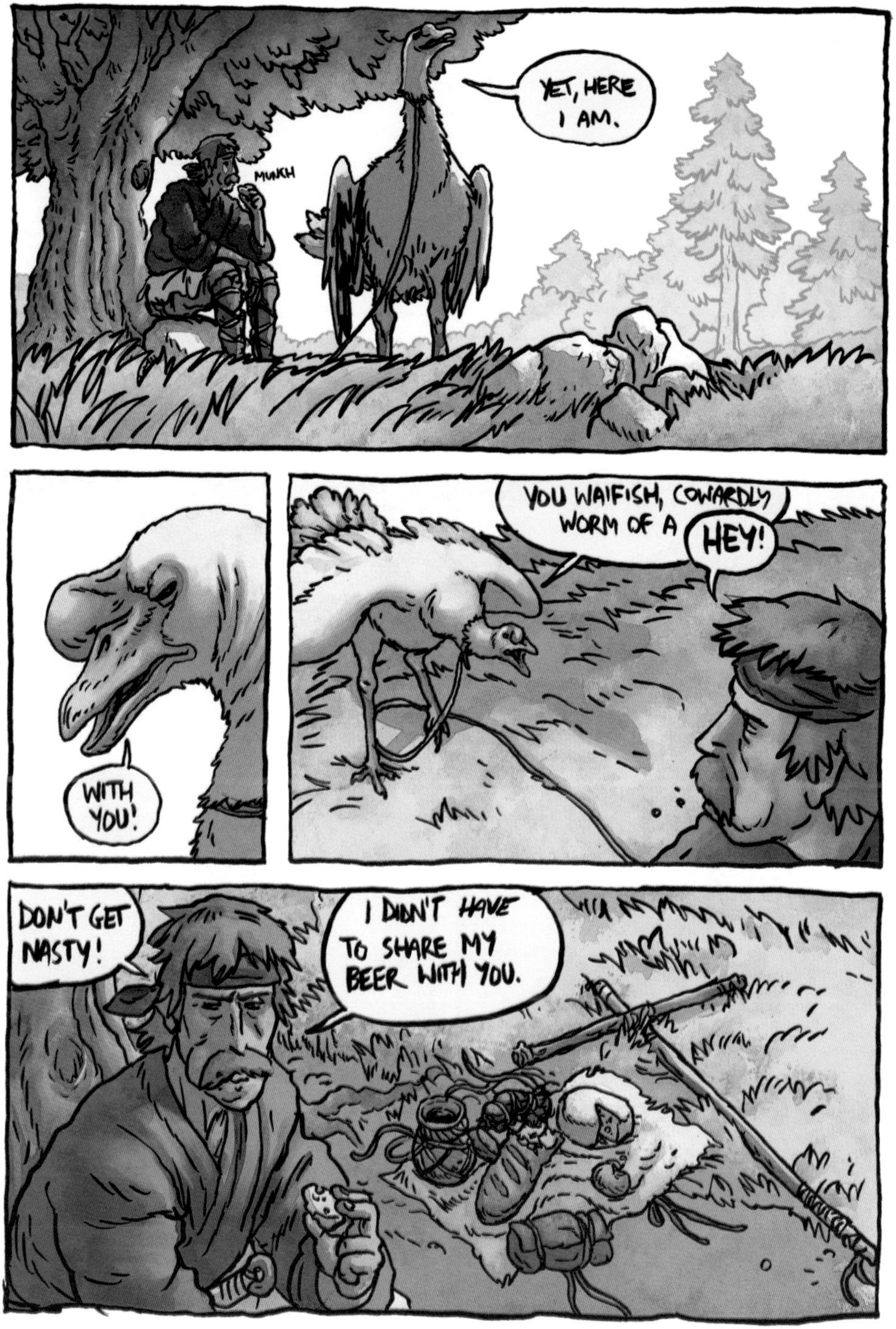
YET, HERE I AM.
MUNCH
WITH YOU!
YOU WAIFISH, COWARDLY WORM OF A
HEY!
DON'T GET NASTY!
I DIDN'T HAVE TO SHARE MY BEER WITH YOU.

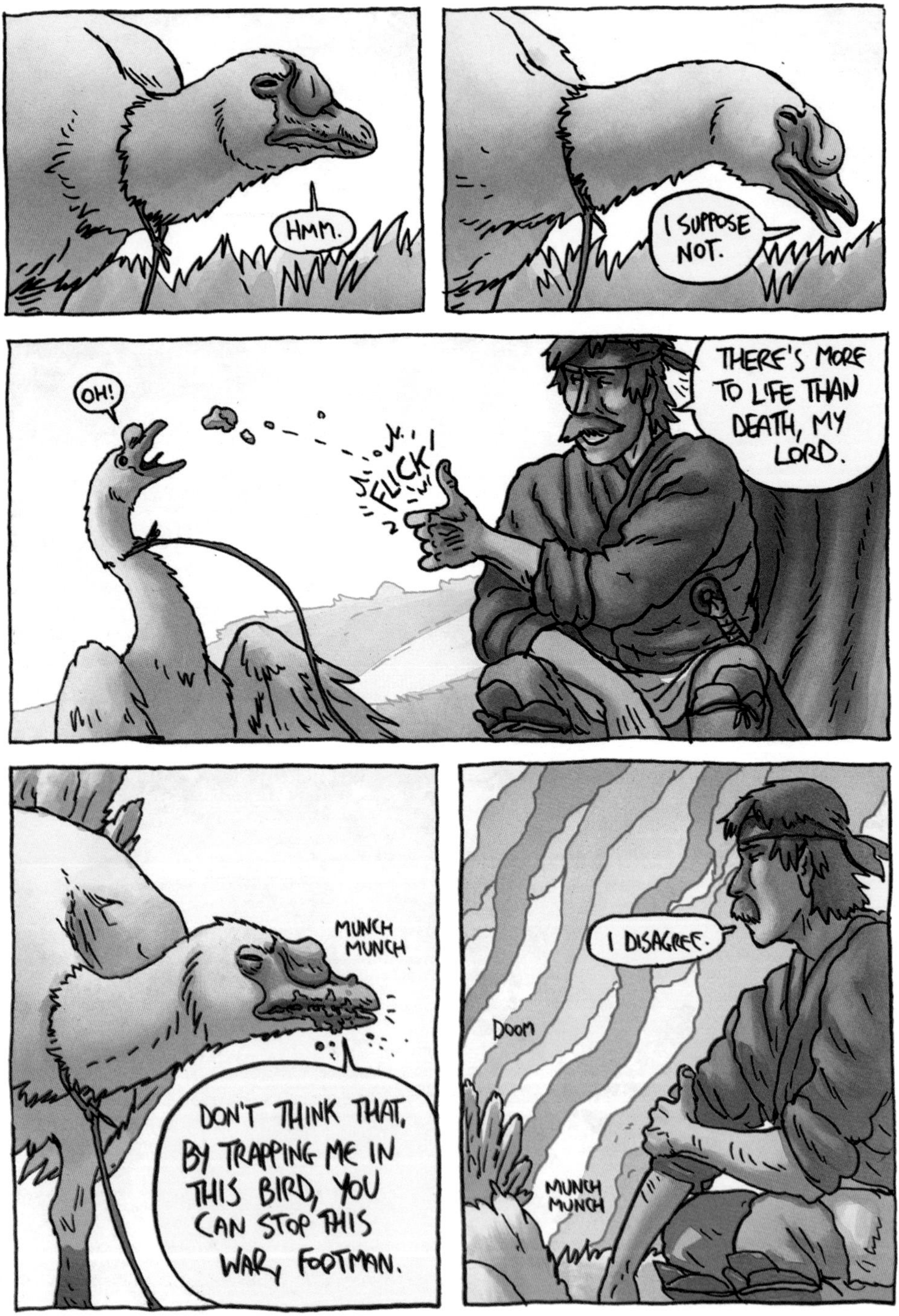
HMM.
I SUPPOSE NOT.
OH!
FLICK
THERE'S MORE TO LIFE THAN DEATH, MY LORD.
MUNCH MUNCH
DON'T THINK THAT, BY TRAPPING ME IN THIS BIRD, YOU CAN STOP THIS WAR, FOOTMAN.
I DISAGREE.
DOOM
MUNCH MUNCH

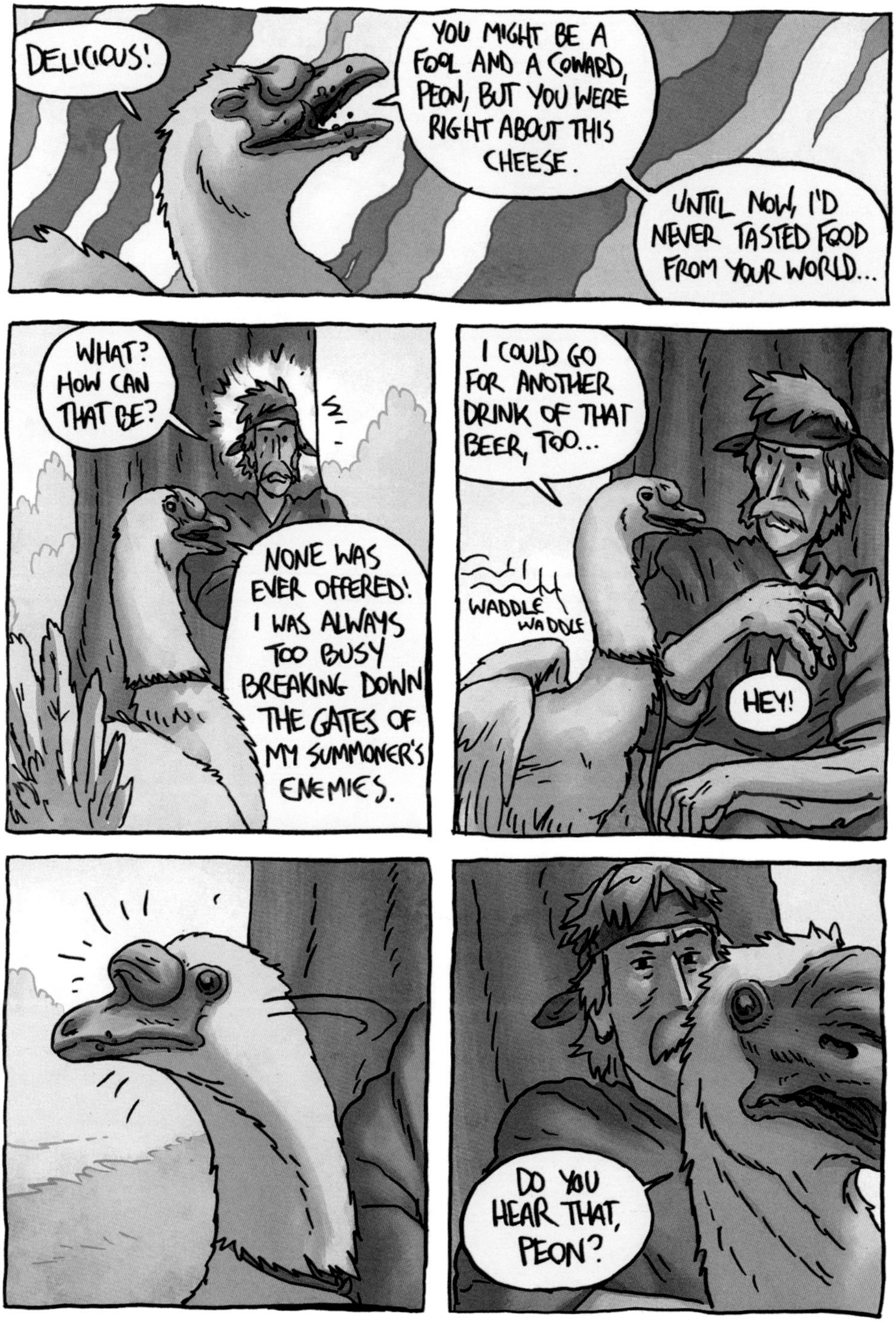
DELICIOUS!
YOU MIGHT BE A FOOL AND A COWARD, PEON, BUT YOU WERE RIGHT ABOUT THIS CHEESE.
UNTIL NOW, I'D NEVER TASTED FOOD FROM YOUR WORLD...
WHAT? HOW CAN THAT BE?
NONE WAS EVER OFFERED! I WAS ALWAYS TOO BUSY BREAKING DOWN THE GATES OF MY SUMMONER'S ENEMIES.
I COULD GO FOR ANOTHER DRINK OF THAT BEER, TOO...
WADDLE WADDLE
HEY!
DO YOU HEAR THAT, PEON?

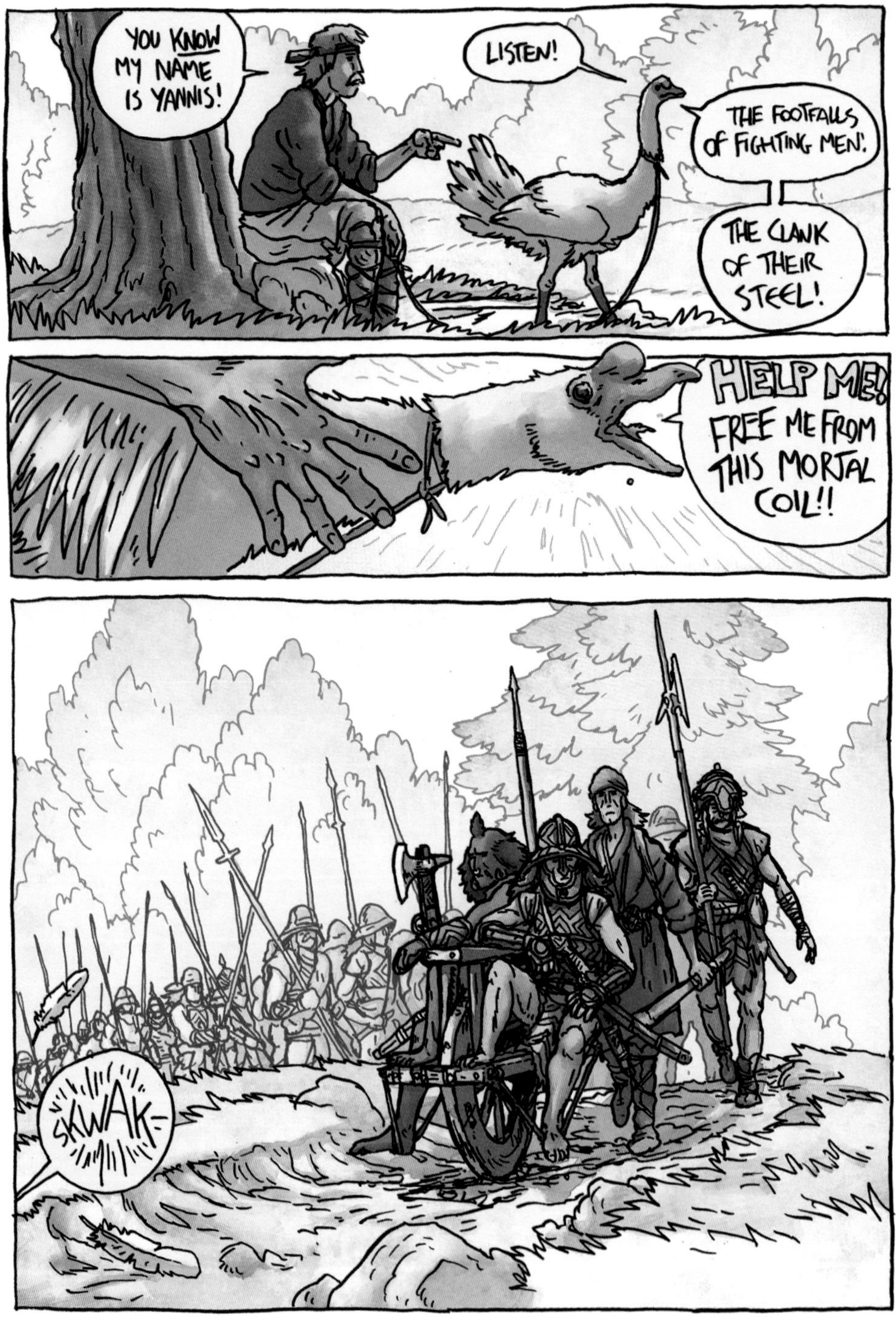
YOU KNOW MY NAME IS YANNIS!
LISTEN!
THE FOOTFALLS OF FIGHTING MEN!
THE CLANK OF THEIR STEEL!
HELP ME! FREE ME FROM THIS MORTAL COIL!!
SKWAK

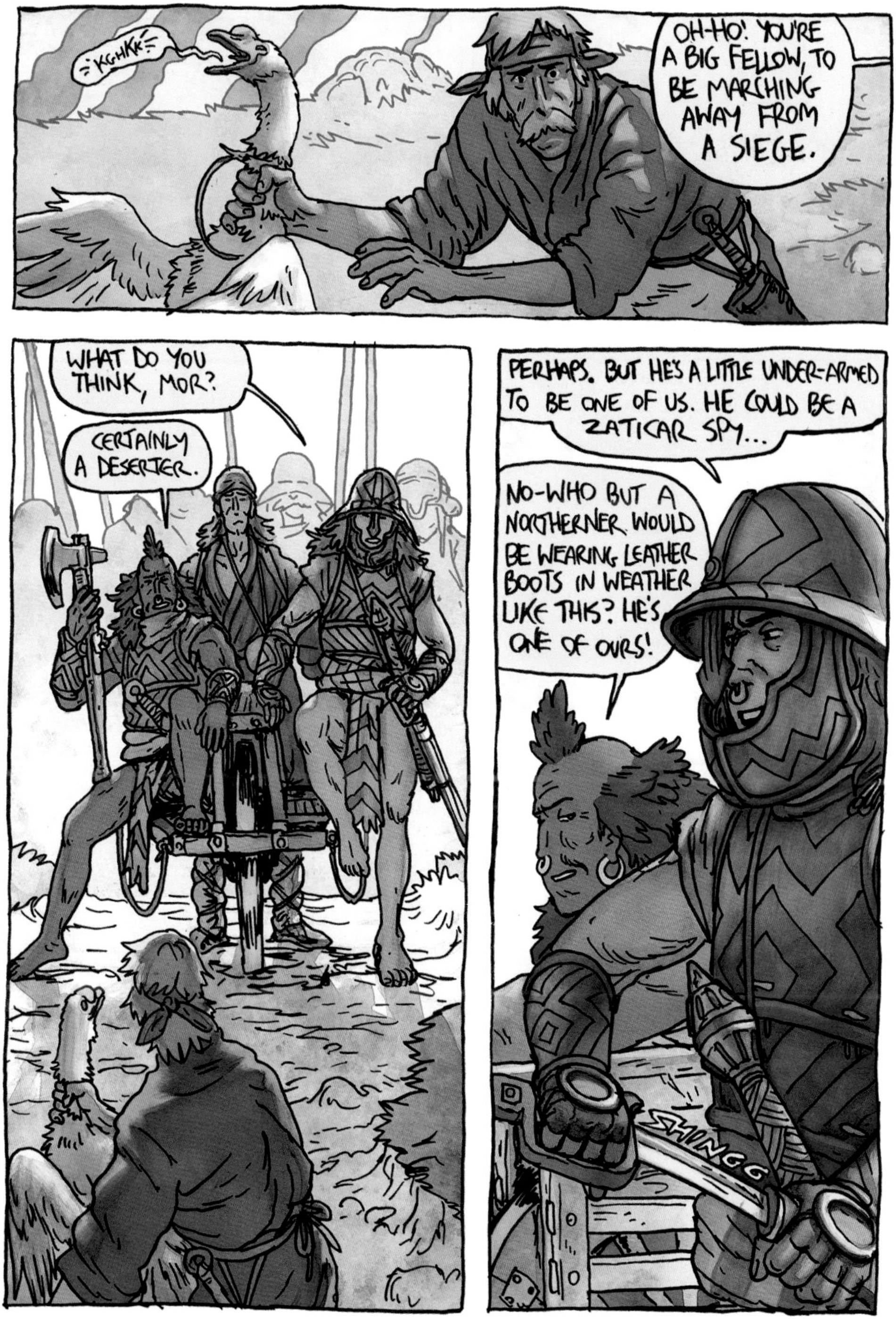
KGHKK
OH-HO! YOU'RE A BIG FELLOW, TO BE MARCHING AWAY FROM A SIEGE.
WHAT DO YOU THINK, MOR?
CERTAINLY A DESERTER.
PERHAPS. BUT HE'S A LITTLE UNDER-ARMED TO BE ONE OF US. HE COULD BE A ZATICAR SPY...
NO-WHO BUT A NORTHERNER WOULD BE WEARING LEATHER BOOTS IN WEATHER LIKE THIS? HE'S ONE OF OURS!
SHNGG

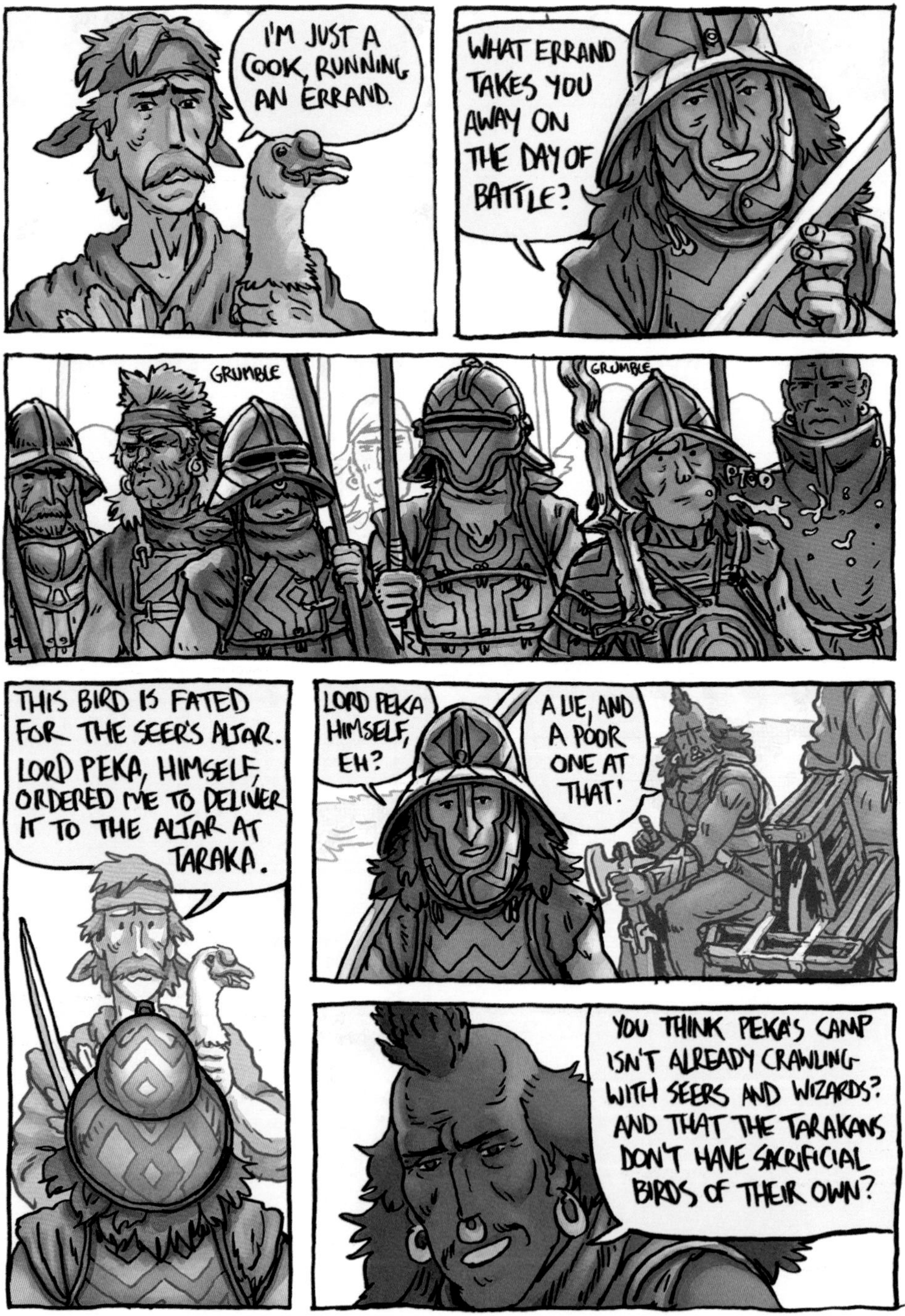
I'M JUST A COOK, RUNNING AN ERRAND.
WHAT ERRAND TAKES YOU AWAY ON THE DAY OF BATTLE?
GRUMBLE
GRUMBLE
PTOO
THIS BIRD IS FATED FOR THE SEER'S ALTAR. LORD PEKA, HIMSELF, ORDERED ME TO DELIVER IT TO THE ALTAR AT TARAKA.
LORD PEKA HIMSELF, EH?
A LIE, AND A POOR ONE AT THAT!
YOU THINK PEKA'S CAMP ISN'T ALREADY CRAWLING WITH SEERS AND WIZARDS? AND THAT THE TARAKANS DON'T HAVE SACRIFICIAL BIRDS OF THEIR OWN?

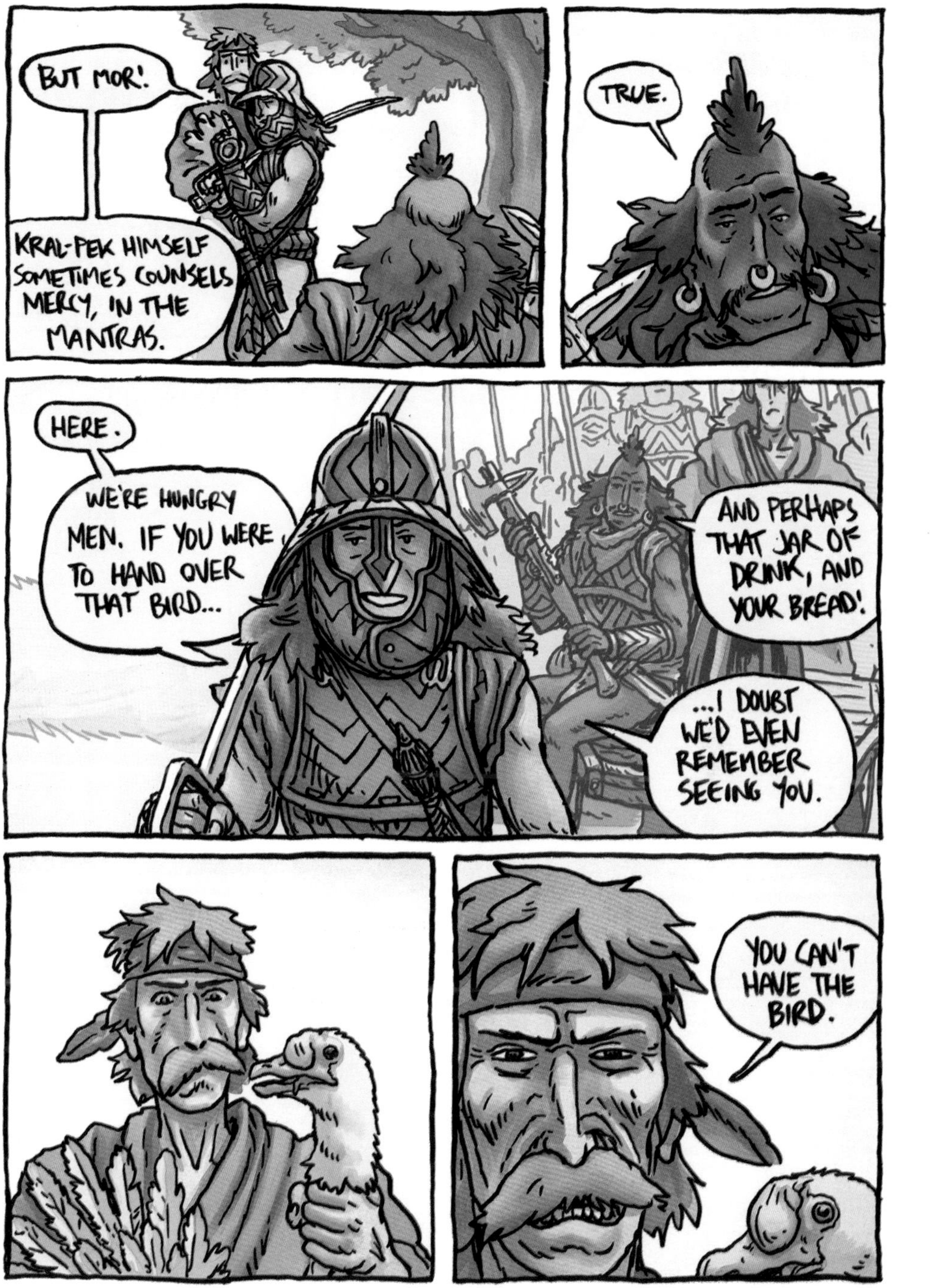
BUT MOR!
KRAL-PEK HIMSELF SOMETIMES COUNSELS MERCY, IN THE MANTRAS.
TRUE.
HERE.
WE'RE HUNGRY MEN. IF YOU WERE TO HAND OVER THAT BIRD...
AND PERHAPS THAT JAR OF DRINK, AND YOUR BREAD!
...I DOUBT WE'D EVEN REMEMBER SEEING YOU.
YOU CAN'T HAVE THE BIRD.

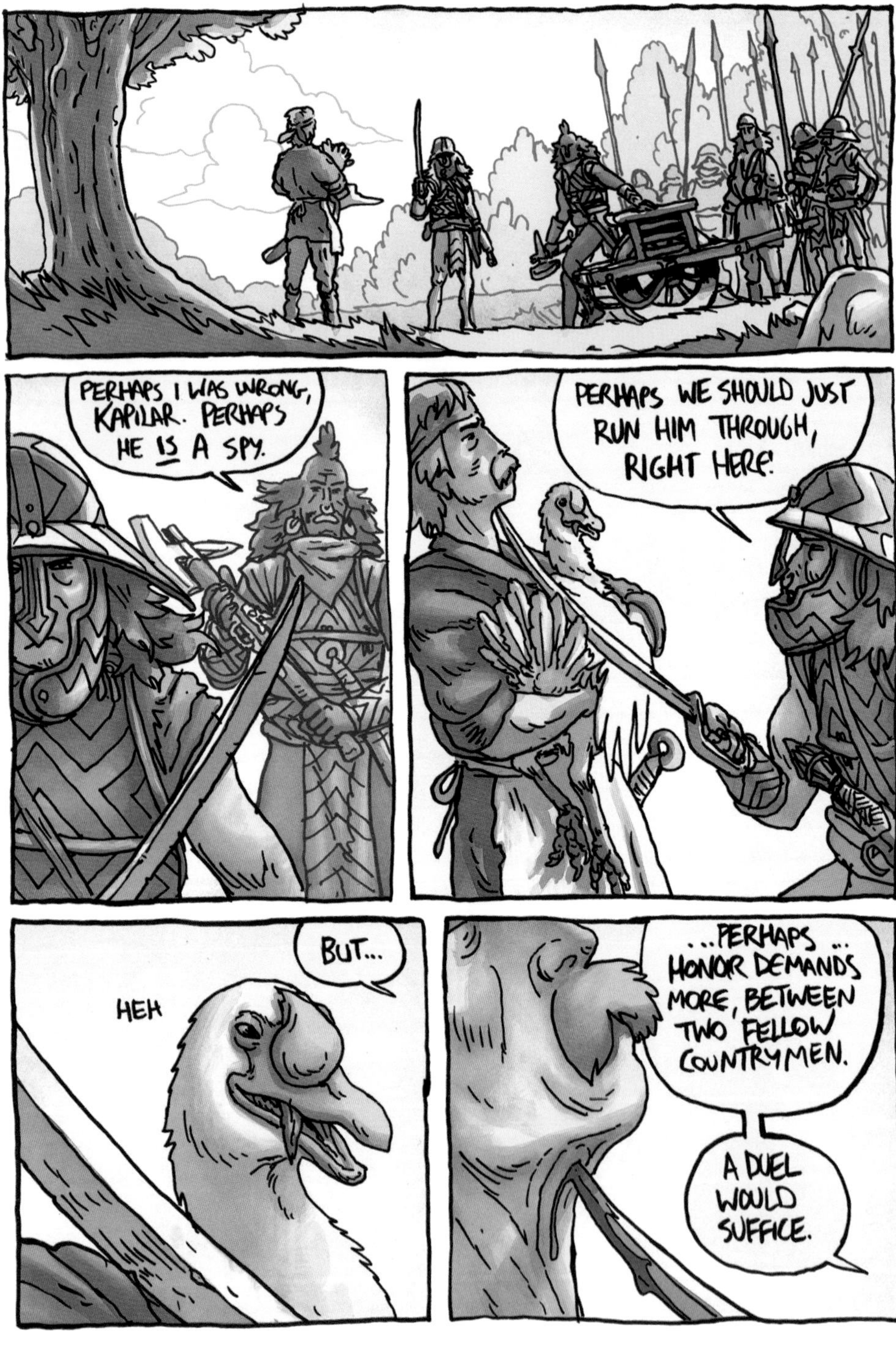
PERHAPS I WAS WRONG, KAPILAR. PERHAPS HE IS A SPY.
PERHAPS WE SHOULD JUST RUN HIM THROUGH, RIGHT HERE!
BUT...
HEH
...PERHAPS... HONOR DEMANDS MORE, BETWEEN TWO FELLOW COUNTRYMEN.
A DUEL WOULD SUFFICE.

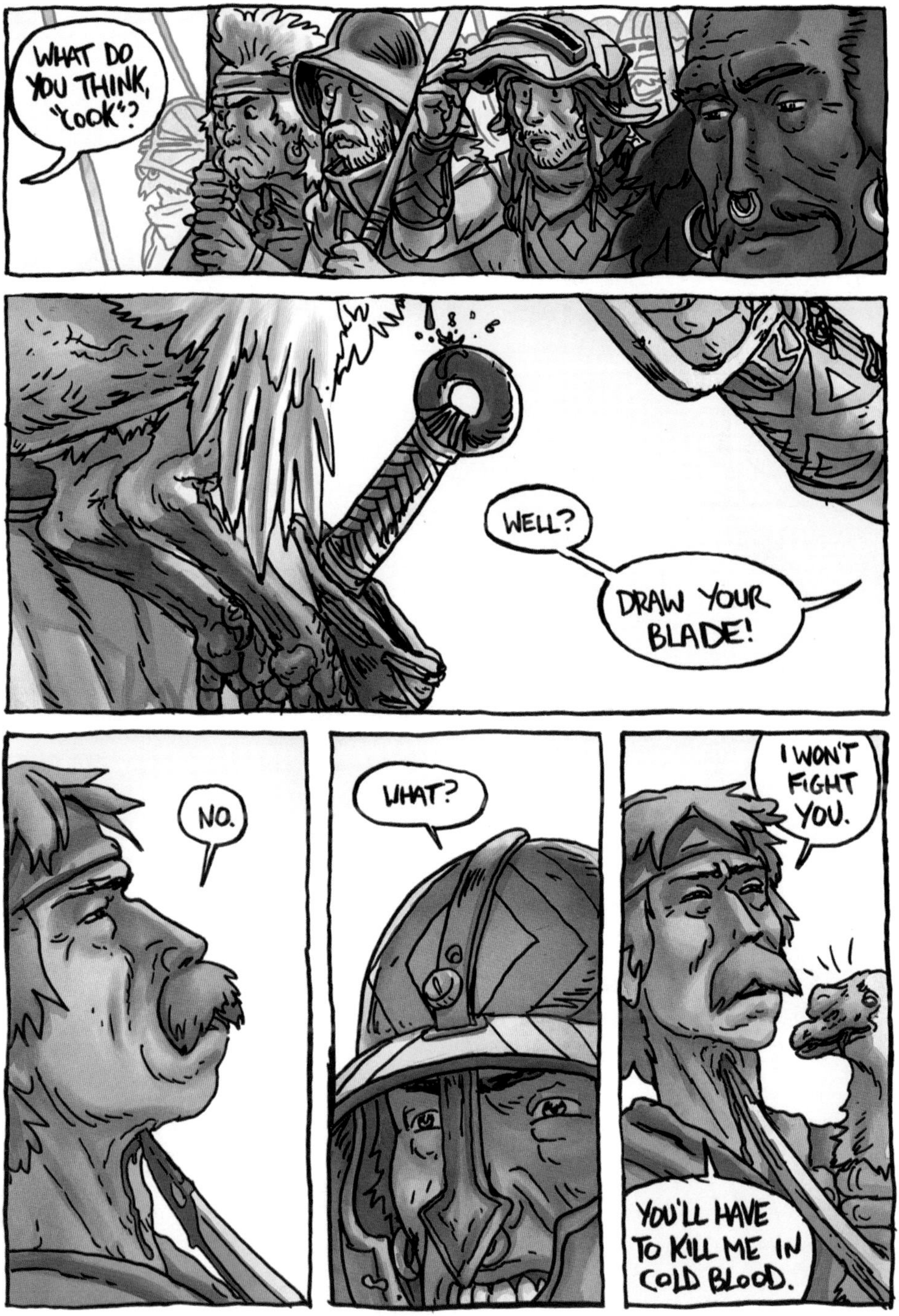
WHAT DO YOU THINK, "COOK"?
WELL?
DRAW YOUR BLADE!
NO.
WHAT?
I WON'T FIGHT YOU.
YOU'LL HAVE TO KILL ME IN COLD BLOOD.

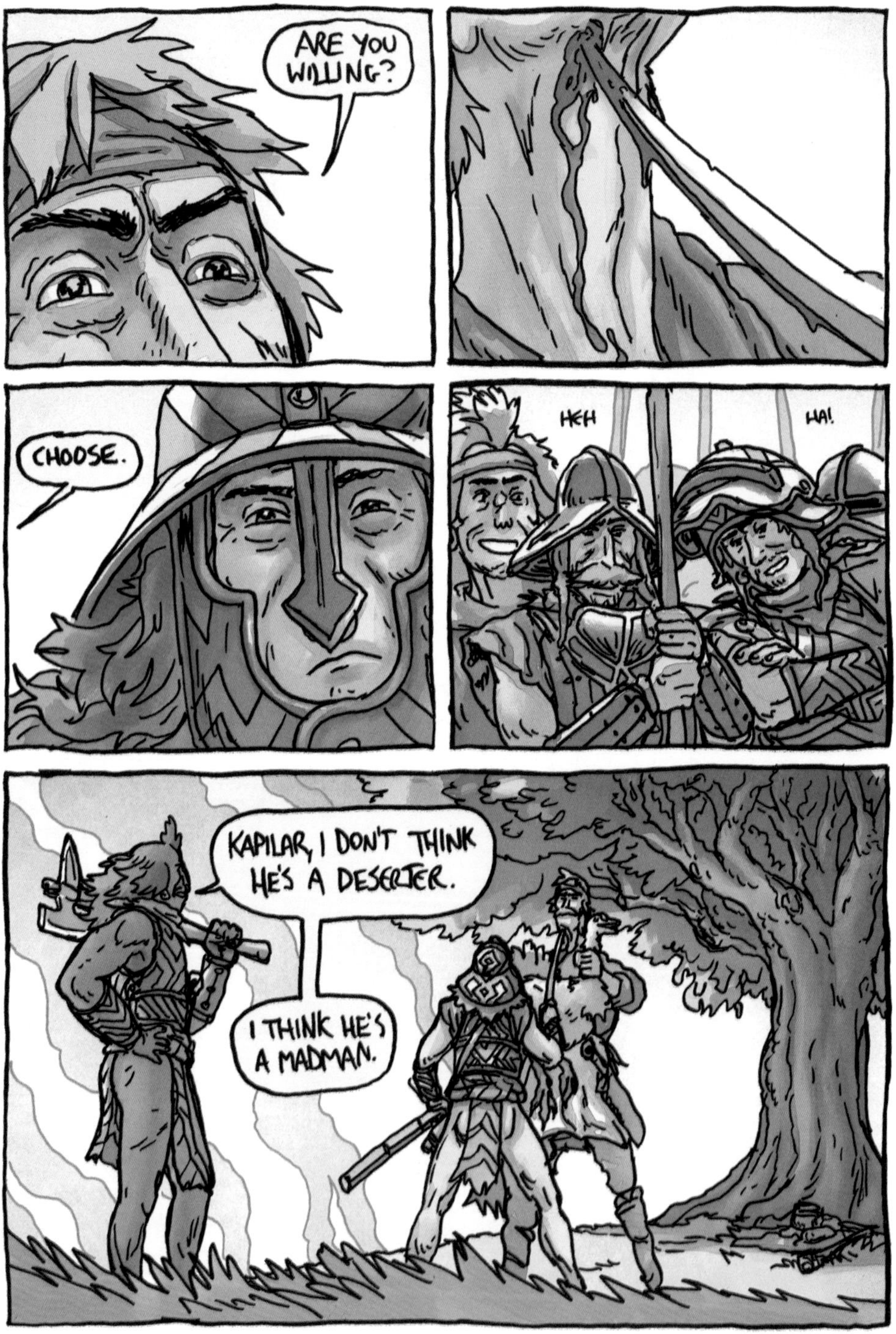
ARE YOU WILLING?
CHOOSE.
HEH
HA!
KAPILAR, I DON'T THINK HE'S A DESERTER.
I THINK HE'S A MADMAN.

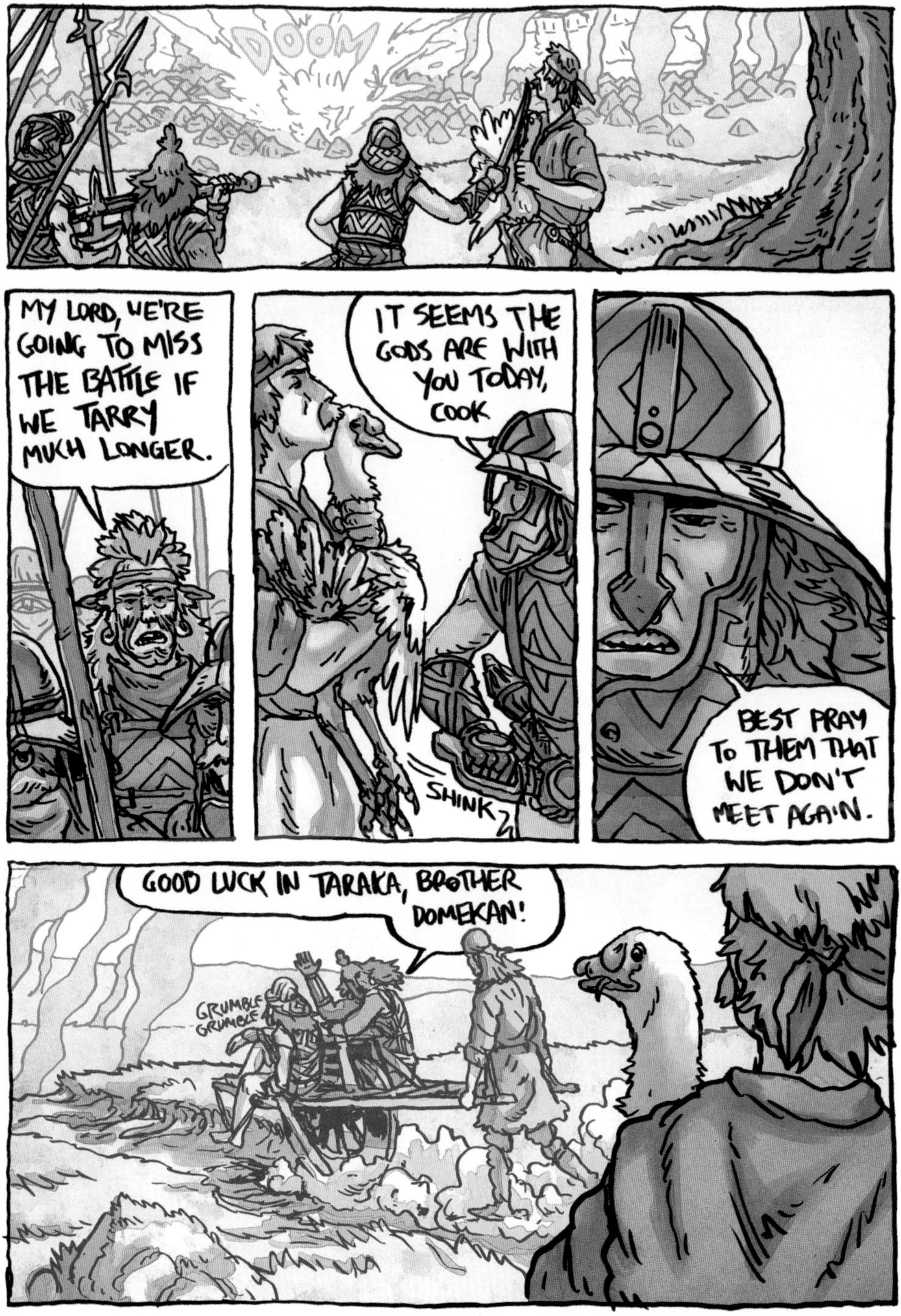
DOOM
MY LORD, WE'RE GOING TO MISS THE BATTLE IF WE TARRY MUCH LONGER.
IT SEEMS THE GODS ARE WITH YOU TODAY, COOK
SHINK
BEST PRAY TO THEM THAT WE DON'T MEET AGAIN.
GOOD LUCK IN TARAKA, BROTHER DOMEKAN!
GRUMBLE GRUMBLE

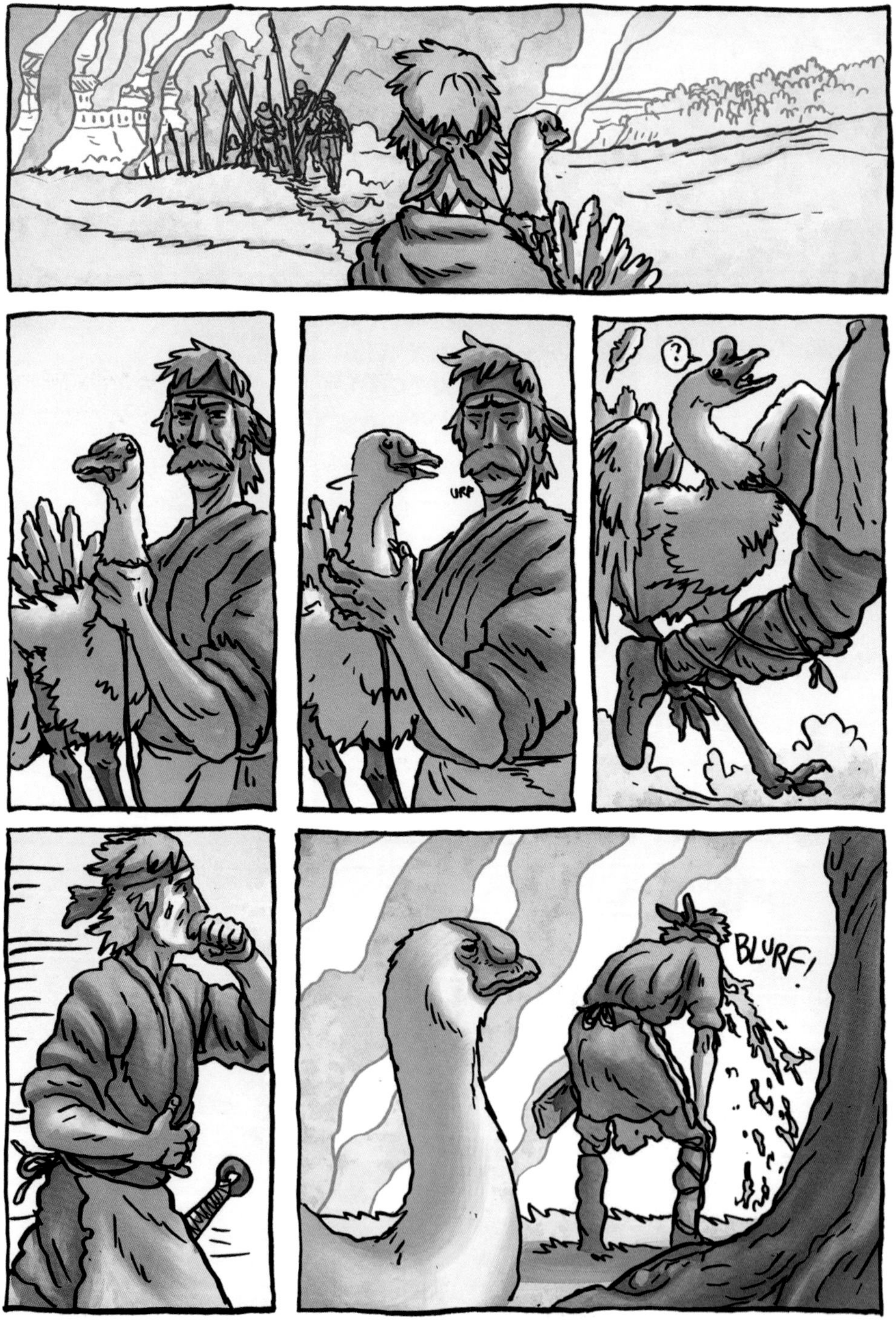
URP
?
BLURF!

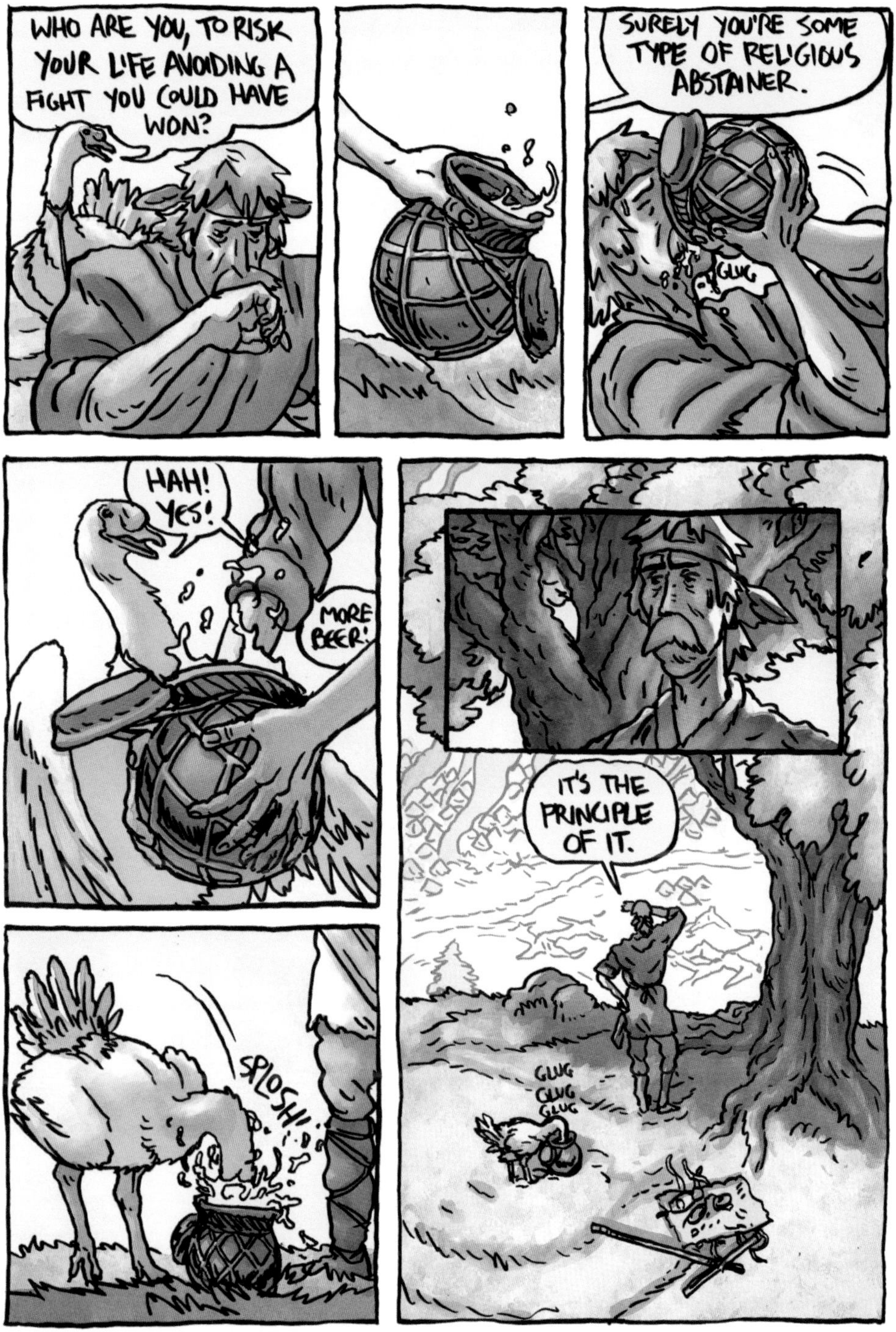
WHO ARE YOU, TO RISK YOUR LIFE AVOIDING A FIGHT YOU COULD HAVE WON?
SURELY YOU'RE SOME TYPE OF RELIGIOUS ABSTAINER.
GLUG
HAH! YES!
MORE BEER!
SPLOSH!
IT'S THE PRINCIPLE OF IT.
GLUG
GLUG
GLUG

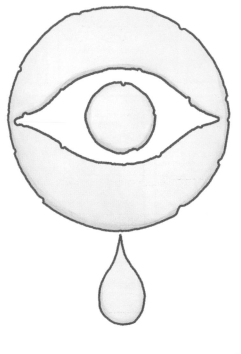

THE HEAD OF ANTON GABRIEL

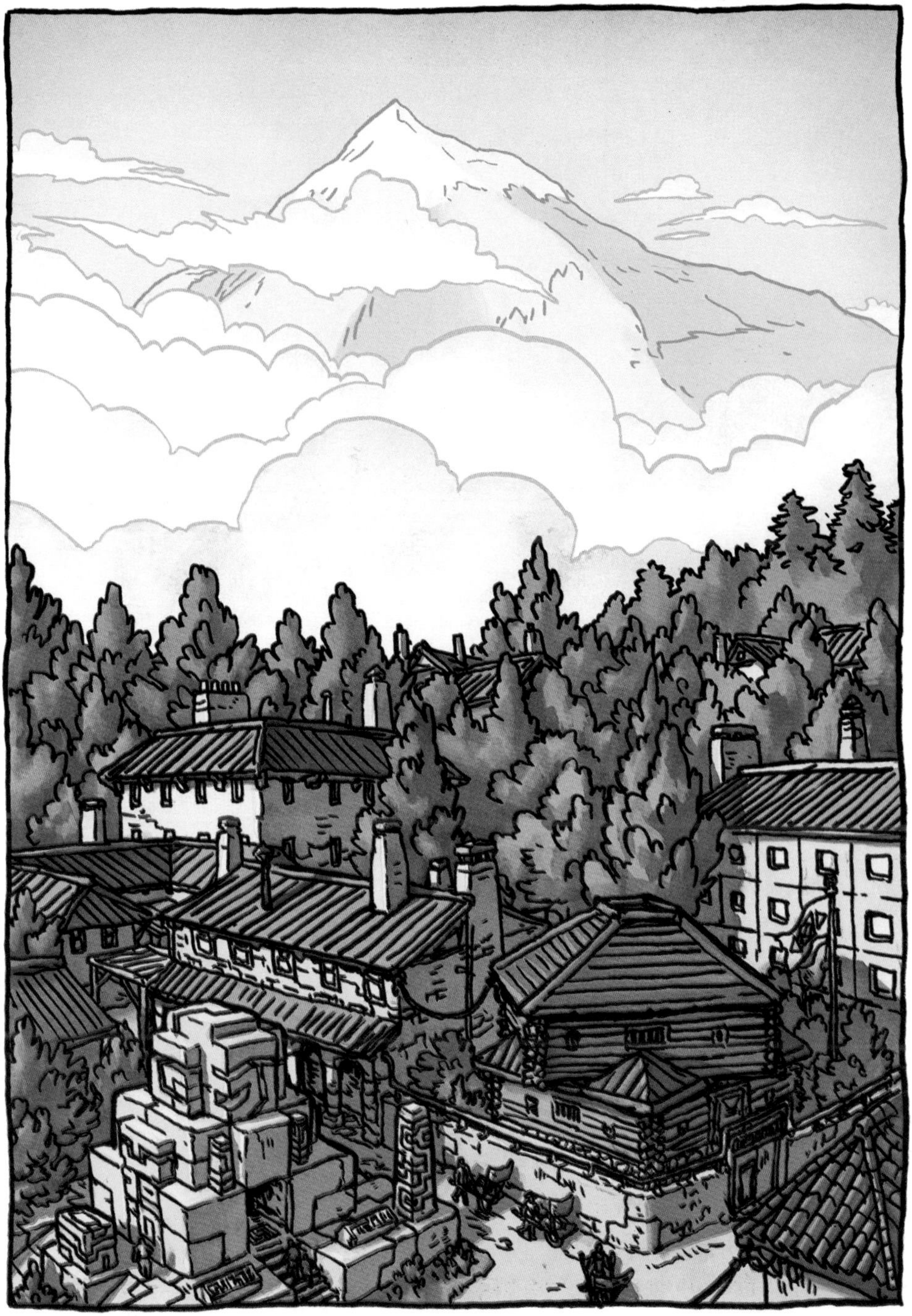

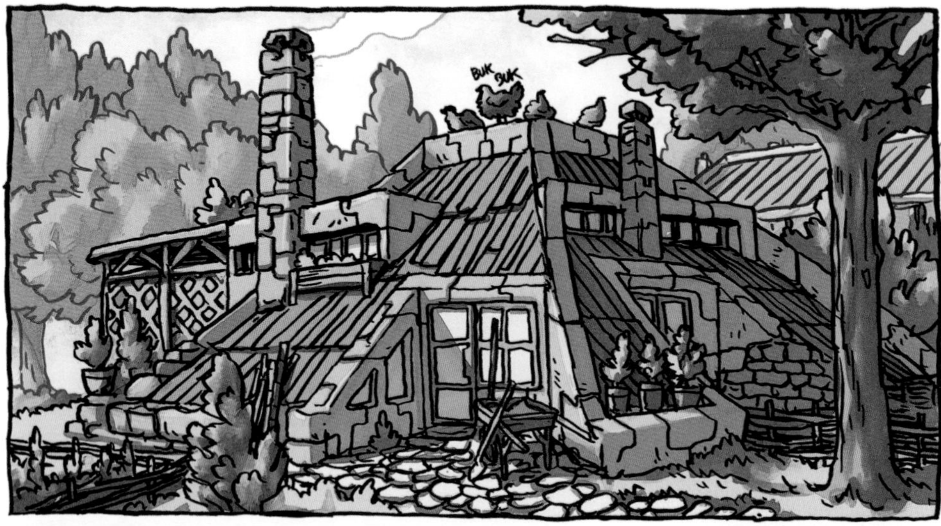
BUK BUK

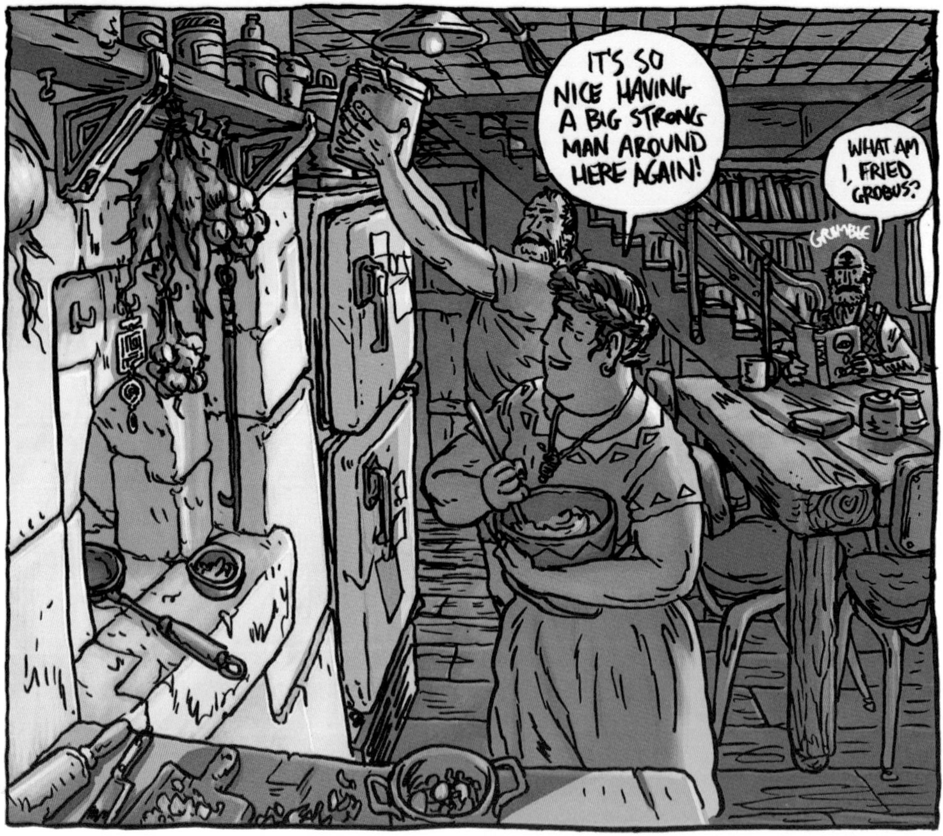
IT'S SO NICE HAVING A BIG STRONG MAN AROUND HERE AGAIN!
GRUMBLE
WHAT AM I, FRIED GROBUS?

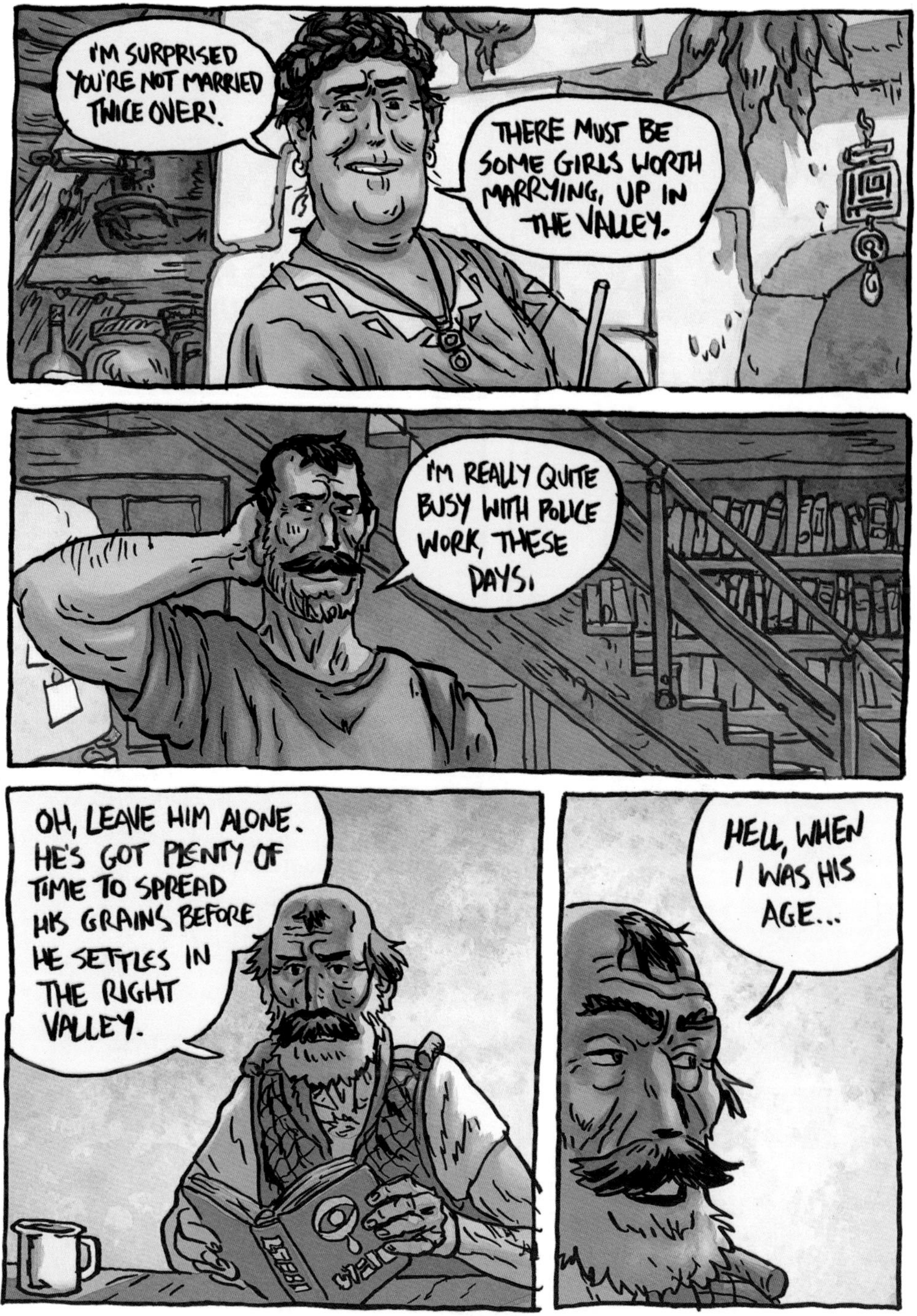

I'M SURPRISED YOU'RE NOT MARRIED TWICE OVER!.
THERE MUST BE SOME GIRLS WORTH MARRYING, UP IN THE VALLEY.
I'M REALLY QUITE BUSY WITH POLICE WORK, THESE DAYS.
OH, LEAVE HIM ALONE. HE'S GOT PLENTY OF TIME TO SPREAD HIS GRAINS BEFORE HE SETTLES IN THE RIGHT VALLEY.
HELL, WHEN I WAS HIS AGE...

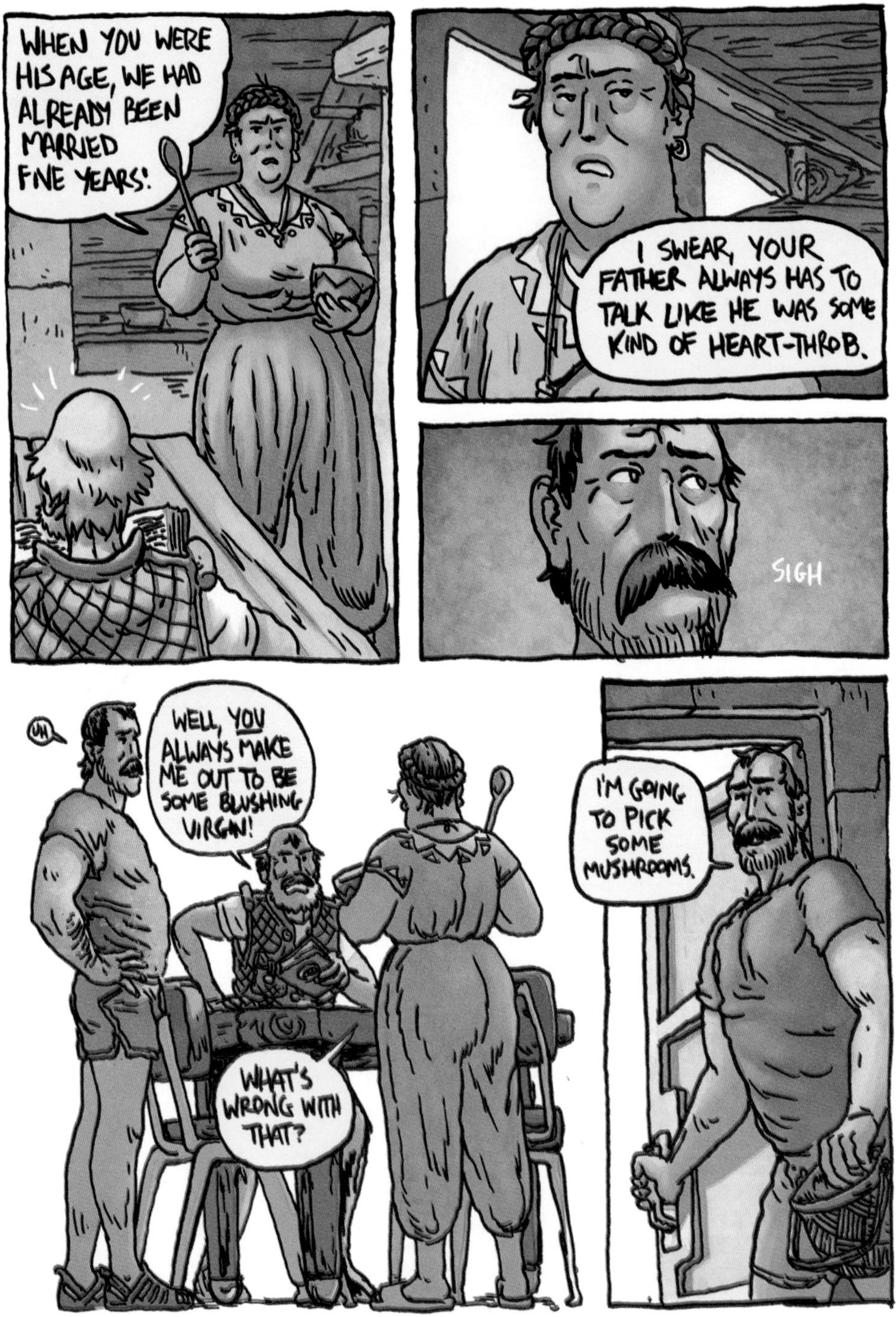
WHEN YOU WERE HIS AGE, WE HAD ALREADY BEEN MARRIED FIVE YEARS!
I SWEAR, YOUR FATHER ALWAYS HAS TO TALK LIKE HE WAS SOME KIND OF HEART-THROB.
SIGH
UH
WELL, YOU ALWAYS MAKE ME OUT TO BE SOME BLUSHING VIRGIN!
WHAT'S WRONG WITH THAT?
I'M GOING TO PICK SOME MUSHROOMS.

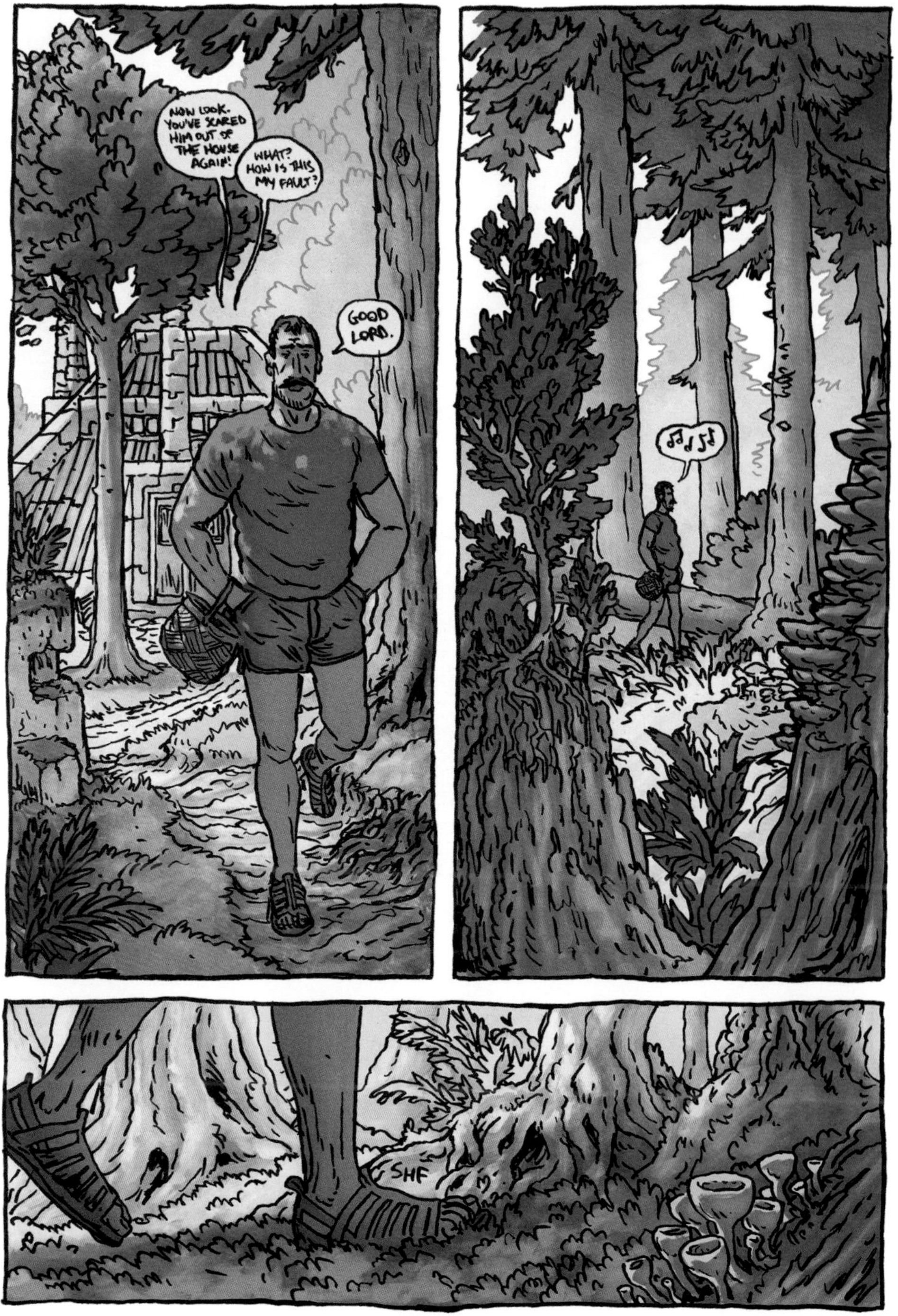
NOW LOOK. YOU'VE SCARED HIM OUT OF THE HOUSE AGAIN!
WHAT? HOW IS THIS MY FAULT?
GOOD LORD.
SHF

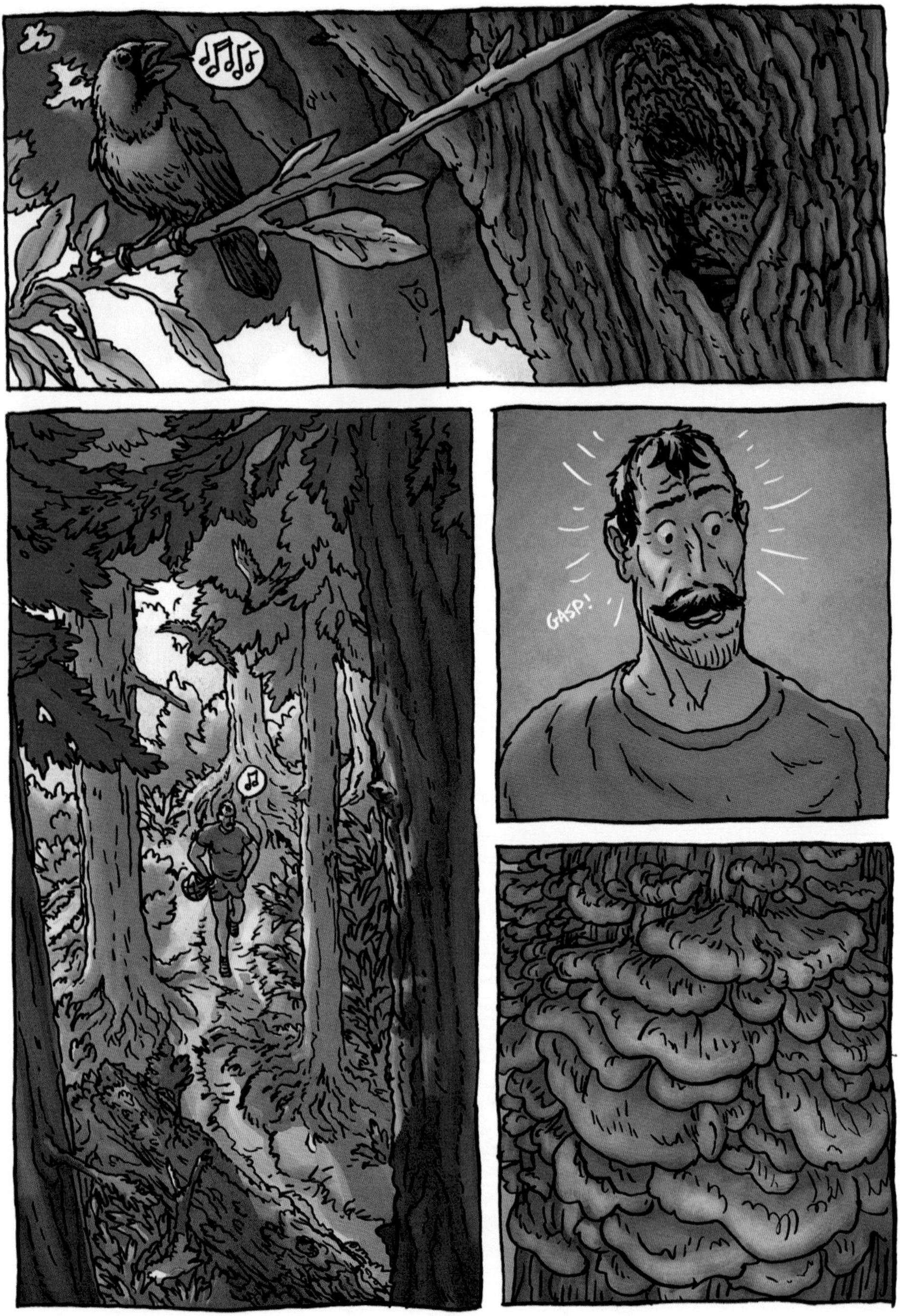
GASP!

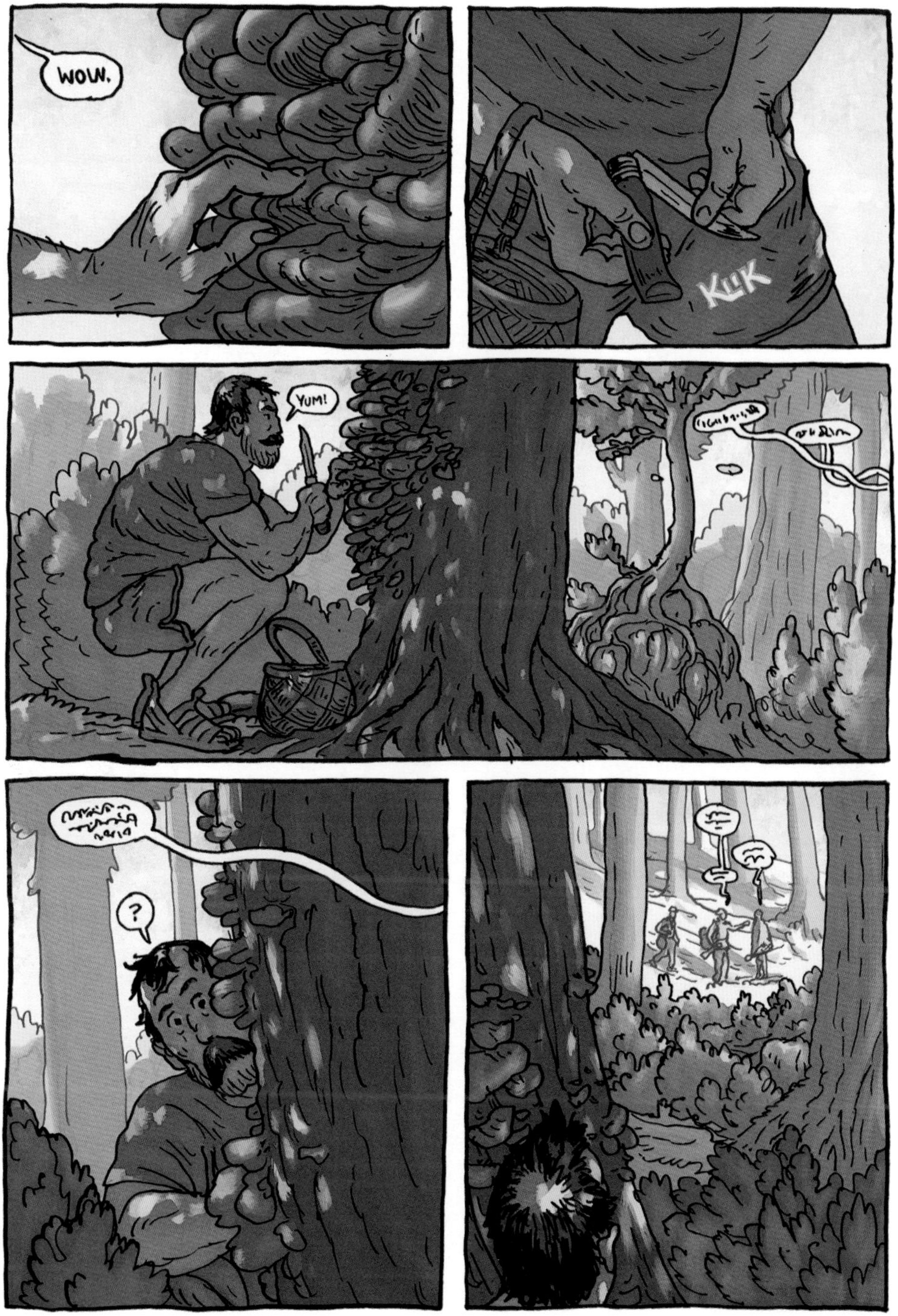
WOW.
KLIK
YUM!
?

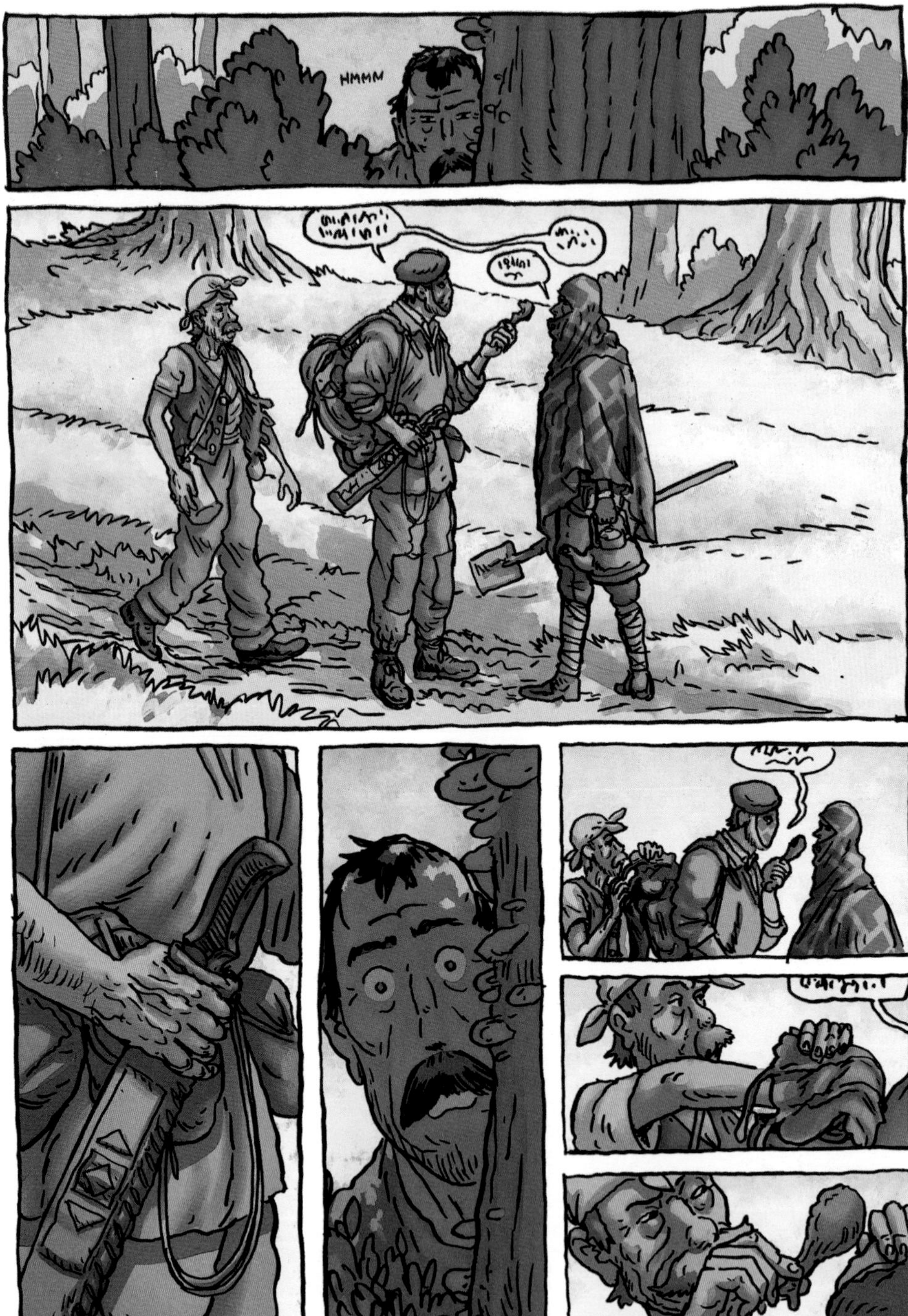
HMMM

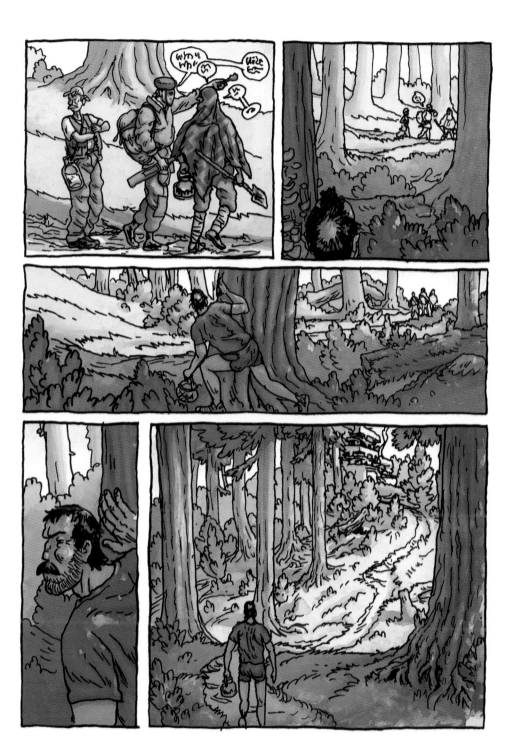

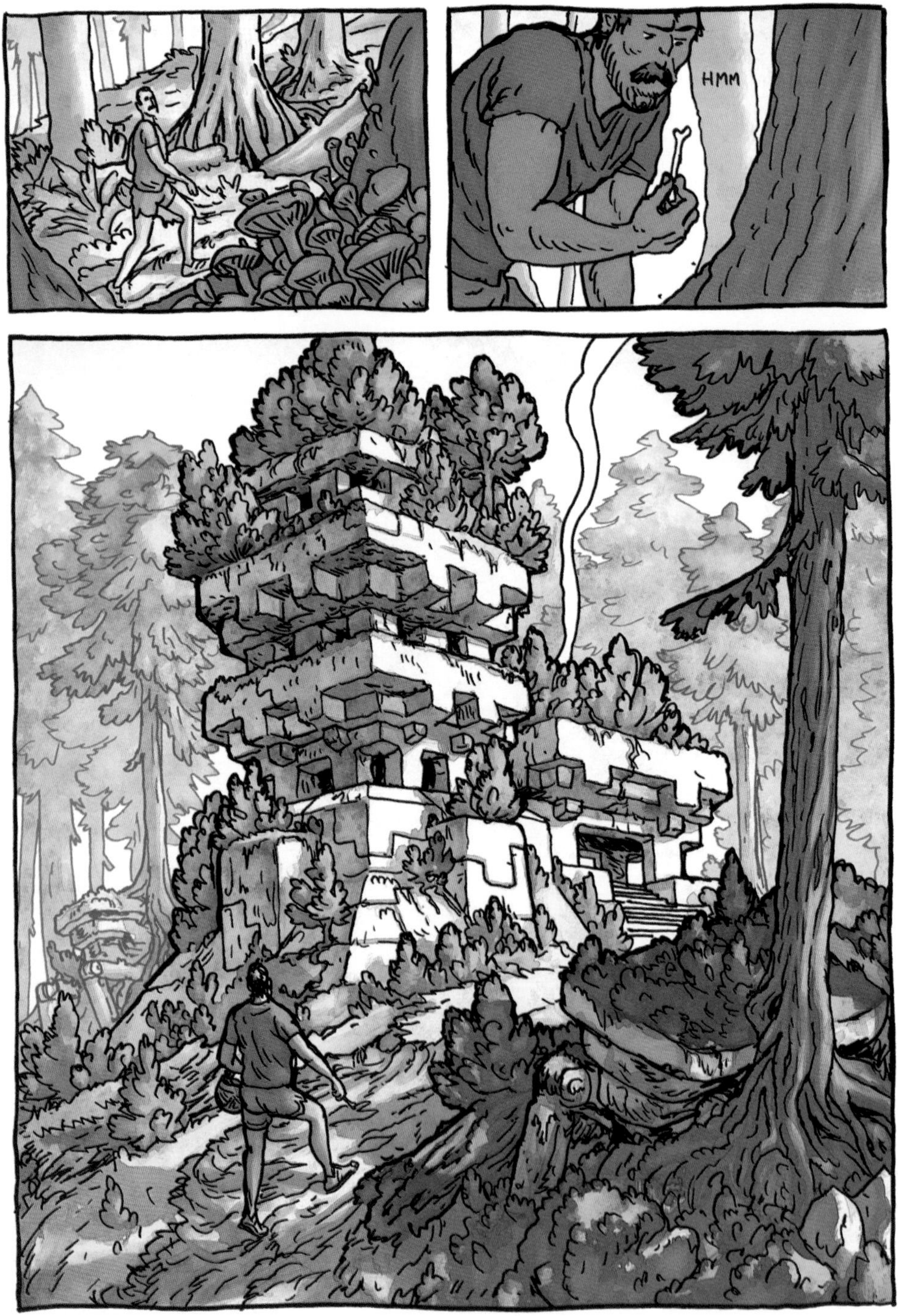
HMM

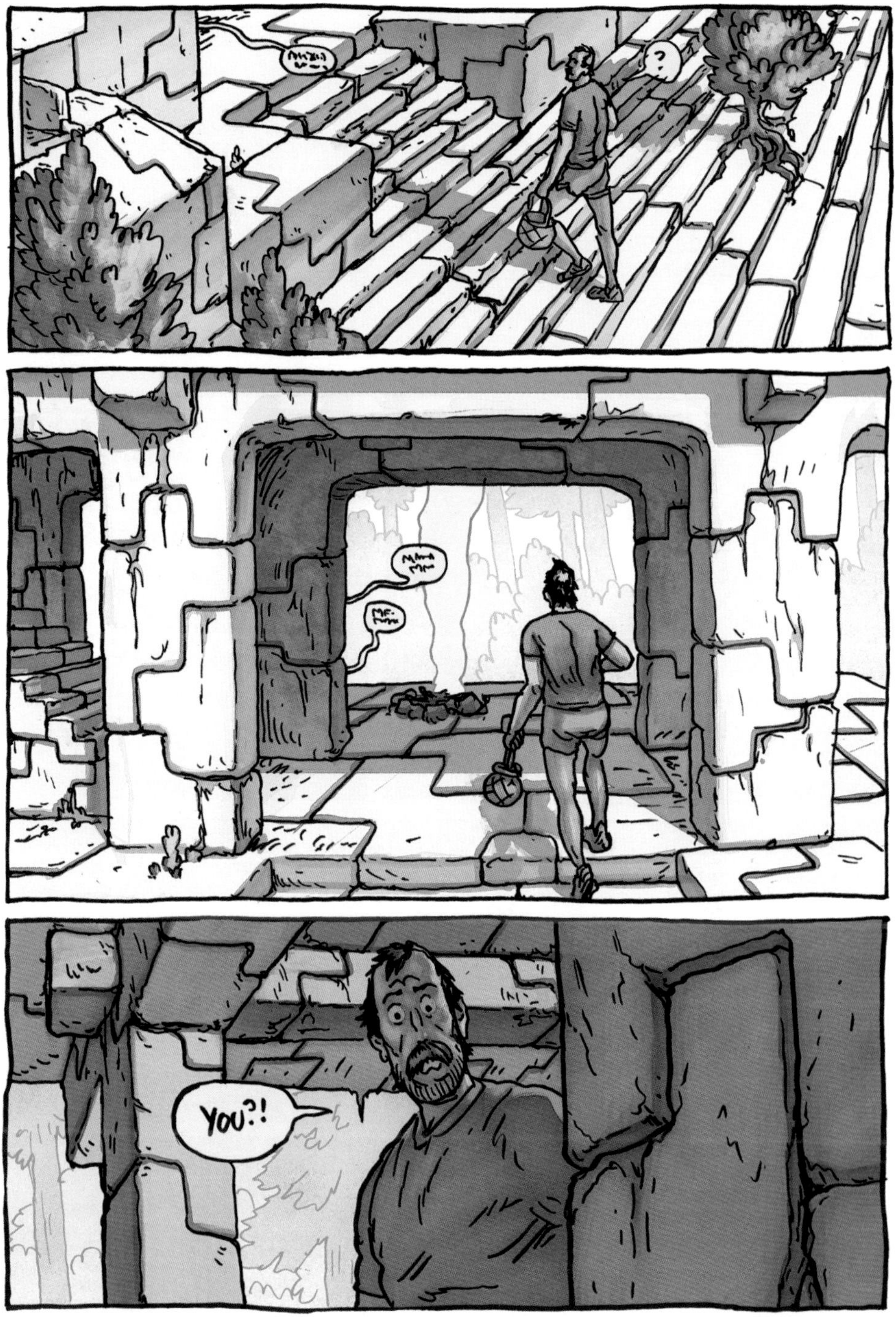
?
YOU?!

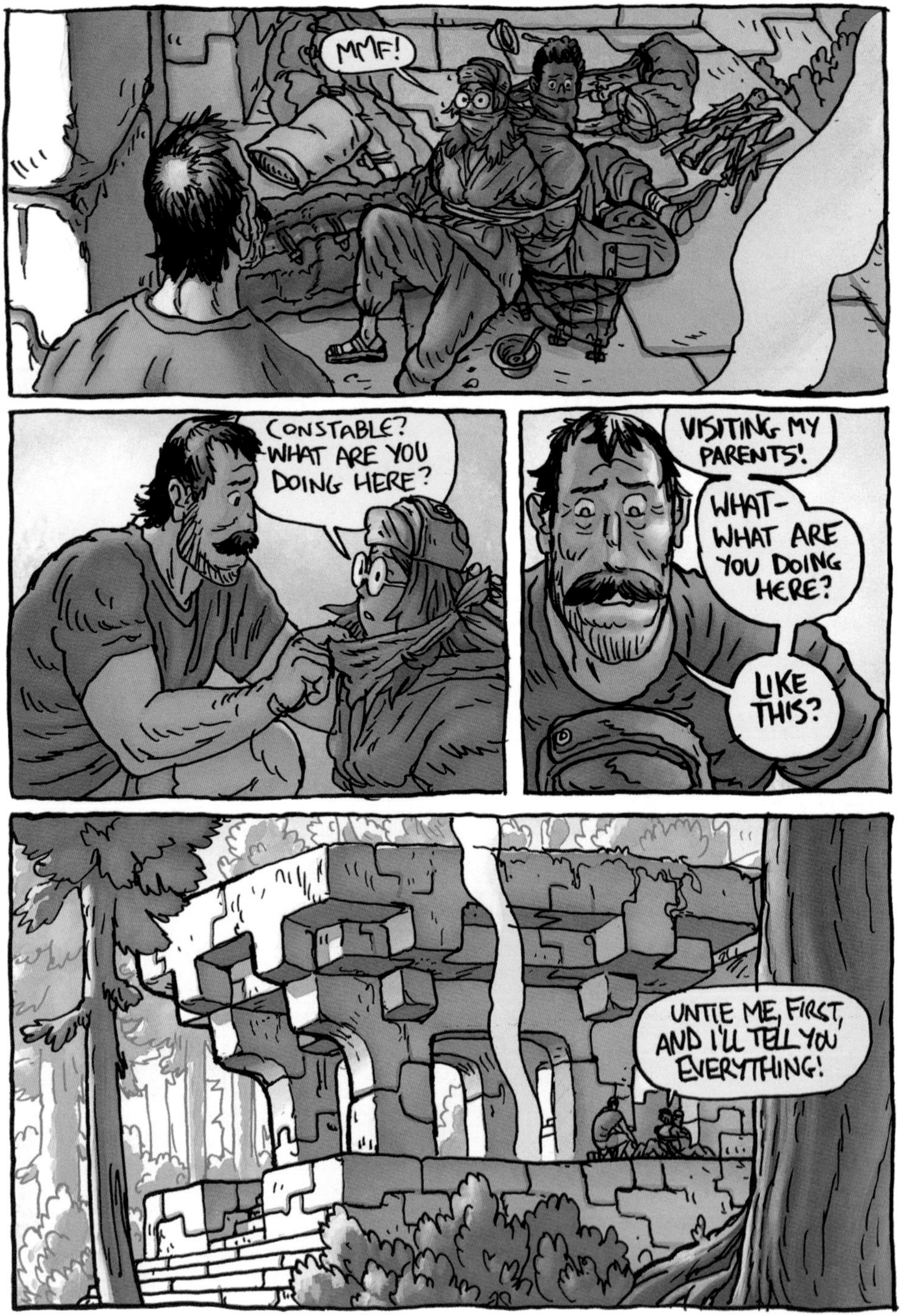
MMF!
CONSTABLE? WHAT ARE YOU DOING HERE?
VISITING MY PARENTS!
WHAT- WHAT ARE YOU DOING HERE?
LIKE THIS?
UNTIE ME, FIRST, AND I'LL TELL YOU EVERYTHING!

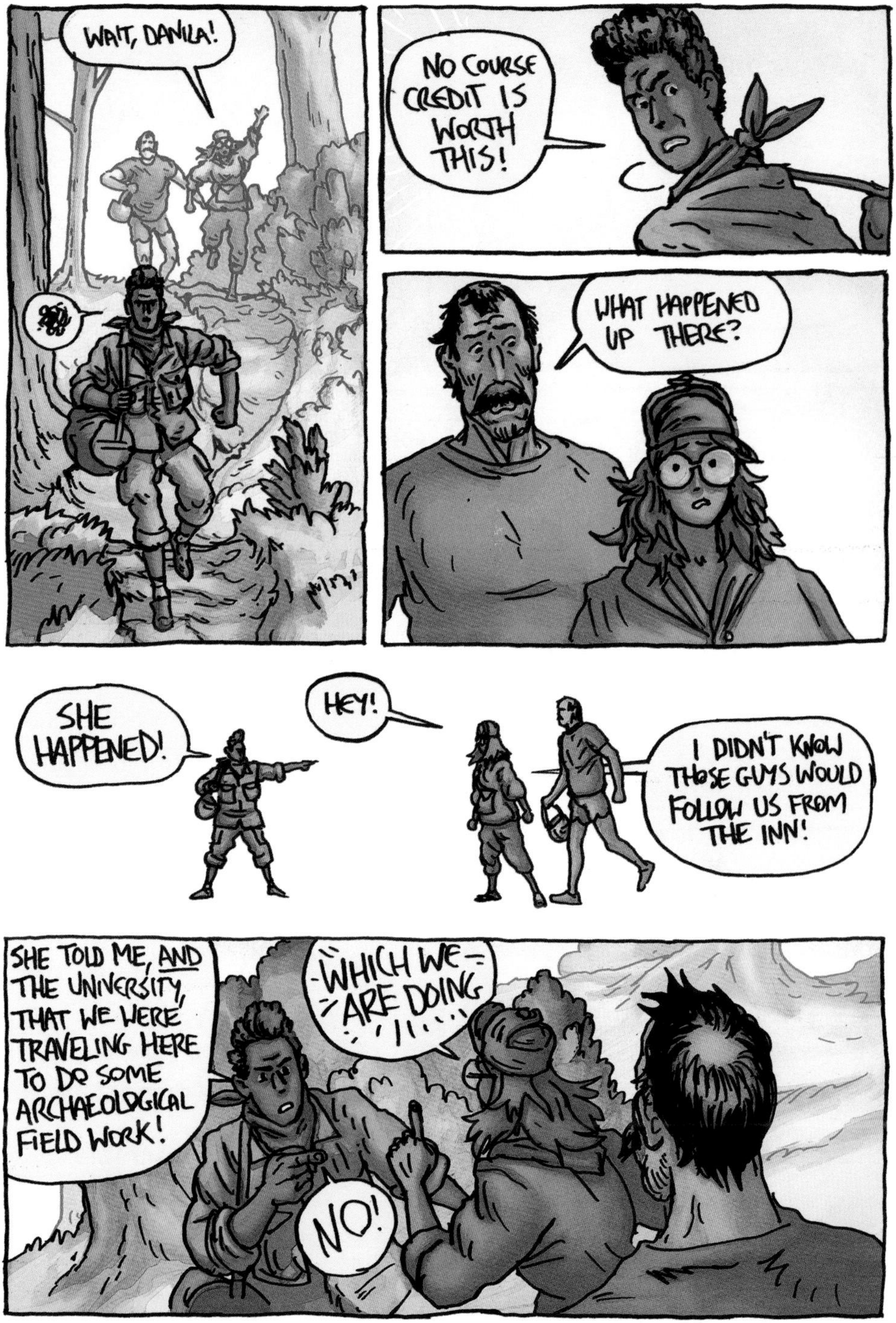
WAIT, DANILA!
NO COURSE CREDIT IS WORTH THIS!
WHAT HAPPENED UP THERE?
SHE HAPPENED!
HEY!
I DIDN'T KNOW THOSE GUYS WOULD FOLLOW US FROM THE INN!
SHE TOLD ME, AND THE UNIVERSITY, THAT WE WERE TRAVELING HERE TO DO SOME ARCHAEOLOGICAL FIELD WORK!
WHICH WE ARE DOING
NO!

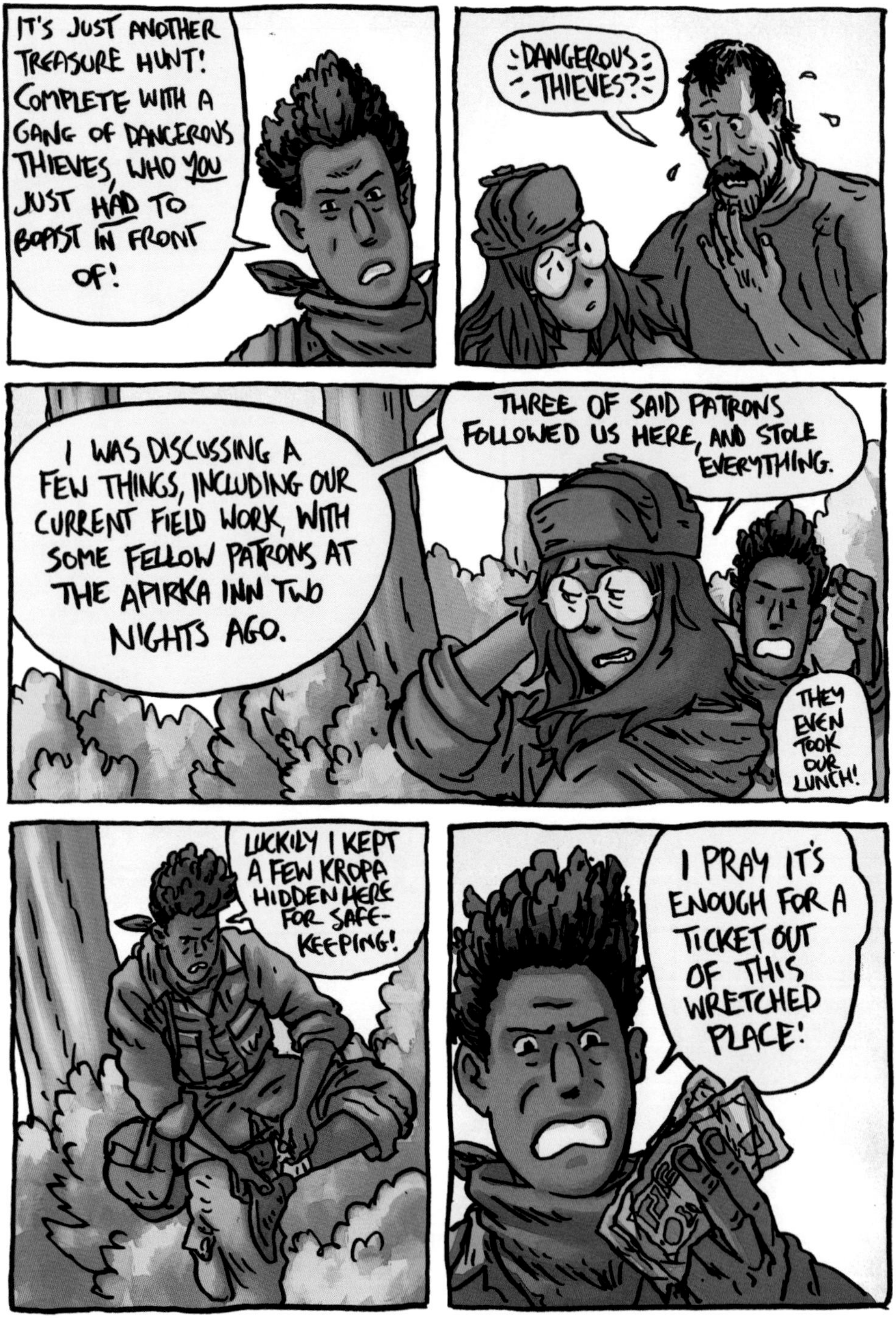
IT'S JUST ANOTHER TREASURE HUNT! COMPLETE WITH A GANG OF DANGEROUS THIEVES, WHO YOU JUST HAD TO BOAST IN FRONT OF!
DANGEROUS THIEVES?
I WAS DISCUSSING A FEW THINGS, INCLUDING OUR CURRENT FIELD WORK, WITH SOME FELLOW PATRONS AT THE APIRKA INN TWO NIGHTS AGO.
THREE OF SAID PATRONS FOLLOWED US HERE, AND STOLE EVERYTHING.
THEY EVEN TOOK OUR LUNCH!
LUCKILY I KEPT A FEW KROPA HIDDEN HERE FOR SAFE-KEEPING!
I PRAY IT'S ENOUGH FOR A TICKET OUT OF THIS WRETCHED PLACE!

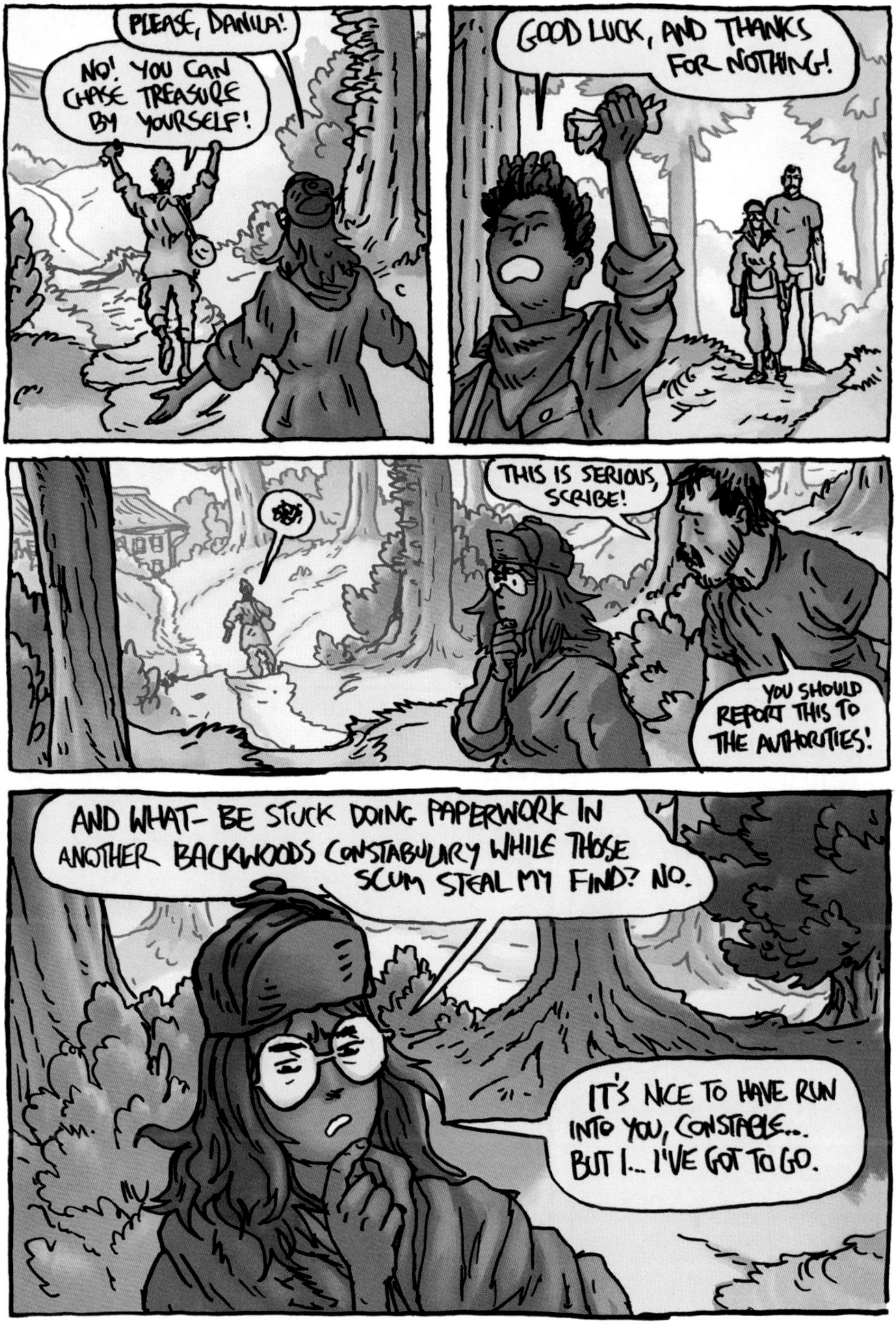
PLEASE, DANILA!
NO! YOU CAN CHASE TREASURE BY YOURSELF!
GOOD LUCK, AND THANKS FOR NOTHING!
THIS IS SERIOUS, SCRIBE!
YOU SHOULD REPORT THIS TO THE AUTHORITIES!
AND WHAT- BE STUCK DOING PAPERWORK IN ANOTHER BACKWOODS CONSTABULARY WHILE THOSE SCUM STEAL MY FIND? NO.
IT'S NICE TO HAVE RUN INTO YOU, CONSTABLE... BUT I... I'VE GOT TO GO.

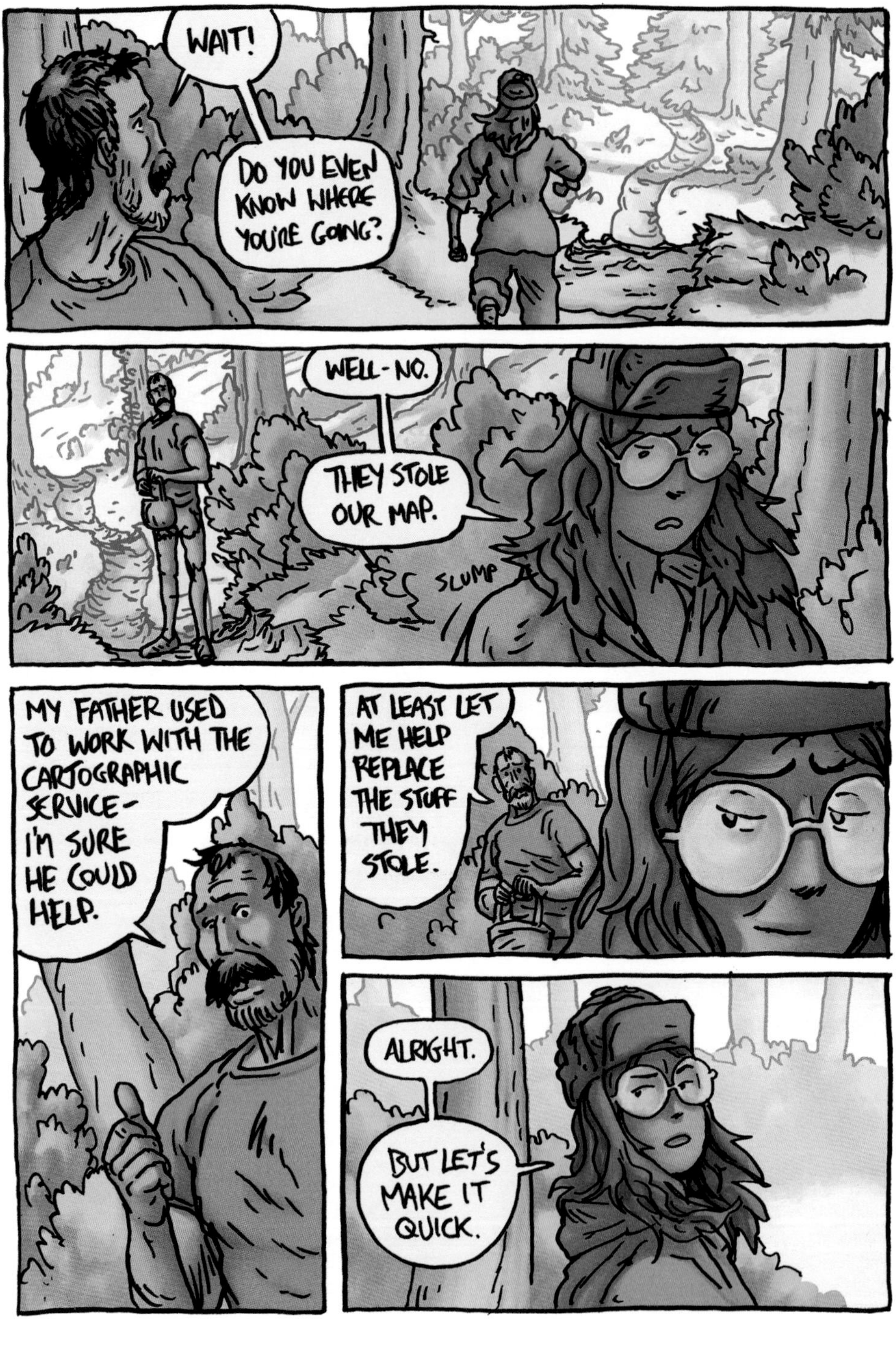
WAIT!
DO YOU EVEN KNOW WHERE YOU'RE GOING?
WELL-NO.
THEY STOLE OUR MAP.
SLUMP
MY FATHER USED TO WORK WITH THE CARTOGRAPHIC SERVICE- I'M SURE HE COULD HELP.
AT LEAST LET ME HELP REPLACE THE STUFF THEY STOLE.
ALRIGHT.
BUT LET'S MAKE IT QUICK.

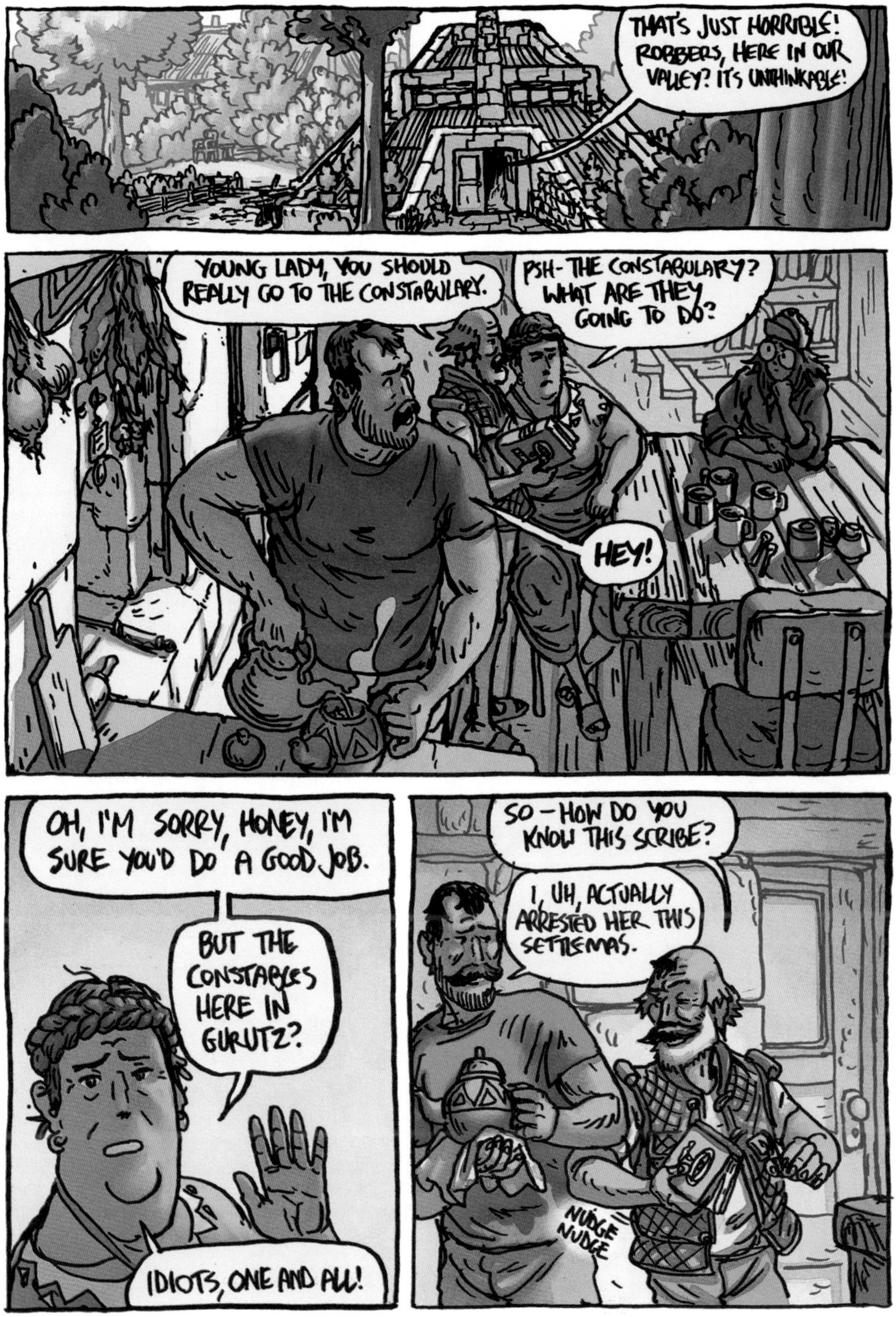
THAT'S JUST HORRIBLE! ROBBERS, HERE IN OUR VALLEY? IT'S UNTHINKABLE!
YOUNG LADY, YOU SHOULD REALLY GO TO THE CONSTABULARY.
PSH- THE CONSTABULARY? WHAT ARE THEY GOING TO DO?
HEY!
OH, I'M SORRY, HONEY, I'M SURE YOU'D DO A GOOD JOB.
BUT THE CONSTABLES HERE IN GURUTZ?
IDIOTS, ONE AND ALL!
SO - HOW DO YOU KNOW THIS SCRIBE?
I, UH, ACTUALLY ARRESTED HER THIS SETTLEMAS.
NUDGE NUDGE

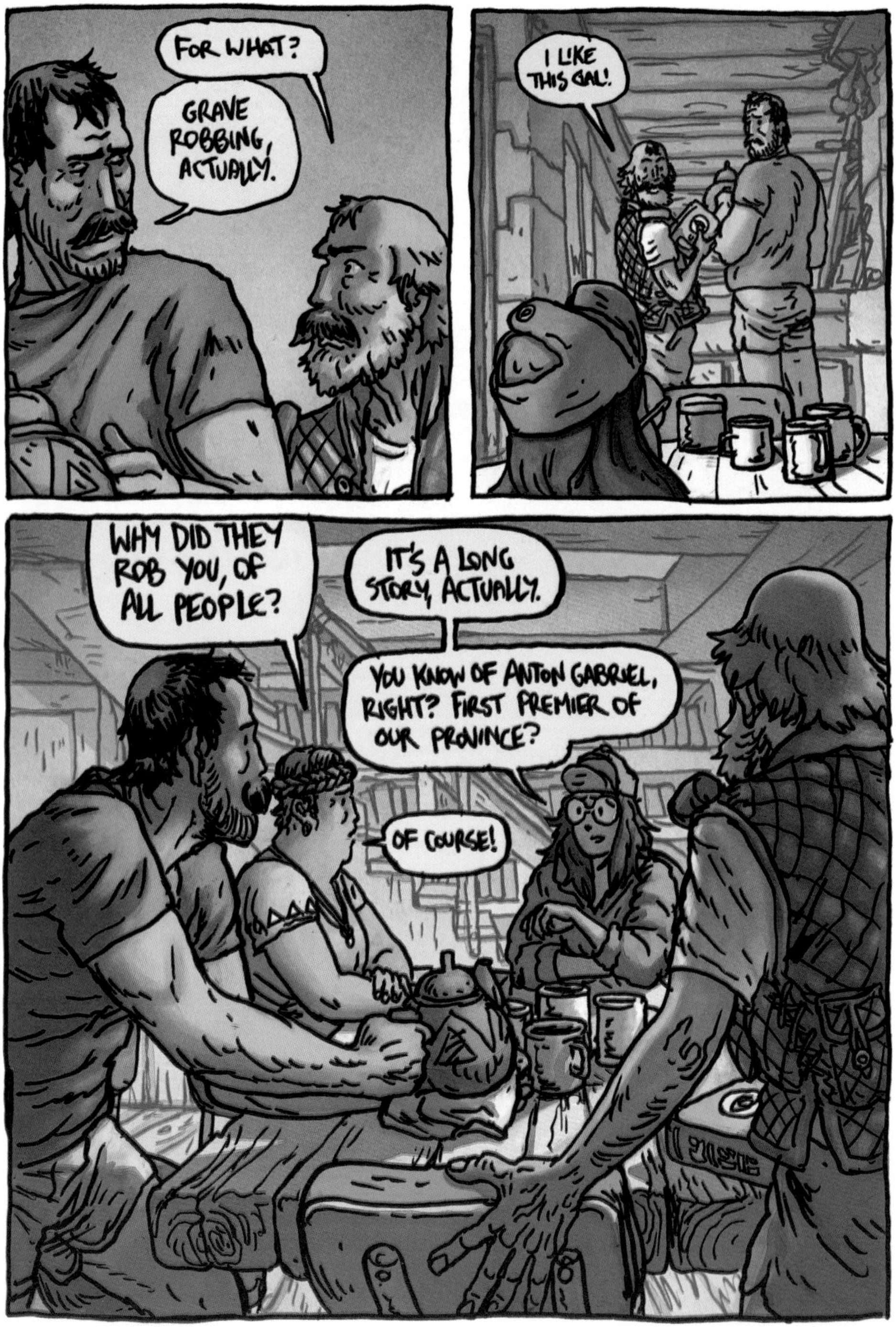
FOR WHAT?
GRAVE ROBBING, ACTUALLY.
I LIKE THIS GAL!
WHY DID THEY ROB YOU, OF ALL PEOPLE?
IT'S A LONG STORY, ACTUALLY.
YOU KNOW OF ANTON GABRIEL, RIGHT? FIRST PREMIER OF OUR PROVINCE?
OF COURSE!

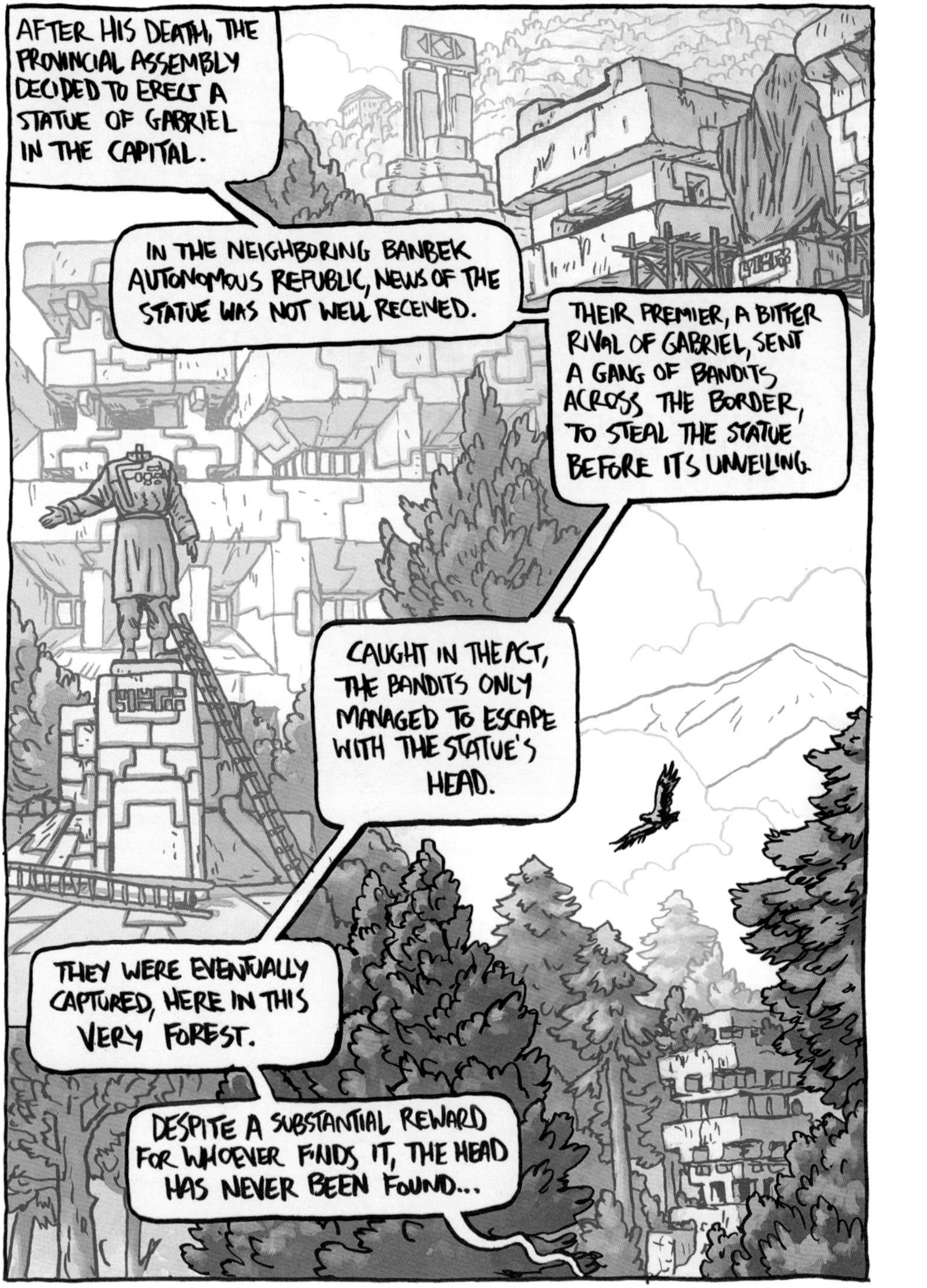
AFTER HIS DEATH, THE PROVINCIAL ASSEMBLY DECIDED TO ERECT A STATUE OF GABRIEL IN THE CAPITAL.
IN THE NEIGHBORING BANBEK AUTONOMOUS REPUBLIC, NEWS OF THE STATUE WAS NOT WELL RECEIVED.
THEIR PREMIER, A BITTER RIVAL OF GABRIEL, SENT A GANG OF BANDITS ACROSS THE BORDER, TO STEAL THE STATUE BEFORE ITS UNVEILING.
CAUGHT IN THE ACT, THE BANDITS ONLY MANAGED TO ESCAPE WITH THE STATUE'S HEAD.
THEY WERE EVENTUALLY CAPTURED, HERE IN THIS VERY FOREST.
DESPITE A SUBSTANTIAL REWARD FOR WHOEVER FINDS IT, THE HEAD HAS NEVER BEEN FOUND...

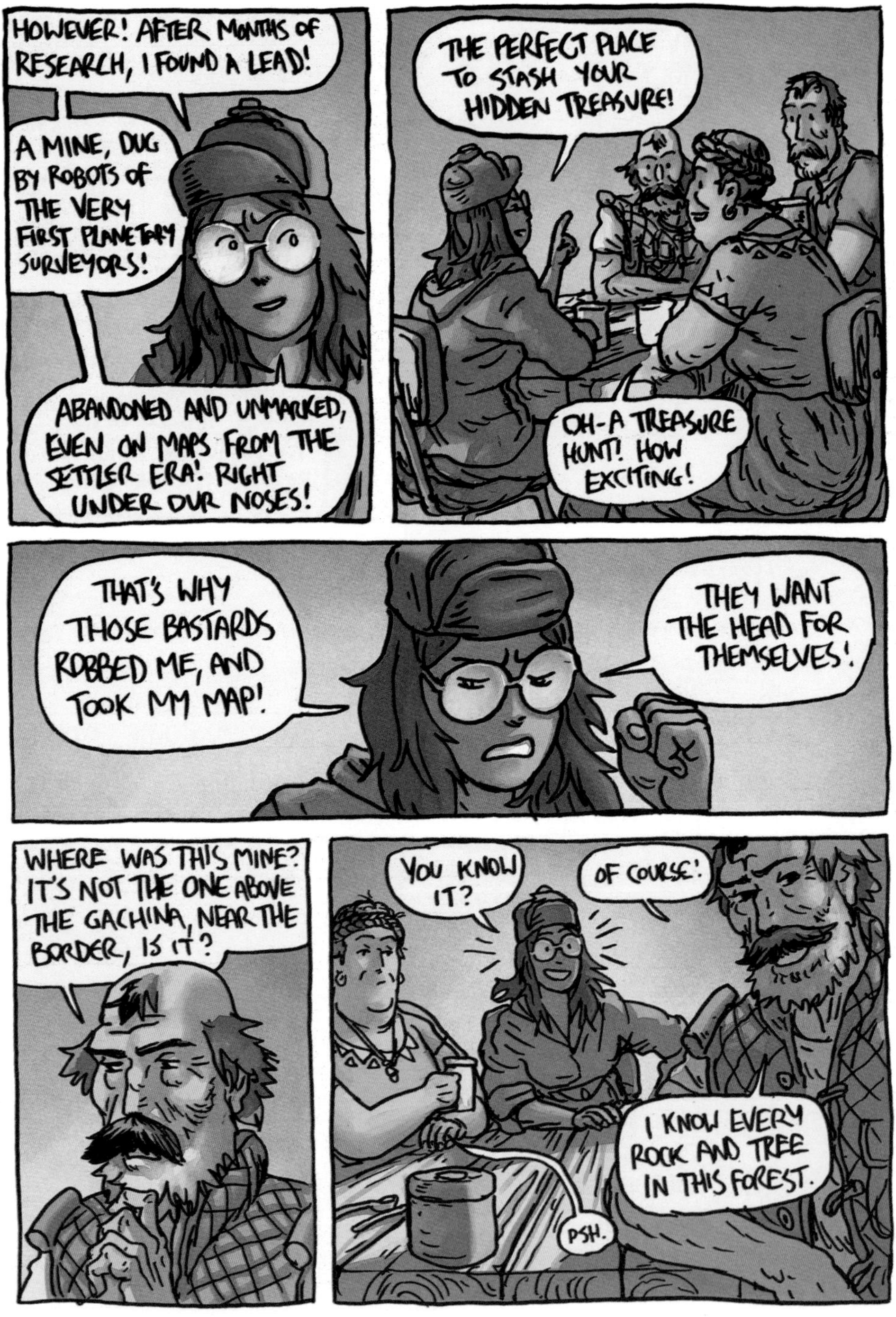
HOWEVER! AFTER MONTHS OF RESEARCH, I FOUND A LEAD!
A MINE, DUG BY ROBOTS OF THE VERY FIRST PLANETARY SURVEYORS!
ABANDONED AND UNMARKED, EVEN ON MAPS FROM THE SETTLER ERA! RIGHT UNDER OUR NOSES!
THE PERFECT PLACE TO STASH YOUR HIDDEN TREASURE!
OH-A TREASURE HUNT! HOW EXCITING!
THAT'S WHY THOSE BASTARDS ROBBED ME, AND TOOK MY MAP!
THEY WANT THE HEAD FOR THEMSELVES!
WHERE WAS THIS MINE? IT'S NOT THE ONE ABOVE THE GACHINA, NEAR THE BORDER, IS IT?
YOU KNOW IT?
OF COURSE!
I KNOW EVERY ROCK AND TREE IN THIS FOREST.
PSH.

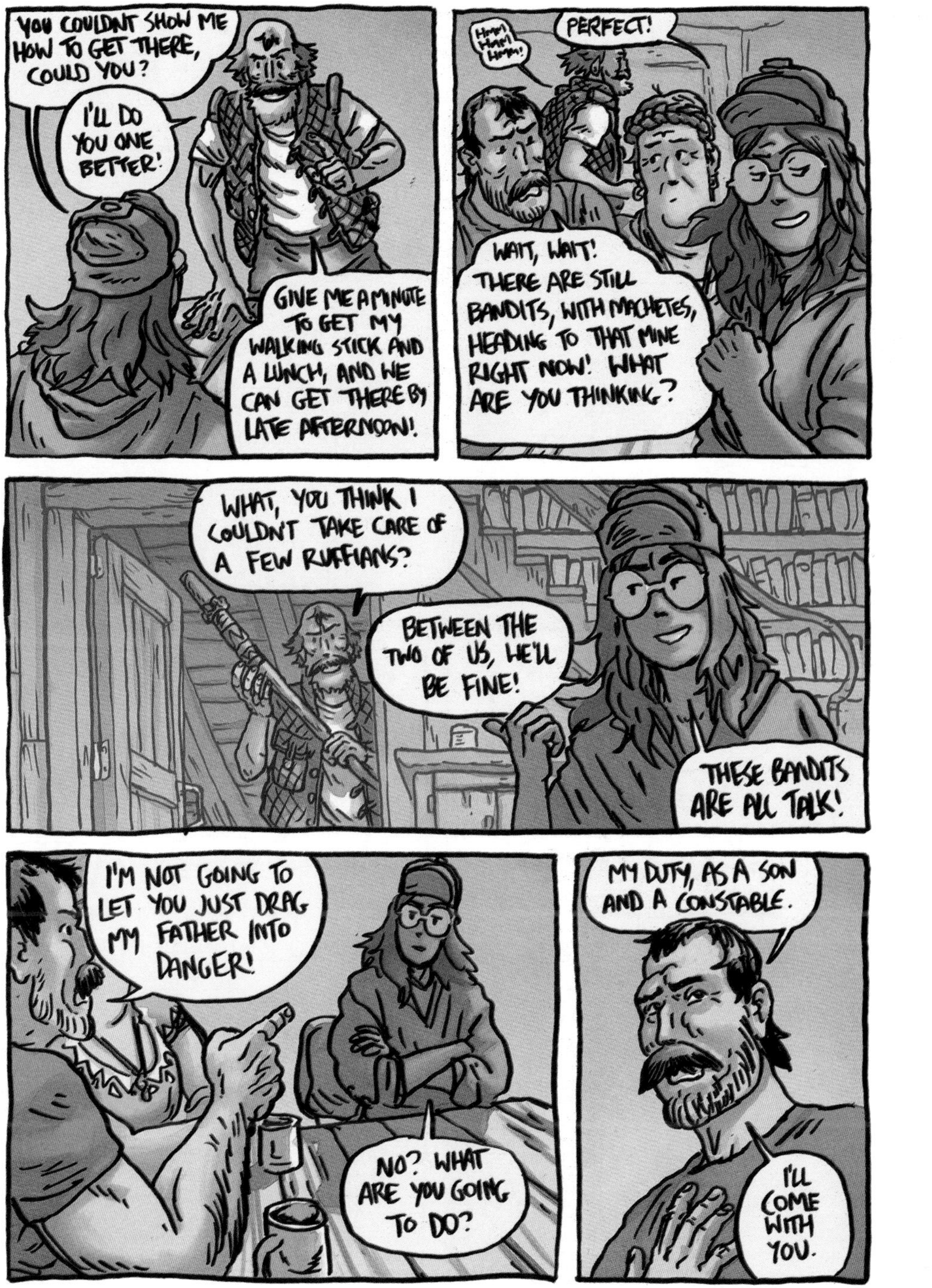
YOU COULDNT SHOW ME HOW TO GET THERE, COULD YOU?
I'LL DO YOU ONE BETTER!
GIVE ME A MINUTE TO GET MY WALKING STICK AND A LUNCH, AND WE CAN GET THERE BY LATE AFTERNOON!
HMM HMM HMM!
PERFECT!
WAIT, WAIT! THERE ARE STILL BANDITS, WITH MACHETES, HEADING TO THAT MINE RIGHT NOW! WHAT ARE YOU THINKING?
WHAT, YOU THINK I COULDN'T TAKE CARE OF A FEW RUFFIANS?
BETWEEN THE TWO OF US, HE'LL BE FINE!
THESE BANDITS ARE ALL TALK!
I'M NOT GOING TO LET YOU JUST DRAG MY FATHER INTO DANGER!
NO? WHAT ARE YOU GOING TO DO?
MY DUTY, AS A SON AND A CONSTABLE.
I'LL COME WITH YOU.

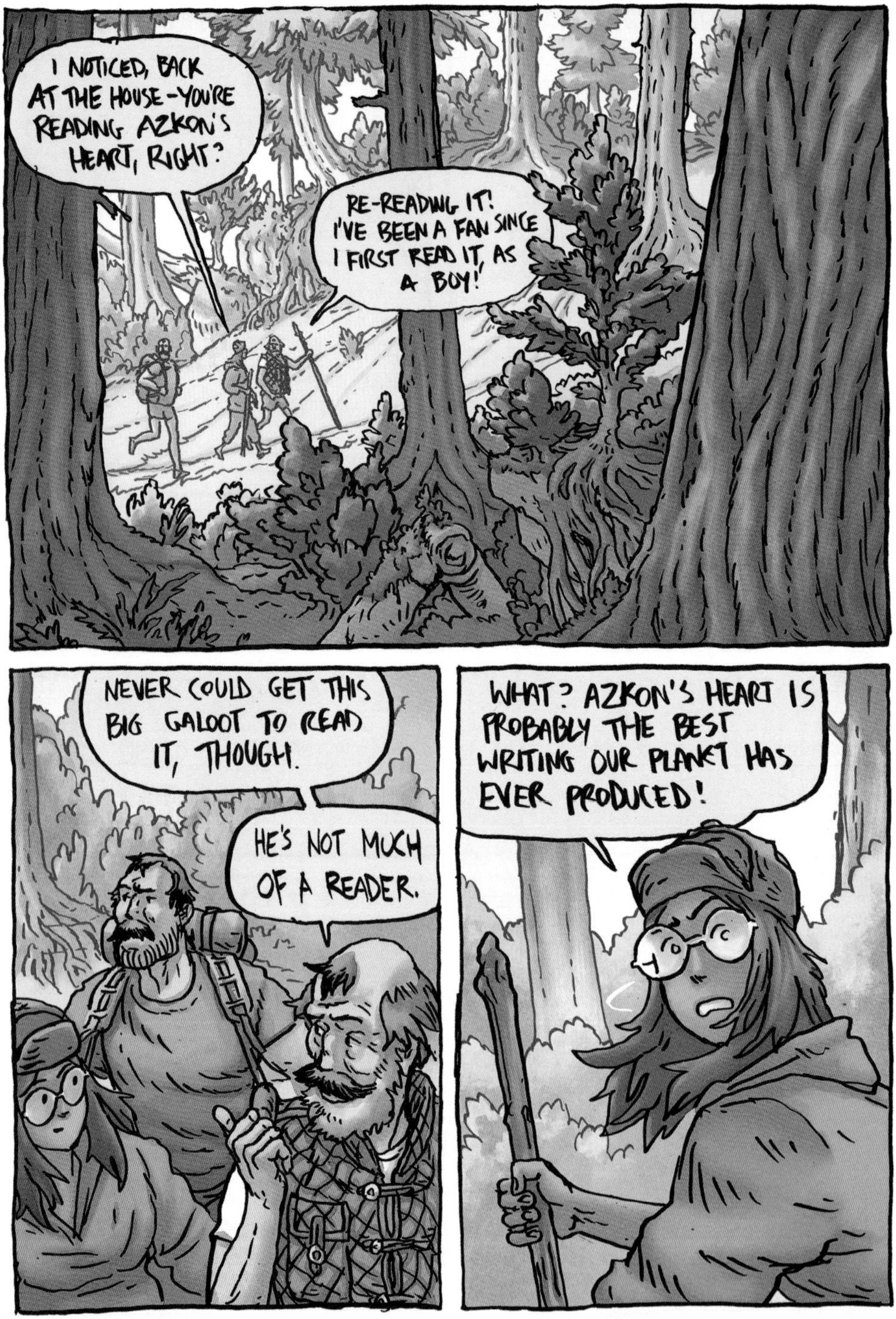
I NOTICED, BACK AT THE HOUSE-YOU'RE READING AZKON'S HEART, RIGHT?
RE-READING IT! I'VE BEEN A FAN SINCE I FIRST READ IT, AS A BOY!
NEVER COULD GET THIS BIG GALOOT TO READ IT, THOUGH.
HE'S NOT MUCH OF A READER.
WHAT? AZKON'S HEART IS PROBABLY THE BEST WRITING OUR PLANET HAS EVER PRODUCED!

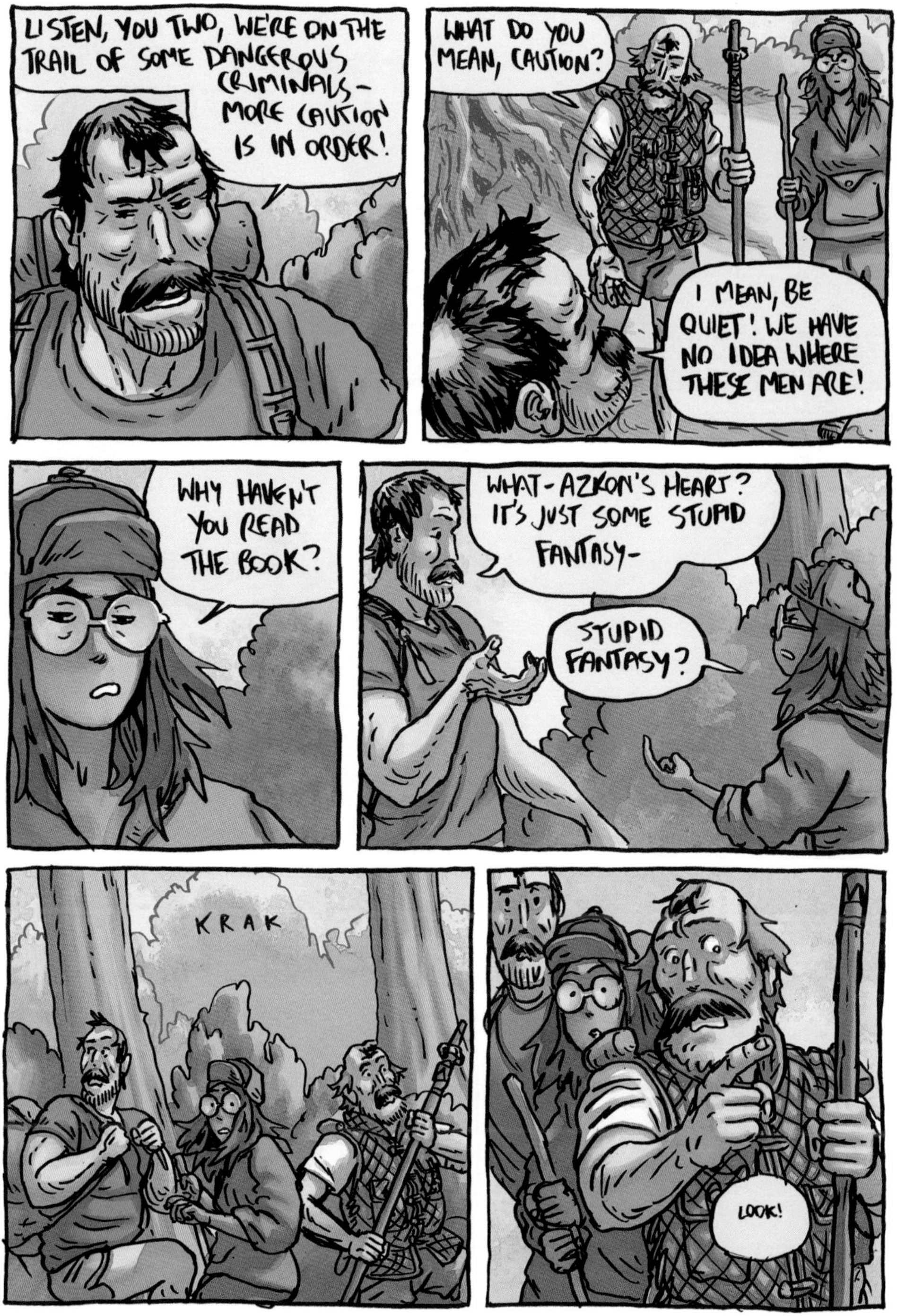
LISTEN, YOU TWO, WE'RE ON THE TRAIL OF SOME DANGEROUS CRIMINALS- MORE CAUTION IS IN ORDER!
WHAT DO YOU MEAN, CAUTION?
I MEAN, BE QUIET! WE HAVE NO IDEA WHERE THESE MEN ARE!
WHY HAVEN'T YOU READ THE BOOK?
WHAT- AZKON'S HEART? IT'S JUST SOME STUPID FANTASY-
STUPID FANTASY?
KRAK
LOOK!

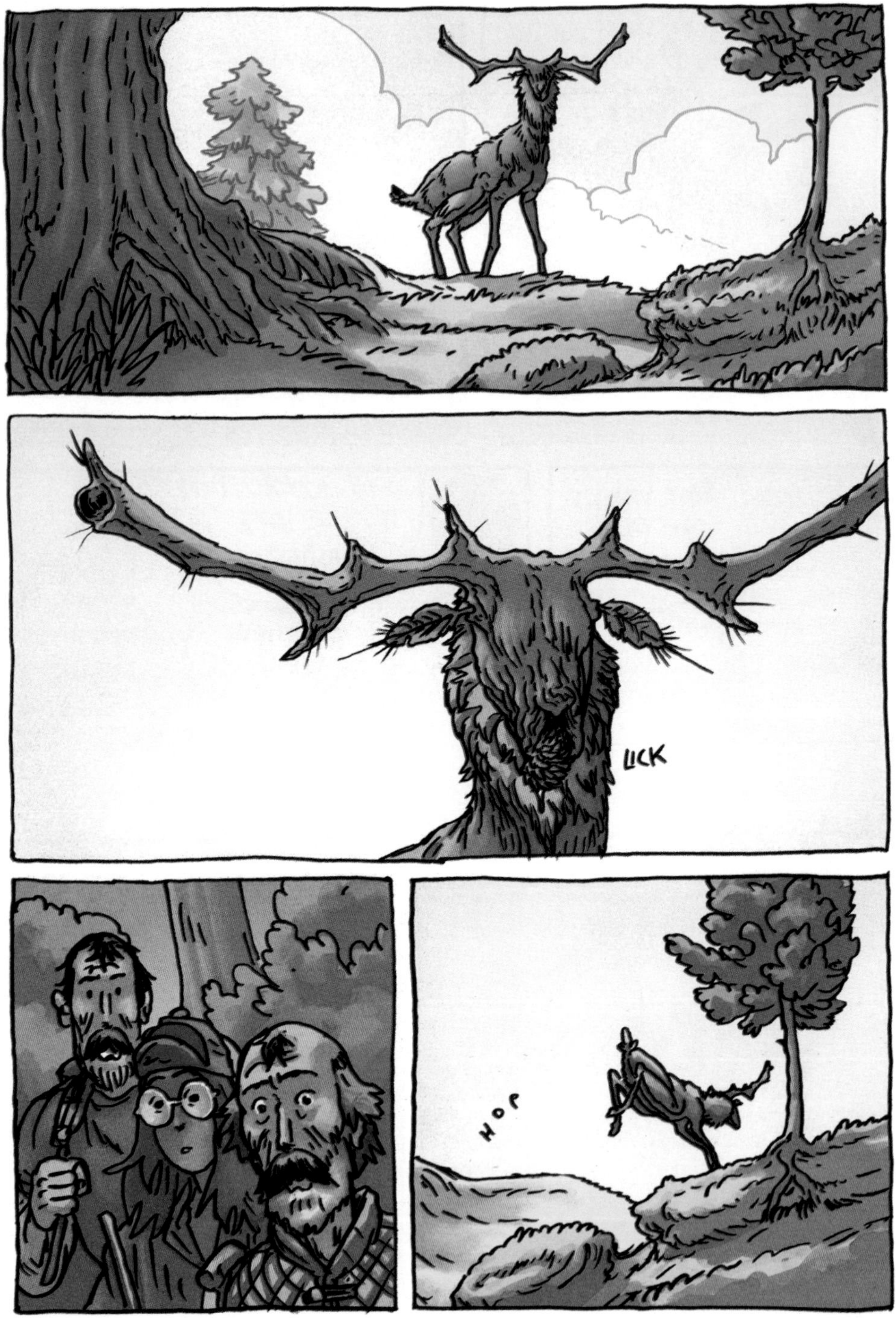
LICK
HOP

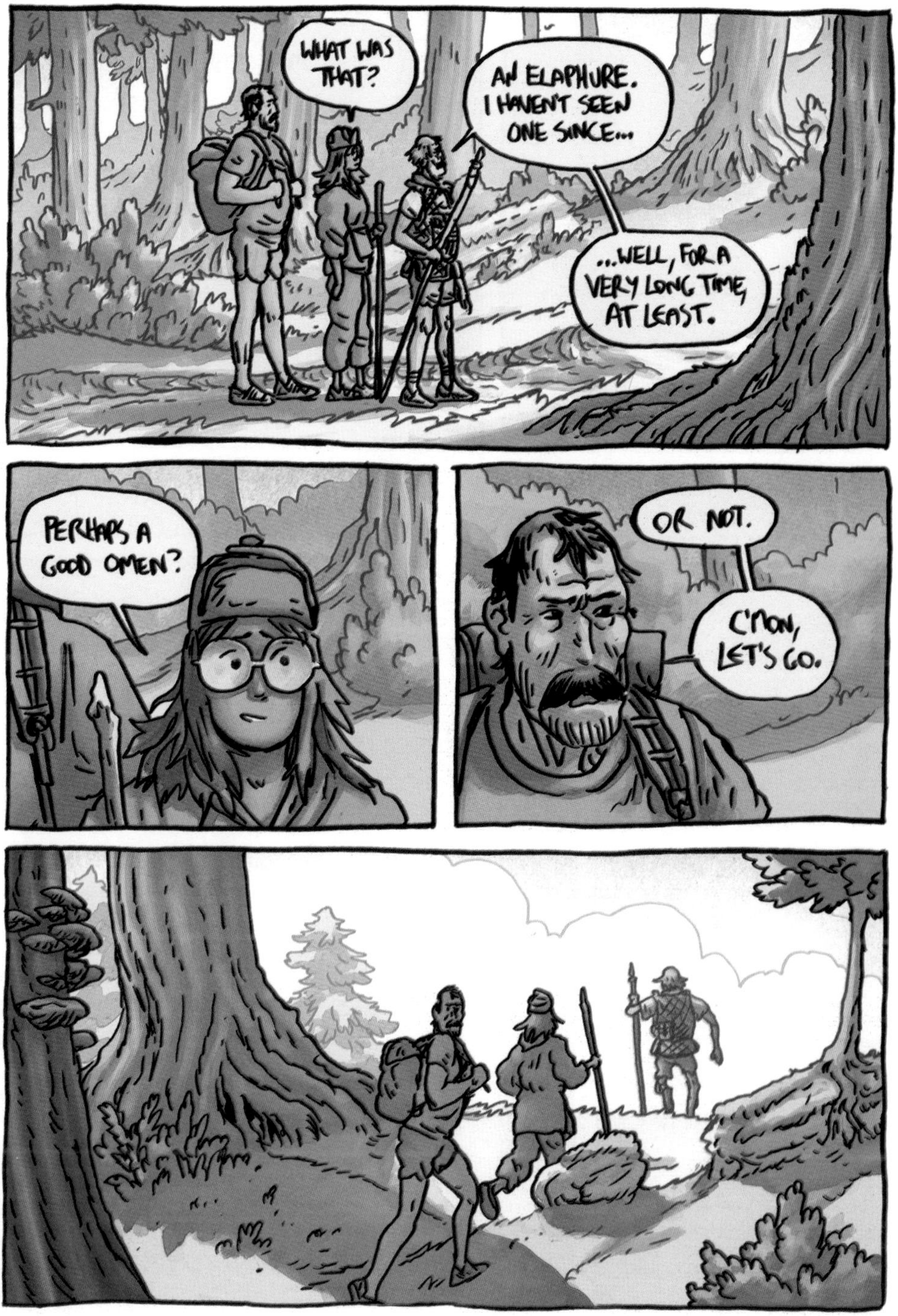
WHAT WAS THAT?
AN ELAPHURE. I HAVEN'T SEEN ONE SINCE...
...WELL, FOR A VERY LONG TIME, AT LEAST.
PERHAPS A GOOD OMEN?
OR NOT.
C'MON, LET'S GO.

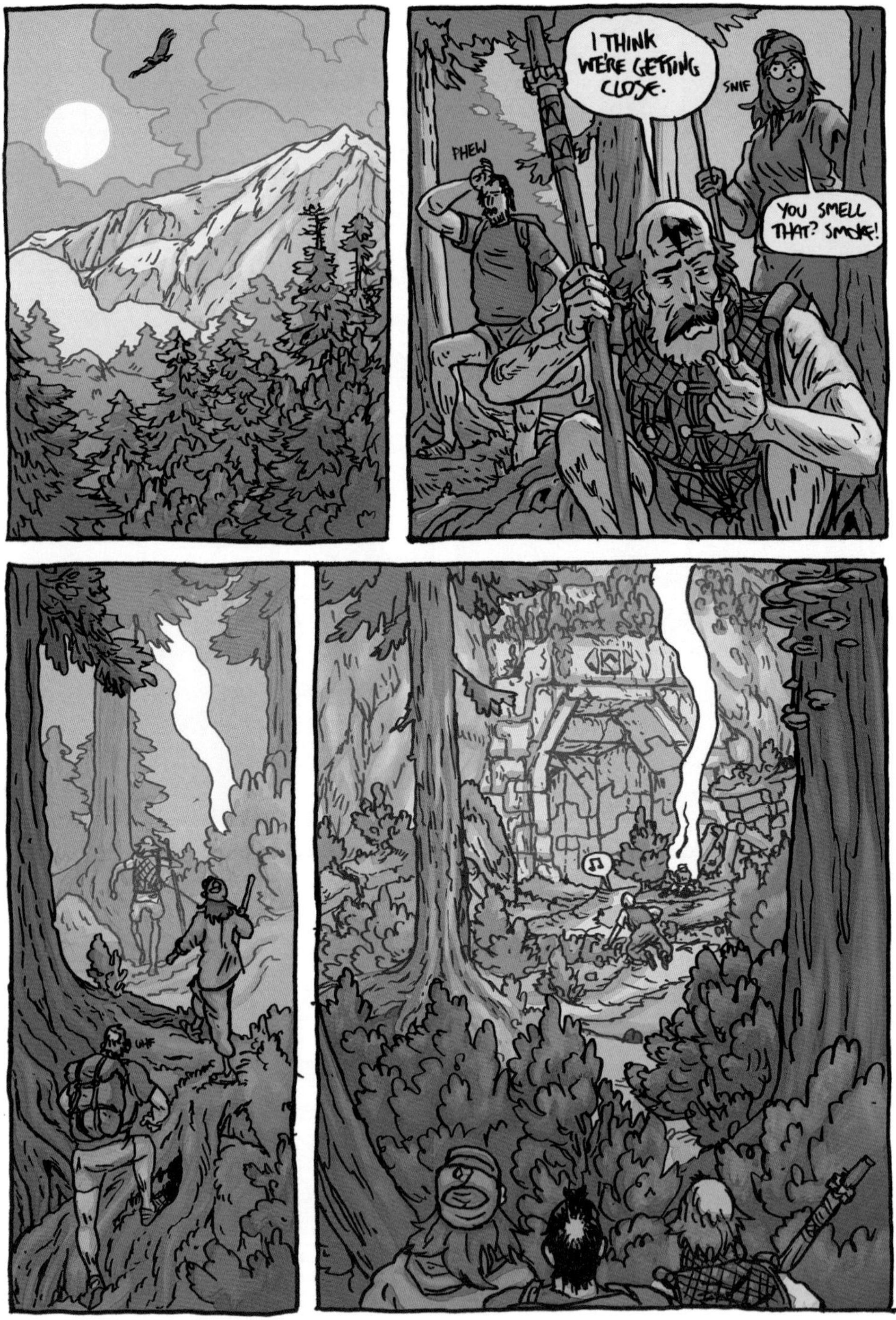
I THINK WE'RE GETTING CLOSE.
SNIF
PHEW
YOU SMELL THAT? SMOKE!
UHF

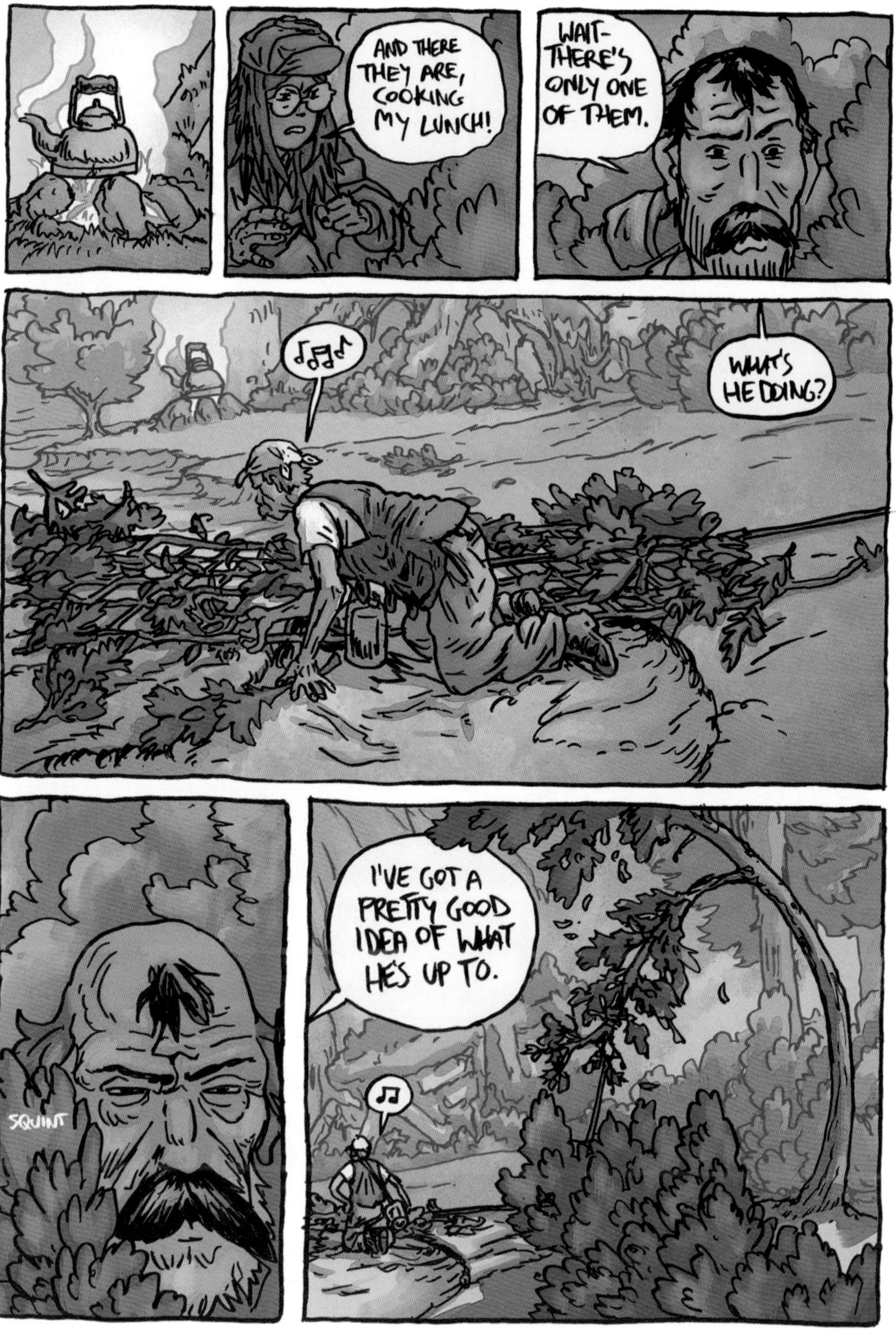
AND THERE THEY ARE, COOKING MY LUNCH!
WAIT- THERE'S ONLY ONE OF THEM.
WHAT'S HE DOING?
SQUINT
I'VE GOT A PRETTY GOOD IDEA OF WHAT HE'S UP TO.

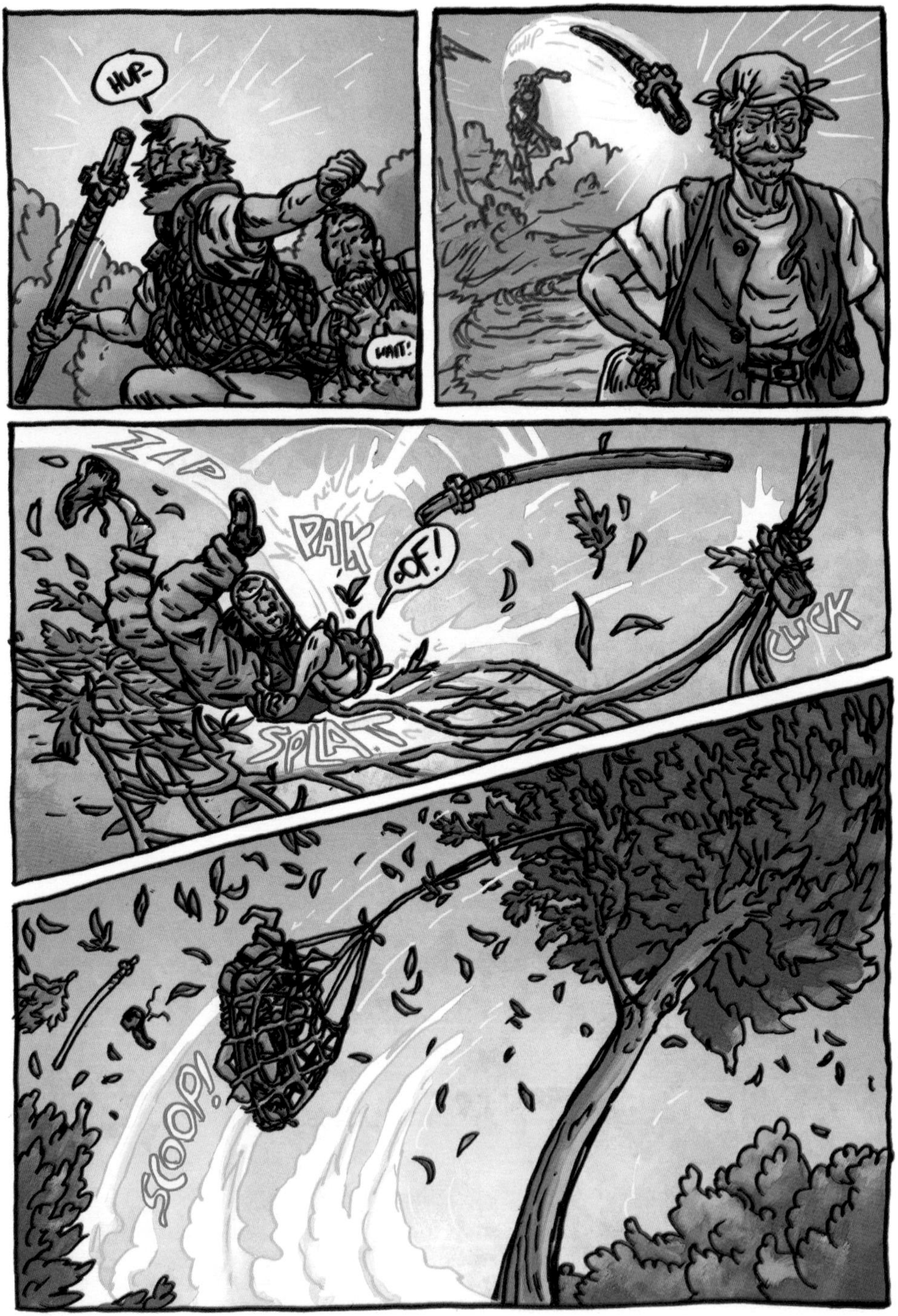
HUP-
WAIT!
WHIP
ZIP
PAK
OOF!
CLICK
SPLAT
SCOOP!

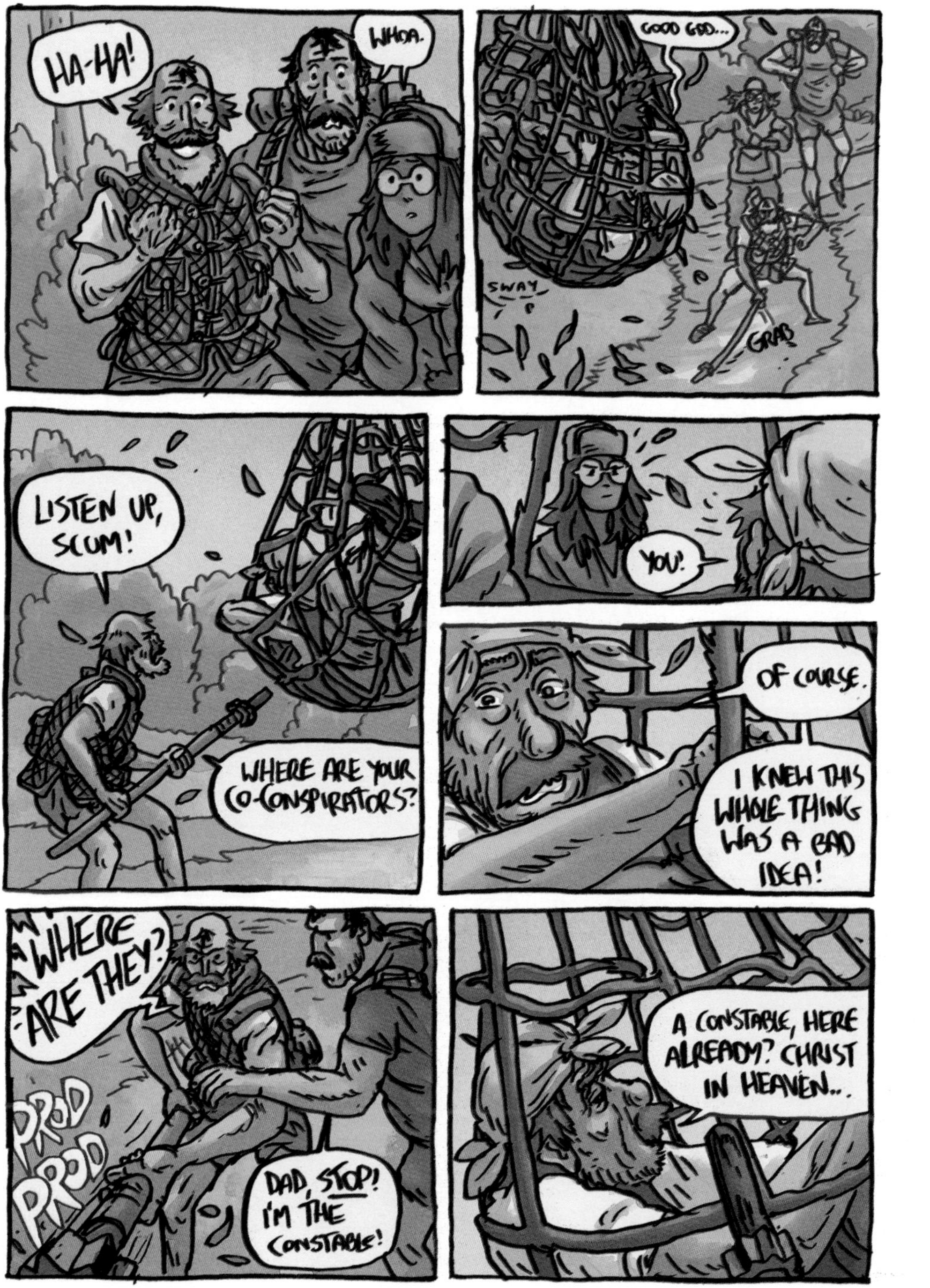
HA-HA!
WHOA.
GOOD GOD...
SWAY
GRAB
LISTEN UP, SCUM!
WHERE ARE YOUR CO-CONSPIRATORS?
YOU!
OF COURSE.
I KNEW THIS WHOLE THING WAS A BAD IDEA!
WHERE ARE THEY?
PROD PROD
DAD, STOP! I'M THE CONSTABLE!
A CONSTABLE, HERE ALREADY? CHRIST IN HEAVEN...

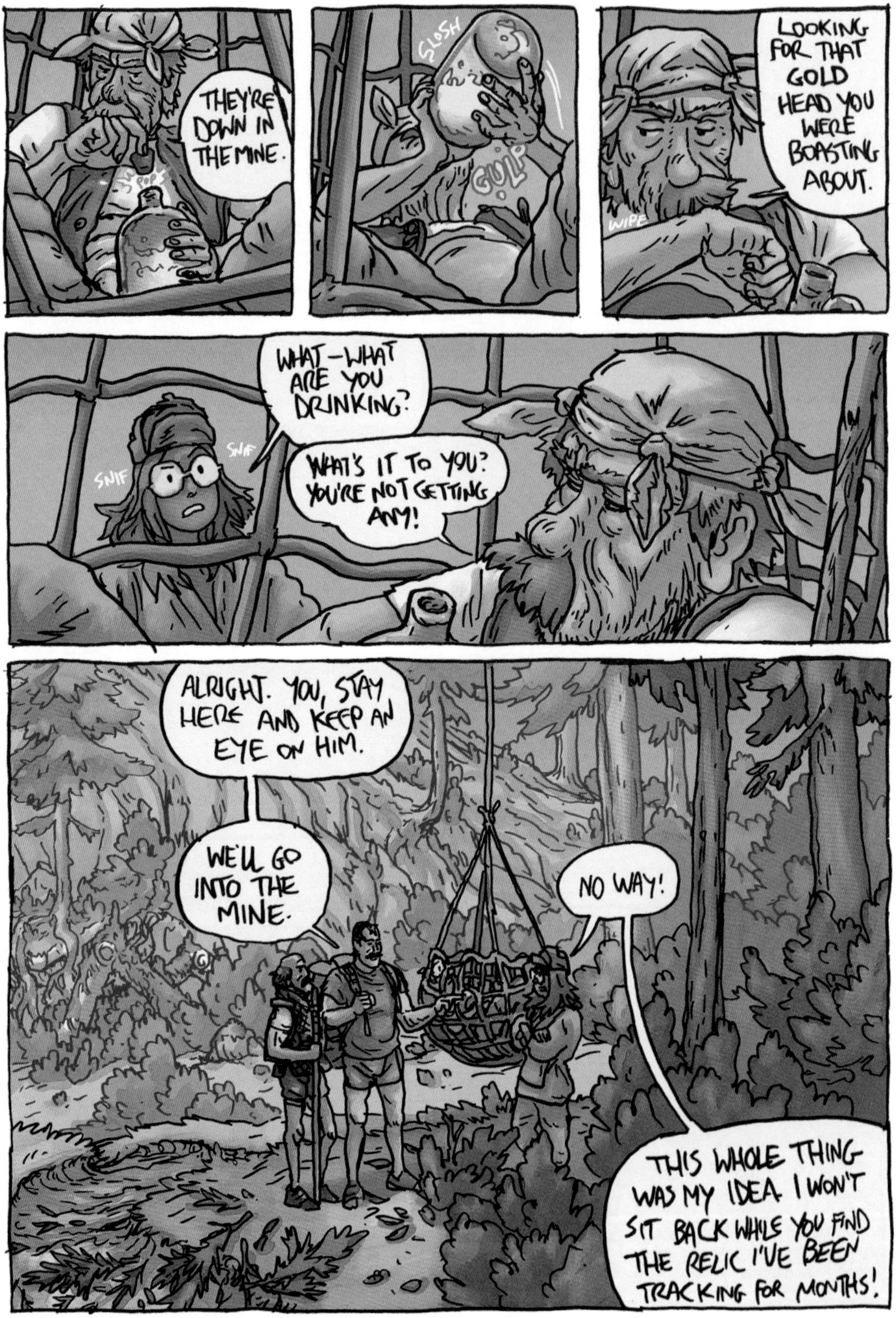
THEY'RE DOWN IN THE MINE.
POP
SLOSH
GULP
LOOKING FOR THAT GOLD HEAD YOU WERE BOASTING ABOUT.
WIPE
WHAT—WHAT ARE YOU DRINKING?
SNIF
SNIF
WHAT'S IT TO YOU? YOU'RE NOT GETTING ANY!
ALRIGHT. YOU, STAY HERE AND KEEP AN EYE ON HIM.
WE'LL GO INTO THE MINE.
NO WAY!
THIS WHOLE THING WAS MY IDEA. I WON'T SIT BACK WHILE YOU FIND THE RELIC I'VE BEEN TRACKING FOR MONTHS!

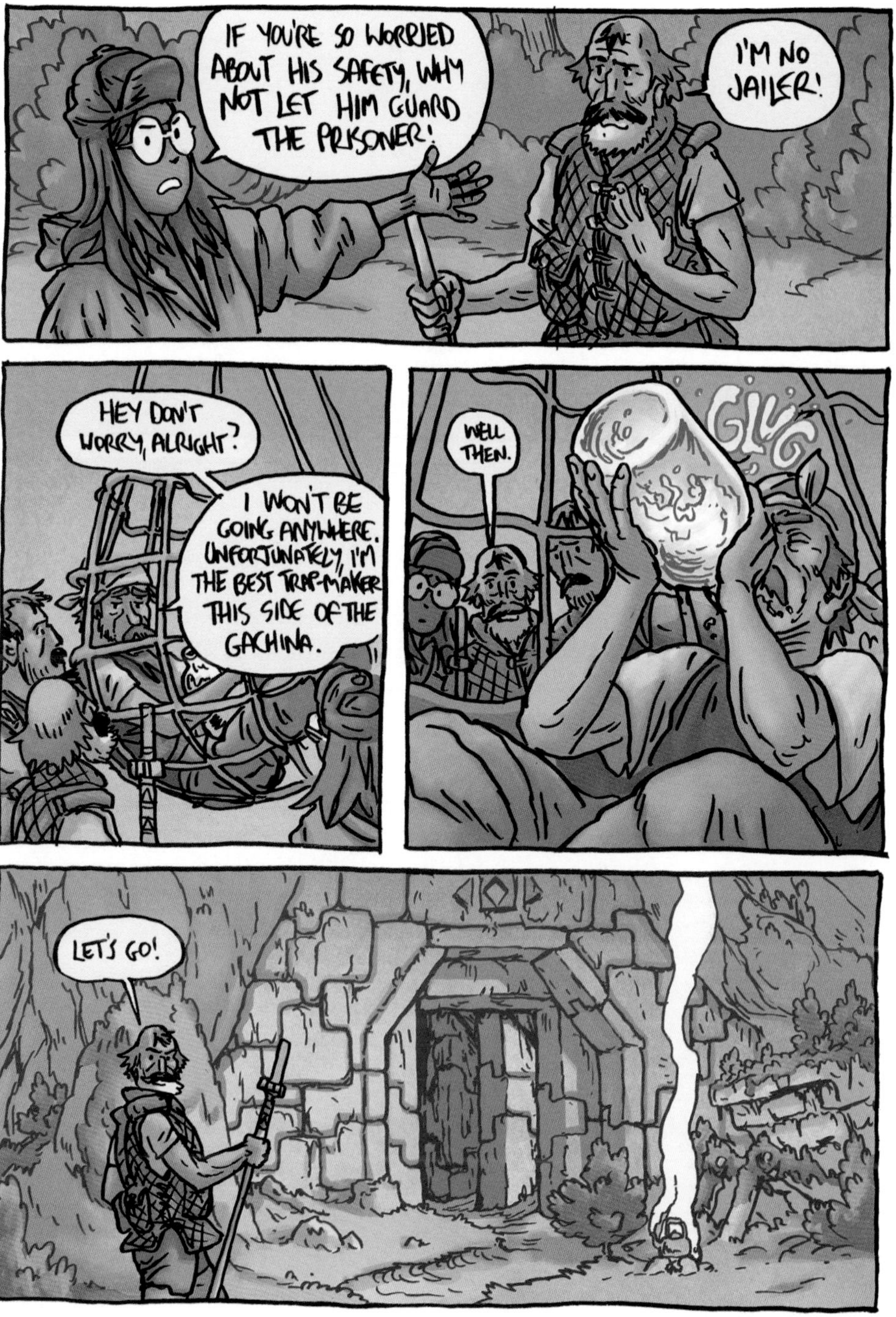

IF YOU'RE SO WORRIED ABOUT HIS SAFETY, WHY NOT LET HIM GUARD THE PRISONER!
I'M NO JAILER!
HEY DON'T WORRY, ALRIGHT?
I WON'T BE GOING ANYWHERE. UNFORTUNATELY, I'M THE BEST TRAP-MAKER THIS SIDE OF THE GACHINA.
WELL THEN.
GLUG
LET'S GO!

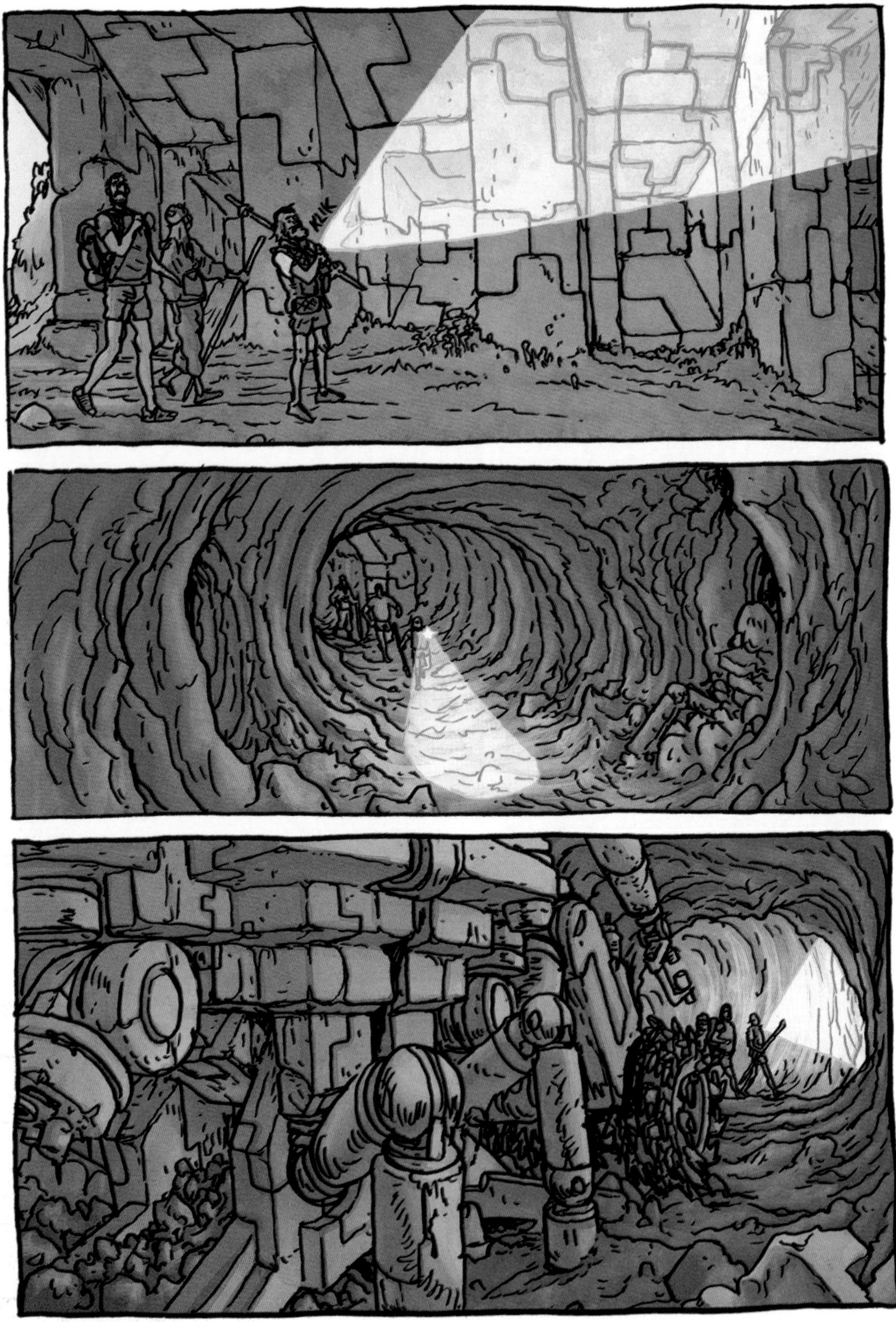
KLIK

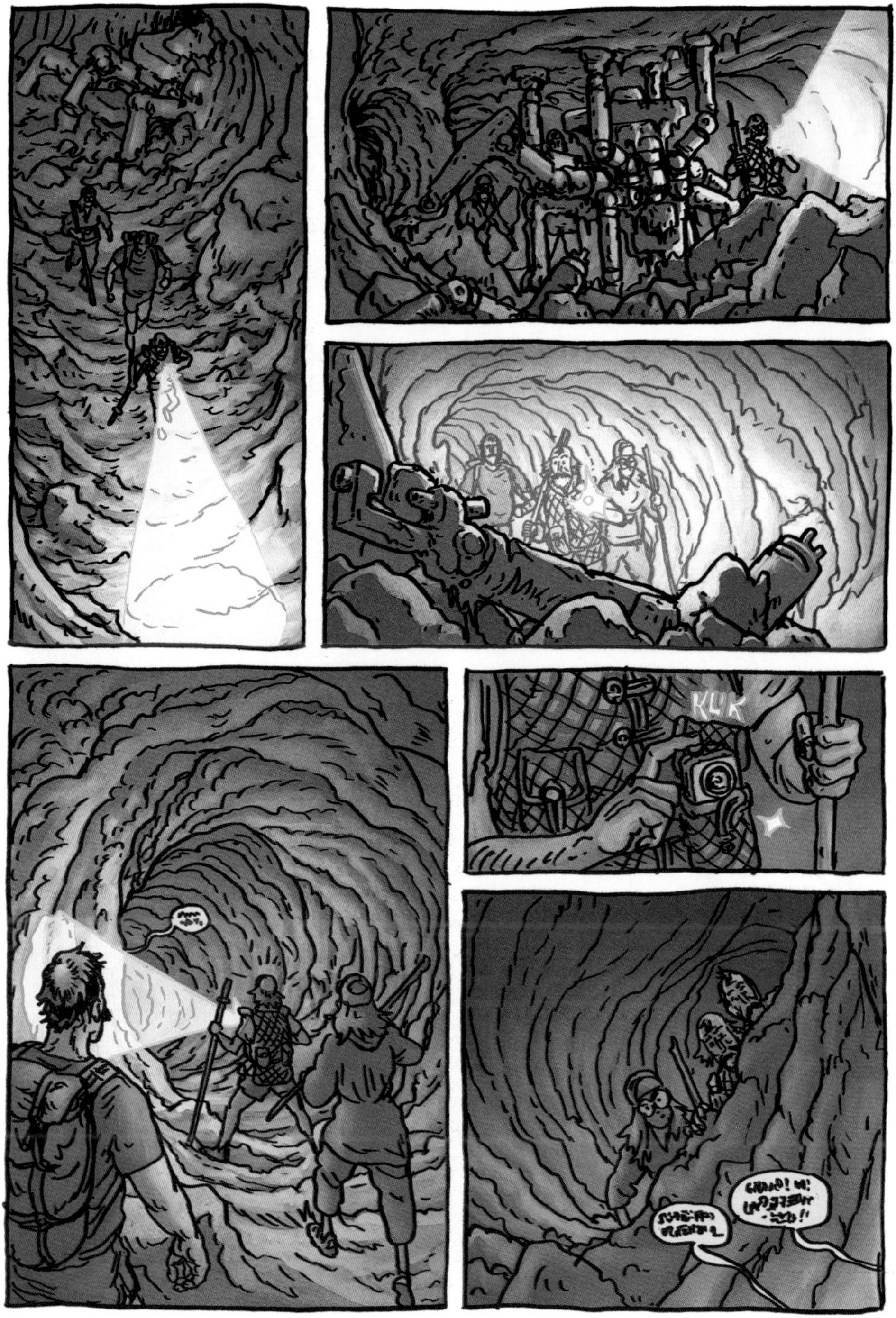
KLIK

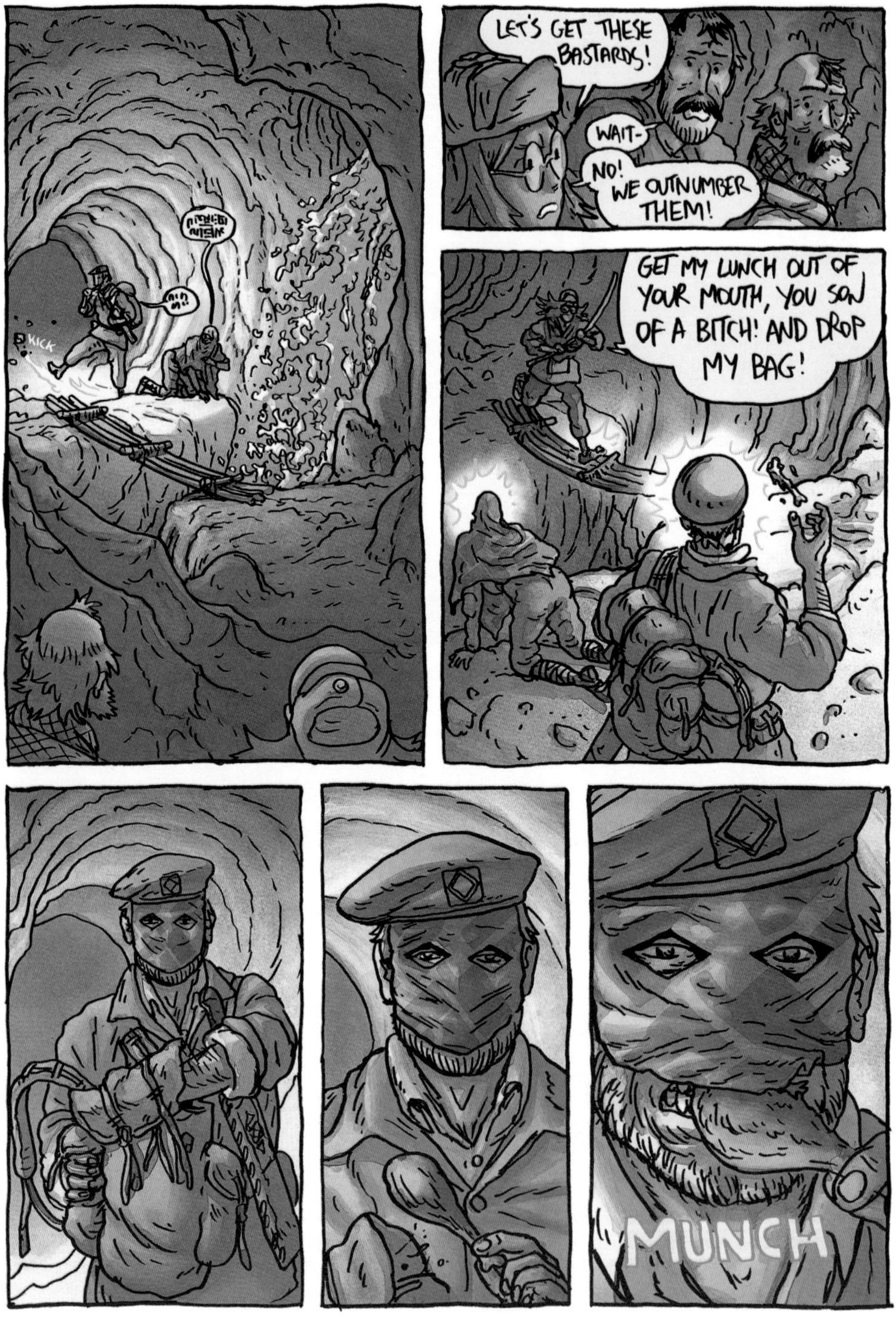
KICK
LET'S GET THESE BASTARDS!
WAIT-
NO! WE OUTNUMBER THEM!
GET MY LUNCH OUT OF YOUR MOUTH, YOU SON OF A BITCH! AND DROP MY BAG!
MUNCH

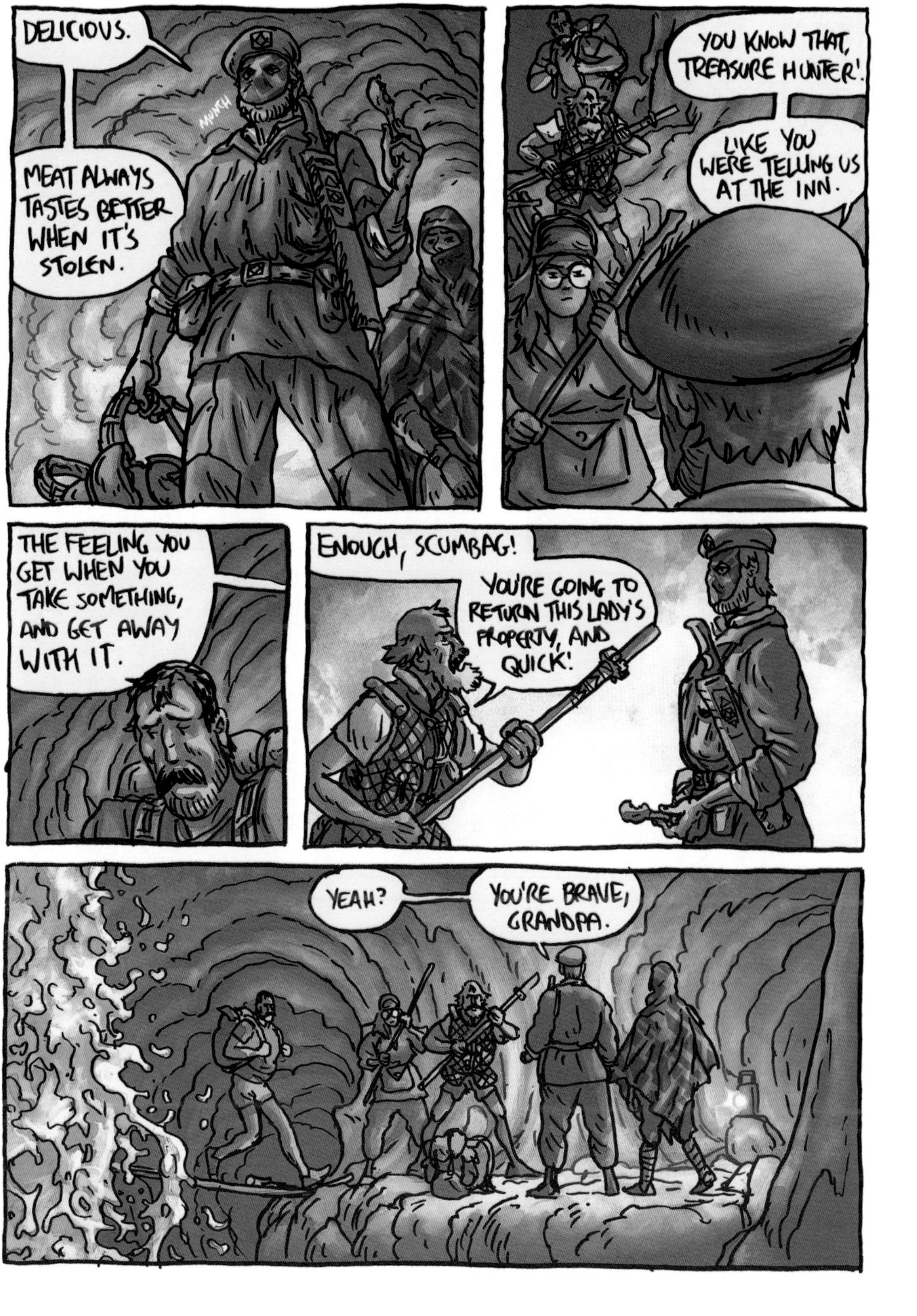
DELICIOUS.
MUNCH
MEAT ALWAYS TASTES BETTER WHEN IT'S STOLEN.
YOU KNOW THAT, TREASURE HUNTER!
LIKE YOU WERE TELLING US AT THE INN.
THE FEELING YOU GET WHEN YOU TAKE SOMETHING, AND GET AWAY WITH IT.
ENOUGH, SCUMBAG!
YOU'RE GOING TO RETURN THIS LADY'S PROPERTY, AND QUICK!
YEAH?
YOU'RE BRAVE, GRANDPA.

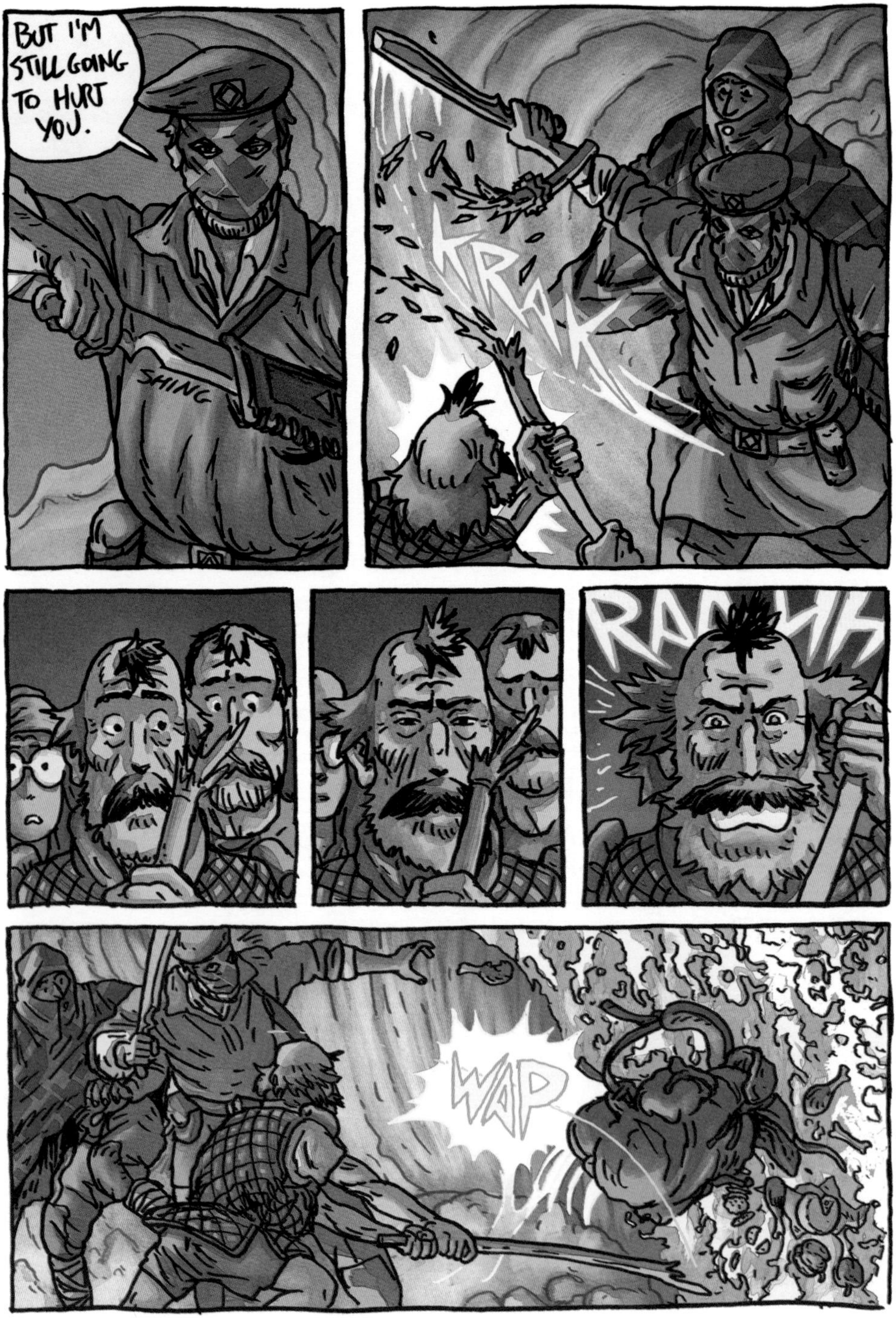
BUT I'M STILL GOING TO HURT YOU.
SHING
KRAK
RAAAH
WAP

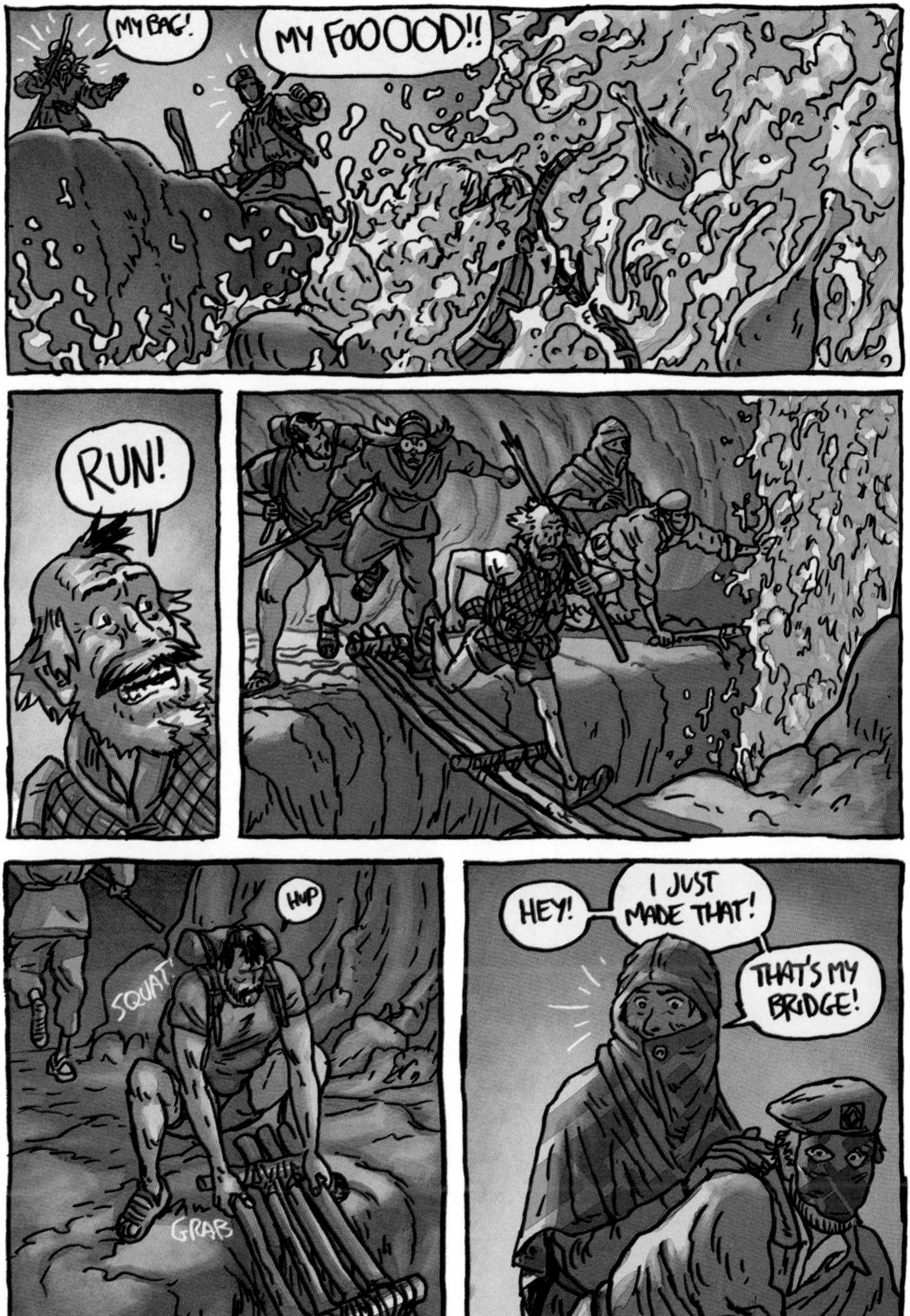
MY BAG!
MY FOOOOD!!
RUN!
HUP
SQUAT!
GRAB
HEY!
I JUST MADE THAT!
THAT'S MY BRIDGE!

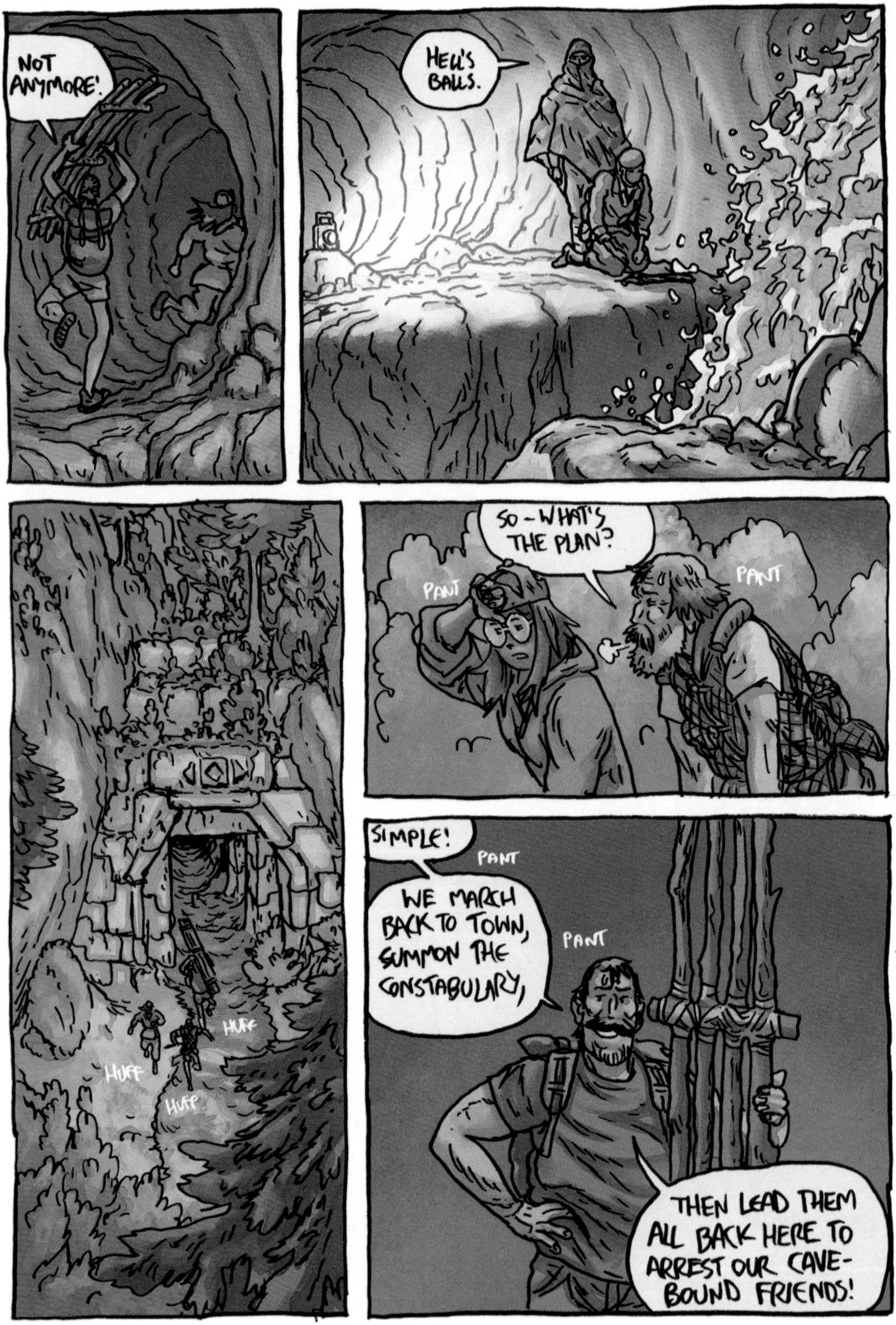
NOT ANYMORE!
HELL'S BALLS.
HUFF
HUFF
HUFF
SO - WHAT'S THE PLAN?
PANT
PANT
SIMPLE!
PANT
WE MARCH BACK TO TOWN, SUMMON THE CONSTABULARY,
PANT
THEN LEAD THEM ALL BACK HERE TO ARREST OUR CAVE-BOUND FRIENDS!

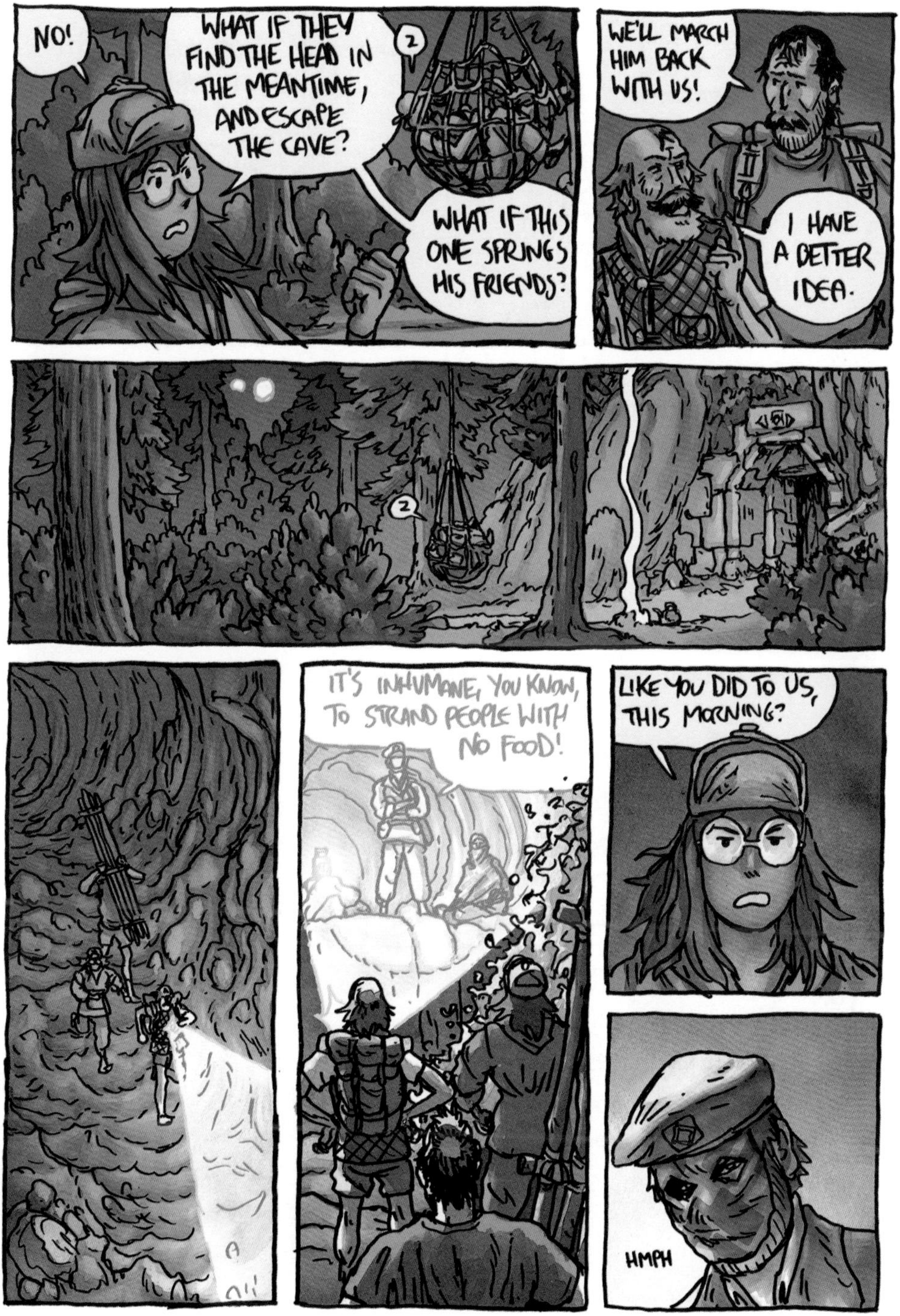
NO!
WHAT IF THEY FIND THE HEAD IN THE MEANTIME, AND ESCAPE THE CAVE?
?
WHAT IF THIS ONE SPRINGS HIS FRIENDS?
WE'LL MARCH HIM BACK WITH US!
I HAVE A BETTER IDEA.
?
IT'S INHUMANE, YOU KNOW, TO STRAND PEOPLE WITH NO FOOD!
LIKE YOU DID TO US, THIS MORNING?
HMPH

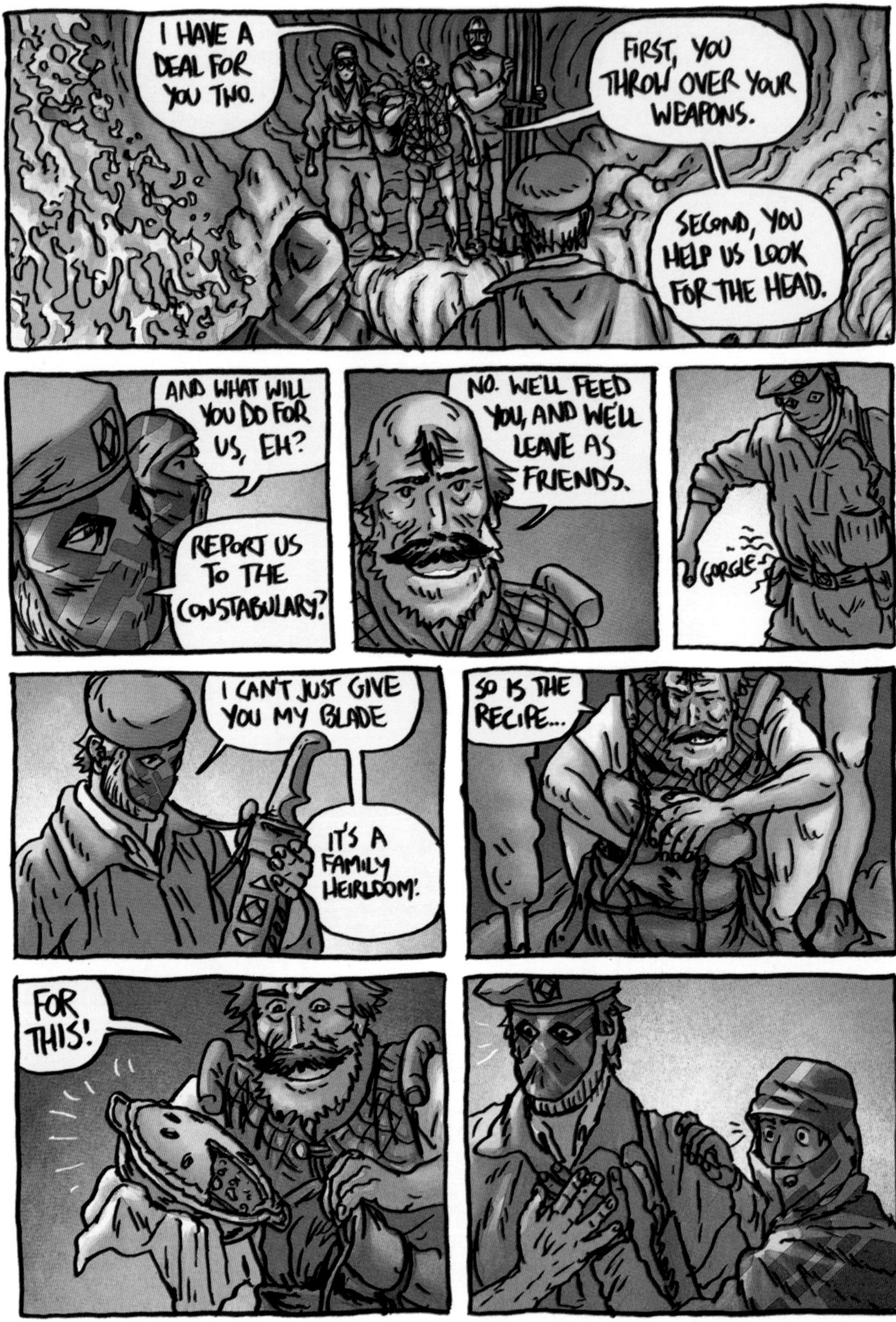
I HAVE A DEAL FOR YOU TWO.
FIRST, YOU THROW OVER YOUR WEAPONS.
SECOND, YOU HELP US LOOK FOR THE HEAD.
AND WHAT WILL YOU DO FOR US, EH?
REPORT US TO THE CONSTABULARY?
NO. WE'LL FEED YOU, AND WE'LL LEAVE AS FRIENDS.
GORGLE
I CAN'T JUST GIVE YOU MY BLADE
IT'S A FAMILY HEIRLOOM!
SO IS THE RECIPE...
FOR THIS!

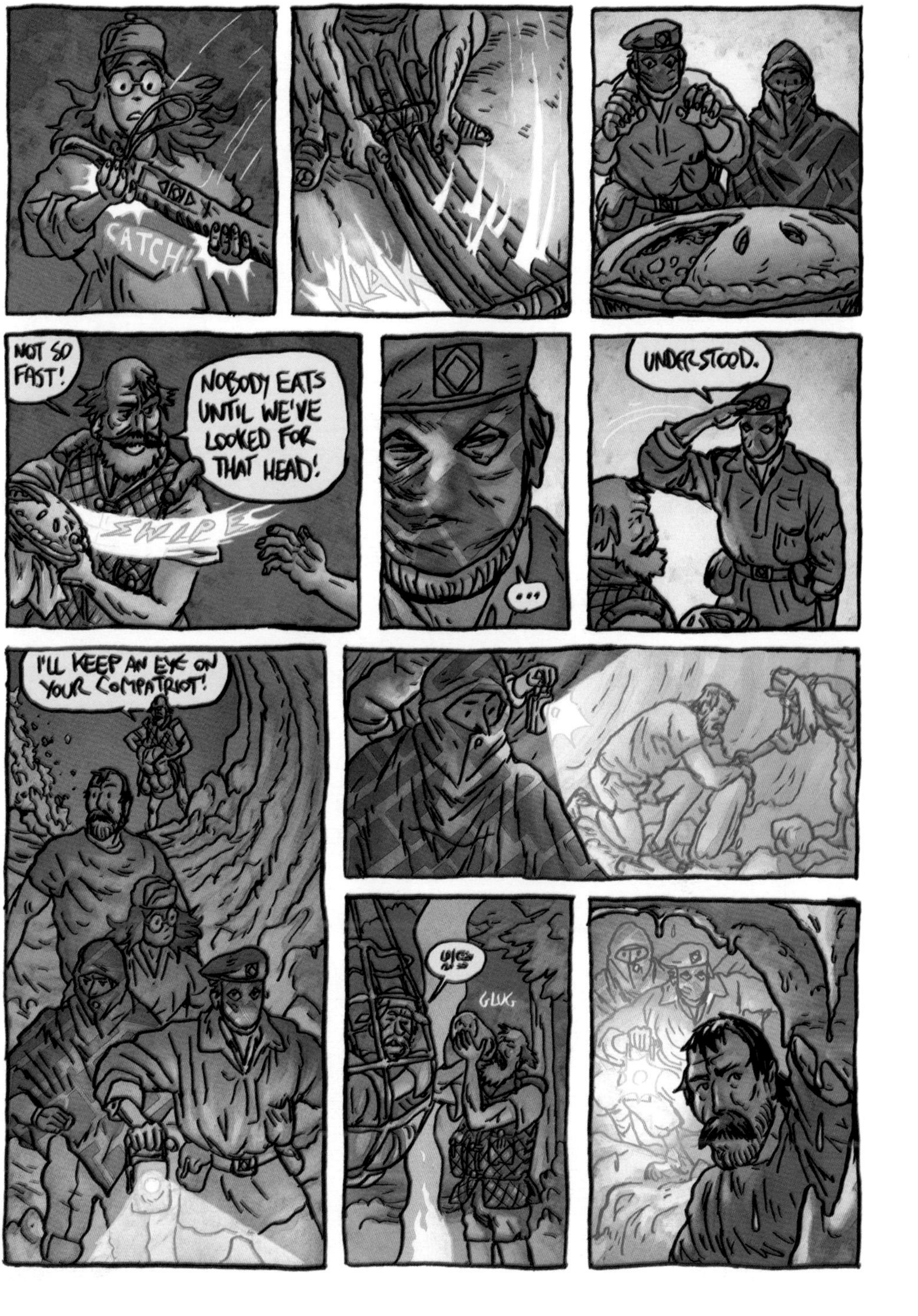
CATCH!
NOT SO FAST!
NOBODY EATS UNTIL WE'VE LOOKED FOR THAT HEAD!
SWIPE
...
UNDERSTOOD.
I'LL KEEP AN EYE ON YOUR COMPATRIOT!
GLUG

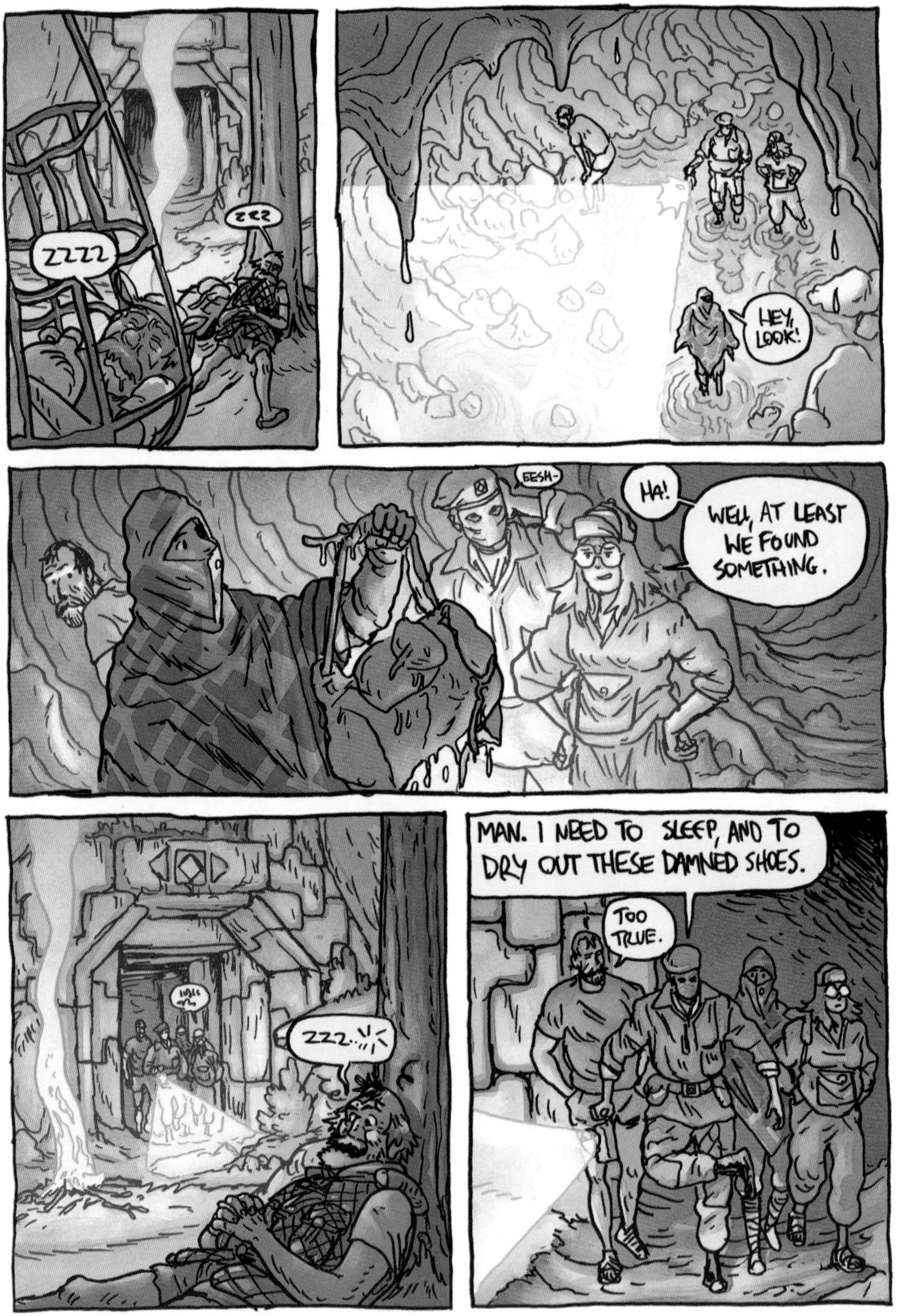
ZZZZ
ZZZ
HEY, LOOK!
EESH-
HA!
WELL, AT LEAST WE FOUND SOMETHING.
ZZZ..
MAN. I NEED TO SLEEP, AND TO DRY OUT THESE DAMNED SHOES.
TOO TRUE.

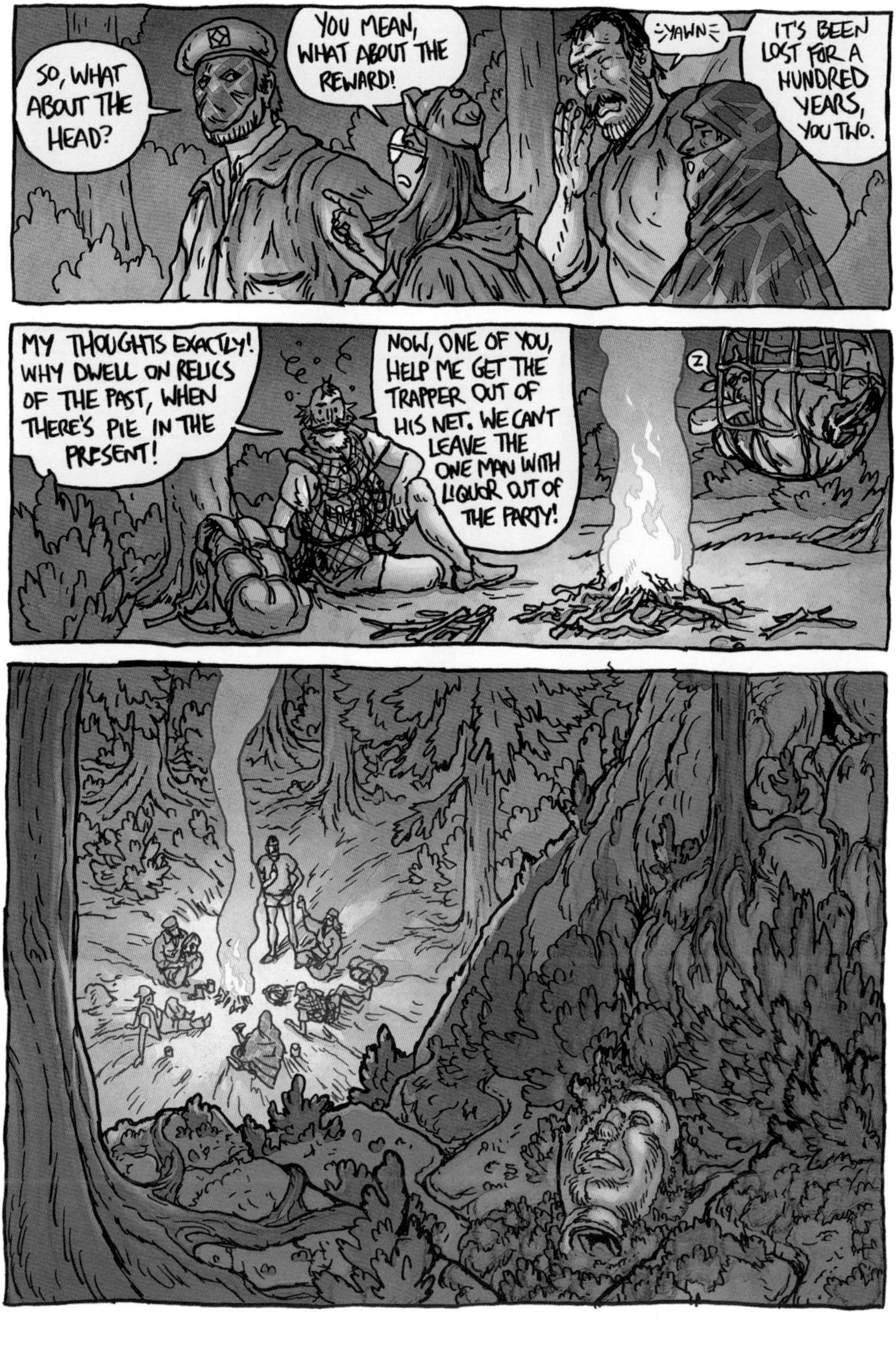

SO, WHAT ABOUT THE HEAD?
YOU MEAN, WHAT ABOUT THE REWARD!
=YAWN=
IT'S BEEN LOST FOR A HUNDRED YEARS, YOU TWO.
MY THOUGHTS EXACTLY! WHY DWELL ON RELICS OF THE PAST, WHEN THERE'S PIE IN THE PRESENT!
NOW, ONE OF YOU, HELP ME GET THE TRAPPER OUT OF HIS NET. WE CAN'T LEAVE THE ONE MAN WITH LIQUOR OUT OF THE PARTY!
Z

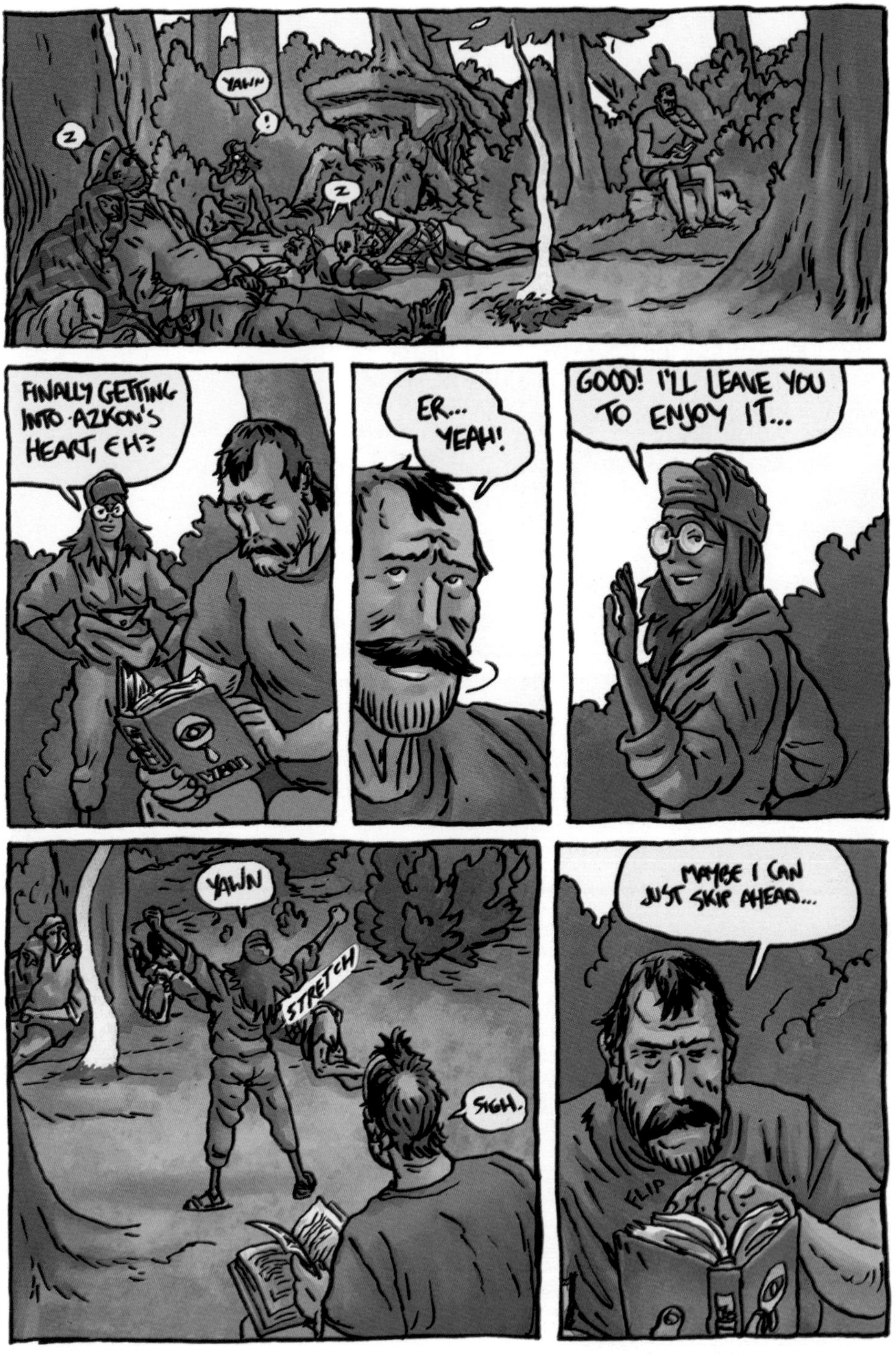
Z
YAWN
!
Z
FINALLY GETTING INTO AZKON'S HEART, EH?
ER... YEAH!
GOOD! I'LL LEAVE YOU TO ENJOY IT...
YAWN
STRETCH
SIGH.
MAYBE I CAN JUST SKIP AHEAD...
FLIP

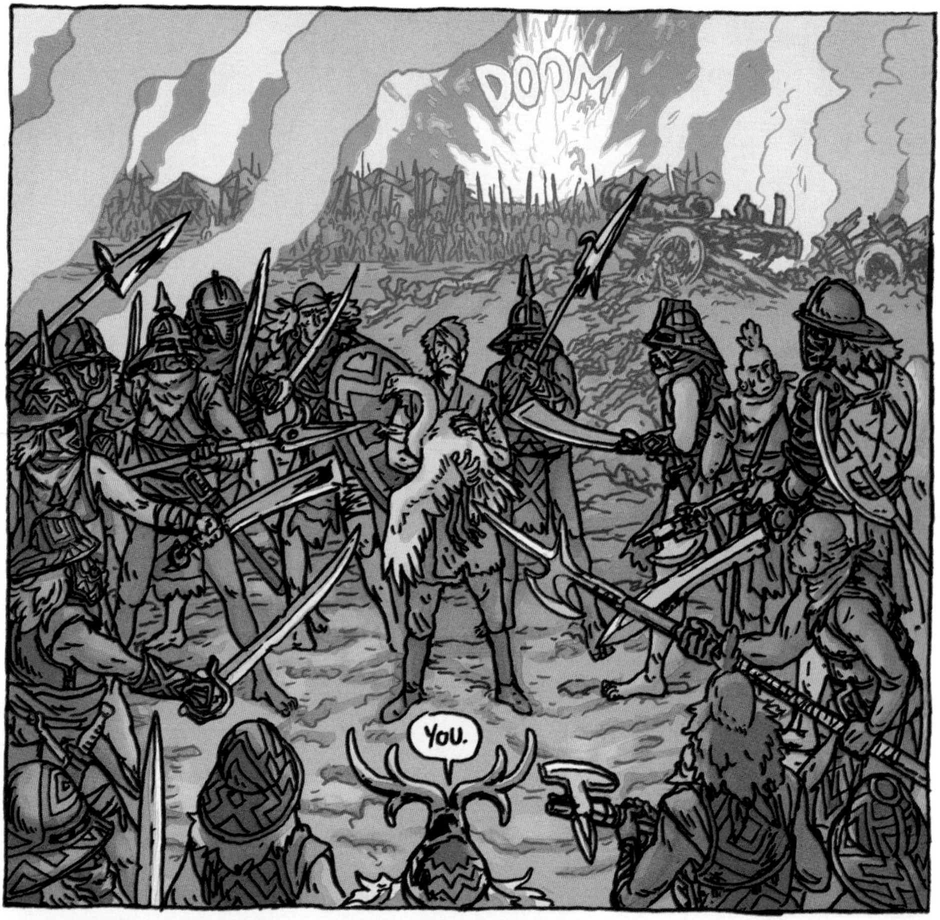
DOOM
YOU.

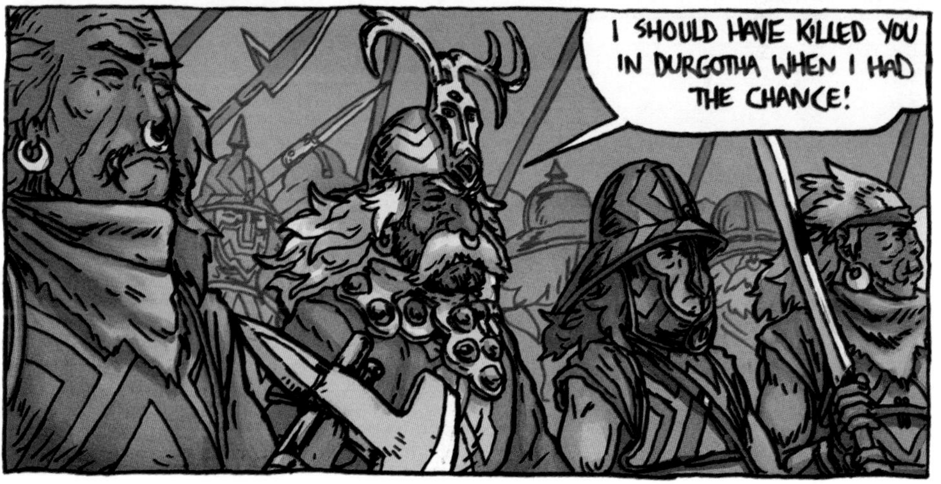
I SHOULD HAVE KILLED YOU IN DURGOTHA WHEN I HAD THE CHANCE!

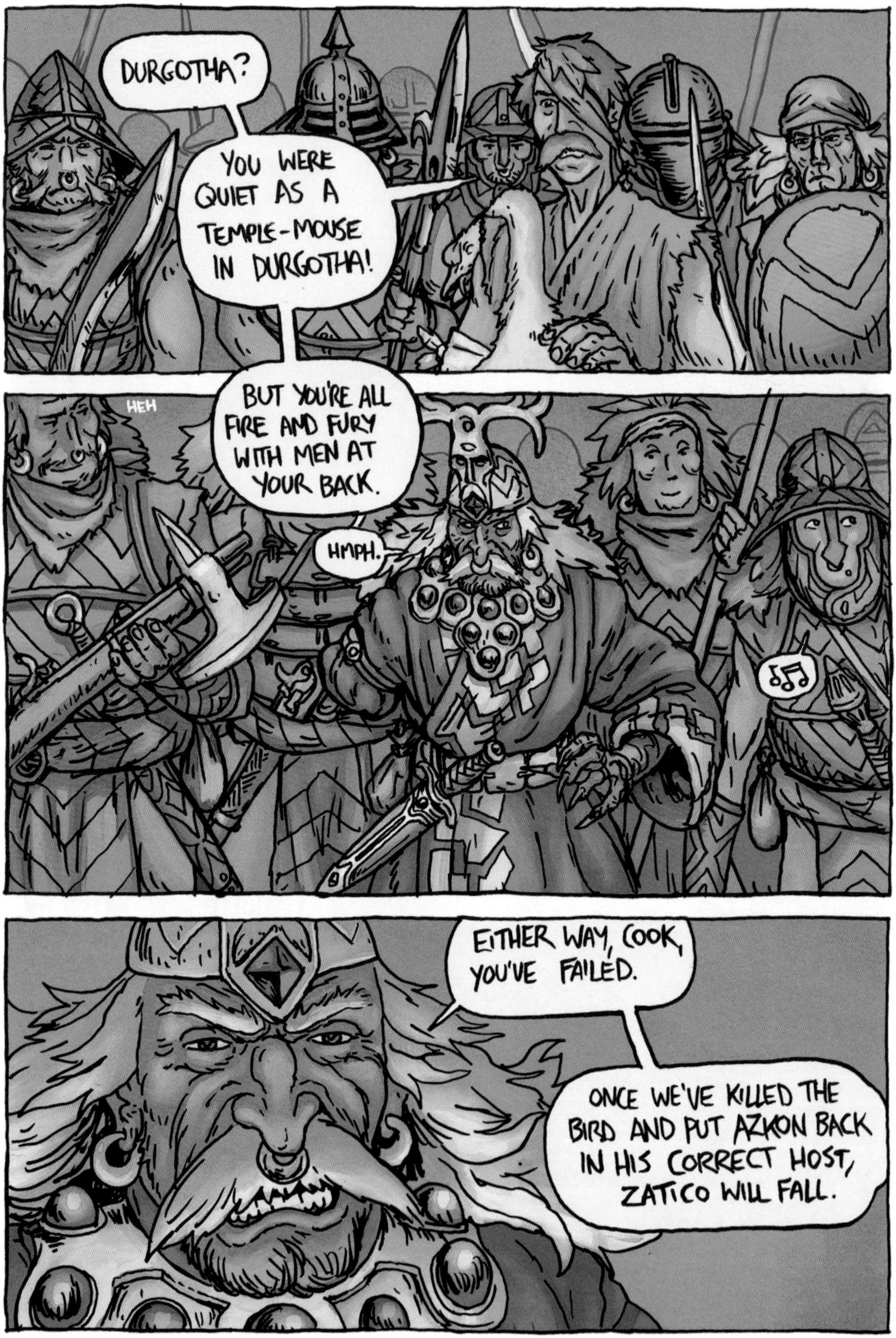
DURGOTHA?
YOU WERE QUIET AS A TEMPLE-MOUSE IN DURGOTHA!
BUT YOU'RE ALL FIRE AND FURY WITH MEN AT YOUR BACK.
HEH
HMPH.
EITHER WAY, COOK, YOU'VE FAILED.
ONCE WE'VE KILLED THE BIRD AND PUT AZKON BACK IN HIS CORRECT HOST, ZATICO WILL FALL.

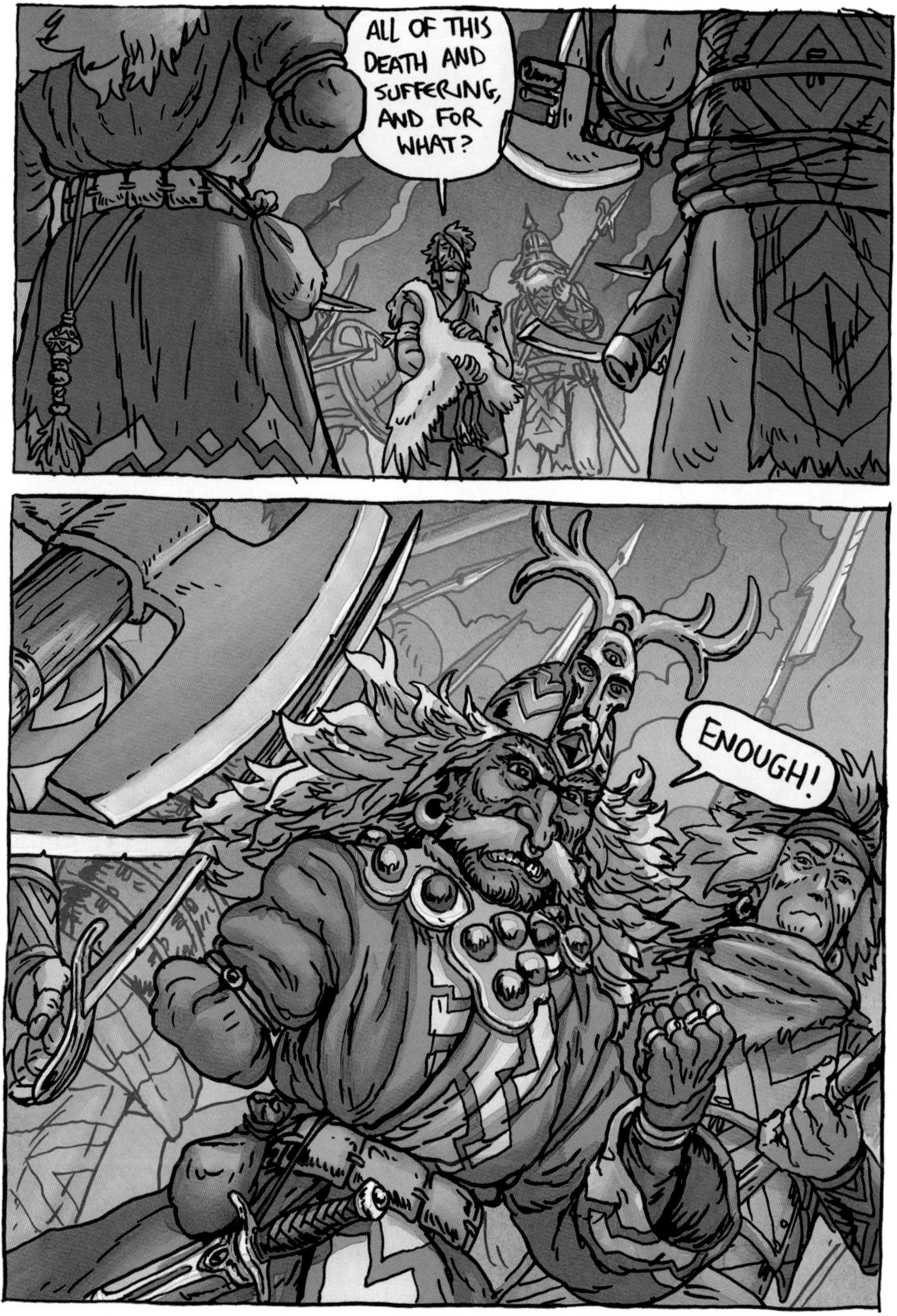
ALL OF THIS DEATH AND SUFFERING, AND FOR WHAT?
ENOUGH!

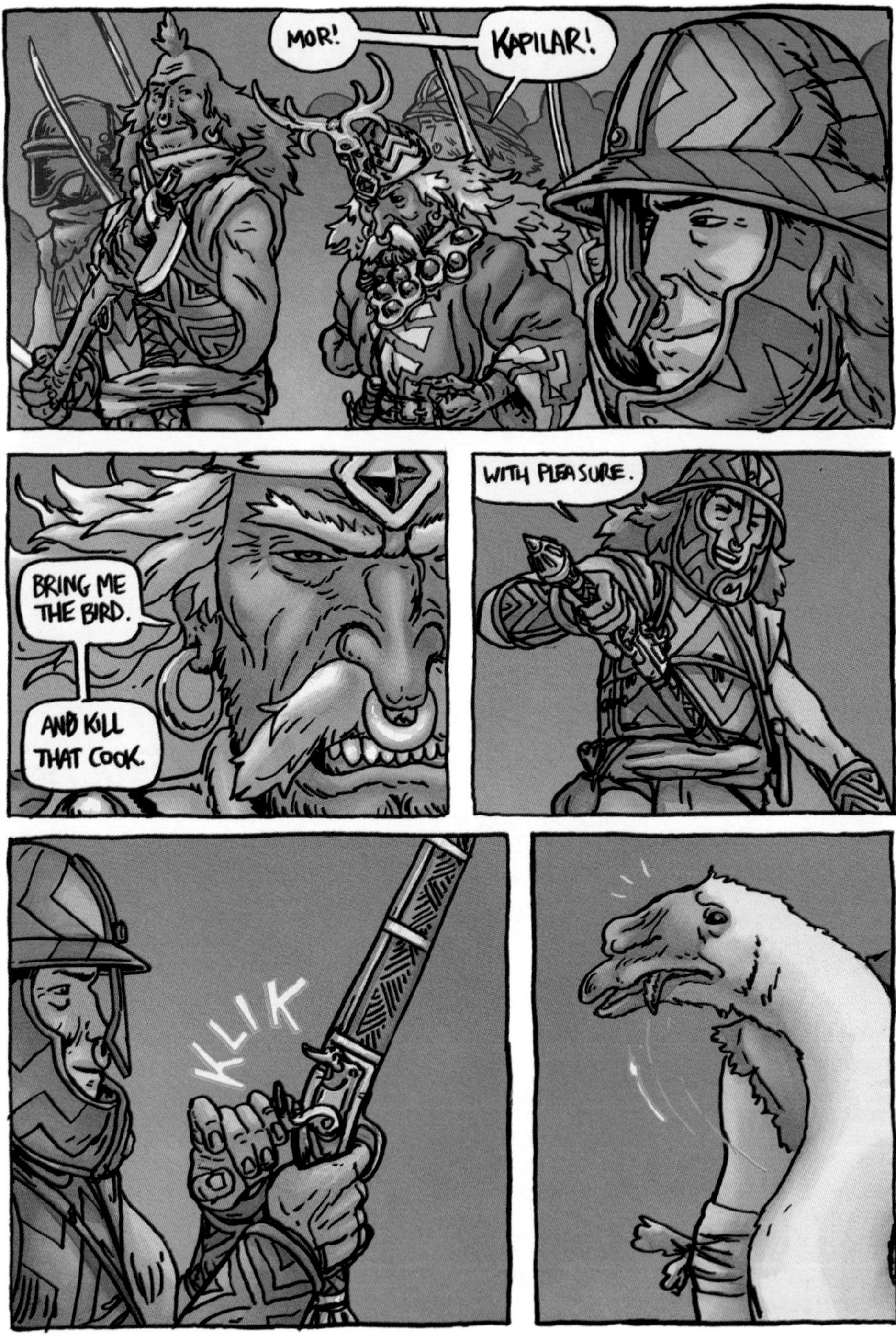
MOR!
KAPILAR!
BRING ME THE BIRD.
AND KILL THAT COOK.
WITH PLEASURE.
KLIK

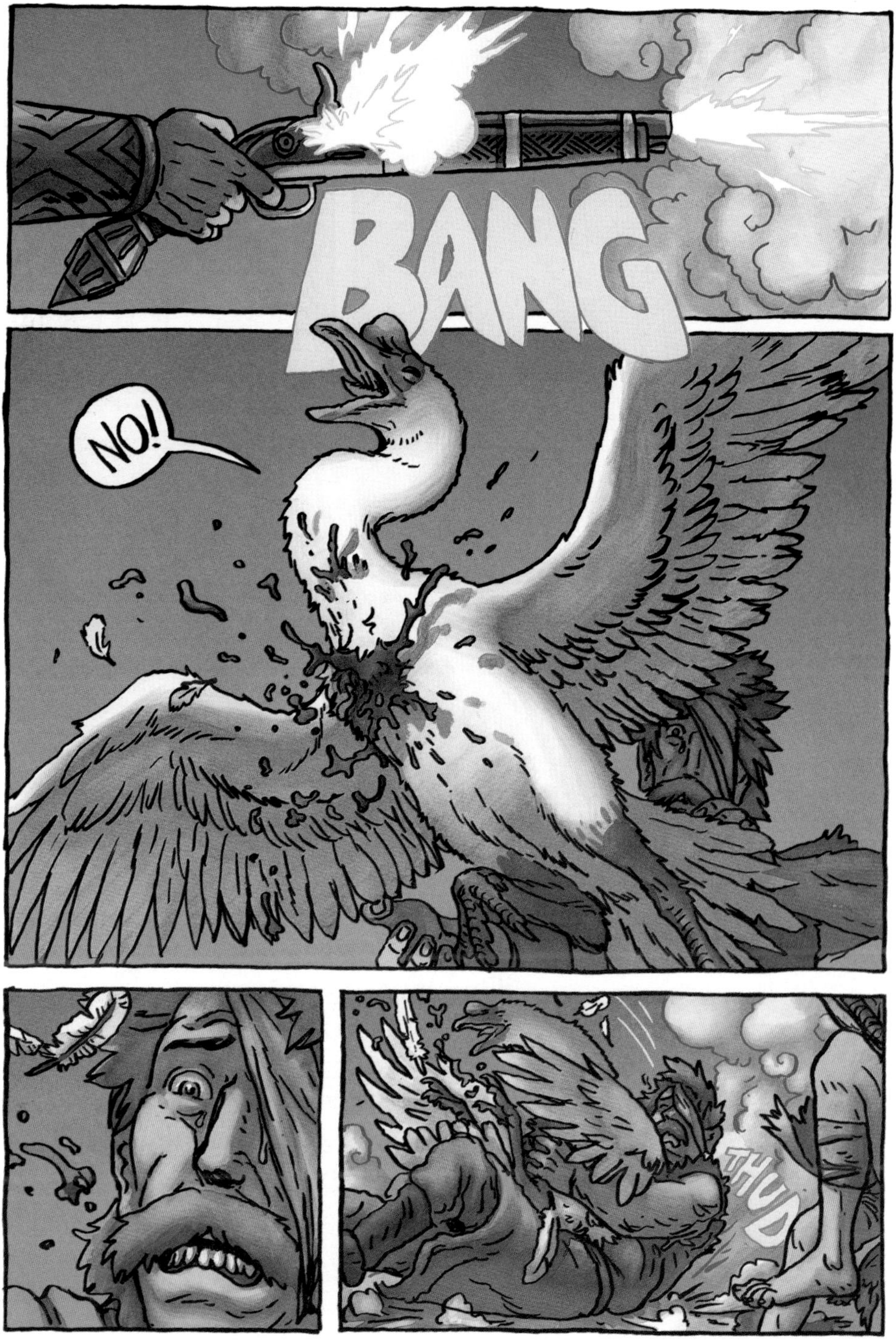
BANG
NO!
THUD

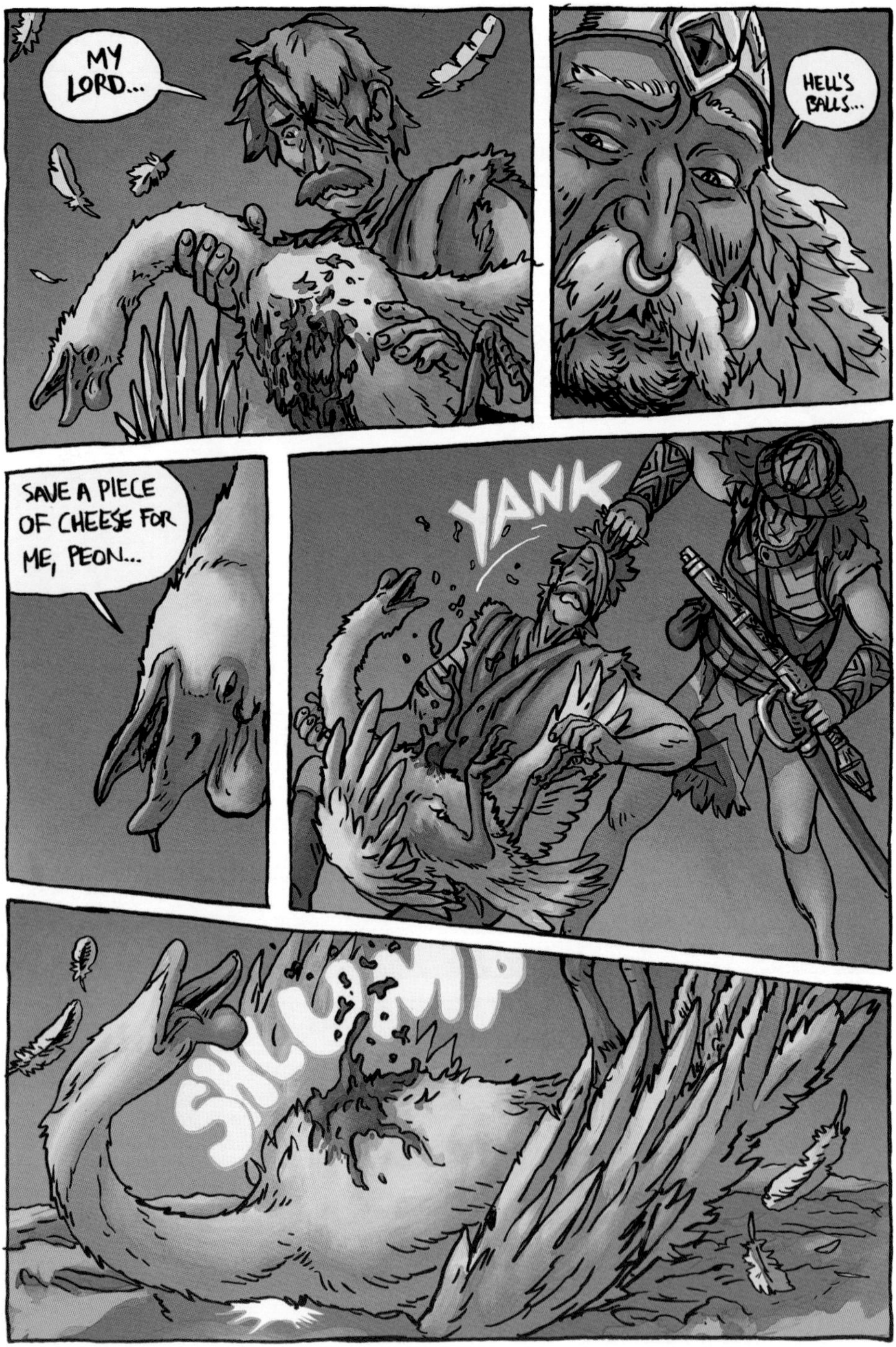
MY LORD...
HELL'S BALLS...
SAVE A PIECE OF CHEESE FOR ME, PEON...
YANK
SHLOMP

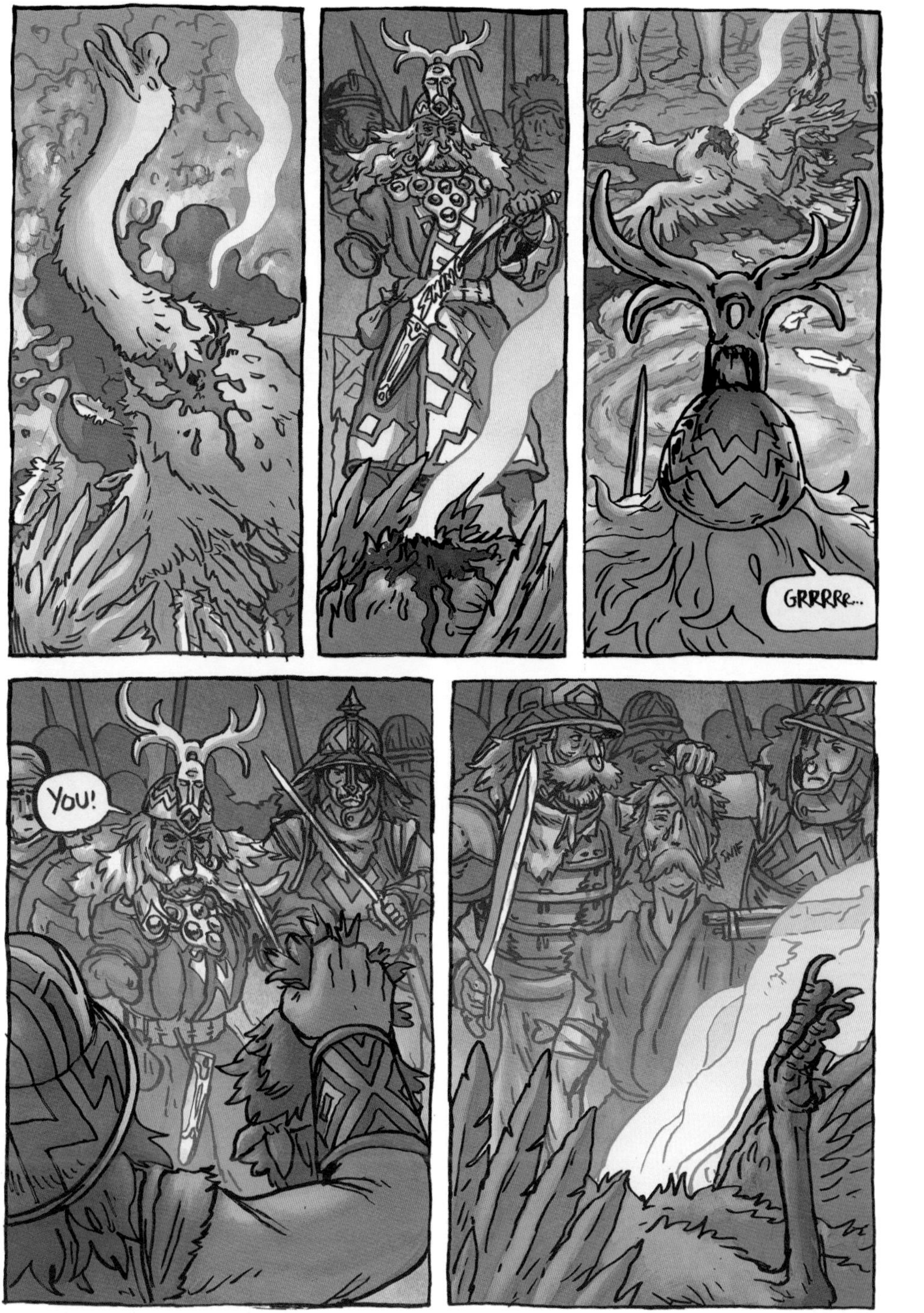
SWING
GRRRRr...
YOU!

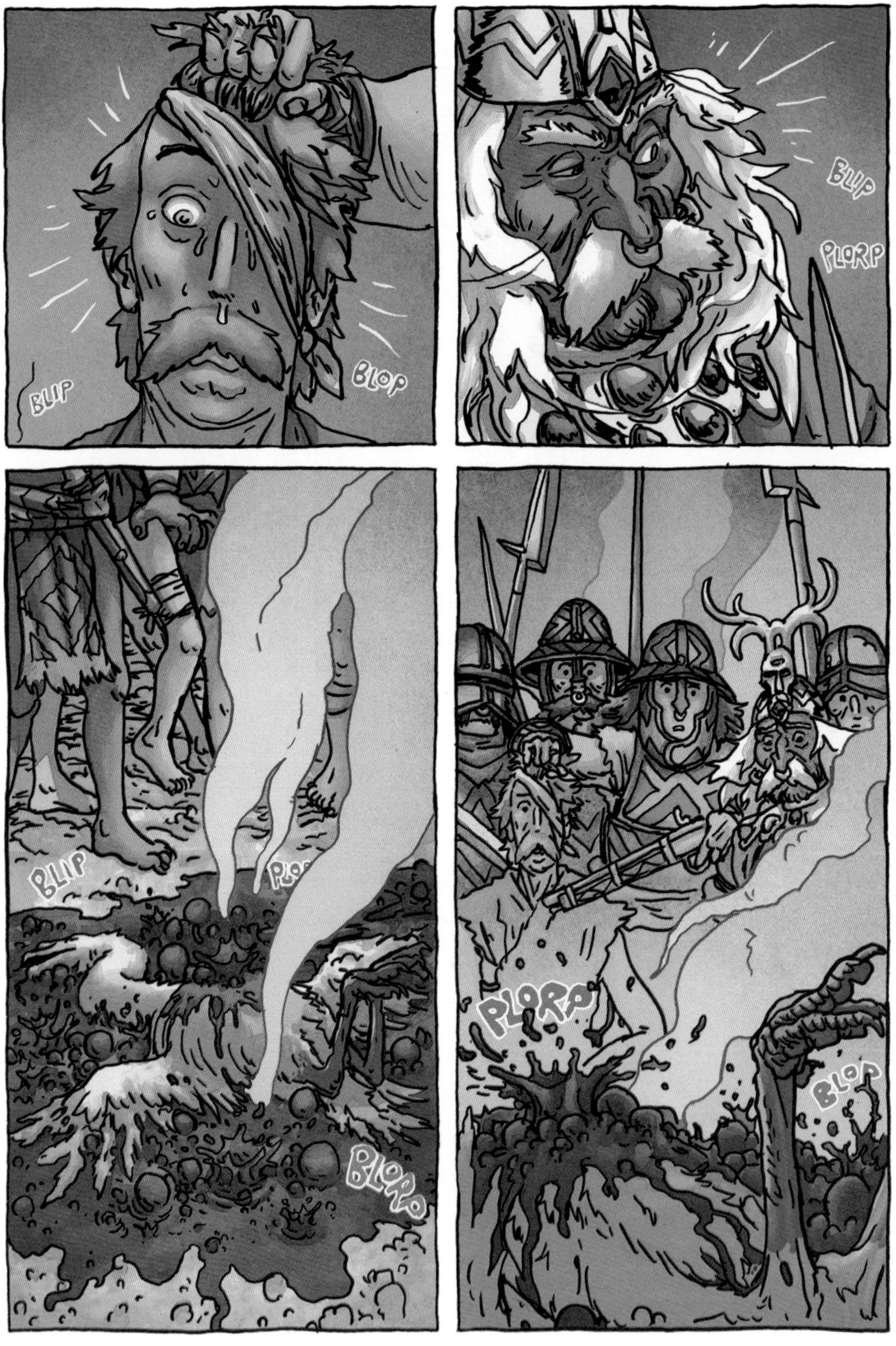
BLIP
BLOP
BLIP
PLORP
BLIP
BLORP
PLORP
BLOP

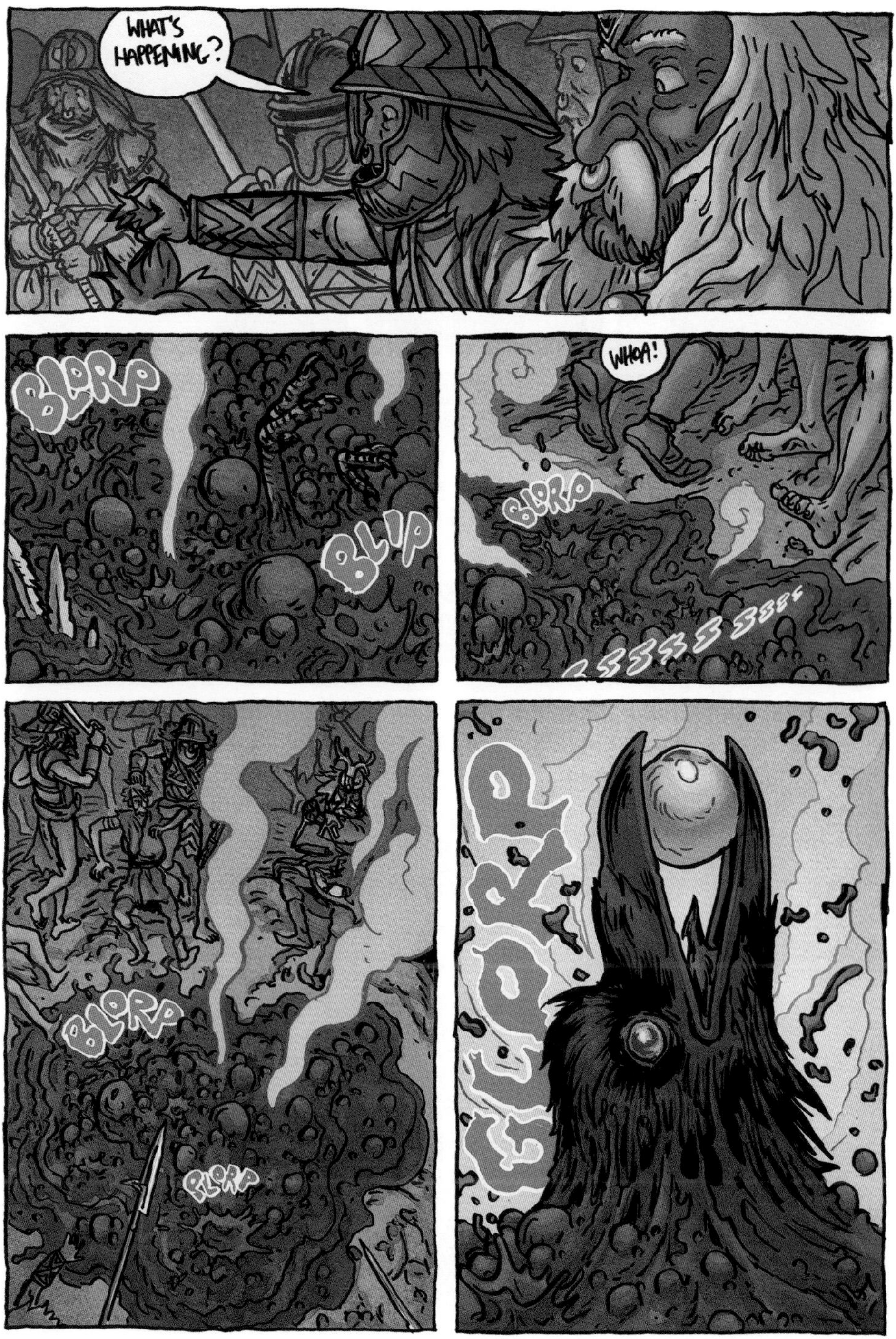
WHAT'S HAPPENING?
BLORP
BLIP
WHOA!
BLORP
SSSSSSSSSS
BLORP
BLORP
GLORP

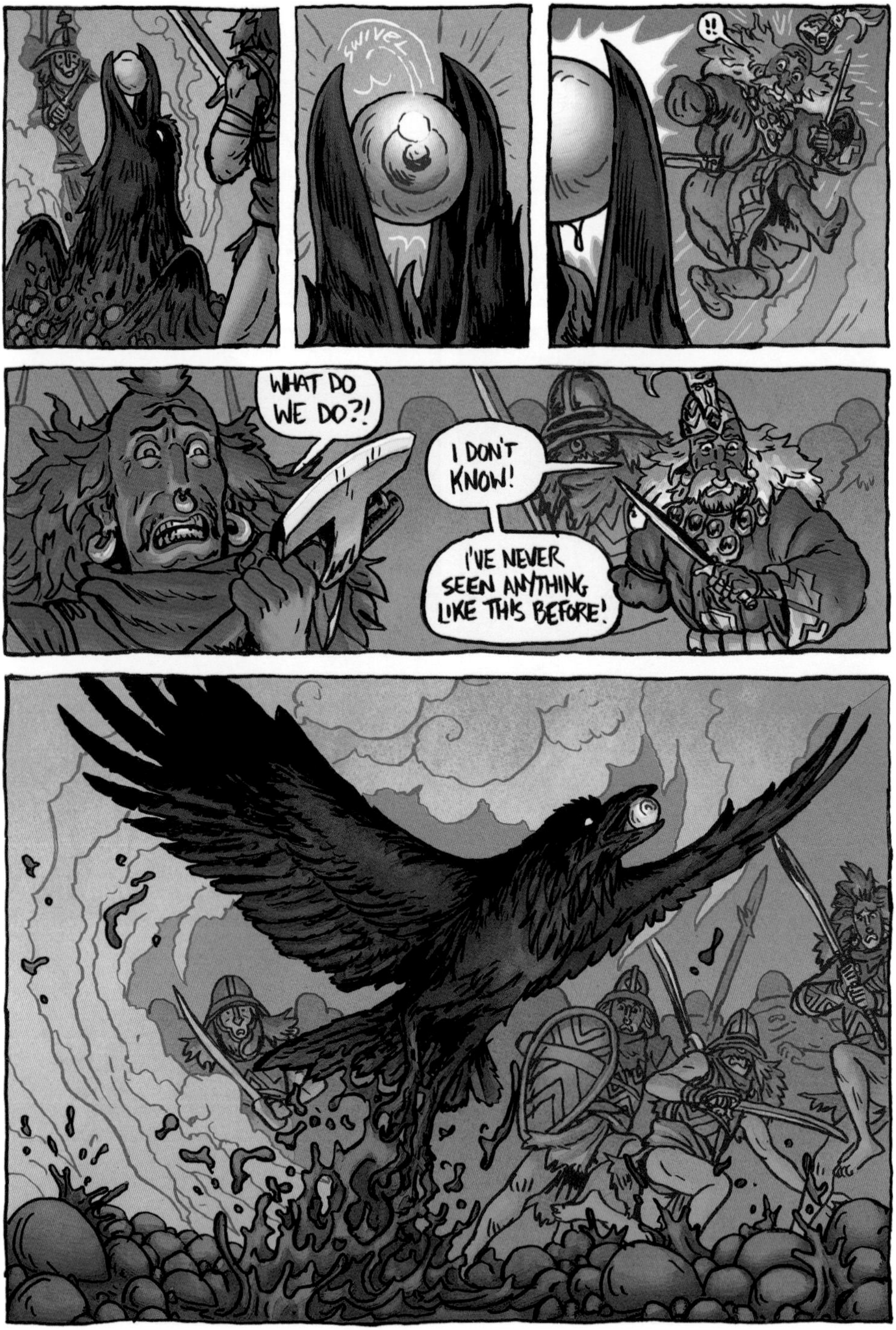
SWIVEL
!!
WHAT DO WE DO?!
I DON'T KNOW!
I'VE NEVER SEEN ANYTHING LIKE THIS BEFORE!

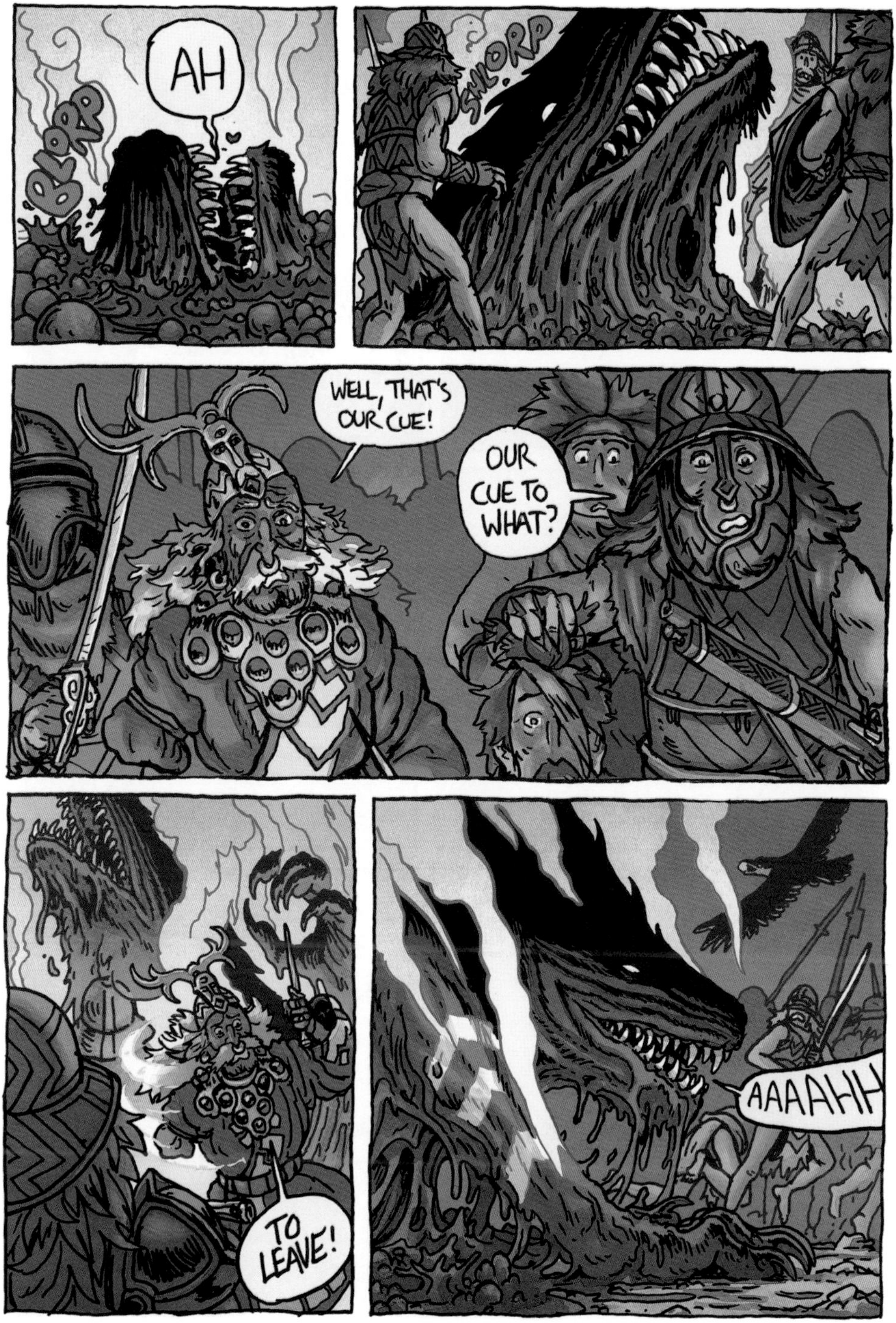
BLORP
AH
SHLORP
WELL, THAT'S OUR CUE!
OUR CUE TO WHAT?
TO LEAVE!
AAAAHH

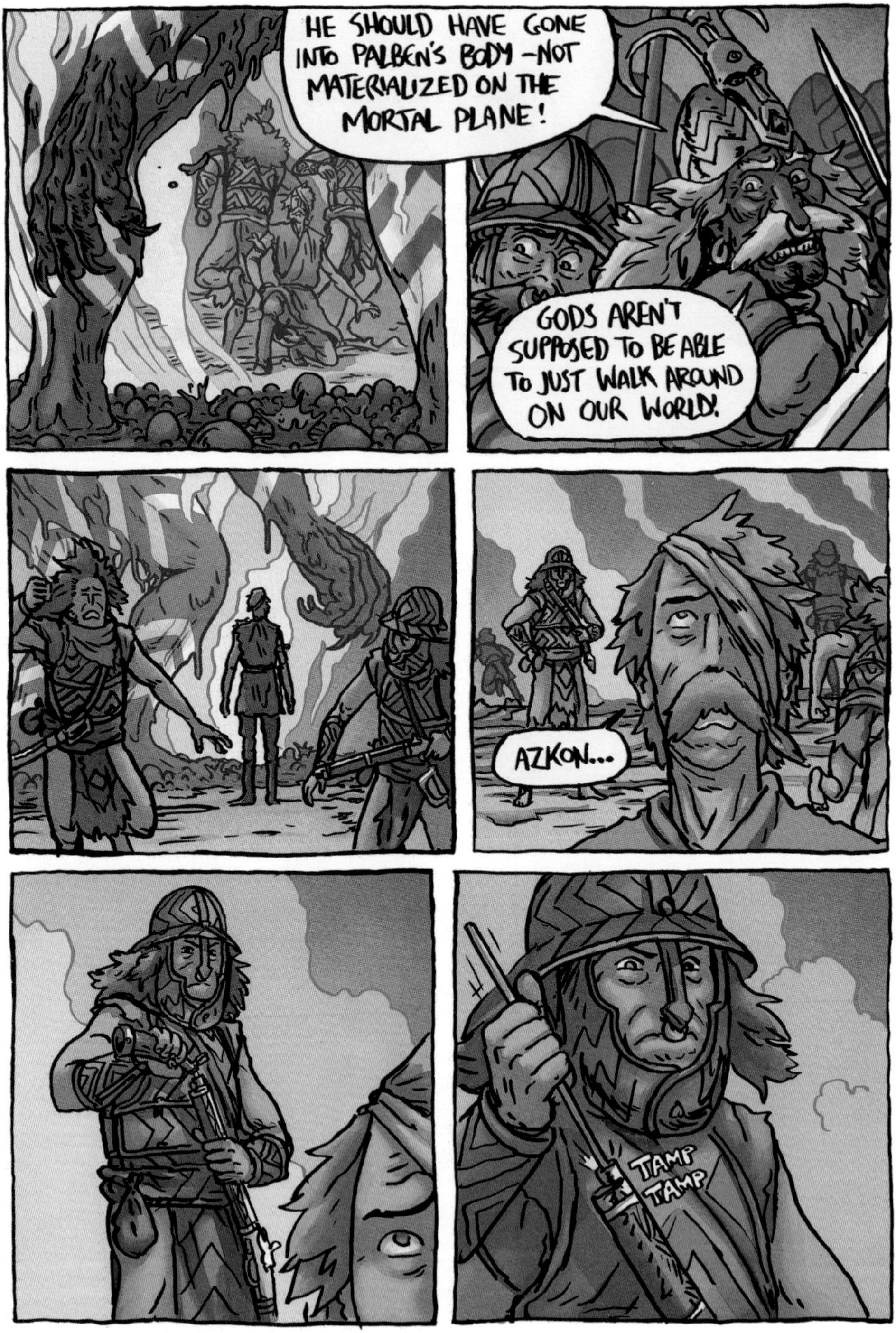
HE SHOULD HAVE GONE INTO PALBEN'S BODY —NOT MATERIALIZED ON THE MORTAL PLANE!
GODS AREN'T SUPPOSED TO BE ABLE TO JUST WALK AROUND ON OUR WORLD!
AZKON...
TAMP TAMP

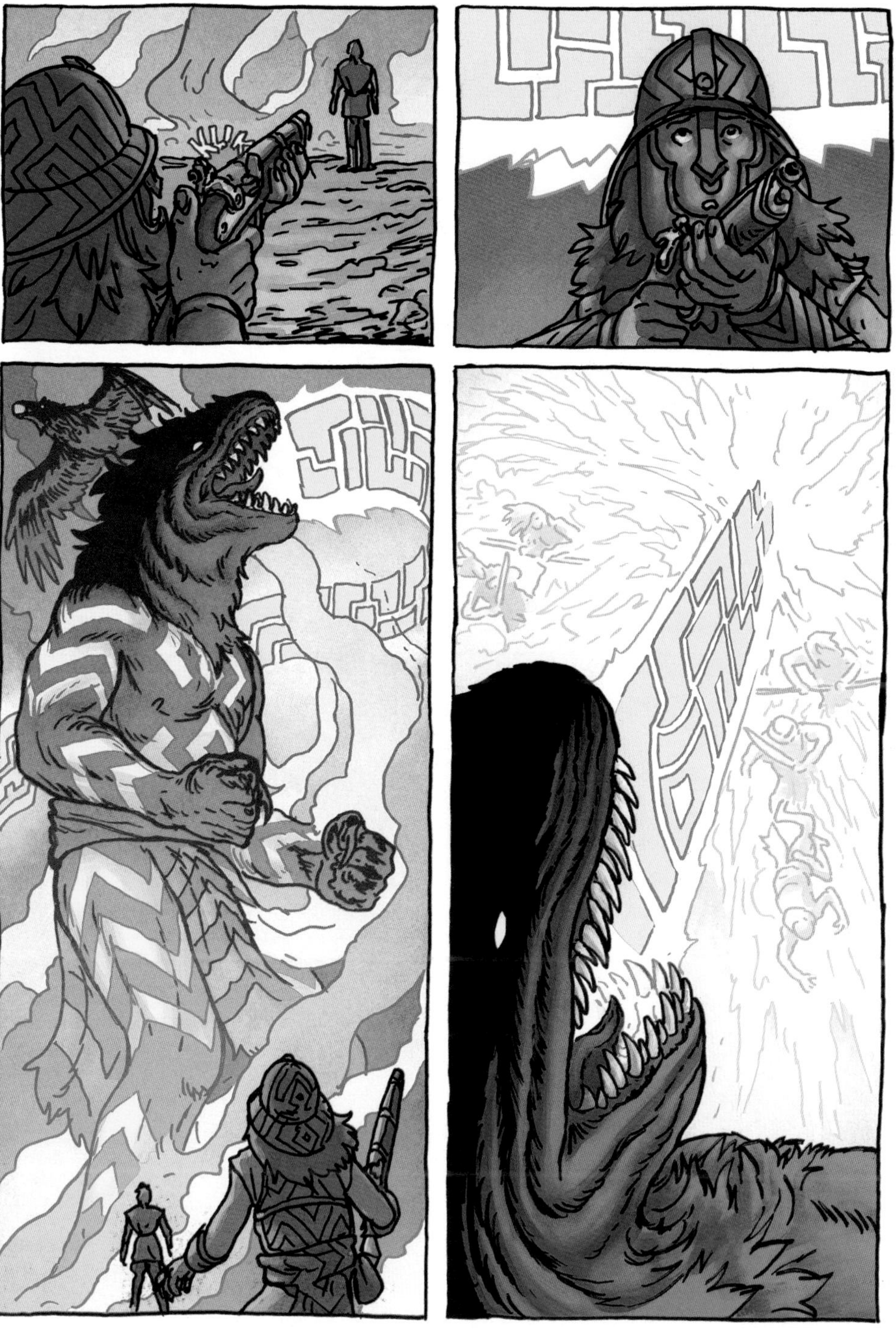
KLIK

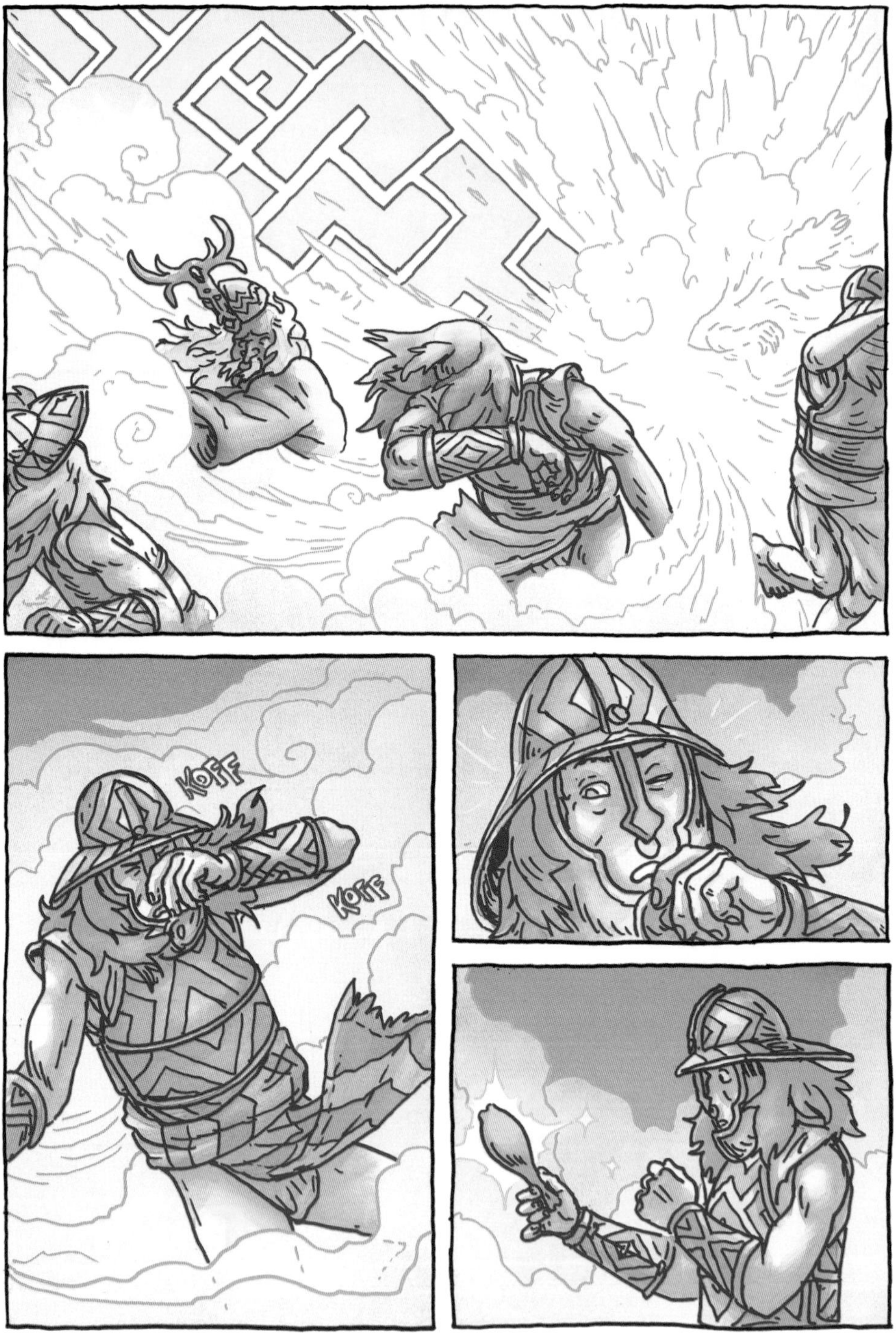
KOFF
KOFF

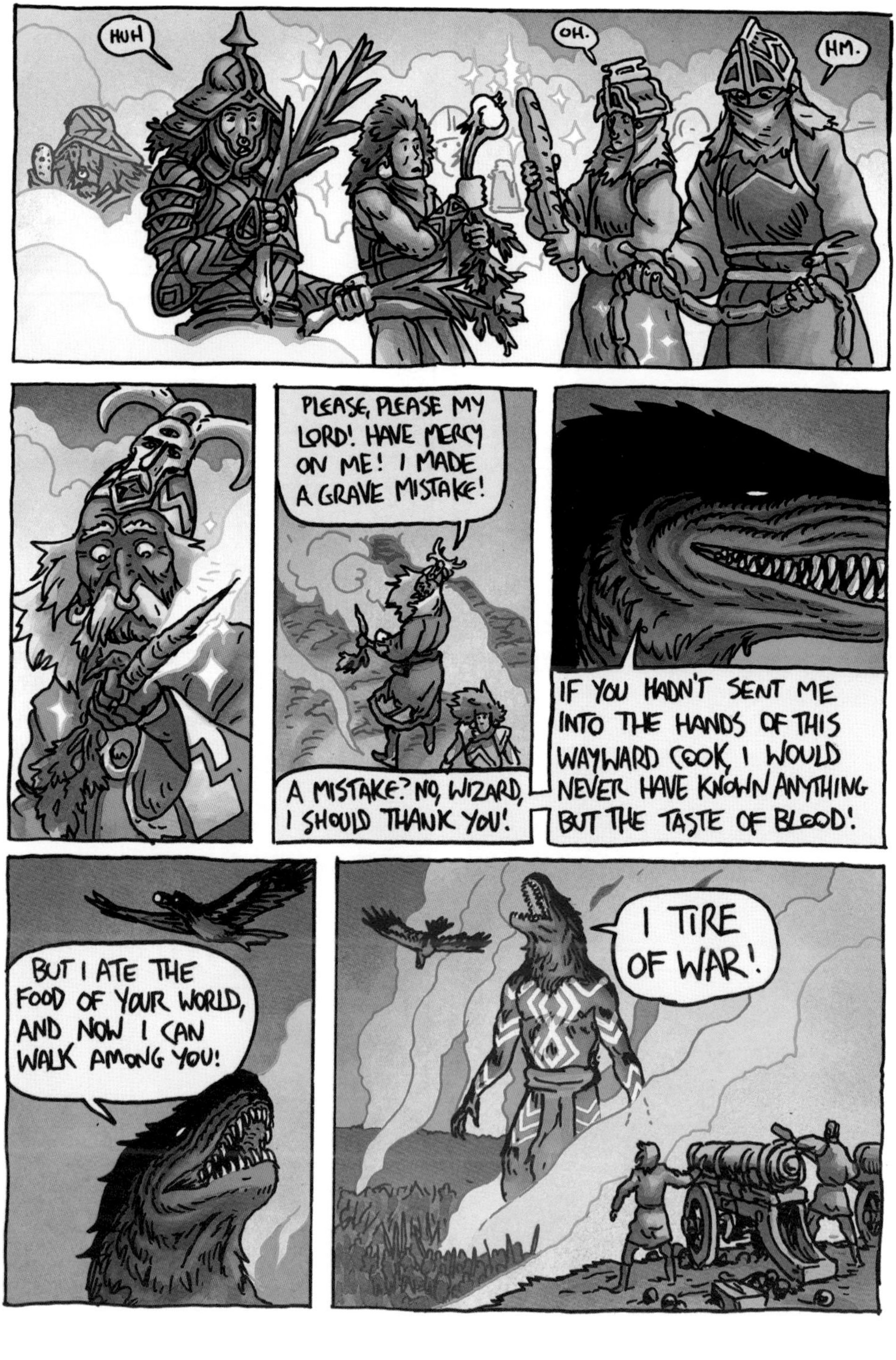
HUH
OH.
HM.
PLEASE, PLEASE MY LORD! HAVE MERCY ON ME! I MADE A GRAVE MISTAKE!
A MISTAKE? NO, WIZARD, I SHOULD THANK YOU!
IF YOU HADN'T SENT ME INTO THE HANDS OF THIS WAYWARD COOK, I WOULD NEVER HAVE KNOWN ANYTHING BUT THE TASTE OF BLOOD!
BUT I ATE THE FOOD OF YOUR WORLD, AND NOW I CAN WALK AMONG YOU!
I TIRE OF WAR!

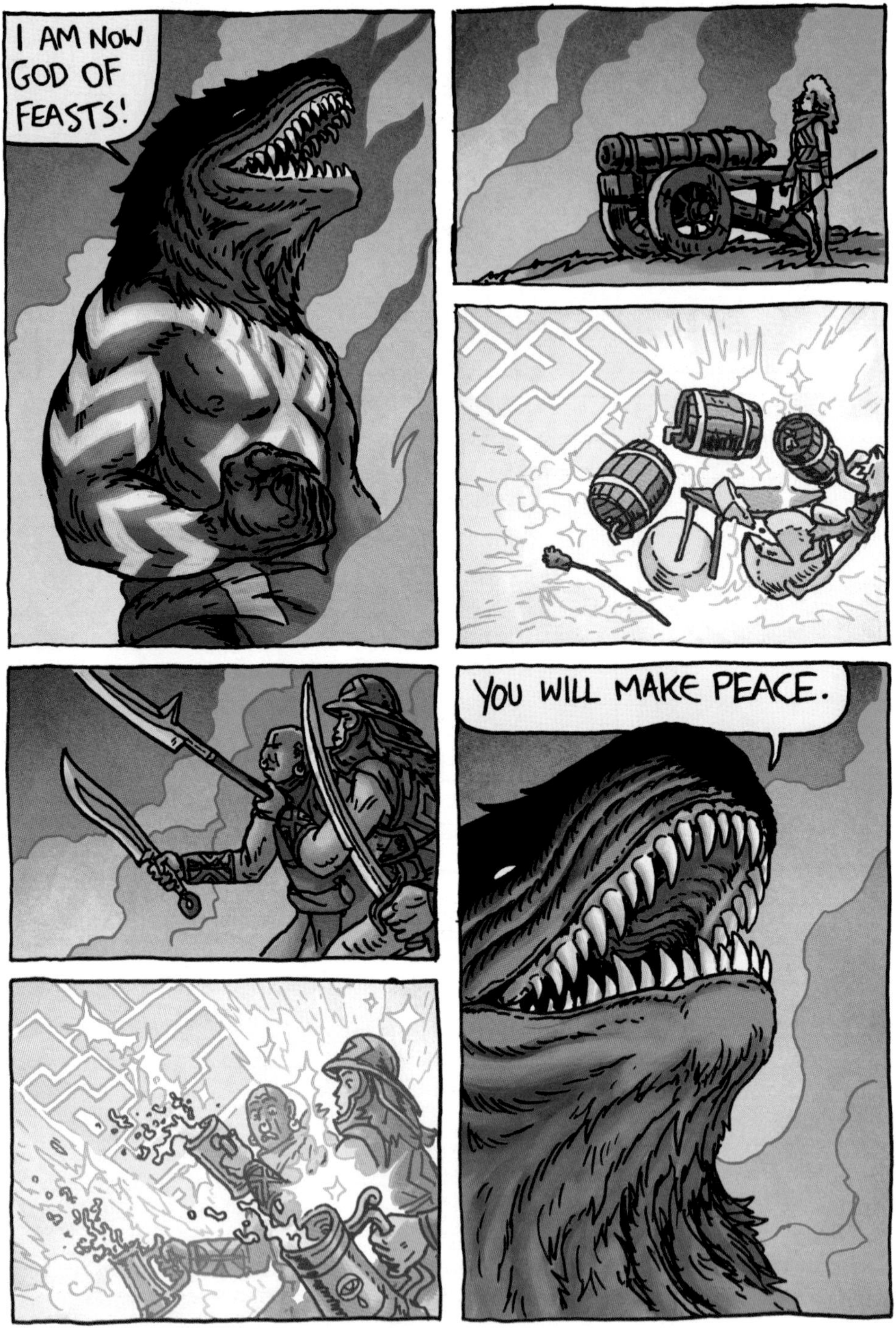
I AM NOW GOD OF FEASTS!
YOU WILL MAKE PEACE.

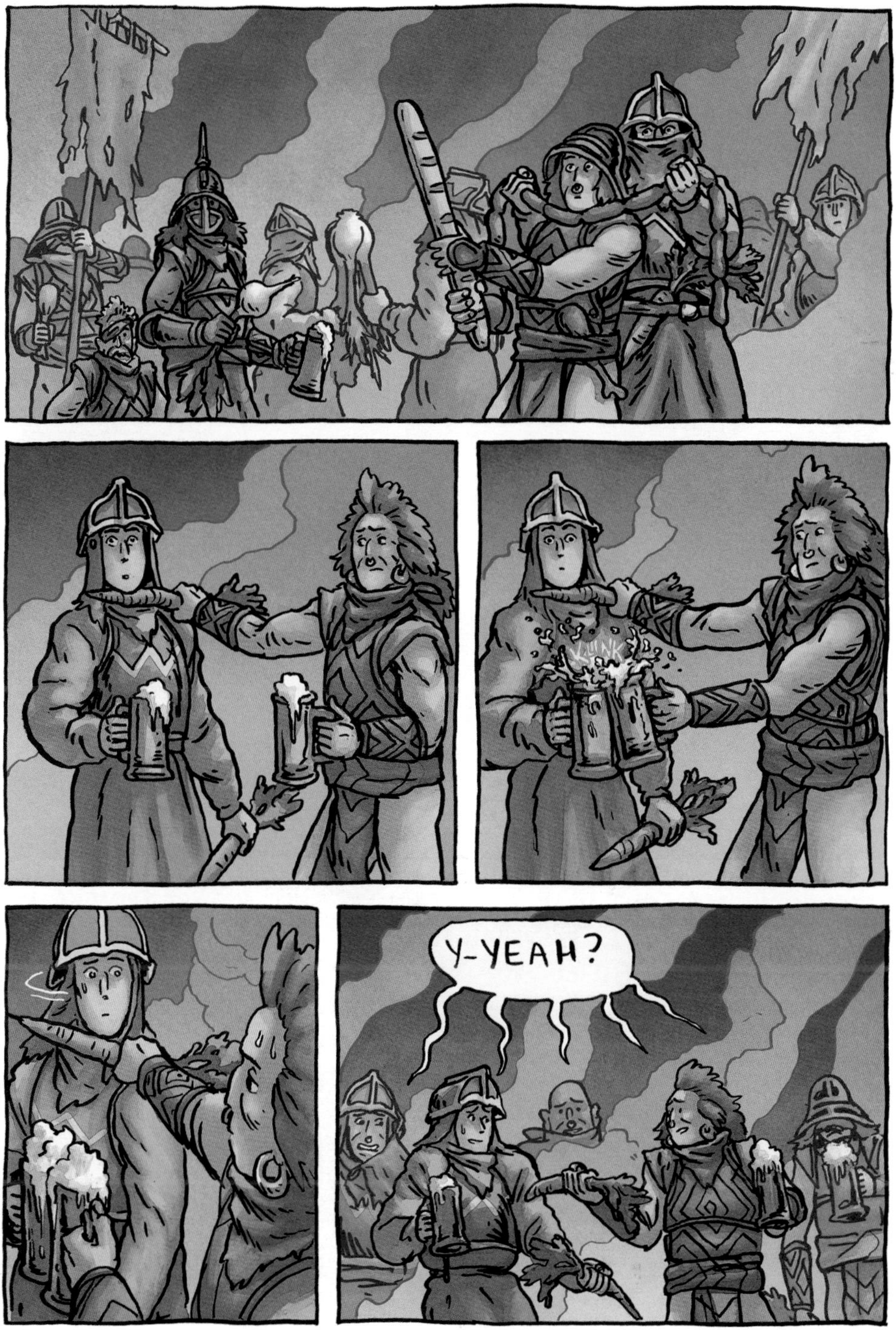
KLUNK
Y-YEAH?

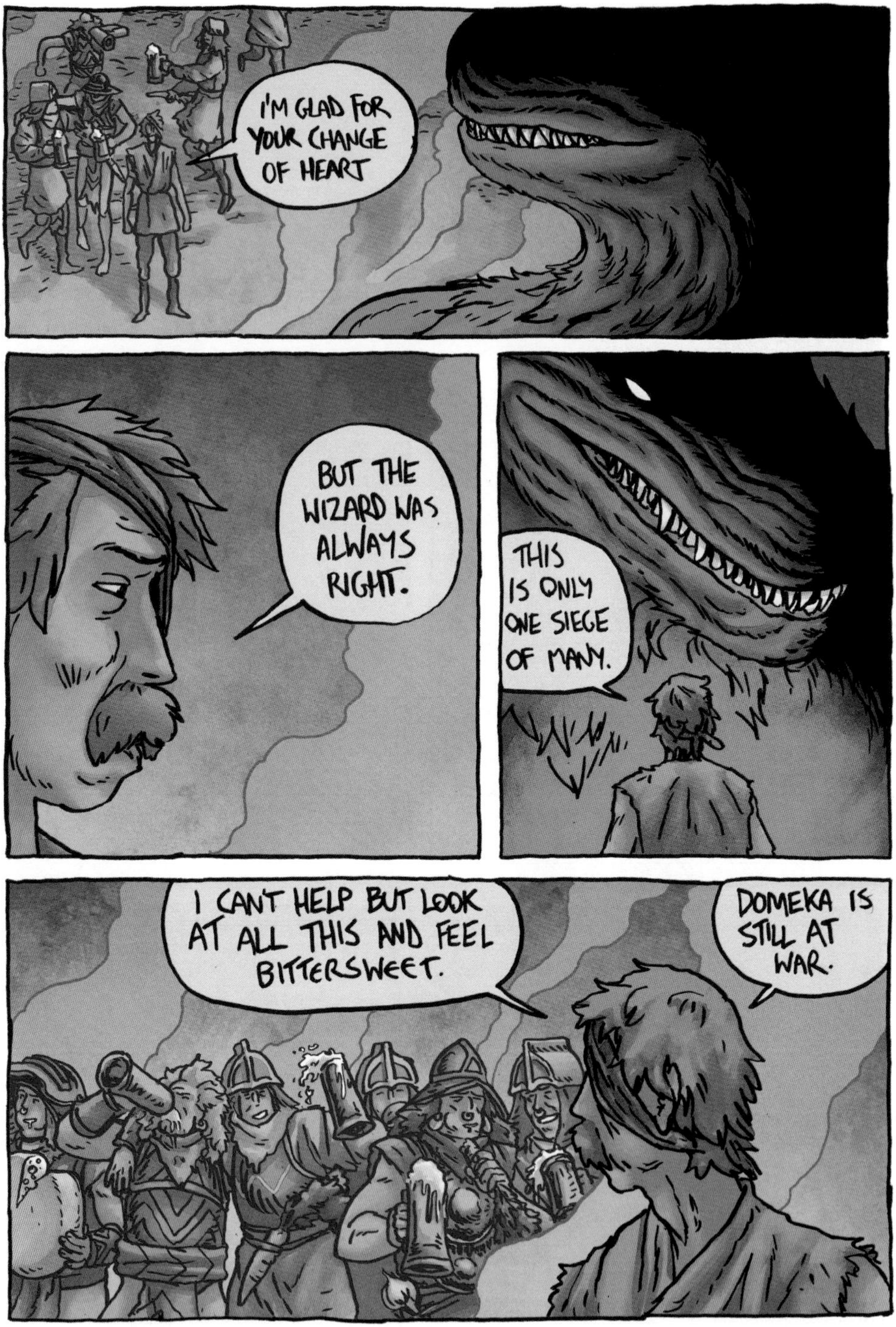
I'M GLAD FOR YOUR CHANGE OF HEART
BUT THE WIZARD WAS ALWAYS RIGHT.
THIS IS ONLY ONE SIEGE OF MANY.
I CAN'T HELP BUT LOOK AT ALL THIS AND FEEL BITTERSWEET.
DOMEKA IS STILL AT WAR.

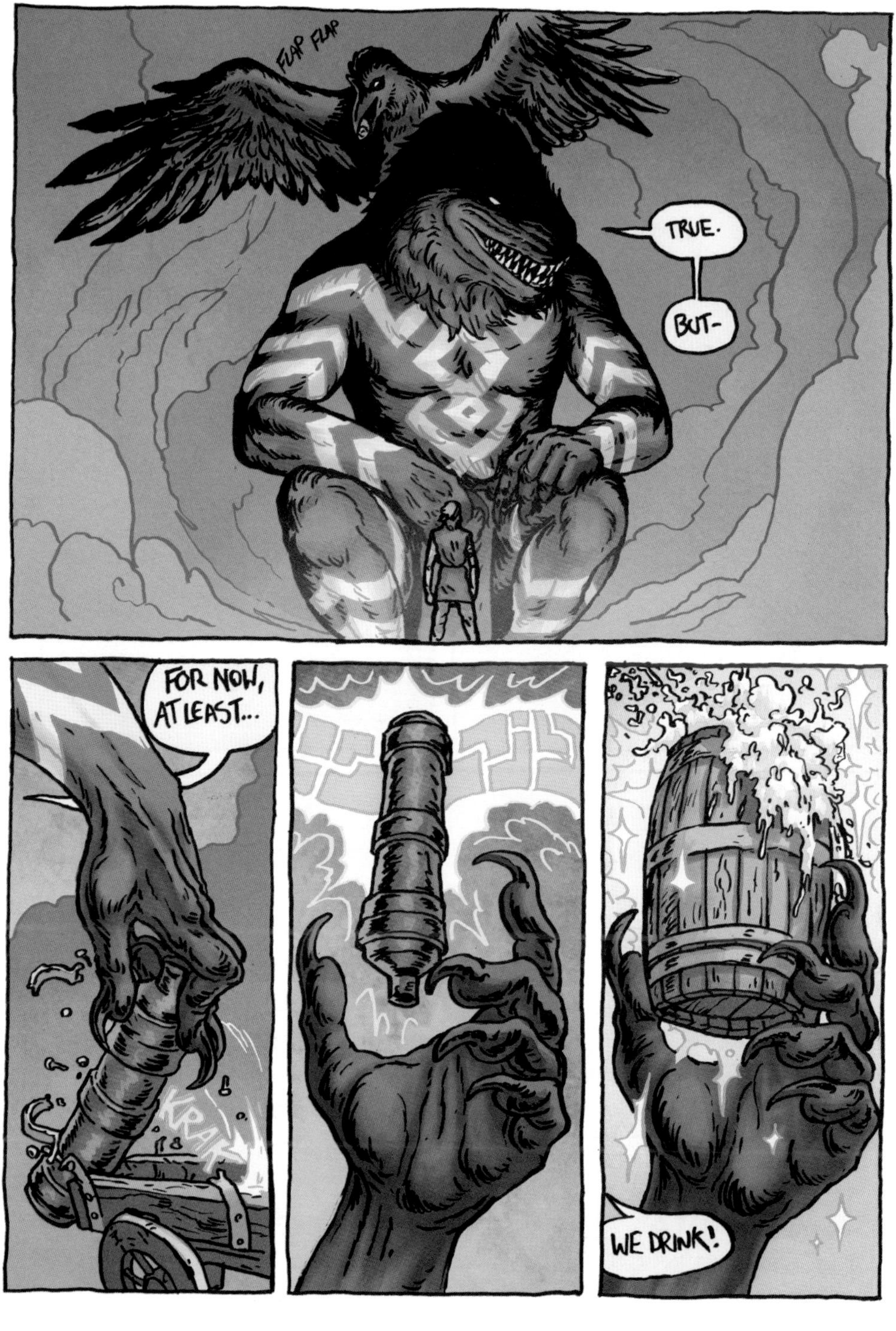
FLAP FLAP
TRUE.
BUT-
FOR NOW, AT LEAST...
KRAK
WE DRINK!

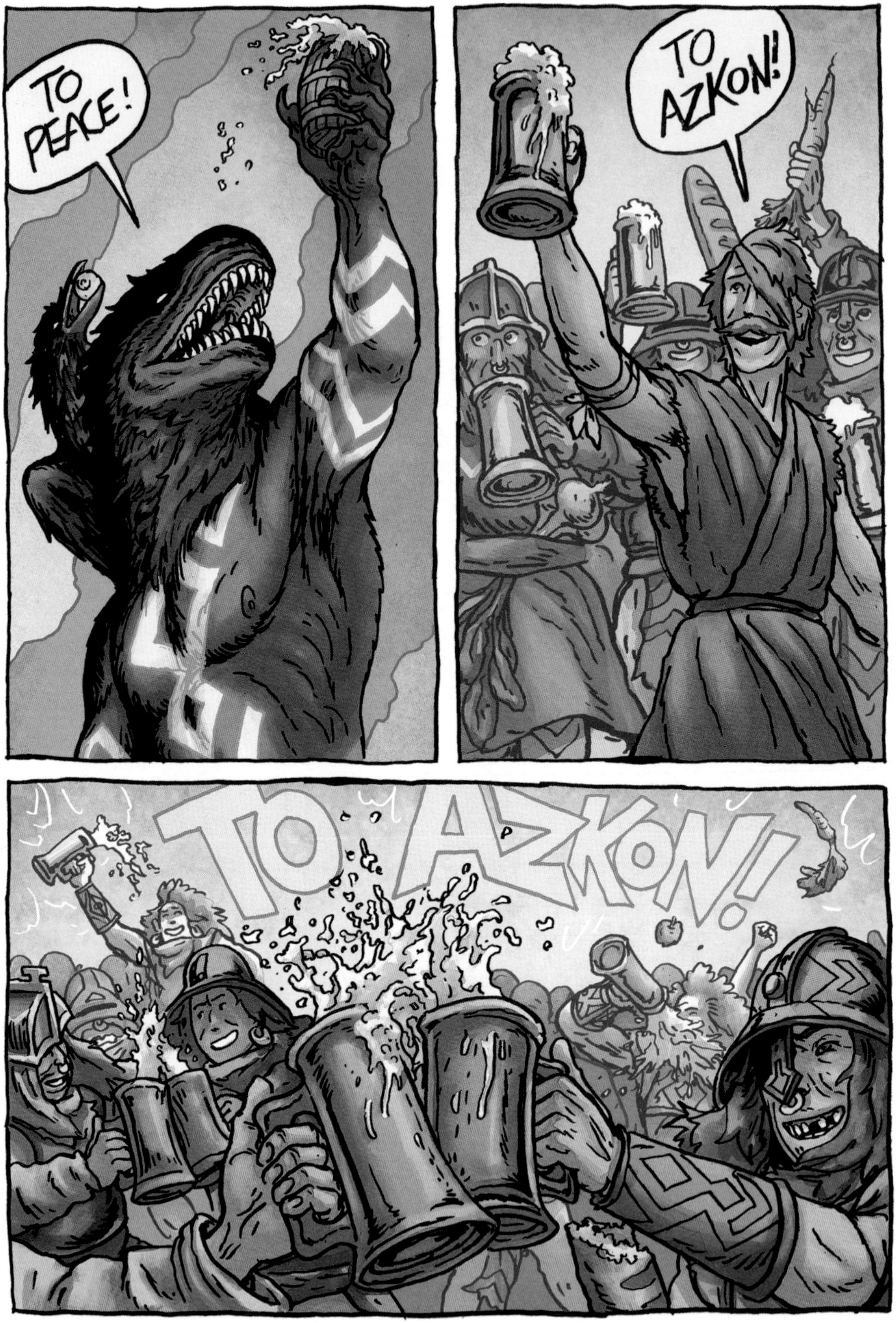
TO PEACE!
TO AZKON!
TO AZKON!

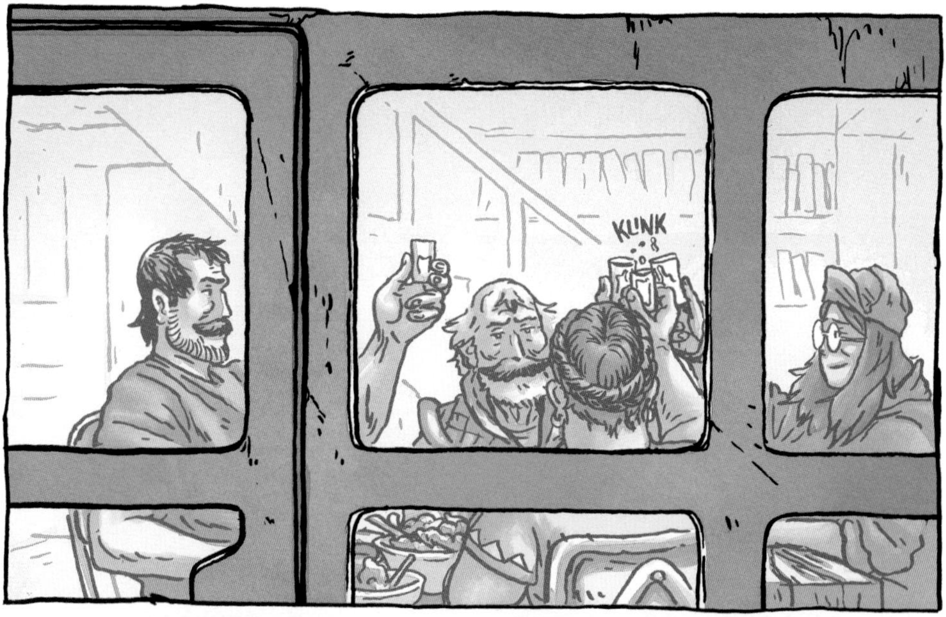
KLINK

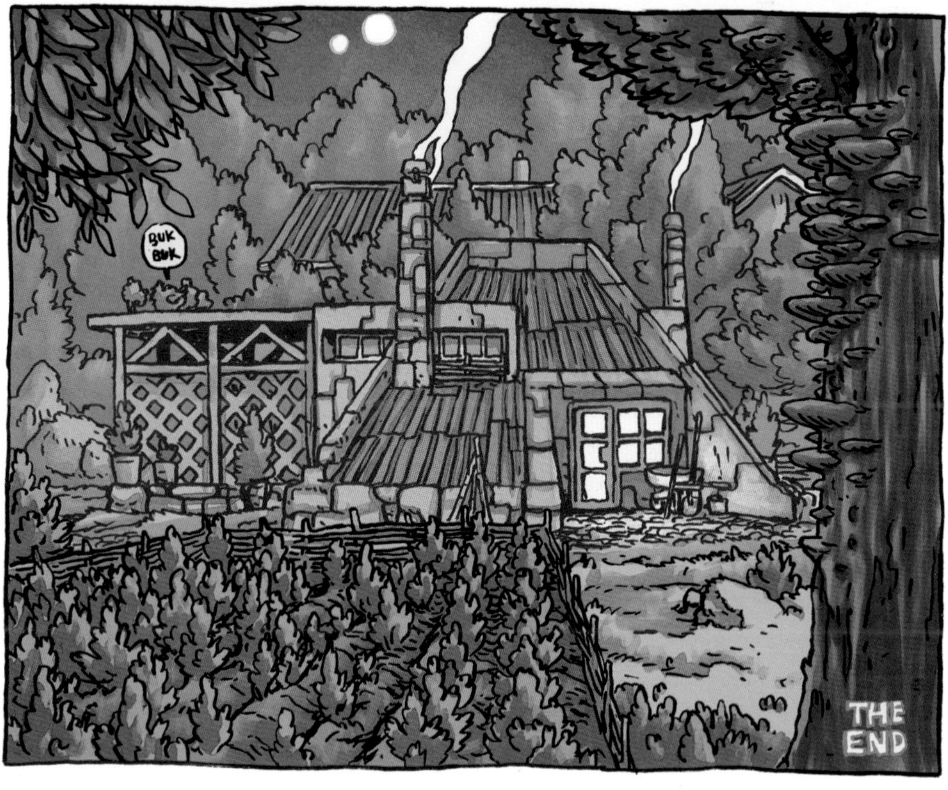
BUK
BUK
THE END

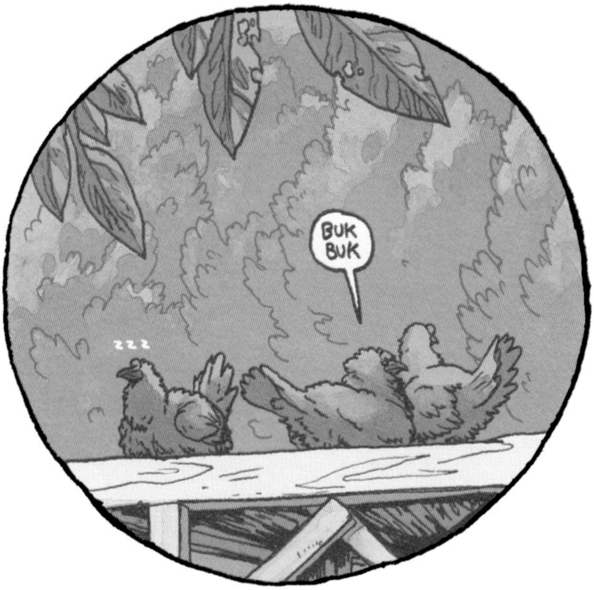
BUK BUK
zzz

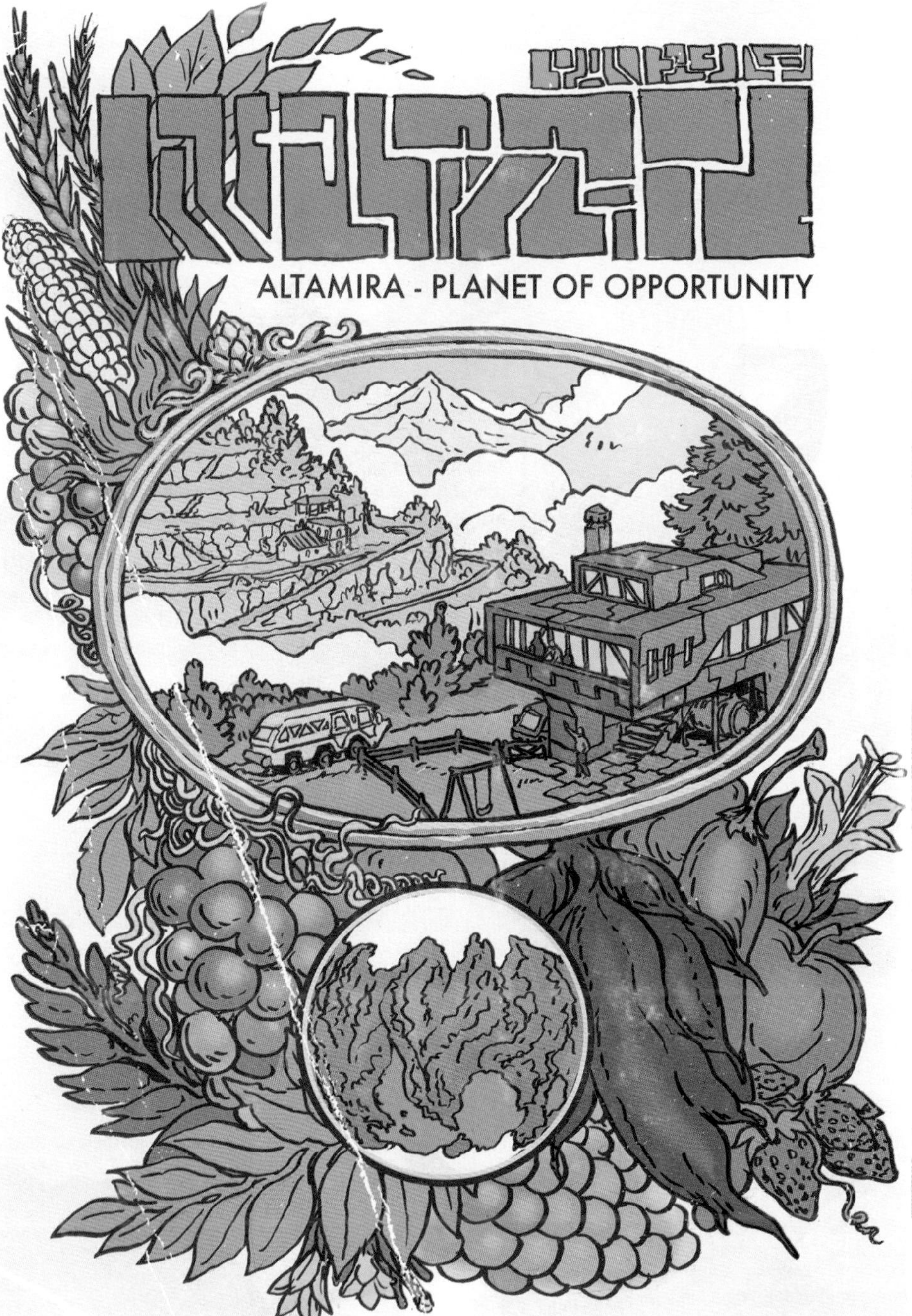
ALTAMIRA - PLANET OF OPPORTUNITY

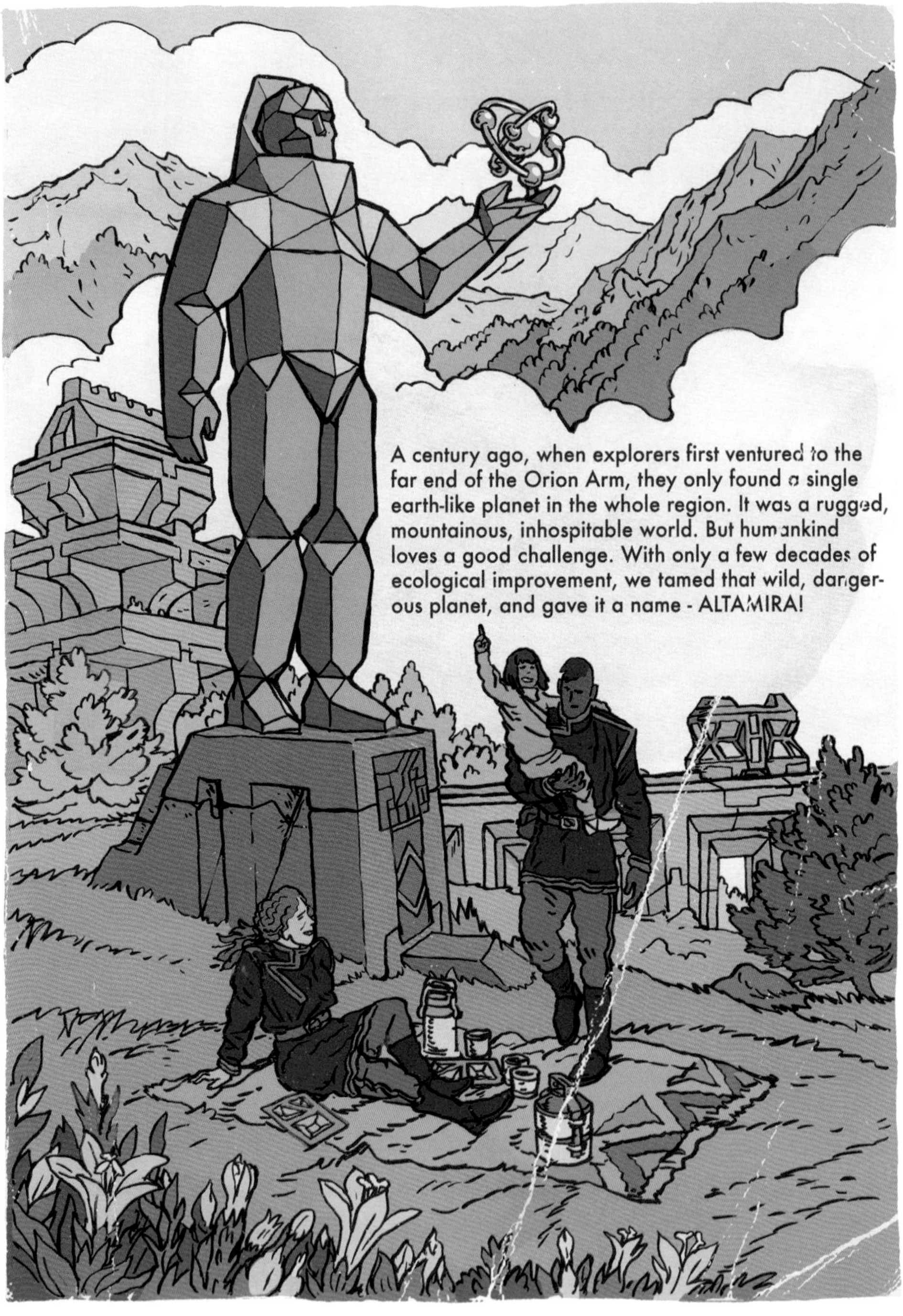
A century ago, when explorers first ventured to the far end of the Orion Arm, they only found a single earth-like planet in the whole region. It was a rugged, mountainous, inhospitable world. But humankind loves a good challenge. With only a few decades of ecological improvement, we tamed that wild, dangerous planet, and gave it a name - ALTAMIRA!

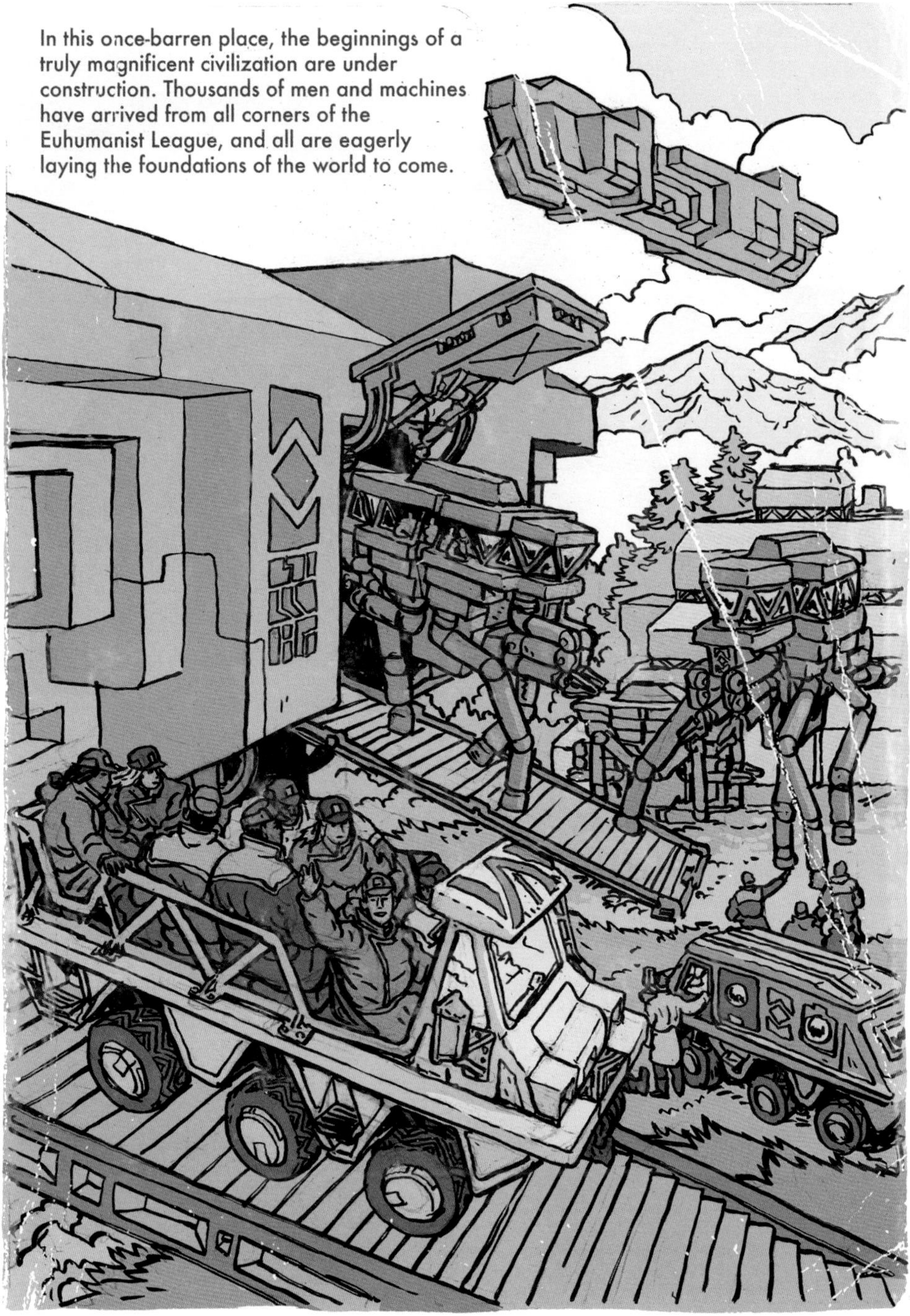
In this once-barren place, the beginnings of a truly magnificent civilization are under construction. Thousands of men and machines have arrived from all corners of the Euhumanist League, and all are eagerly laying the foundations of the world to come.

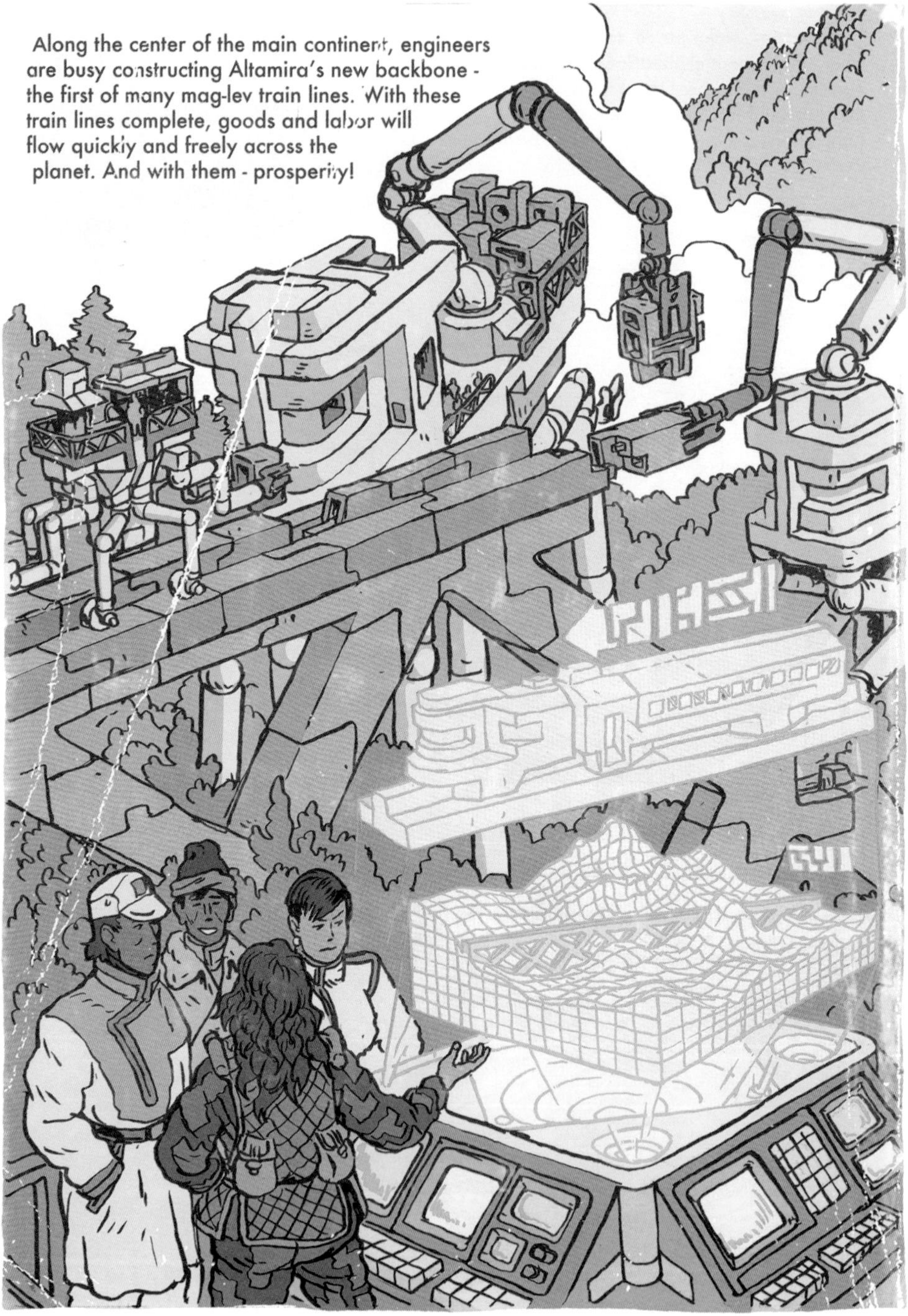
Along the center of the main continent, engineers are busy constructing Altamira's new backbone - the first of many mag-lev train lines. With these train lines complete, goods and labor will flow quickly and freely across the planet. And with them - prosperity!

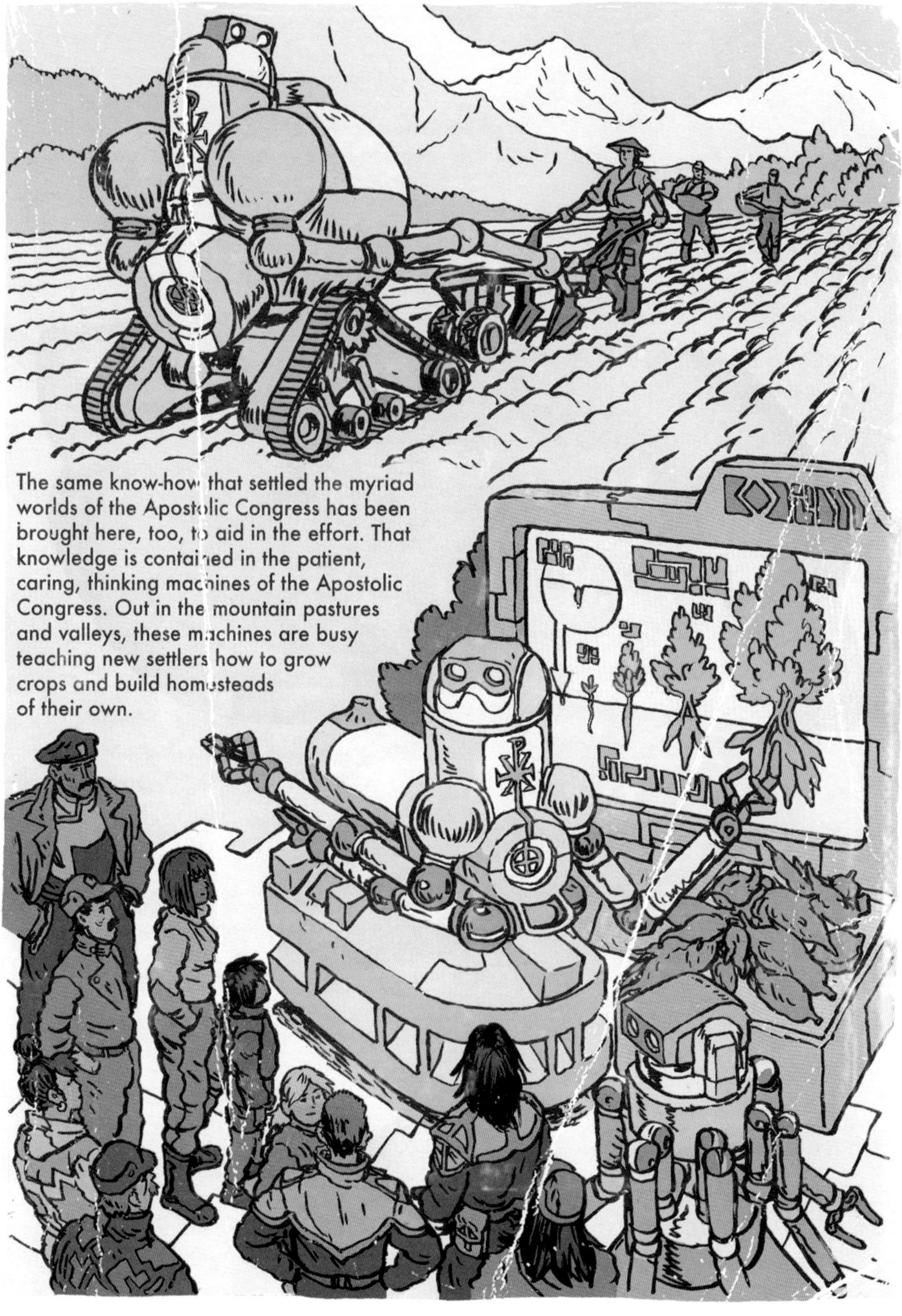
The same know-how that settled the myriad worlds of the Apostolic Congress has been brought here, too, to aid in the effort. That knowledge is contained in the patient, caring, thinking machines of the Apostolic Congress. Out in the mountain pastures and valleys, these machines are busy teaching new settlers how to grow crops and build homesteads of their own.

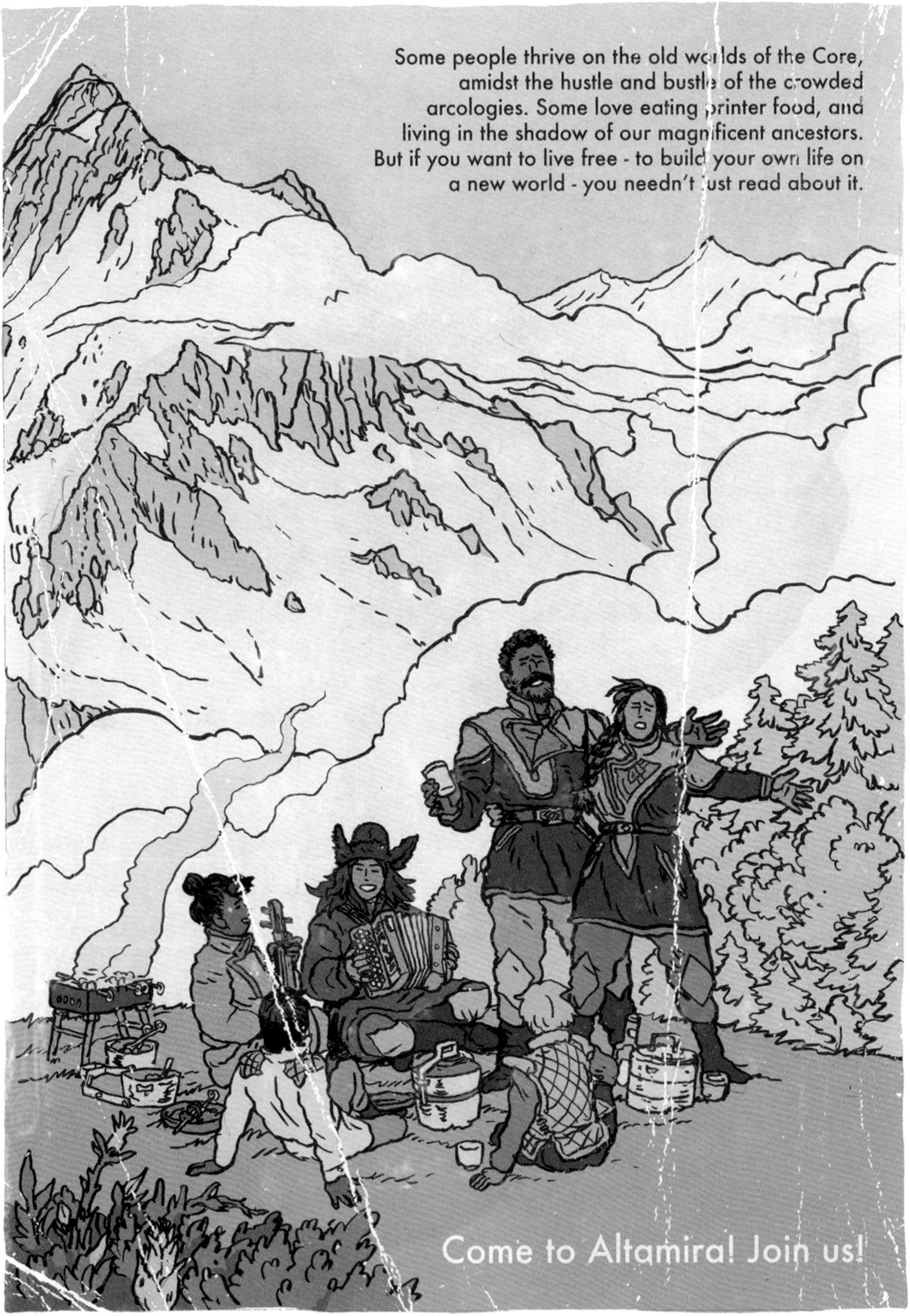
Some people thrive on the old worlds of the Core, amidst the hustle and bustle of the crowded arcologies. Some love eating printer food, and living in the shadow of our magnificent ancestors. But if you want to live free - to build your own life on a new world - you needn't just read about it.
Come to Altamira! Join us!

I WANTED TO GIVE SPECIAL THANKS TO ALL THE FOLKS WHO SUPPORTED
THE BOOK'S GENESIS ON PATREON, FOLLOWED THE SERIALIZATION
ONLINE, AND, OF COURSE, PLEDGED ON KICK STARTER. WITHOUT
YOUR SUPPORT, THIS LITTLE BOOK WOULDN'T EXIST.

SINCERELY,
SIMON ROY

THE ILLUSTRIOUS OFFICIAL GRIZ GROBUS PIN-UP GALLERY

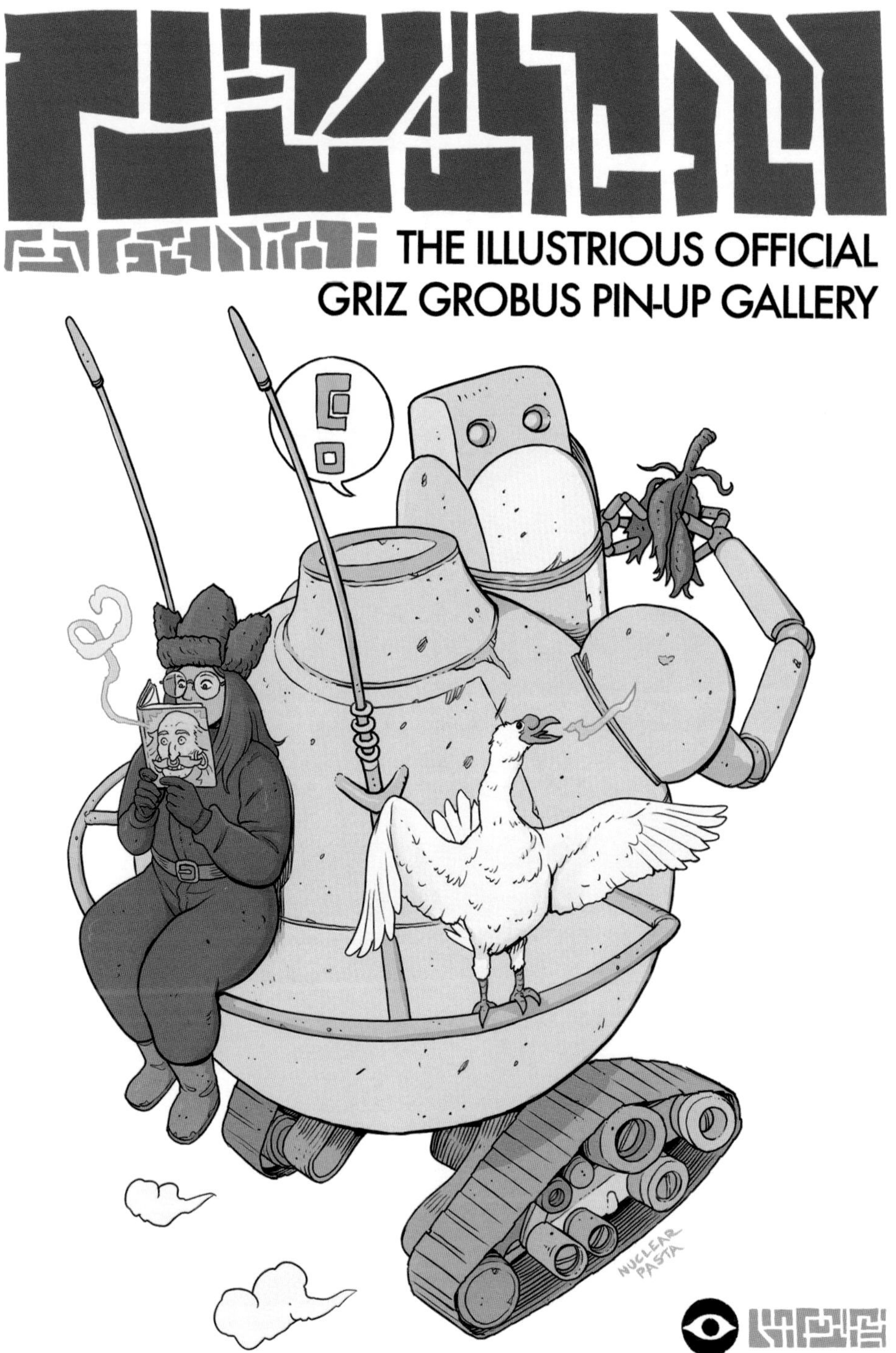
NUCLEAR PASTA

WILL TEMPEST!

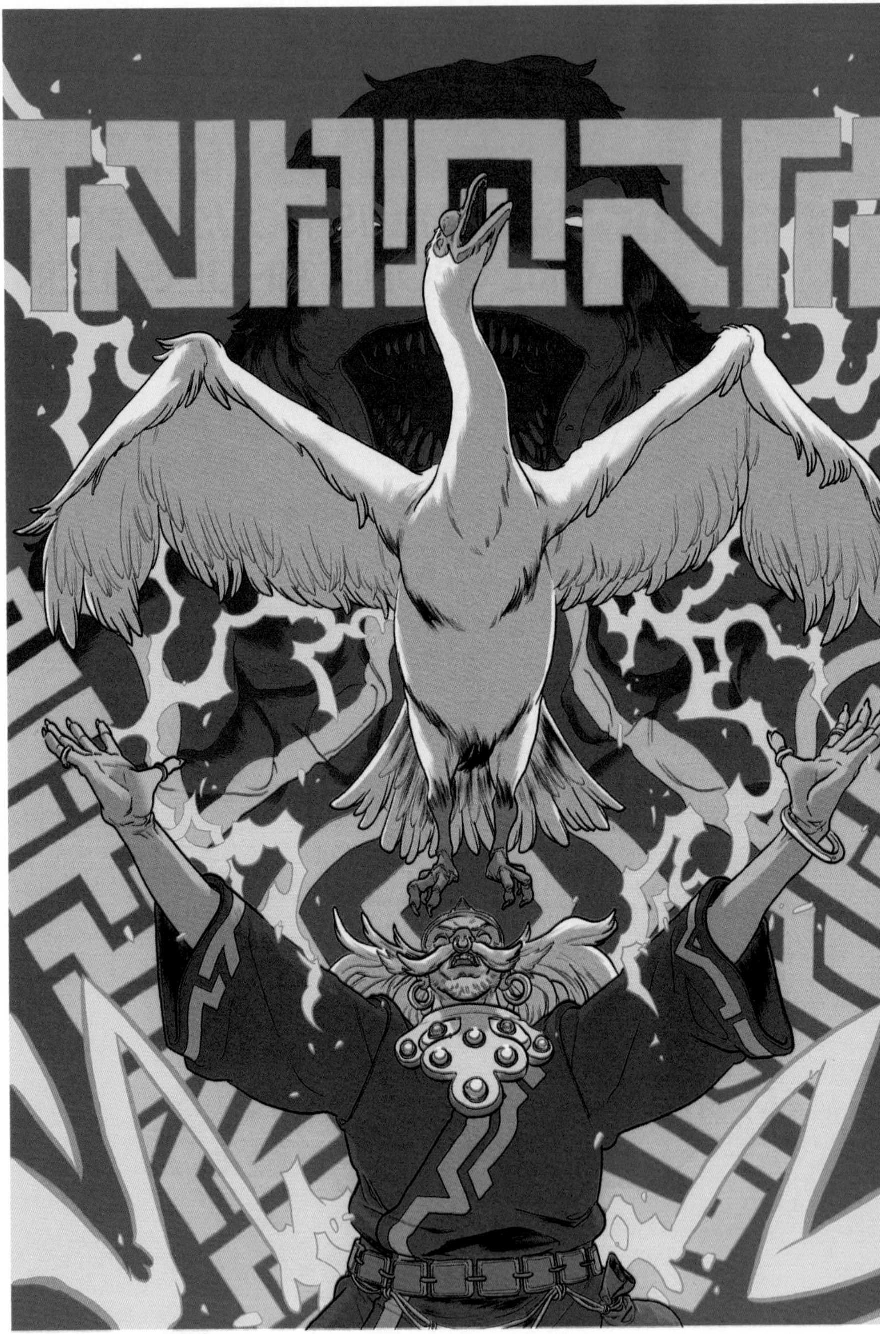

WILL
TEMPEST!

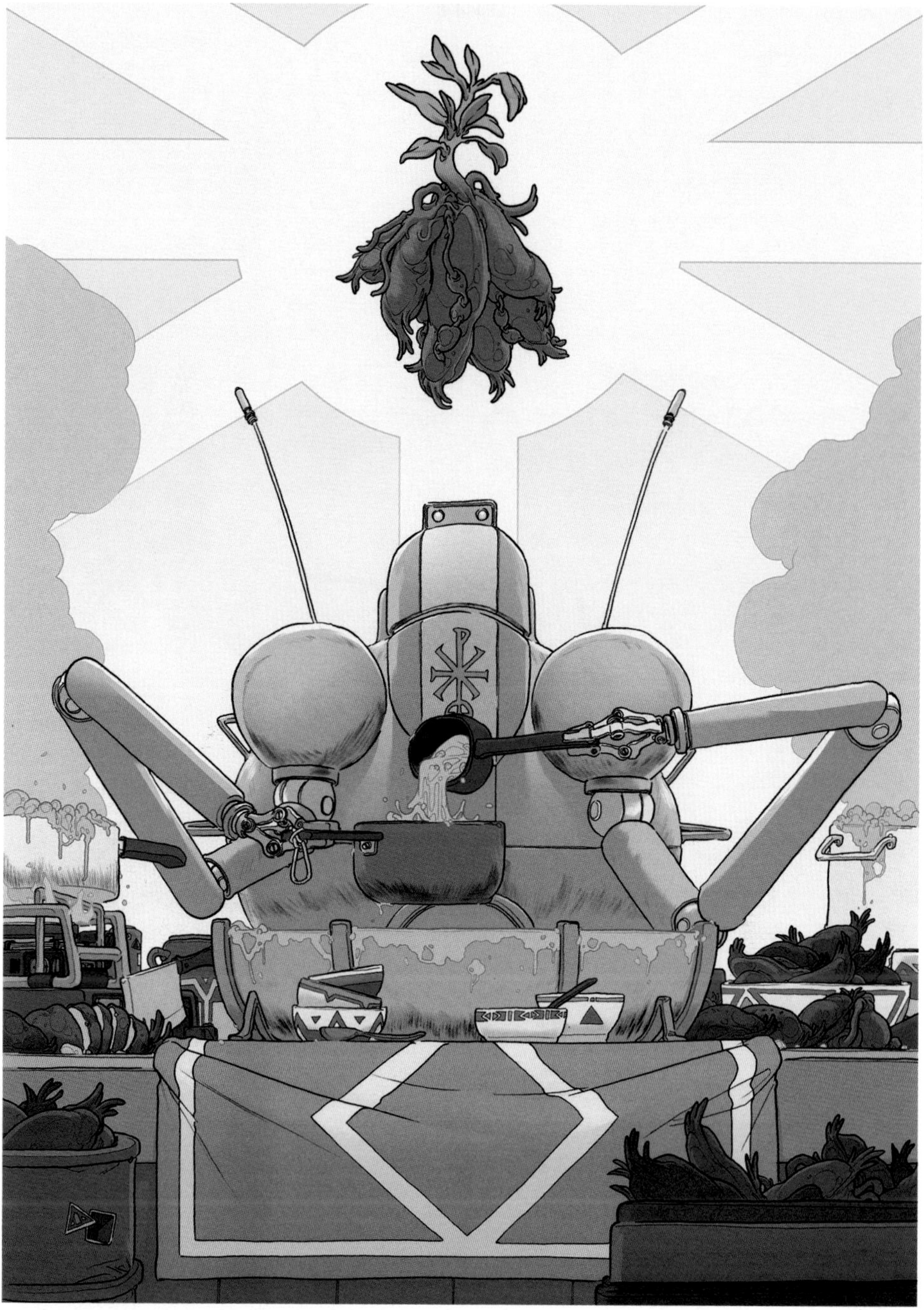

CALLUM DIGGLE!

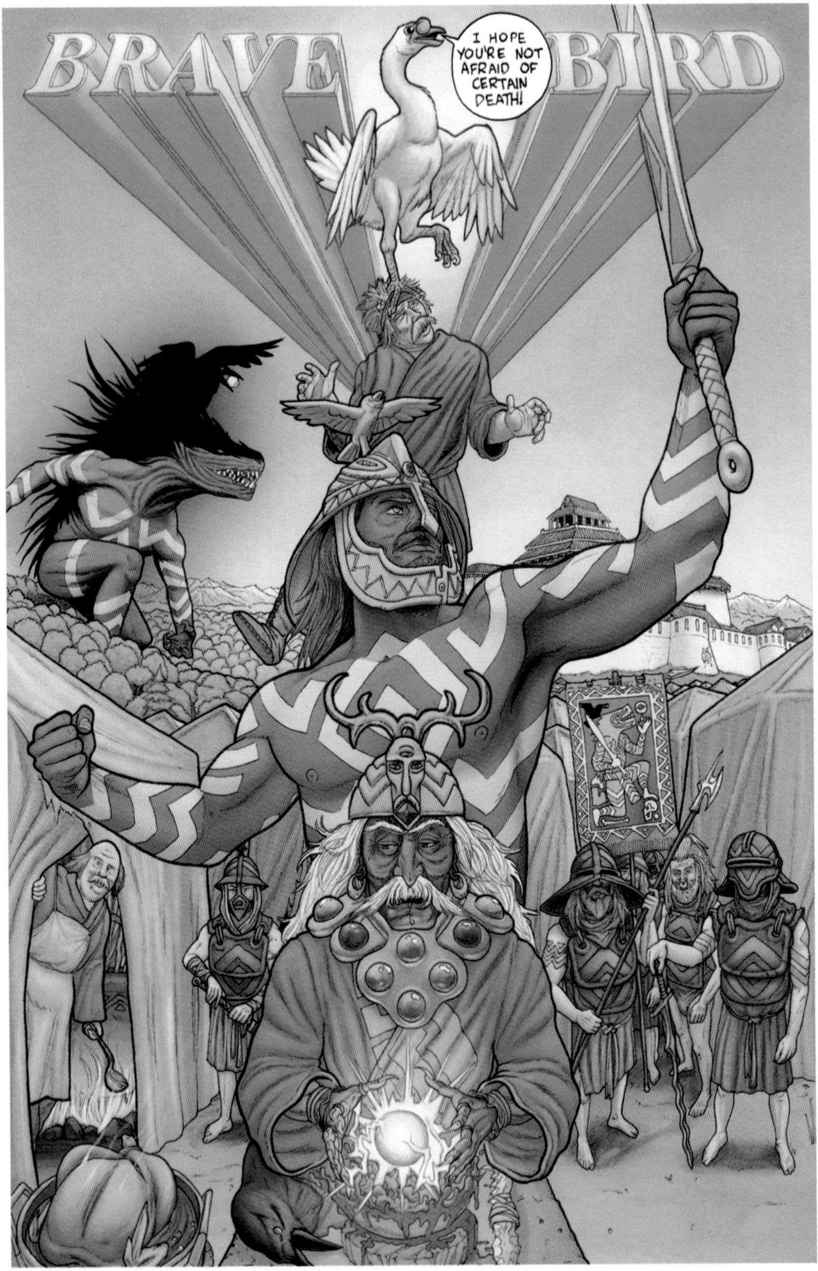
BRAVE BIRD
I HOPE YOU'RE NOT AFRAID OF CERTAIN DEATH!

TIFFANY TURRILL!

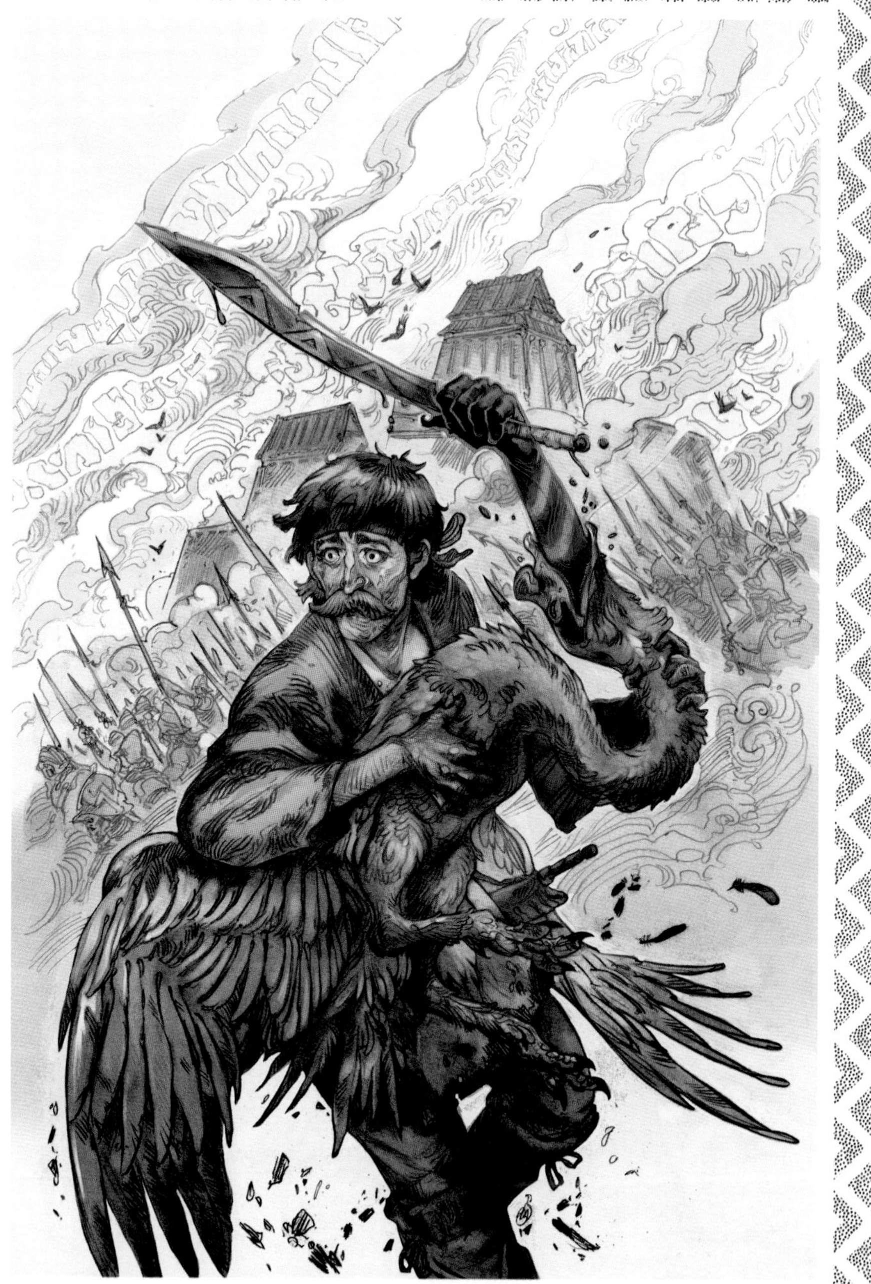

EVAN DAHM!

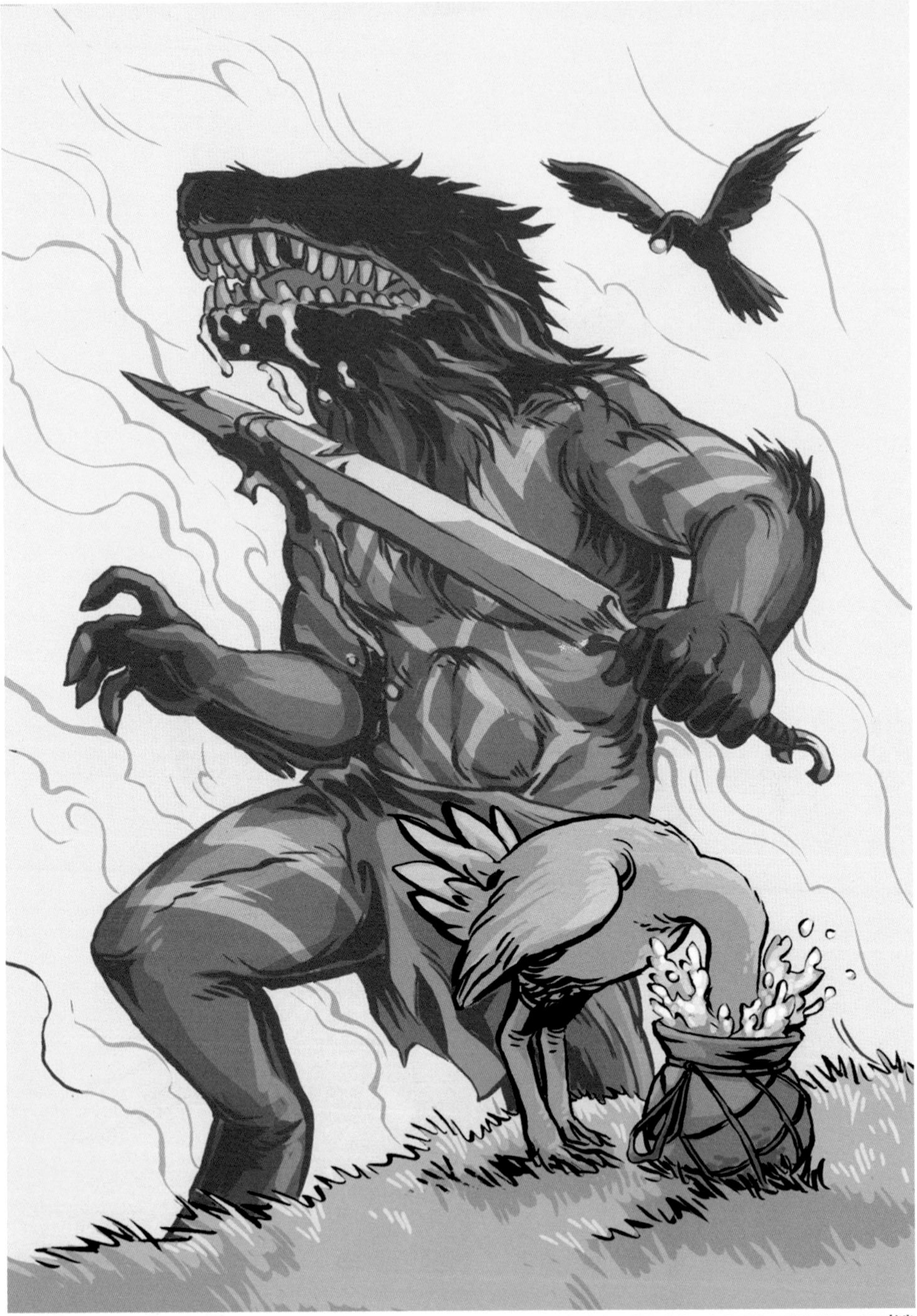

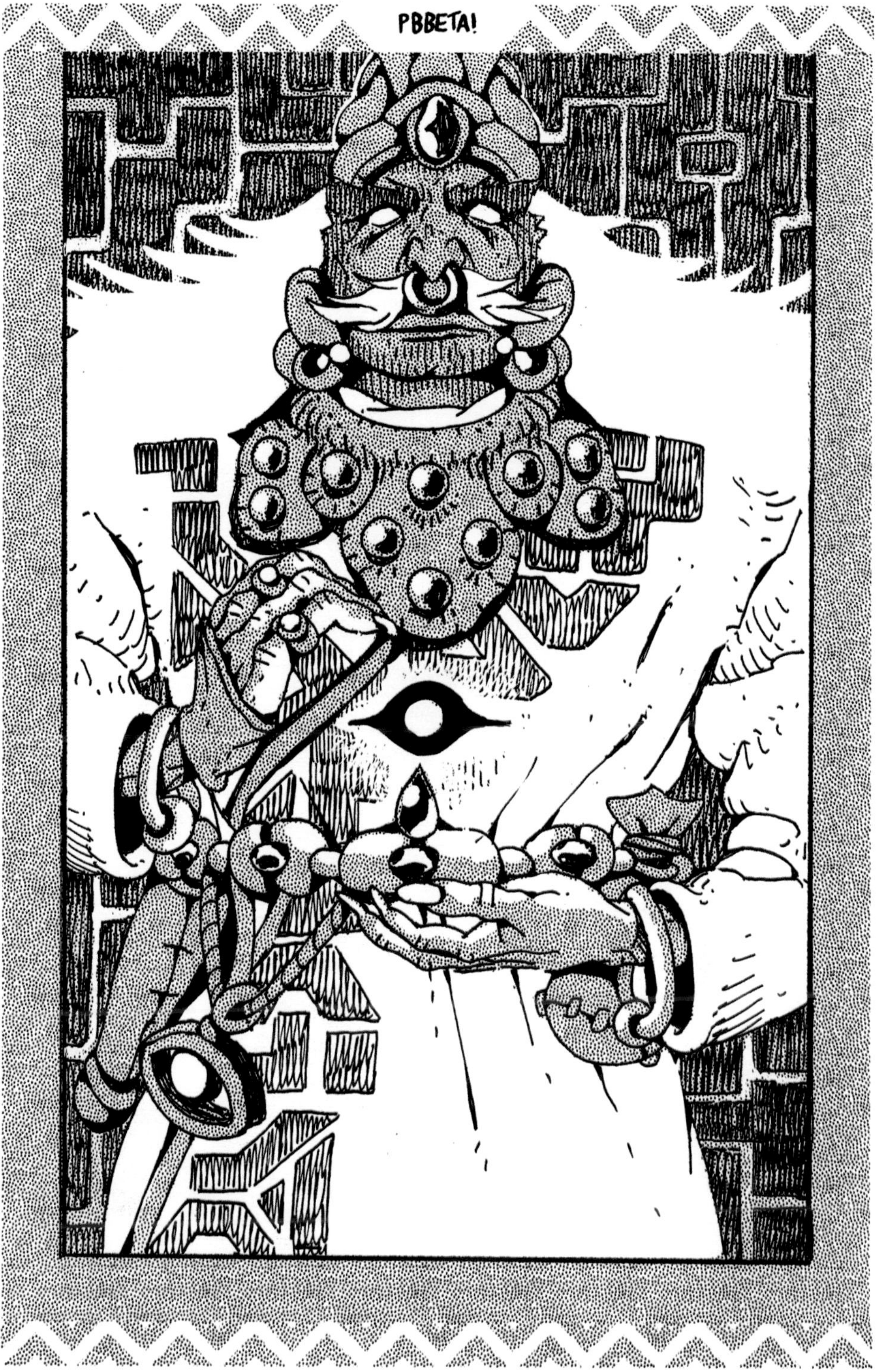
PBBETA!

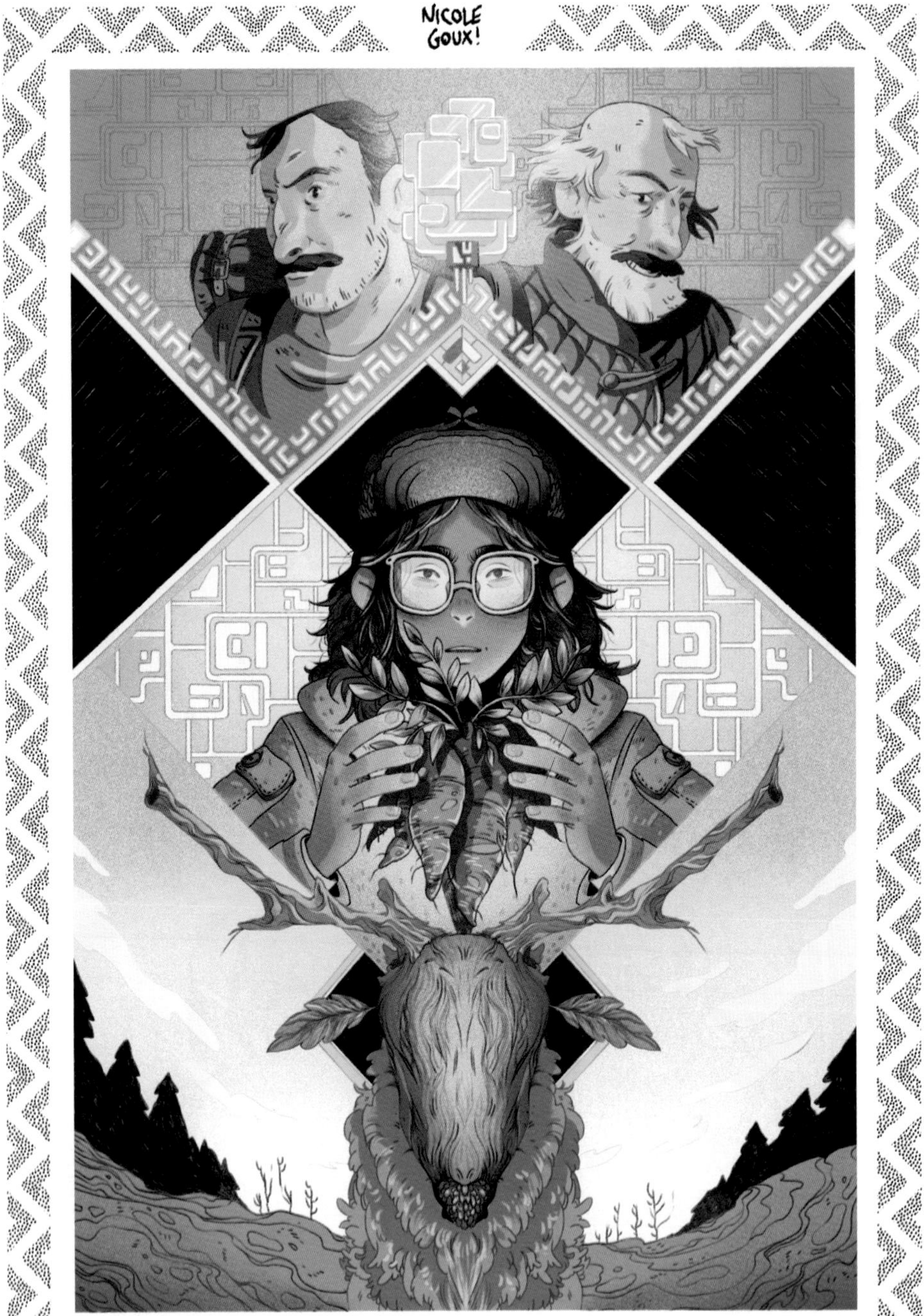
NICOLE GOUX!

VLAD
LEGOSTAEV!

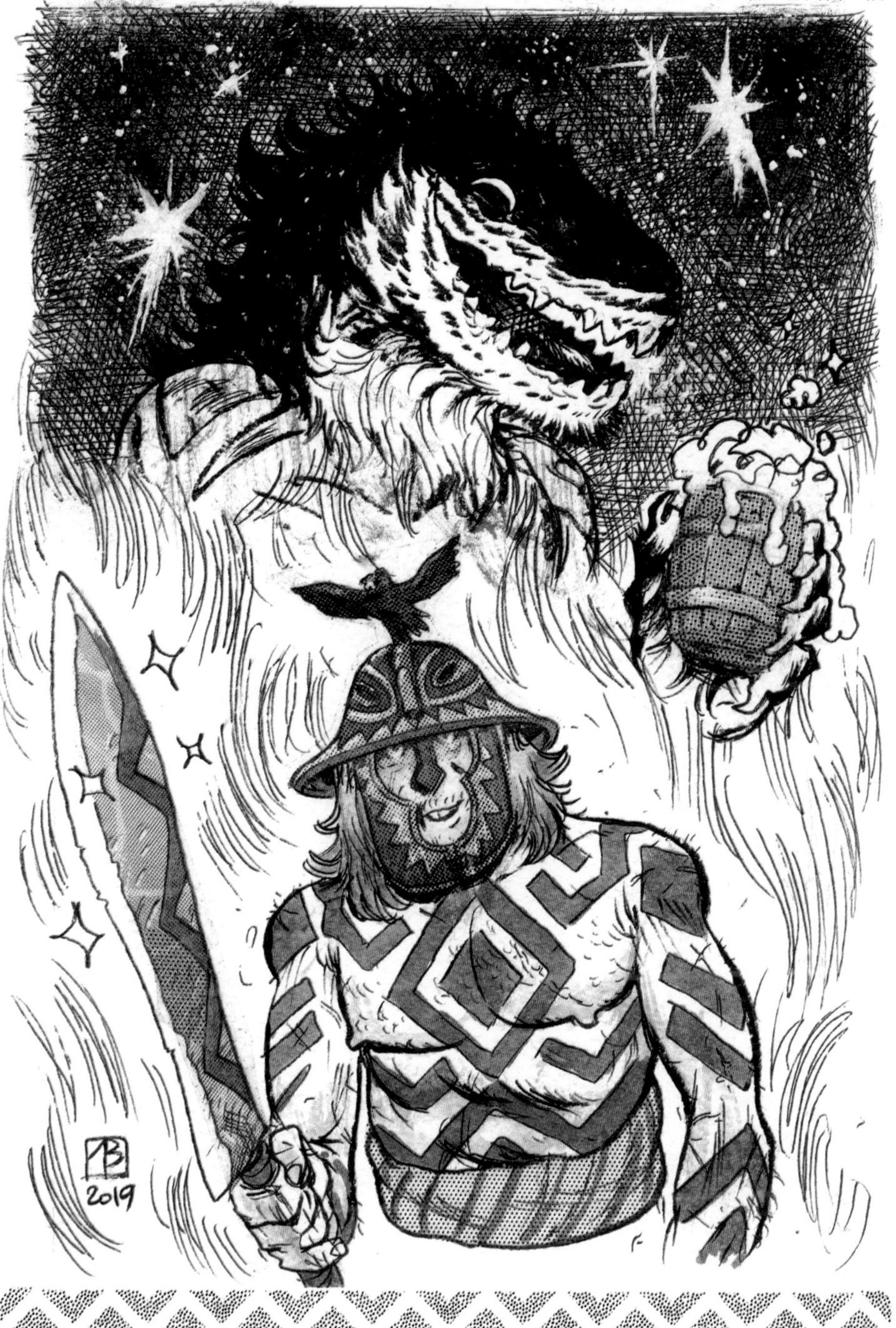
2019

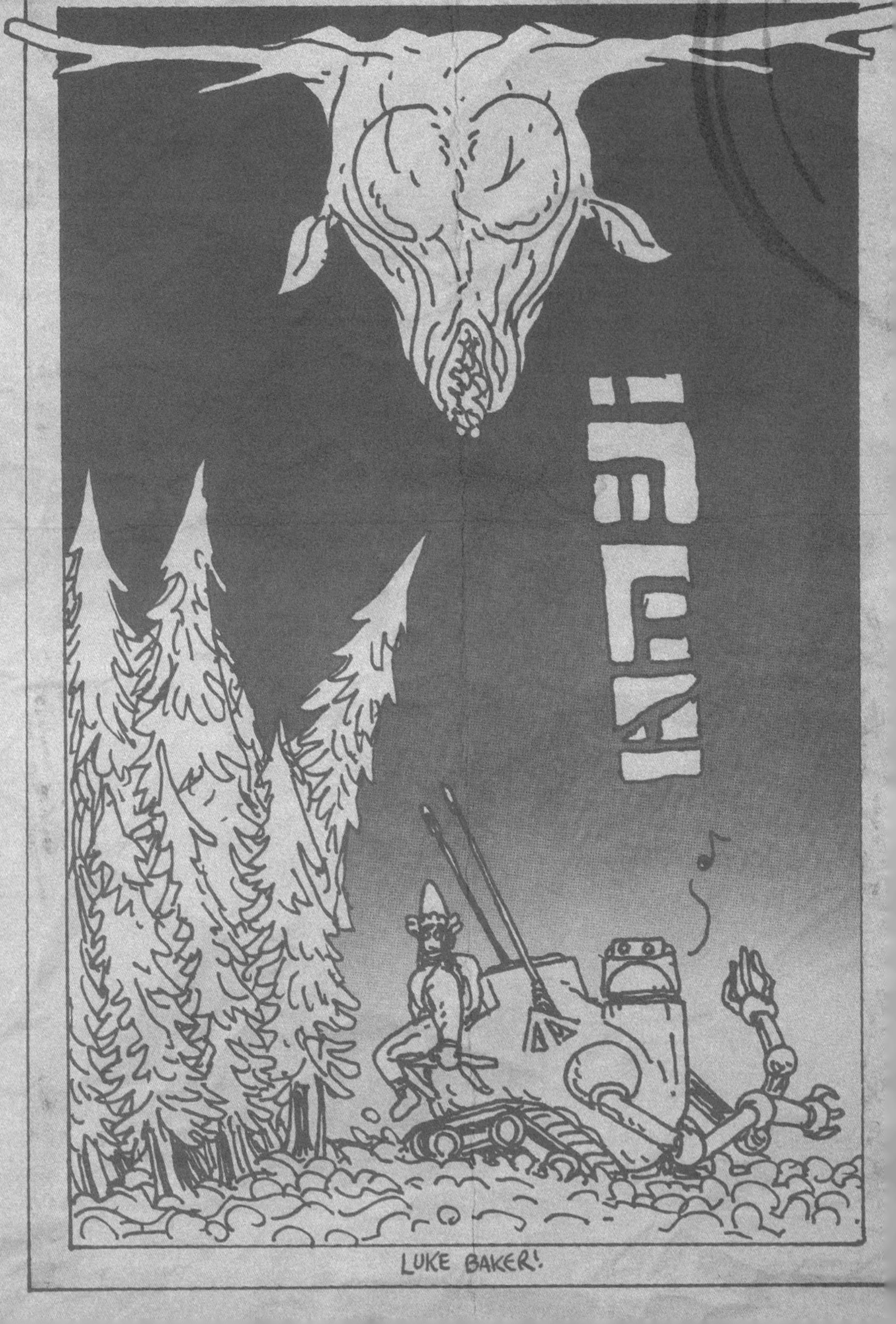

LUKE BAKER!

JACK T COLE!

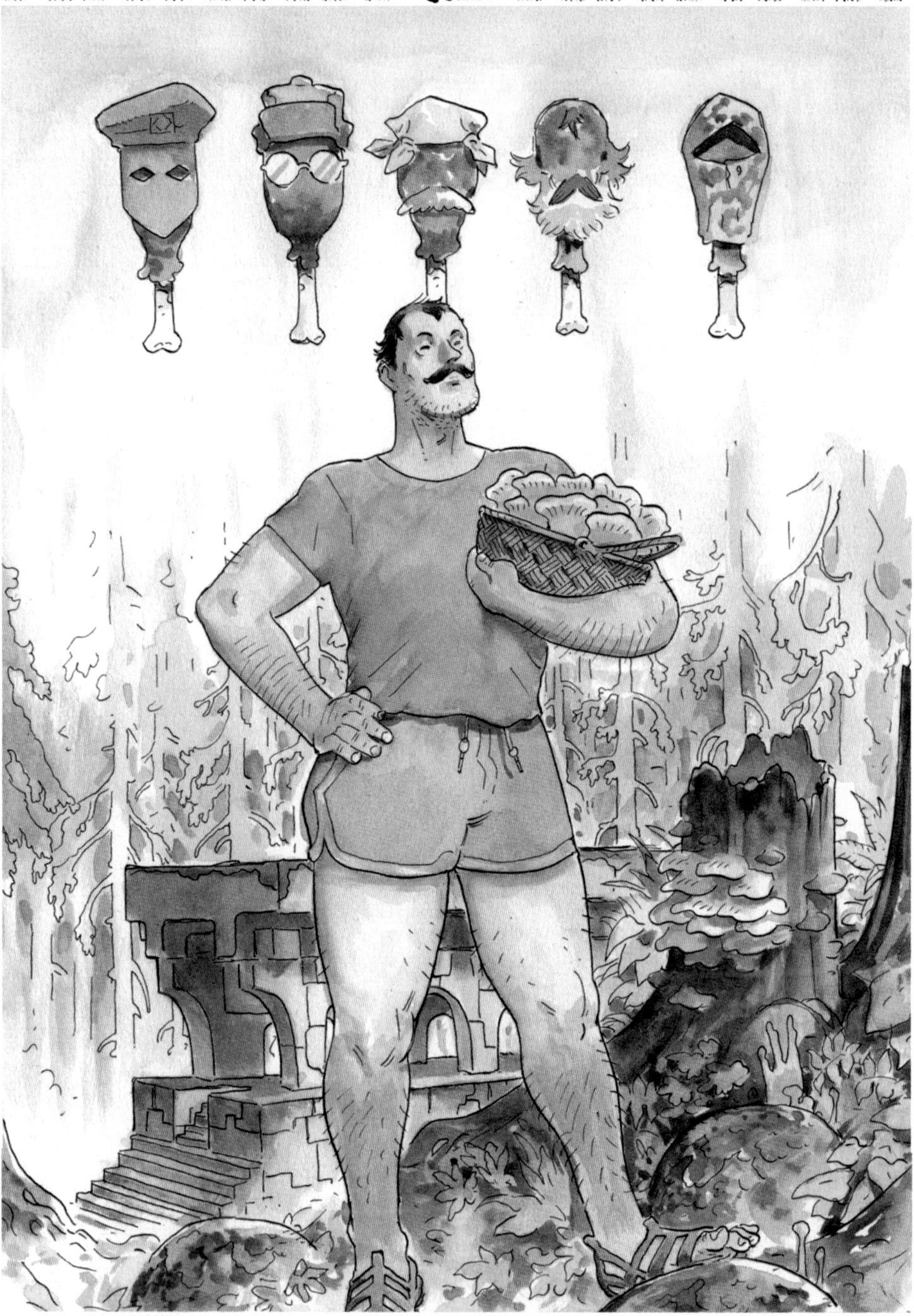

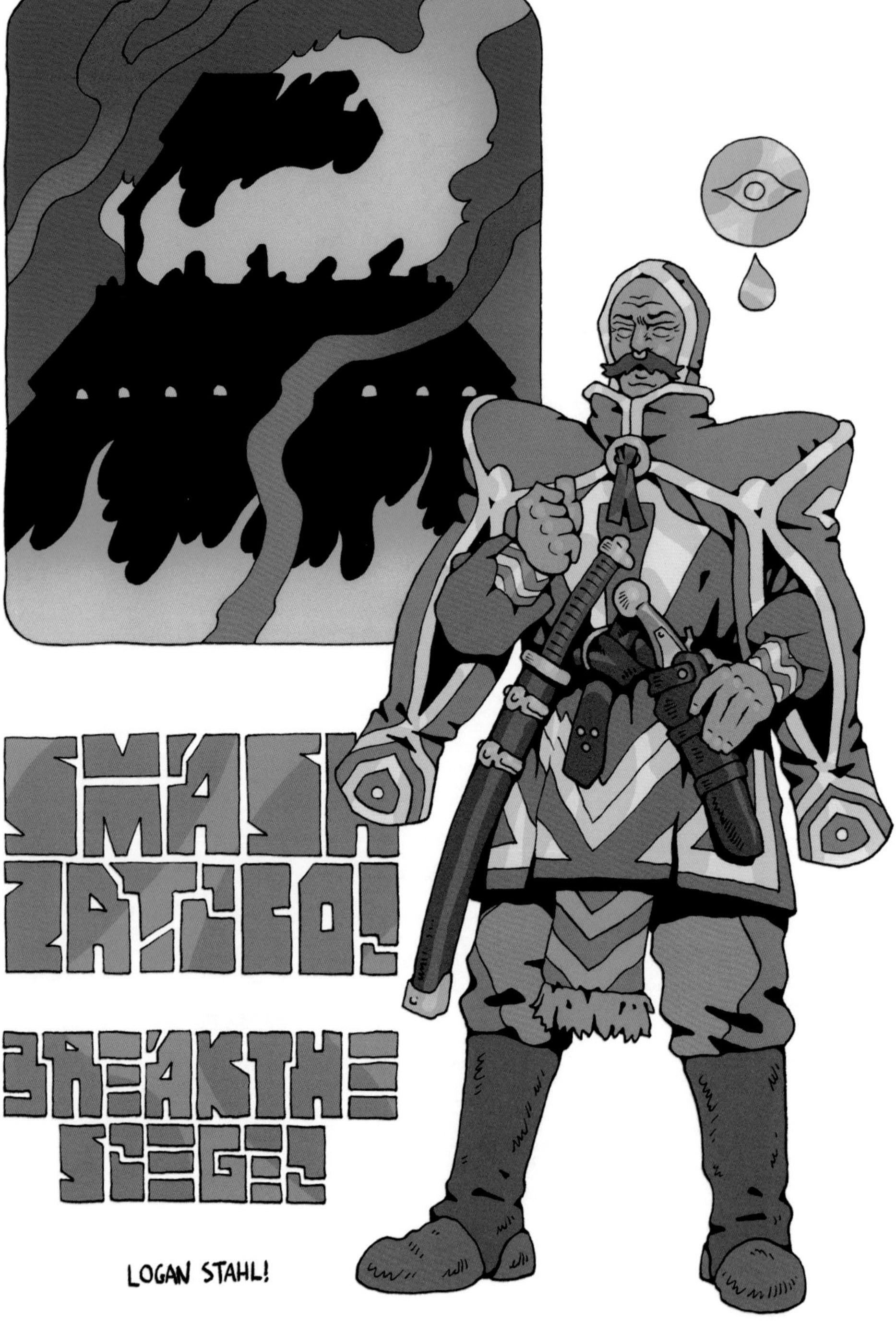
LOGAN STAHL!

DER-SHING HELMER!

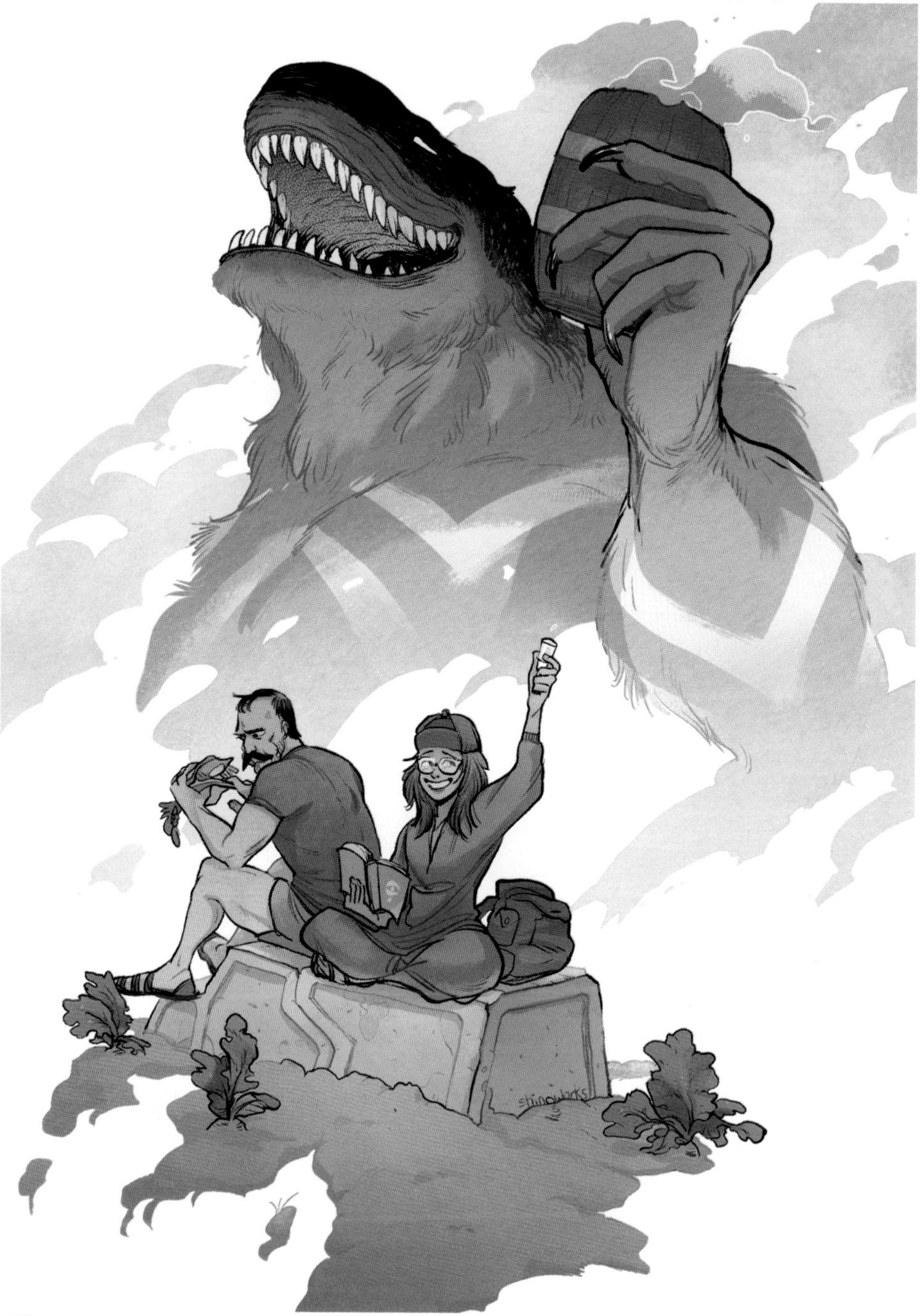
shingworks

REBECCA
KIRBY!

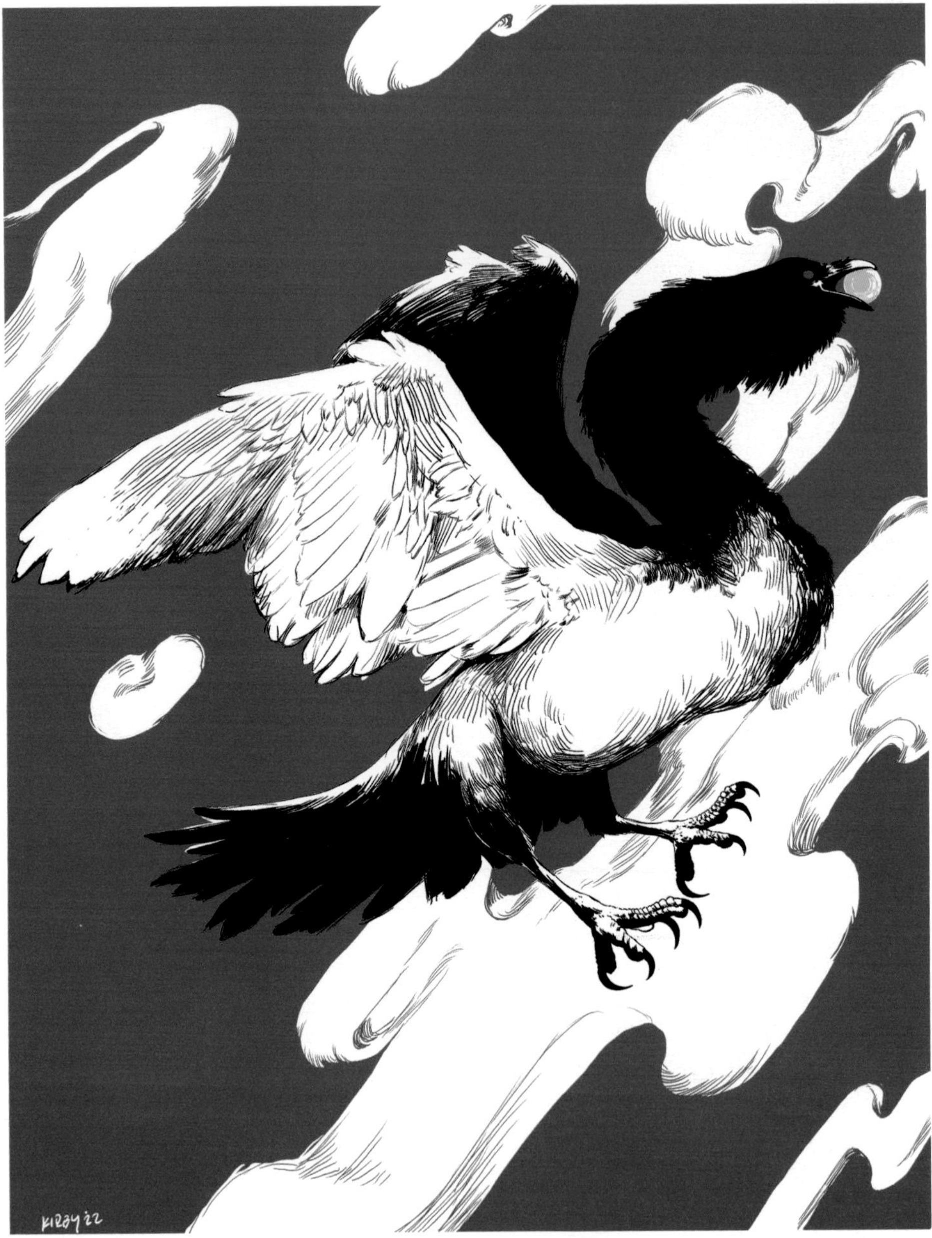
KIRBY '22

Drew Shields

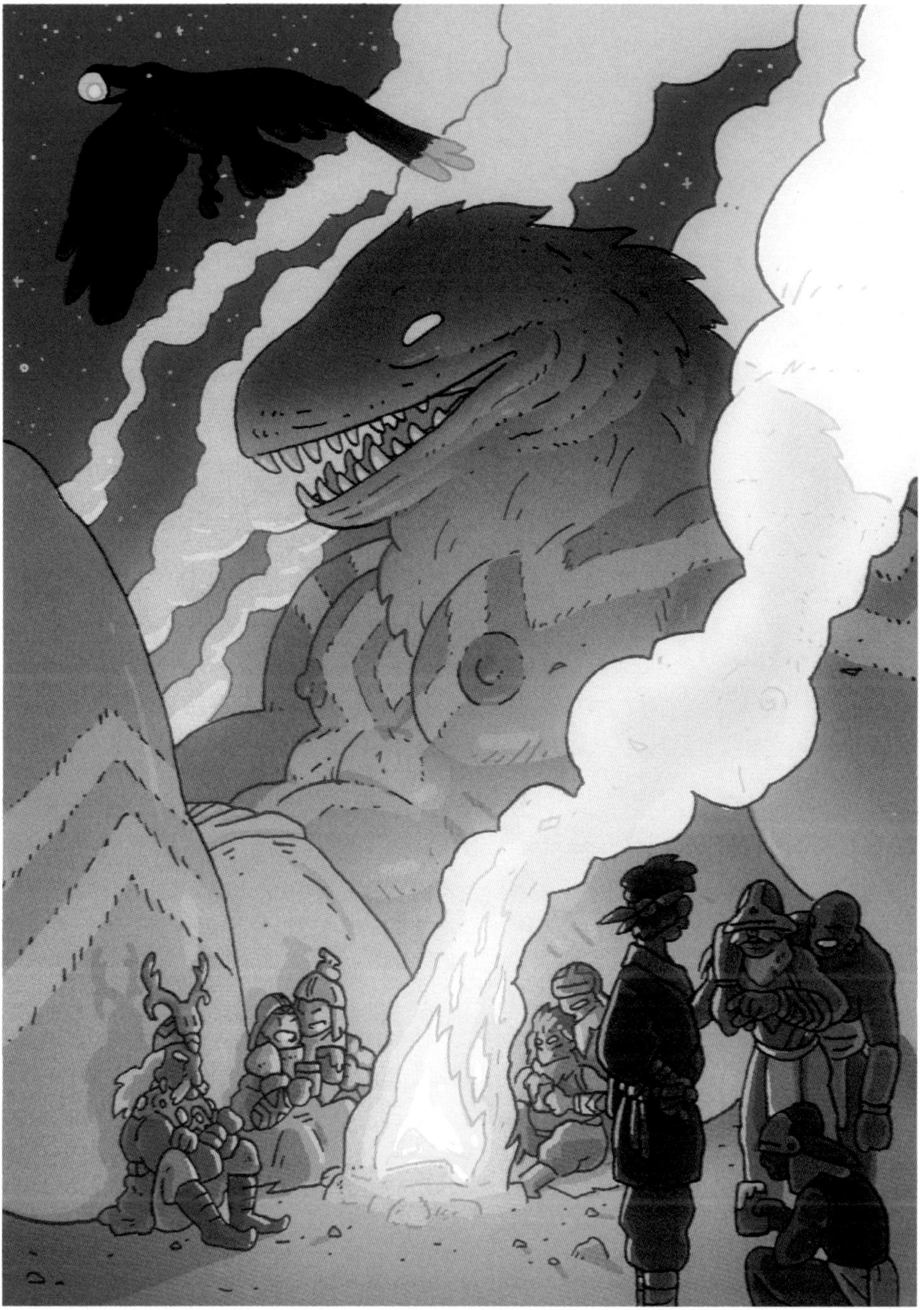

AND, OF COURSE,
ARTYOM TRAKHANOV!

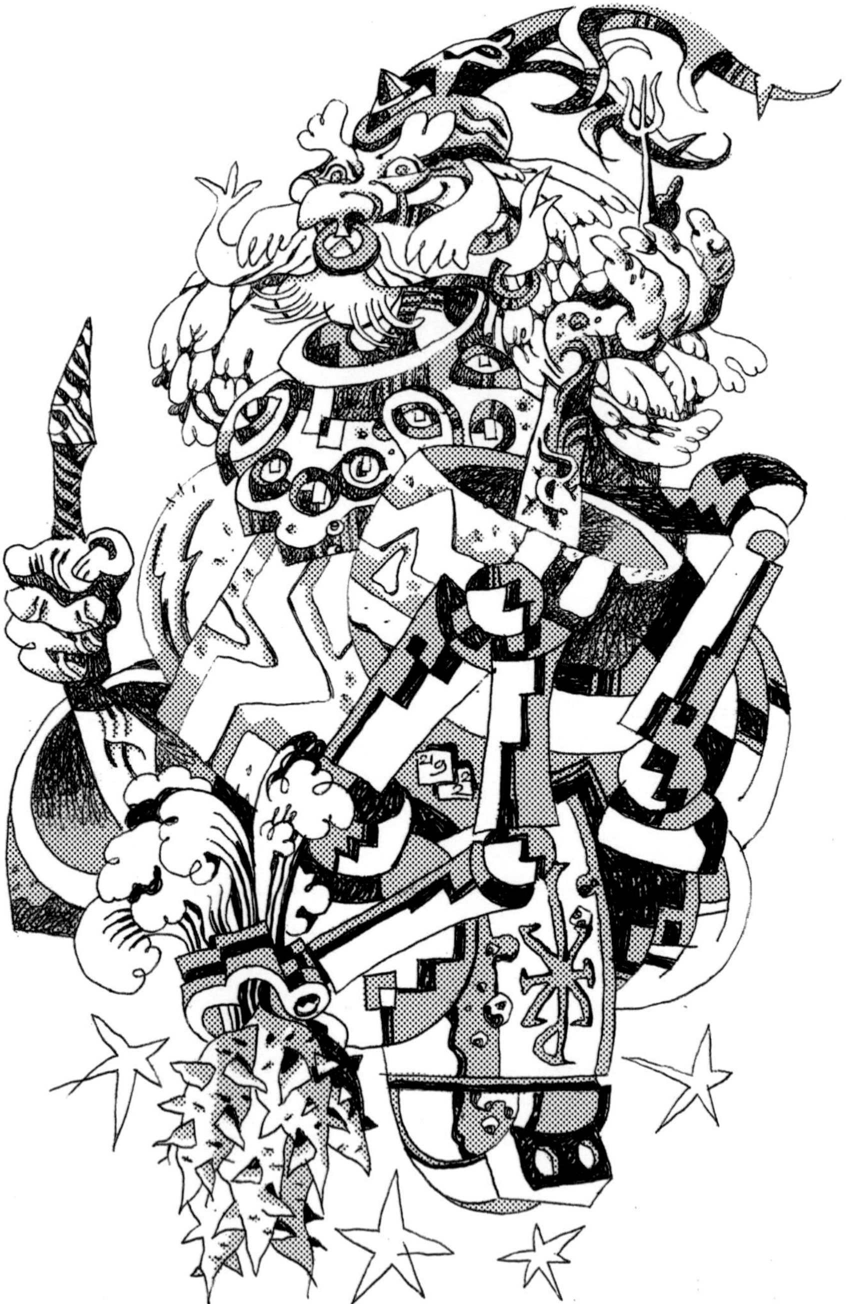